In April 1970 the International Economic Association organised a conference on growth models, at Ma'ale Hachamisha, near Jerusalem. The papers presented at that meeting are printed in this volume, and the discussions to which they gave rise are summarised.

Growth models have been the subject of much work and no little controversy for a number of years. Though most of the participants already knew one another well, the papers do not generally assume a very thorough acquaintance with previous literature, and several of them bring together the main results in their fields.

The first paper in the volume, by E. Helmstadter, uses a growth model in the study of economic history. This is followed by two papers (H. Rose and H. Uzawa) on monetary problems, and two (K. Shell and C. C. von Weizsäcker) on inventive activity. Four papers (two by J. E. Stiglitz, the others by L. Spaventa and F. H. Hahn) explore the controversial issues of capital theory by means of growth models, including reswitching and the heterogeneity of capital. Five papers are devoted to various aspects of optimal growth: P. A. Diamond relates optimal taxation and growth; M. Inagaki offers an unorthodox view of intertemporal optimality; D. McFadden summarises and extends theorems on the existence of optimal plans; P. J. Hammond and J. A. Mirrlees propose and analyse a concept to replace optimality; and B. Peleg and M. Yaari report some new results on the prices associated with optimal plans. The final paper, by A. Dixit, surveys some of the growth models that have been applied to the developing economies.

A summary of the discussions among participants, prepared by N. H. Stern, is included. The final session was devoted to a general discussion of the role of growth models in economic analysis. In it disagreements were clarified, but not resolved. The volume as a whole demonstrates the wide range of growth models that economists have developed, and the diverse uses to which they have been put, while reflecting the dissatisfaction which the participants felt, in varying degrees, with the present state of the art.

Models of Economic Growth

OTHER INTERNATIONAL ECONOMIC ASSOCIATION PUBLICATIONS

Latin America in the International Economy

Science and Technology in Economic Growth

Allocation Under Uncertainty

Models of Economic Growth

Proceedings of a Conference held by the International Economic Association at Jerusalem

EDITED BY
JAMES A. MIRRLEES AND N. H. STERN

A HALSTED PRESS BOOK

JOHN WILEY & SONS
New York – Toronto

Published in the United Kingdom 1973 by
The Macmillan Press Ltd.

Published in the U.S.A. and
Canada by Halsted Press, a
Division of John Wiley & Sons, Inc.,
New York

Library of Congress Cataloging in Publication Data

IEA Conference on the Essence of a Growth Model, Jerusalem, 1970.
Models of economic growth.

"A Halsted Press book."
Bibliography: p.
1. Economic development—Mathematical models.
I. Mirrlees, James A., and Stern, N. H., eds. II. International Economic Association. III. Title.
HD82.I18 1970 330.9'172'4 73-531
ISBN 0-470-60918-4

Printed in Great Britain

Contents

Acknowledgements

The International Economic Association wishes to express its gratitude to all those organisations and persons who contributed to the realisation of this volume. Thanks are due to the Bank of Israel, which bore practically all the local expenses, and to the Ford Foundation, whose grant made possible the participation of a number of young specialists.

The Conference was held in the agreeable surroundings of the Ma'ale Hachamisha Kibbutz near Jerusalem, and the local organisation was most efficiently carried out by the Israel Political Sciences Association.

The Association would also like to thank Professor Robert Solow, Chairman of the Programme Committee, and the other members of that committee, who were responsible for framing the work of the meeting. In particular our gratitude goes to Professor Michael Bruno who made the local arrangements, and, with the rest of the Programme Committee, undertook the direction of the conference in Israel, when Professor Solow was unable to attend. This volume was edited by Professor James A. Mirrlees and Dr N. H. Stern, who was also responsible for summarising the discussion. The editors would like to thank Charlotte Stiglitz for making a tape-recording of the discussion.

List of Participants

Mr A. B. Atkinson, University of Cambridge, U.K.
Dr Yoram Ben-Porath, The Hebrew University, Jerusalem, Israel
Dr Eytan Berglas, Tel Aviv University, Israel
Professor Claude Berthomieu, Université de Lille, France
Mrs Krishna Bharadwaj, University of Cambridge, U.K.
Dr C. J. Bliss, University of Cambridge, U.K.
Dr Jean-Marc Boussard, Institut National de la Recherche Agronomique, Paris, France
Professor Michael Bruno, The Hebrew University, Jerusalem, Israel
Professor Peter A. Diamond, Massachusetts Institute of Technology, Cambridge, U.S.A.
Dr Avinash K. Dixit, University of Oxford, U.K.
Professor Luc Fauvel, Université de Paris, France
Professor P. Garegnani, University of Pavia, Italy
Professor F. H. Hahn, London School of Economics and University of Cambridge, U.K.
Professor Ernst Helmstädter, University of Münster, Federal German Republic
Professor M. Inagaki, Sir George Williams University, Montreal, Canada
Dr David Levhari, The Hebrew University, Jerusalem, Israel
Professor Erik Lundberg, University of Stockholm, Sweden
Professor James A. Mirrlees, University of Oxford, U.K.
Professor Yair Mundlak, The Hebrew University, Faculty of Agriculture, Rehovot, Israel
Dr Luigi Pasinetti, University of Cambridge, U.K.
Professor D. Patinkin, The Hebrew University, Jerusalem, Israel
Dr Bezalel Peleg, The Hebrew University, Jerusalem, Israel
Professor Hugh Rose, University of Rochester, N.Y., U.S.A.
Professor Karl Shell, University of Pennsylvania, Philadelphia, U.S.A.
Dr Eytan Sheshinski, The Hebrew University, Jerusalem, Israel
Professor Luigi Spaventa, University of Perugia, Italy
Mr N. H. Stern, University of Oxford, U.K.
Professor Joseph E. Stiglitz, Yale University, New Haven, U.S.A., and University of Cambridge, U.K.
Dr Morris Teubal, The Hebrew University, Jerusalem, Israel
Professor Hirofumi Uzawa, University of Tokyo, Japan
Professor C. C. von Weizsäcker, University of Bielefeld, Federal German Republic
Professor Menahem E. Yaari, The Hebrew University, Jerusalem, Israel

Introduction

James A. Mirrlees

It is not self-evident that economists should construct models of economic growth; far less that they should construct more and more complicated models of economic growth. The question is whether the models are likely to prove useful. I write this with some feeling, since some authors leave the purposes of their work unclear, and some critics attack the models without regard to their uses. One should not insist that all professional papers be at pains to explain to everyone where they might lead, nor that they be immune to criticism until the allowable applications have been specified. But it seems better to discuss a man's actions than his soul, and I would like to apply the same principle to economic models.

Discussion of the uses of growth models is not easy; for the relationship between an economist's models and economic reality and policy is necessarily tenuous. Since real economies are untidy and complicated, no one can hope to project the workings of the real economy in his mind: simplification is essential if anything is to be done with our knowledge of it. The art of economics is to choose good simplifications. At least in the first place, the choice is made by a leap of intuition. The leap may, as we all know, be casually and carelessly made. It may also be distilled by years of struggle, or achieved by inexplicable inspiration. The result can be criticised and improved. Perhaps some economists would find no significance in the leap of intuition, regarding the development of economic theory rather as a progress from simple initial models back towards the full economic reality. For them, the working out of each particular model, be it a growth model or a general equilibrium model, provides little more than practice, and its contemplation a preparation for adding new complications. The models are to be judged by their fruitfulness, not their usefulness. I am not sure what attraction there may be in that view. At any rate it is not, I think, the usual view of growth theorists. Many of them would willingly acknowledge the leap of intuition to a model used for a specific purpose. Since the aim is not to capture reality, but to gain partial understanding of some particular aspect, they would not suppose – or should not suppose – that a model used once for one purpose is the right one to use for a different problem.

Yet simple models – such as the 'one-sector neoclassical' model – are used for many purposes. Any model that has become popular in this sense deserves to be vigorously criticised. If the criticism is telling, perhaps better models will be developed, or we shall become more careful about applying it. No doubt the critic will be more effective if he offers a new model. He will not deserve to be effective if he merely points out that the model is not fully realistic, or that more complicated models – which may well be less realistic – could lead to more confused conclusions.

Consider some of the uses to which growth models have been put.

(1) *The Historical*

A growth model can suggest how history could have happened the way it did. The paper by Helmstädter in this volume is an example of the technique. Perhaps the best-known example is the introduction of 'technical progress' into the one-good model, to show how capital accumulation could go on without the rate of profit falling over time. We know now that capital accumulation and a rising rate of profit can coexist in models where there is no technological change, and we are not sure that the rate of profit does not fall. But without question we were made to look at history in new ways.

(2) *The Predictive*

In a similar way, models are used to formulate and support conjectures about the effects of major changes in current economic behaviour and policy on the future. Probably there is no other way of discussing how increased saving (brought about by new habits of thriftiness, or changes in taxation) can affect the distribution of wealth and income. The direction and effects of technological change have been the subject of much work of this kind, especially in recent years, though few economists are satisfied with the results so far. Two of the papers in the present volume, by Professors Shell and von Weizsäcker, are directed to these questions.

(3) *The Interpretative*

The working of the economic system throws up a great deal of information, which economists, in their role as reformers, would like to be able to use, especially to reveal otherwise unsuspected economic possibilities. The most famous proposal here is that the rate of profit earned in an economy can be used as an estimate of the 'social rate of return', that is, as a measure of the effects a society could expect from increased saving. Professor Solow has given considerable attention to this idea (Solow [1963], [1967]). His work has been criticised by Pasinetti [1969], whose interest, however, appears to be concentrated on a different interpretation of the asserted equality between the rate of profit and the social rate of return (as an 'explanation of the rate of profit'). Successful criticism of this use of observed profit rates would have widespread consequences, since it is closely related to the work of Denison and others on the contributions of various factors to economic growth. Because of the importance of the issue – and the obscure status of the criticism offered – I discuss it further below.

(4) *The Revelatory*

The most striking and convincing use of growth models is to demonstrate previously unsuspected possibilities, as when, for example, Samuelson [1958] showed that intertemporal equilibrium could be inefficient, and others have since shown that a real rate of interest less than the rate of growth if continued for ever implies dynamical inefficiency.

(5) *The Philosophical*

For similar reasons, simple growth models are used when we try to understand what kinds of consideration bear upon the choice of optimum investment plans. A leading example is the discussion of the existence of optimum growth paths. If this strikes more practical economists as an obviously unimportant issue, they should at least consider how closely related it is to the sensitivity of economic proposals. Economists often say that there is little need to consider future economic possibilities and values beyond a time horizon of twenty, or at most fifty years. Yet when the standard everyday methods of cost-benefit analysis are pushed towards their logical conclusion in plausible models (with as many commodities as you want, if a single capital good offends you) current policies *may* be highly sensitive to the specification of economic possibilities far in the future. That is one malady of which the non-existence of optimum growth is a symptom. No doubt one seeks a cure, or better, a way of ignoring the problem 'for all practical purposes'. But no one has yet shown how.

The papers by Hammond and Mirrlees, Inagaki, and McFadden provide diverse contributions to this issue.

(6) *The Institutional*

The study of growth models has shown that economists cannot straightforwardly carry over their notions of price-guided systems and their properties to intertemporal economics. The most obvious difficulty, that most forward markets do not and if they could probably should not exist has been explored more in the general equilibrium context than by means of growth models. Perhaps the simpler models of growth theory could provide illuminating examples to guide these difficult developments. Until now, growth models have been used to discuss two other sets of problems: the stability of equilibrium growth; and the possibility of identifying dynamically efficient growth paths from their associated prices, or of realising a dynamically efficient path through the use of prices. This last problem, a natural extension of older welfare economics to the intertemporal case, receives attention from Pelag and Yaari in their contribution to the present volume.

The stability problem has attracted more attention than any other in this area, since it was made precise by Solow in his justly famous 1956 paper. One might rephrase it by asking whether, if one assumes that the economy is so completely in equilibrium that all expectations about prices are sure, and actually fulfilled, the implied growth path will be sufficiently regular to support the initial hypothesis of fulfilled expectations. Hahn [1966] has shown that, even when one assumes full employment of labour, and describes consumer behaviour by fixed savings coefficients, there may be divergent growth paths along which expectations are satisfied (at least for a considerable time). Probably one ought to conclude that any theory of equilibrium growth with fulfilled expectations would, at least, put too great weight on expectations about prices in the distant future. This phenomenon is not unrelated to the optimum growth problems just referred to.

No one needs to be told that, in the real world, future prices are predicted with uncertainty, and growth does not, therefore, follow an equilibrium path in the sense of the Solow stability theory. It would, however, be satisfactory if we could with good reason suppose that actual growth is approximated by equilibrium growth – for surely equilibrium growth is easier to analyse than a sequence of temporary equilibria, and prices in equilibrium growth give evidence about economic possibilities that may be rather easy to interpret.

It seems to me that, in the light of the various results about divergent equilibrium paths, we must expect that actual growth paths, even if approximately competitive, need not be at all close to the full equilibrium growth path of the economy, even when that is unique. It is an important task for growth theory to look at this problem directly, and find, for example, whether observed prices and interest rates still give the outside observer some useful information. The papers by Hahn and Stiglitz in the present volume look at a number of models which may be useful for that task.

Another institutional use of growth models is in the analysis of monetary and public finance issues, either to assess the long-run effects of particular fiscal proposals, or to elucidate the nature of the policy choices available. Diamond's work on the National Debt [1965] is an instance of both types of analysis, and he contributes a paper to this volume showing how growth models and optimum tax theory can be related. The papers by Rose and Uzawa on monetary and fiscal questions also illustrate the application of growth models to understanding government policies and their interrelations.

(7) *Estimation*

One of the most controversial uses of growth models is as a theoretical or empirical tool for estimating parameters, which might, for example, be used to guide public policy. Thus, a growth model designed to apply to developing countries, or to a particular developing country, may yield growth rates, interest rates, and wage rates which could be used in project appraisal, or to support general judgements about economic prospects and the emphasis of government policy. Dixit discusses some of these models in his paper. Many – with diverse time horizons, technological assumptions, and degrees of disaggregation – have been constructed. It is no little part of their value that they reveal to their makers the lack of reliable data on which to base the desired estimates. This prompts two observations.

First, is it not strange that economists find it so hard to construct believable models that rely only on the available data for their implementation? We use less aggregated models, because we know that is how the world is; and then we cannot find out anything about alternative techniques at the sectoral level, or we cannot assess the effects of investment and migration on agricultural output and its distribution. The difficulties should not be exaggerated, but they deserve to be thought about, especially by those who believe more disaggregation is always better.

Second, the unreliability of some of the data, and the resulting uncertainty of the estimated parameters, is no ground for ignoring them. It is just in the case of developing countries, where the models are perhaps particularly crude, that the alternative techniques of relying on direct economic intuition, or on completely *ad hoc* 'models', have been notably unsuccessful.

(8) *The Exploratory*

Growth models are also used, very frequently, as a kind of Marshallian mathematics, '[to help] a person to write down quickly, shortly and exactly, some of his thoughts for his own use: and to make sure that he has enough, and only enough, premises for his conclusions'. It is possible that, as Marshall would have claimed, work of this exploratory kind is useful mainly to the author. The chief exception is the use of models in education. Models are popular with teachers, because communication of at least some aspects is readily testable. That is no bad motive. Fine phrases usually convey mood rather than argument. Models, on the other hand, suit a non-authoritative educational system: the student can check them and use them for himself, and decide for himself whether he knows why each component is there. Of course models, like diagrams, focus the attention narrowly and divert it from important considerations; and of course the intuitive leap of which I spoke before is harder to talk about and too often ignored. But without diagrams and models it is hardly possible to convey what we know about growth. Spare a thought, therefore, for the educational uses of growth models – and hope that the students will learn to criticise them as well as they manipulate them.

Another important exception is the use of models to ease, clarify, or demonstrate the difficulty of, capital theory and similar puzzling aspects of the economy. Here, too, one tries to see how things fit together, and also to develop better-trained intuitions about crude (though appealing) notions like capital, 'the' rate of interest, 'the' period of production, and so on. Malinvaud's paper on capital accumulation [1953] is a beautiful example, with its clear explanation of the sense in which the marginal product of capital can be equal to the rate of interest. The papers by Spaventa and Stiglitz in the present volume in part perform tasks of this kind.

I suppose the above list of uses for growth models is incomplete. It should be enough to suggest that the models deserve neither abandonment nor wholesale condemnation; though one may wonder whether the growth model is always the best tool – or weapon – to use. Modern welfare economics, to take one example, demonstrates what evidence may be contained in observed prices better than growth models have succeeded in doing.

A more interesting observation is that some uses depend much more on leaps of intuition than others – and must, from that point of view, be more open to criticism. If a growth model is used to demonstrate a possibility, or contradict a conjecture, it normally requires little credulity to see the general relevance of the result. When, on the other hand, a particular model is used for evaluating policy in a particular country, the relation of model to reality is the central justification. I do not think it is easy to criticise a proposed relationship between model and reality – to show that it is *too* unrealistic for the purpose at hand: but it can be done. (Stern and I have elsewhere made some limited suggestions about possible procedures [1972].) One can show that the model does not capture relevant aspects of reality – 'Surely, if you want to make long run predictions you must allow for capital with diverse labour-productivities'; suggest it does not raise the right questions – 'If you are discussing monetary policy, had you not better allow expectations to be unfulfilled?'; or show that its most striking properties fail to survive natural generalisations – 'But it is only in the one-good model that the rate of profit is determined by the existing stock of capital goods'.

Criticisms of another kind have been directed against growth models, and particularly 'neoclassical growth models' (which we may take to be models that use production functions and make competitive assumptions). The criticisms I have in mind claim that neoclassical growth models provide illegitimate support to *laissez-faire* philosophy and private enterprise economy; or that the theory which these models represent fails to provide a determinate outcome (or equilibrium). The first of these criticisms is hard to substantiate, though it is not to be denied that the defenders of capitalism find comfort in strange places. But perhaps it is necessary to point out to the critics that when an economist says 'Assume there is no government', he does it, not because he has failed to notice that there is, or because he thinks there should not be one, but because he believes he can make his particular points most clearly, or develop his argument with least confusion, if he ignores it. Even if equilibrium is determinate, it can be affected by government policy and political or co-operative action.

One might have thought that Hahn and Matthews [1964] had dealt effectively with the view that neoclassical theory is incomplete, because it 'lacks a theory of the rate of profit' except in special models. But Pasinetti and others seem to hold that view still, and put forward reswitching phenomena in support [1969]. It will not do. Neoclassical theorists know what assumptions are needed for a generally determinate theory: they need to assume something about demand, i.e. saving behaviour, as well as supply. They also need reasons for full employment. For example, one might assume that only one rate of interest would be consistent with a particular growth rate of consumption per head, because of intertemporal preferences. Then the long run production equilibrium is implied by that interest rate, and one has a determinate theory – over-simple no doubt, but no worse than theories with fixed savings propensities and unrealistic class divisions. Reswitching causes no problem for that theory: there may be reswitching, but equilibrium is still determinate, even unique.

In general, there may be more than one equilibrium: that has been known at least since Walras. The claim that equilibrium is *determinate*, though possibly not unique, is a claim that further assumptions cannot be consistently added to those already made (at least when they are important enough to be expressed as equations). If one wants, reasonably enough, to incorporate, say, co-operative behaviour by workers into the model, some of the competitive assumptions must be abandoned – of course.

Having said, once more, that neoclassical *steady-rate* theory is, whatever its faults, at least a determinate theory, one must point out that intertemporal equilibrium may well be indeterminate – in quite a different way – since the assumptions of perfect competition and fulfilled expectations are not enough to exclude the possibility of such unlikely phenomena as an infinitely prolonged tulip mania. For example, if all consumers are perfectly altruistic in Meade's sense (Meade (1968), Chapter 13), a continuum of equilibria is possible, just as in optimum growth models there are in general infinitely many 'locally optimal' or 'competitive' paths (cf. Hammond and Mirrlees in this book). These possibilities cannot be lightly dismissed; but they are symptoms of the unsatisfactory treatment of expectations. As theorists we analyse either models where expectations are certain and fulfilled, or theories in which they are much too loosely linked to past experience. It was not unreasonable of Joan Robinson to insist that, in growth theory, only steady balanced growth makes sense as an equilibrium. But if we remain restricted to these cases, neoclassical theory is determinate, and no useful discussion of stability is possible.

Pasinetti's doubts about the determinacy of equilibrium under neoclassical assumptions arise from his observation that Solow's attempt ([1963] and [1967]) to show that the rate of profit is equal to the social rate of return fails when the latter cannot be (uniquely) defined – as happens when there is reswitching. I think he is wrong if he supposes that the equation 'rate of profit = rate of return' is an essential part of neoclassical theory – that theory rests on profit maximisation and rational consumer behaviour, which are meaningful even when reswitching is possible. That equality is proposed as an implication of neoclassical theory, which is of interest because of its interpretative value (the third use of models in my list). If we observe that the rate of profit (gross of tax) is 15 per cent, it would be nice if we were entitled to deduce that the economy could, by sacrificing consumption now, achieve increases in future consumption in perpetuity at a rate of nearly 15 per cent. Even under competitive assumptions, we are not entitled to make that deduction.

The reason is rather simple. There may be no efficient way of turning a sacrifice of present consumption into a perpetual constant increase in future consumption: the best one can do in this way may give a much lower return. That is the most interesting implication of reswitching. It can hold even if the number of techniques available to the economy is very large, provided that the different techniques of production all involve rather different kinds of capital equipment. Generally, the economy would be capable of changes in production plans that involve reductions in consumption immediately, and in a number of future years also, and provide increased consumption in the other years, such that the changes in consumption discount to zero when a discount rate of 15 per cent is used. But these consumption changes may also have zero present value when a discount rate of 5 per cent is used (if the same technical choices are consistent with 5 per cent as with 15 per cent, because of reswitching). So what is a representative member of the economy, who thinks his rate of time preference is 10 per cent, to do? The moral, which should surprise no economist, is that the effects of economic programmes on aggregate consumption cannot in general be adequately summarised by internal rates of return. It would be interesting to know when one *can* do that, but discussions about the 'likelihood' that reswitching would occur bear little on the question of realism so far. In any case, the rate of profit in a competitive economy would still give us some information about investment possibilities: for example there can be no feasible plan for turning a present sacrifice of consumption into a perpetual increase in future consumption that will yield a rate of return greater than the rate of profit. Furthermore no one should suppose that reswitching in any way weakens the proposition that wage rates and rental rates are equal to the marginal products of labour and other services. The reason for caution in regarding wage rates as estimates of marginal products is quite different and much less recondite: competitive conditions do not prevail.

Another area in which the evidence of market prices – such as wages and profit rates – is used in evidence too freely for the purist is the explanation of growth, culminating in the work of Denison ([1962] and [1967]). Here too it is valuable to ask what the (implicit) models are being used for, and why. One can certainly ask of a particular country whether the data suggests there has been more productivity growth than one would expect if technology remained constant. That was how Griliches and Jorgenson [1967] saw the matter. But after Denison's criticisms of their work [1969], it is hard to resist the view that there has been technological change if one accepts the hypothesis of approximately competitive conditions; and it is not clear where that conclusion should lead. Yet, if one reads anything else into the discussion of 'contributions to growth', one can easily fall into error. If, in a particular country, it is found that the measured rate of growth of capital (at constant prices, naturally – if one can get it!), multiplied by the measured share of profits is 1 per cent per year, while the rate of growth of national product has been 4 per cent, what is one to conclude? Does it mean that a doubling of the rate of investment would have added 1 per cent to the growth rate of output; or that zero net investment would have implied a 3 per cent growth rate of output? It does not – unless, as is most unlikely for the countries I know, the economy is well described by a one-good neoclassical growth model.

This has been pointed out often enough in various ways (cf., e.g., Sen [1970]). The various inputs may be complementary to one another, or substitutes. To put it another way, one must expect in general that the marginal products of the various inputs – capital goods, labour, and so on – depend, possibly quite sensitively, on the growth rates of the inputs, not just on their current levels. They also depend on future growth rates, through expectations. Therefore, even if one is prepared to assume competitive conditions as a reasonable approximation, and fairly accurate expectations, the factor shares cannot indicate, except in special circumstances, even the effect of *small* changes in the factor growth rates on the overall growth rate. If that is granted, what do calculations of contributions to growth tell us? They surely do not provide a satisfactory basis for 'explaining' the differences in growth rates between countries. Differences in growth rates presumably are explained in part by differences in factor growth rates: but it is hard to believe that factor shares tell us much, in a direct way, about the manner in which the causation operates.

This is not to say that the collection and analysis of data on growth rates is useless: far from it. The careful study of this evidence is an achievement, and deserves our admiration. I think it also deserves better models, for it is the kind of thing one ought to be able to do. The one-good neoclassical model is too simple. Models with innumerable different kinds of capital goods are of no use at all. One item on the agenda for growth theorists is the development and application of better, but not over-complex, models.

This introduction has been devoted to an attempt to show that growth models can be useful, and that their uses can be criticised. When one considers what dynamic phenomena economists would now most like to think about – my own list would include the formation of expectations, the role of management and supervision, the generation of inventions and innovations, the implications of the costs of economic change, methods for obtaining long-term predictions and bringing them to bear on government policy, and the relationship between long-term and short-term aims in government policy – when one considers such problems, one must consider whether growth models are the right method for studying them. One may also wonder whether there have been enough creative attempts to apply growth models to these issues. No one likes dull models, mechanically put through their paces. But good economic intuition can produce illuminating models, and good economic analysis can make them generate insights, even deep insights, into the workings of economies. It has been done. Without intuitive leaps and simple models, I doubt whether we shall learn much more about these issues.

The model of research behaviour on which these remarks have been based may be a poor one, and I shall not try to make it more explicit. Perhaps I may demonstrate my bias most clearly if I conclude by (diffidently) suggesting four morals, from the history of growth theory. *First*, it is usually best to build models with an eye to particular uses. *Second*, one should criticise the uses of the models, not the models alone. *Third*, one should not expect too much from *n*-sector models – most of the ideas and applications have arisen from simple models and examples. *Fourth*, one should not fully believe in models – one can use a model without being committed to it. I suppose the last is the hardest. If anything explains the heat of debates in growth theory, it is the difficulty thinkers in the scholastic tradition have in appreciating that, for workers in the scientific tradition, it makes sense to entertain a model and use it without being committed to it; while the scientists cannot imagine why mere models should be the object of passion. I think that, in this, the scientists are right.

JAMES A. MIRRLEES

December 1972

REFERENCES

E. F. Denison, *The Sources of Economic Growth in the United States and the Alternatives before Us* (Allen & Unwin, 1962).
—— *Why Growth Rates Differ* (Brookings Institution, 1967).
—— 'Some Major Issues in Productivity Analysis: An Examination of Estimates by Jorgenson and Griliches', *Survey of Current Business*, May 1969 (Part II).
P. A. Diamond, 'National Debt in a Neoclassical Growth Model', *American Economic Review*, 1965.
Z. Griliches and D. W. Jorgenson, 'The Explanation of Productivity Change', *Review of Economic Studies* (1967).
F. H. Hahn and R. C. O. Matthews, 'The Theory of Economic Growth: A Survey', *Economic Journal* (1964).
F. H. Hahn, 'Equilibrium Growth with Heterogeneous Capital Goods', *Quarterly Journal of Economics* (Nov 1966).
E. Malinvaud, 'Capital Accumulation and the Efficient Allocation of Resources', *Econometrica*, 1953. Reprinted in *Readings in Welfare Economics*, ed. Arrow and Scitovsky (A.E.A., 1969).
J. E. Meade, *The Growing Economy* (Allen & Unwin, 1968).
J. A. Mirrlees and N. H. Stern, 'Fairly Good Plans', *Journal of Economic Theory*, (1972).
L. L. Pasinetti, 'Switches of Technique and the "Rate of Return" in Capital Theory', *Economic Journal* LXXIX (Sept 1969).
P. A. Samuelson, 'An Exact Consumption-Loan Model of Interest with or without the Social Contrivance of Money', *Journal of Political Theory*, 1958.
A. K. Sen, Introduction to *Growth Economics*, ed. Sen (Penguin Books, 1970).
R. M. Solow, 'A Contribution to the Theory of Growth', *Quarterly Journal of Economics* (1956).

R. M. Solow, *Capital Theory and the Rate of Return* (Amsterdam, 1963).
—— 'The Interest Rate and Transition Between Techniques' in *Socialism, Capitalism and Economic Growth*, ed. C. H. Feinstein (Cambridge, 1967).

Part 1

Experience of Growth

1 The Long-Run Movement of the Capital–Output Ratio and of Labour's Share

Ernst Helmstädter
UNIVERSITY OF MÜNSTER, GERMANY

In growth theory the capital–output ratio as well as labour's share of output have been frequently considered as stable parameters. According to Klein,[1] both of them belong to the set of *celebrated ratios*. The parametric nature of those ratios is established either as an empirical observation or as a basic pattern of rational behaviour.

But what do the statistical results really show us? If we look at a time series of the capital–output ratio, for instance, we usually find certain changes in this ratio in the long run. Surely they do not seem to be very large. This situation leads some economists to the conclusion that the ratio is indeed stable, while others reject the hypothesis of stability. Thus the participants at the Corfu Conference of the International Economic Association could not reach a consensus on this question.[2]

In the case of income shares the state of affairs is quite similar. There is some evidence that the income ratios follow one or the other trend in the long run. But these facts do not seem to be convincing enough to invalidate the assumption of a long-run stability of the wage share.

Our own position is that in the long run the capital–output ratio as well as the income quotas are not stable but follow a certain movement. These movements along the time axis may be approximated linearly. Whenever during the course of some decades the capital–output ratio shows a linear upward trend, the wage–income ratio exhibits a downward trend. The inverse movement of these ratios may be observed throughout the following time period of several decades.

Thus, we can speak of a 'law' of opposedly directed linear long-run trends of both ratios. The time series for Germany, Great Britain and the United States clearly indicate this regularity.

The goal of this paper is to make evident the opposedly directed movement of the capital–output and the wage–income ratio by

[1] Klein (1962) p. 183.
[2] Lutz and Hague (1961) pp. x–xi.

graphical presentation of the available data. Two ways of explaining the facts by simple economic models will then be proposed. The content of this paper is more or less an English version of some parts of a book recently published by the author.[1]

I. THE FACTS AND THEIR STYLISED PATTERN

Let us now consider the development of the wage–income ratio and the capital–output ratio for the three countries mentioned above. This development is graphically demonstrated in Figs. 1.1–1.4. In these figures the *annual* values of these ratios are shown throughout a time span of six decades (Germany), four decades (Great Britain) and three decades (United States). We have been interested in such annual values in order to see which interactions between the two ratios may occur.

The time series presented for Germany and Great Britain end with the First World War. In the time span between the two world wars, according to the basic statistical sources, the ratios considered show important structural changes.[2] Therefore we did not present those ratios in Figs. 1.1–1.3.

To underscore the long-term variations of both ratios we have included free graphical approximations of long-run trends. It may be justified to take linear time trends as representative of this movement. Any further accuracy (e.g. by econometric analysis) is irrelevant for our later considerations.

If we now look at the movement of both ratios we may understand the 'law' of opposedly directed time trends mentioned above. We find turning-points of the trends of both ratios around 1880 and 1895 for Germany and Great Britain respectively. This raises the question whether we should speak of something like Kondratieff cycles[3] or of cycles of a shorter time lapse such as those proposed by Burns[4] and Hoffmann.[5]

We do not think that we should use the notion of 'cycles' at all. Instead of 'cycles' we prefer to speak of 'basic trends' (in French, '*mouvement de fonds*') as they have been described by Dupriez.[6] Such basic trends in the movement of the two ratios may last for two to four decades, and then change directions. Fig. 1.5 shows a synoptical presentation of these basic trends.

[1] Helmstädter (1969).
[2] Helmstädter (1969) pp. 54, 55.
[3] Schumpeter (1939).
[4] Burns (1934).
[5] Hoffmann (1940).
[6] Dupriez (1951).

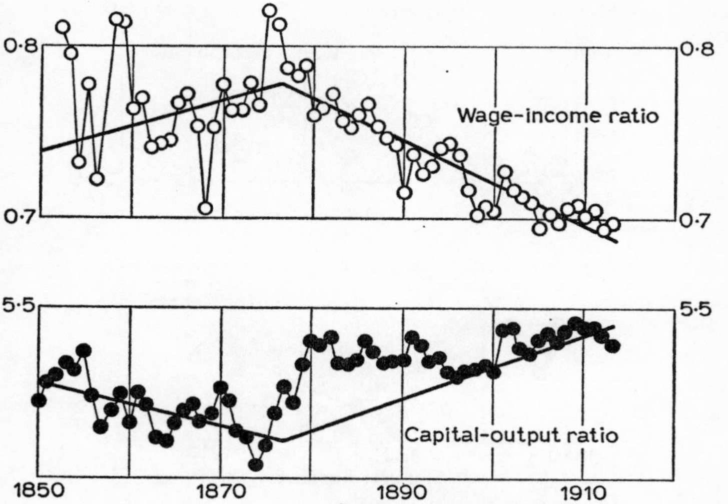

Sources: *Kapitalkoeffizient*, pp. 261–2

FIG. 1.1 The development of the wage–income ratio and the capital–output ratio in Germany, 1850–1913

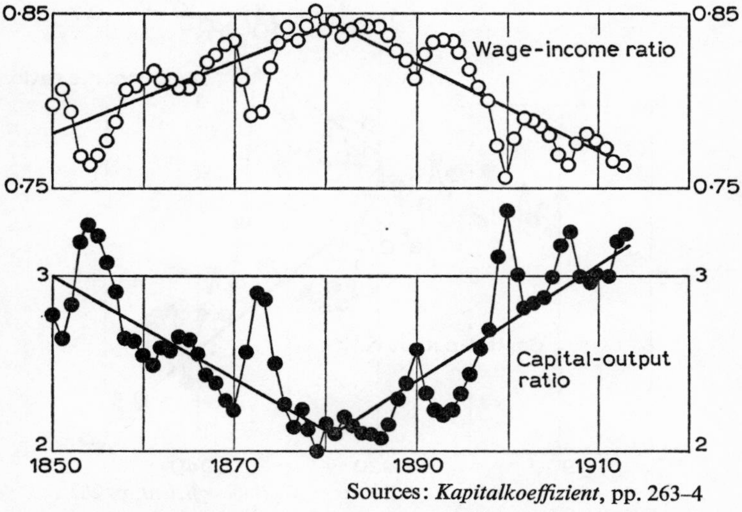

Sources: *Kapitalkoeffizient*, pp. 263–4

FIG. 1.2 The development of the wage–income ratio and the capital–output ratio in the manufacturing industries of Germany, 1850–1913

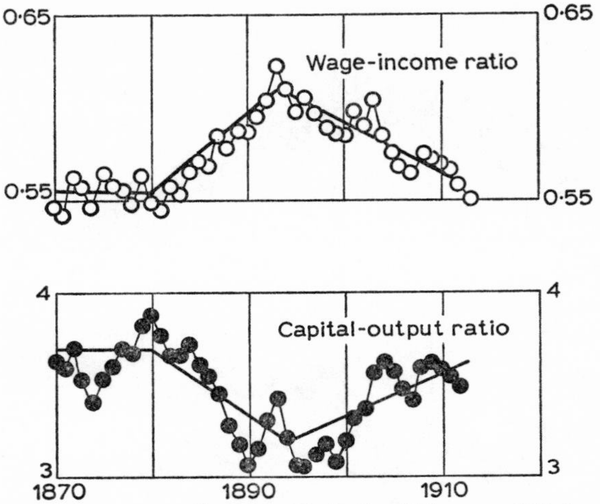

Sources: *Kapitalkoeffizient*, pp. 265–6

FIG. 1.3 The development of the wage–income ratio and the capital–output ratio in Great Britain, 1870–1913

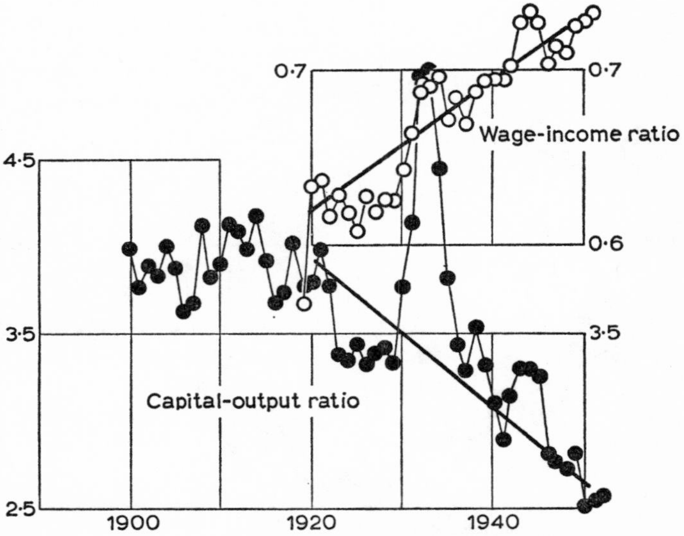

Sources: *Kapitalkoeffizient*, p. 267

FIG. 1.4 The development of the wage–income ratio and the capital–output ratio in the U.S.A., 1900–53

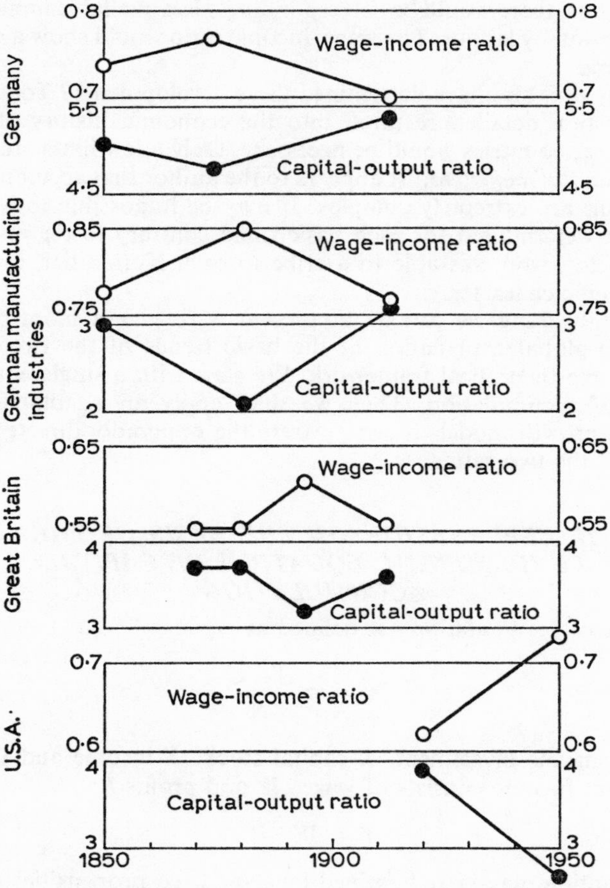

FIG. 1.5 The stylised development of the wage–income ratio and the capital–output ratio in three countries

By using the term 'basic trend' instead of 'cycle' we wish to avoid any implication that the movements might create the turning-points by themselves. Such turning-points may be caused by the rise of important new conditions of accumulation, which, for a complete absorption throughout the economy, need a time span of several decades. The new conditions may demand a higher capital–output ratio. Then, during the next decades, this ratio would increase. That would mean that more of the current product is needed for accumulation. Thus, there would be correspondingly less available immediate consumption by labour. The wage–income ratio would show a downward trend.

Which variables have determined these developments? To answer this question detailed research into the economic history of each of the three countries would be necessary. Only a few hints are given in *Der Kapitalkoeffizient.*[1] It appears to the author that accumulation conditions are extremely complex. It may be impossible to localise *the* basic determinant for each basic trend contrary to the result of Schumpeter, who was able to ascribe to each Kondratieff cycle its own specific character.[2]

The only thing we can do at present is to give a more or less plausible global explanation of the basic trends of the two ratios by a simple theoretical framework. We start with a single equation model of accumulation. Then we shall apply an adaptable neoclassical growth model to demonstrate the opposedly directed time trends of the two ratios.

II. EXPLANATION ON THE BASIS OF THE FUNDAMENTAL EQUATION OF CAPITAL ACCUMULATION

The rate of accumulation r is defined as

$$r \equiv \frac{I}{K} \equiv \frac{Y-C}{K} \tag{1.1}$$

where I means investment, K capital stock, Y income and C consumption. Income consists of wages W and profits P:

$$Y = W+P. \tag{1.2}$$

Consumption may be determined by some fixed propensities c_w and c_p:

$$C = c_w W + c_p P = (c_w - c_p)W + c_p Y. \tag{1.3}$$

Replacing C in (1.1) by the last expression of (1.3) and dividing by Y gives us:

$$r = \frac{1-c_p-(c_w-c_p)\lambda}{k} \tag{1.4}$$

[1] Helmstädter (1969) chap. 7.

[2] First Kondratieff cycle (until 1842): Industrial Revolution; second Kondratieff cycle (1842–97): steam and steel; third Kondratieff cycle (since 1898): electricity, chemistry, motor.

where λ stands for the wage–income ratio and k for the capital–output ratio. Now, we may assume that $c_p = 0$ and $c_w = 1$. Thus, we arrive at the 'fundamental equation of capital accumulation':

$$r = \frac{1-\lambda}{k}. \tag{1.4A}$$

If we now take r as relatively constant in the long run and let k follow a certain trend movement, then λ will show an opposite movement.

In reality r is not constant. But if we take the 'stylised' values of λ and k of Fig. 1.5, we may calculate an artificial value of r. This value is indeed more or less constant, as Table 1.1 shows. These

TABLE 1.1

LONG-RUN AVERAGE VALUES OF THE WAGE–INCOME RATIO AND THE CAPITAL–OUTPUT RATIO AS SHOWN IN FIG. 1.5

		Year	*Labour share* λ	*Capital–output ratio* k	*Calculated accumulation rate* $r = \frac{1-\lambda}{k}$
GERMANY	National economy	1850	0·74	5·1	0·051
		1874	0·77	4·8	0·048
		1913	0·70	5·4	0·056
	Manufacturing industries	1850	0·78	3·0	0·073
		1881	0·85	2·1	0·072
		1913	0·77	3·2	0·072
GREAT BRITAIN		1870 1880	0·555	3·7	0·120
		1894	0·61	3·2	0·122
		1912	0·56	3·6	0·122
U.S.A.		1920	0·62	3·9	0·097
		1950	0·73	2·7	0·102

calculated values of r are too high because non-wage income is not, in reality, completely invested. Furthermore, they show more constancy than the real values of r do.[1] In spite of that it is useful as a first approximation to take r as relatively constant, and to assume an independent movement of k, and to draw the conclusions for the movement of λ out of (1.4) or (1.4A).

[1] See Helmstädter (1969) p. 60.

So far the interpretation of the opposedly directed movement of λ and k is a Kaldorian type of distribution theory, given the condition $c_w > c_p$. Under the assumption of a constant accumulation rate r, an increasing k is necessarily accompanied by an increasing $s\,(= I/Y)$, which reduces λ. When k decreases, s will decrease also and λ will increase. The only modification with respect to the Kaldorian static distribution model is that we dynamise it through the introduction of the identity

$$s \equiv rk. \tag{1.5}$$

If we substitute rk in equation (1.4) by s, we arrive at the Kaldorian static model.

In characterising this approach we may say that we proceed from identity (1.1), introduce a hypothesis about consumption behaviour (1.3), assume accumulation rate a long-run constant, and vary the capital–output coefficient, thus drawing conclusions about the movement of the wage–income ratio. Such a procedure may be useful in bringing to light certain basic tendencies of the historical process. Incidentally, Marx used the same procedure when he explained his 'Gesetz des tendenziellen Falls der Profitrate'.[1]

Another remark concerning our assumptions: There may be no objection to the assumption that $c_w > c_p$ or even $c_w = 1$, $c_p = 0$, prevails during the time under consideration. But the assumption that the accumulation rate is constant is not realistic. There are ascertainable movements of this ratio too. This holds especially for the United States. There, the long-run accumulation rate decreased from 3 per cent in 1920 to 2 per cent in 1950, contrary to our calculated accumulation rate (see Table 1.1) which increased from 9·7 per cent to 10·2 per cent. This difference in the tendency of the two rates may be explained by an increase of c_p or c_w. As we know, the average consumption–income ratio was increasing during that time.[2]

The foregoing explanation is unsatisfactory, since the movement of k is exogenously given. To avoid this difficulty, one has to introduce another type of production function, as we do in the next section.

III. EXPLANATION WITHIN THE FRAMEWORK OF NEO-CLASSICAL GROWTH THEORY

Neo-classical growth theory is mainly concerned with the fundamental problems of the existence, stability and the determinants of equilibrium growth paths. As far as the author can see, no attempts

[1] Helmstädter (1969) pp. 79–84.
[2] Helmstädter (1969) p. 200.

have been made to date upon the problem of relating observable growth paths of real national economies to the concept of dynamic equilibrium.

We shall try to sketch some tentative ideas of long-run disequilibrium analysis. *A priori*, it is certainly apparent that an economy which shows long-run changes of the capital–output ratio and the labour share cannot move along one unique equilibrium path during that time. Does such an economy move towards an equilibrium path, or do the equilibrium conditions themselves change continuously?

With respect to the neo-classical production function, which is the core of that theory, we may ask whether there is one such function for a single basic trend, and, after a turning-point has been reached, whether another production function may hold for the following basic trend with its reversed movements of the capital–output ratio and the wage–income ratio. But should we not rather think of one production function only, which is capable of enclosing both the basic trends of the two ratios throughout a longer time span?

From the standpoint of neo-classical growth theory this last idea may be the more reasonable one. Furthermore, it seems reasonable to try to reproduce the movement of the two ratios with a minimum of alterations of production function parameters, since each alteration would necessitate its own special explanation.

Thus we are looking for a neo-classical production function which does not call for an essential alteration of its parameters whenever a turning-point of the basic trends appears. Furthermore, we limit ourselves to the application of the simplest instruments of neo-classical theory.

(1) *First Case: Cobb–Douglas Production Function*

Given the Cobb–Douglas production function

$$Y_t = (e^{\alpha t}L_t)^{\lambda}(e^{\beta t}K_t)^{1-\lambda} \tag{1.6}$$

with

L = labour input

λ = partial elasticity of labour

$1-\lambda$ = partial production elasticity of capital

α = growth rate of the labour augmentation factor } caused by technical progress

β = growth rate of the capital augmentation factor } caused by technical progress

the equilibrium rate of growth $\bar{g}$ is given by:

$$\bar{g} = \frac{\dot{L}}{L}+\alpha+\left(\frac{1}{\lambda}-1\right)\beta. \tag{1.7}$$

If we now take into account that on the equilibrium path

$$\bar{g} = \frac{\dot{K}}{K} = \frac{s}{k^*} \tag{1.8}$$

where k^* is the capital–output ratio on the equilibrium path, we may rewrite (1.7) as follows:

$$\frac{s}{k^*} = \frac{\dot{L}}{L} + \alpha + \left(\frac{1}{\lambda} - 1\right)\beta. \tag{1.9}$$

This equation implies 'non-neutral' technical progress, if $\alpha \neq \beta > 0$. For the usual definitions of 'neutral' technical progress the growth rates of the augmentation factors have the following classification:

$$\left.\begin{array}{lll} \alpha > 0; & \beta = 0: & \text{Harrod-} \\ \alpha = \beta > 0: & & \text{Hicks-} \\ \alpha = 0; & \beta > 0: & \text{Solow-} \end{array}\right\} \text{neutral technical progress.}$$

So, for neutral technical progress, (1.9) has to be rewritten:

$$\left.\begin{array}{lll} (1.9\text{A}) & \dfrac{s}{k^*} = \dfrac{\dot{L}}{L} + \alpha & \text{Harrod-} \\ (1.9\text{B}) & \dfrac{s}{k^*} = \dfrac{\dot{L}}{L} + \dfrac{\alpha}{\lambda} & \text{Hicks-} \\ (1.9\text{C}) & \dfrac{s}{k^*} = \dfrac{\dot{L}}{L} + \left(\dfrac{1}{\lambda} - 1\right)\beta & \text{Solow-} \end{array}\right\} \begin{array}{l}\text{neutral} \\ \text{technical} \\ \text{progress.}\end{array}$$

If we assumed that s is constant, and the economy were continually on its long-run growth path, in the cases (1.9), (1.9B) and (1.9C) we would have to assume that λ changes continuously. Then k^* would move in the same direction, which would contradict the fact of opposedly directed long-run movements of both ratios. In the case of Harrod neutrality k^* and λ are independent of each other. Under this condition both ratios can evidently make movements quite independently of one another.

Now let us drop the assumption of s being constant. The production elasticity of labour may still change continuously. Then, in the cases of (1.9), (1.9B) and (1.9C) a *decreasing* value of λ would imply an *increasing* value of s/k^* and vice versa. Let us assume a basic trend of decreasing λ. If s decreases, k^* decreases even more, which contradicts the observed trends even more sharply. Thus, s has to increase. But the increase of k^* must be slower. On the other hand, an increasing λ would call for a decreasing s and a still faster reduction of k^*.

Until now we have assumed that s is always connected with k^*. This assumption is not very realistic. The long-run investment ratio s can be changed immediately, but not the long-run value of the capital–output ratio. If under these circumstances we increase s, it will take a longer time until the new k^* is reached. During this time k, the actual capital–output ratio, will increase. A decreased s would evoke the decreasing of k during a longer period of time. It seems reasonable to assume such an adjustment period for k^*.

Under the assumption that an alteration of the long-run s evokes a changing of k in the same direction, a Cobb–Douglas production function with independently changing production elasticities may be used to portray the basic trends of the two ratios. But this function remains unsatisfactory for the explanation of the interdependence of these two ratios. Certainly, it may be possible to introduce some interrelationship. However, the use of a production function which itself already contains such an interconnection may surely be preferred.

(2) *Second Case: C.E.S. Production Function*

The C.E.S. production function contains the production elasticity of labour λ as an implicit variable if the substitution elasticity is unequal to 1. The introduction of such a function demands the assumption of Harrod-neutral technical progress. Otherwise we would have to give up the possibility of equilibrium growth. We may write this production function as follows:

$$Y_t = \{(1-\delta)E_t^{-\rho}+\delta K_t^{-\rho}\}^{-(1/\rho)} \tag{1.10}$$

with δ a distribution parameter
ρ a substitution parameter
E = labour, measured in constant efficiency units.

For E we have

$$E_t = a(t)L_t \tag{1.11}$$

which means that Harrod neutrality of technical progress is given.

Let us define

$$\left[\frac{(\partial Y/\partial K)}{(\partial Y/\partial L)}\right] \equiv w \tag{1.12}$$

$$\frac{K}{L} \equiv v \tag{1.13}$$

$$\frac{K}{E} \equiv u. \tag{1.14}$$

Then, the production function (1.10) yields

$$v = \left[\frac{\delta a(t)^{\rho}}{(1-\delta)w}\right]^{1/(1+\rho)} \tag{1.15}$$

and

$$u = \left[\frac{\delta}{(1-\delta)\,a(t)\,w}\right]^{1/(1+\rho)}. \tag{1.16}$$

From (1.15) and (1.16), we find the substitution elasticity σ as

$$-\left[\frac{dv/v}{dw/w}\right] = \left[\frac{du/u}{dw/w}\right] = \sigma = \frac{1}{1+\rho}. \tag{1.17}$$

We see that it does not matter whether we relate σ to v or u. It is more convenient to take the latter, with respect to the conditions of equilibrium growth under Harrod-neutral technical progress:

$$\bar{g} = \frac{\dot{Y}}{Y} = \frac{\dot{K}}{K} = \frac{\dot{E}}{E}. \tag{1.18}$$

We may take $\dot{E}/E$ as an exogenously given constant. Let us also assume a certain change of the long-run s as given, and let the capital–output ratio adapt to it. What are the conclusions for λ? The answer depends apparently on the value of ρ or σ.

If $0 < \sigma < 1$ holds, then an increased value of s makes K grow faster than Y during a period of disequilibrium expansion:

$$\frac{\dot{K}}{K} > \frac{\dot{Y}}{Y}. \tag{1.19}$$

That means that k is increasing. At the same time we have

$$\frac{\dot{K}}{K} > \frac{\dot{E}}{E}. \tag{1.20}$$

With $0 < \sigma < 1$, that would mean an increasing λ, which contradicts the observable facts. If we begin with a decreased value of the long-run s, k would decrease and K would grow at a lower rate than E:

$$\frac{\dot{K}}{K} < \frac{\dot{E}}{E}. \tag{1.21}$$

That implies, under the condition $0 < \sigma < 1$, a decrease of λ, which again contradicts the observable facts. In the case of $\sigma > 1$, the movement of the labour share would be in the opposite direction. A high s increases k, lets K grow faster than E, so decreasing labour's share, and vice versa.

Our conclusion is that a given constant growth rate of E ($\dot{E}/E =$ const.) demands $\sigma > 1$ in order to demonstrate the observed movements of k and λ.

If we allow for endogenous Harrod-neutral technical progress, we could assume

$$a_{(t)} = f(t, s); \quad a_i > 0; \quad i = t, s. \tag{1.22}$$

Now, a higher s would increase the growth rates of K as well as that of E. Only if s accelerates $\dot{E}/E$ more than $\dot{K}/K$, the substitution elasticity would have to be less than 1. We shall not discuss the case of endogenous Harrod-neutral technical progress further.

To give a further explanation of these considerations by means of a concrete example, let us assume a certain C.E.S. production function. We take an augmentation factor for L:

$$a_{(t)} = \prod_{\theta=0}^{t-1} \left(1 + \frac{d}{\lambda_\theta}\right) \tag{1.23}$$

with $d = 0{\cdot}03$ (rate of exogenous technical progress). Labour grows at the rate

$$\frac{\dot{L}}{L} = 0{\cdot}02. \tag{1.24}$$

The original factor input in period 0 is given:

$$\left.\begin{aligned} L_0 &= 100 \\ K_0 &= 400 \end{aligned}\right\} \tag{1.25}$$

and the distribution parameter

$$\delta = 0{\cdot}7. \tag{1.26}$$

s is constant at

$$s = 0{\cdot}25 \tag{1.27}$$

for 25 periods, and for the next 25 periods at

$$s = 0{\cdot}16. \tag{1.28}$$

During the first 25 periods a high s makes k increase; during the next 25 periods s makes k decrease.

Now let us assume three values of ρ or σ:

1. $\rho = 0; \quad \sigma = 1$
2. $\rho = -\frac{1}{5}; \quad \sigma = 1{\cdot}25$
3. $\rho = -\frac{1}{3}; \quad \sigma = 1{\cdot}5.$

Fig. 1.6 shows the time paths of the growth rates of output and capital and the movement of the capital–output ratio and the wage–income ratio. In the case of $\sigma = 1{\cdot}5$, this example is compatible with the observable facts, as far as these two ratios are concerned.

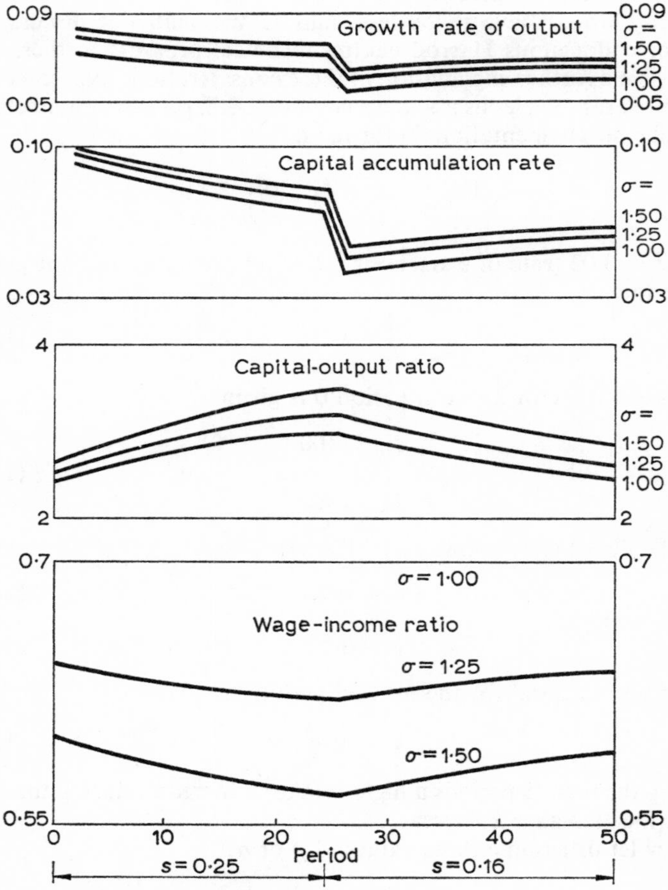

FIG. 1.6 The development of the wage–income ratio and the capital–output ratio in a neo-classical model with different elasticities of substitution (σ) and exogenously given investment–income ratios (s)

IV. CONCLUSIONS

Long-term movements of the capital–output ratio and the wage–income ratio, as observed in these three countries, may be described by a dynamised version of the static Kaldorian income distribution theory. That may be useful for a preliminary inspection. But because of the lack of a production function the capital–output ratio has to be taken as an exogenously given parameter, which follows a long-run time trend.

The instruments of the neo-classical growth theory can deliver a model of greater completeness. But the model has to be used for disequilibrium paths of growth. It seems reasonable to regard s as the only exogenous variable, to which the capital–output ratio has not yet adjusted. An investment ratio that is too high (and possibly still growing) induces an adjustment in k, which increases; and vice versa. If Harrod-neutral technical progress is exogenously given, the substitution elasticity must be greater than 1. In addition, endogenous variations in the growth rate of the labour augmentation factor that are weaker than the variations of the capital accumulation rate call for $\sigma > 1$.

REFERENCES

A. F. Burns, *Production Trends in the United States since 1870* (New York, 1934).

L. H. Dupriez, *Des mouvements économiques généraux*, 2e éd. (Louvain, 1951).

E. Helmstädter, *Der Kapitalkoeffizient: Eine kapitaltheoretische Untersuchung* (Stuttgart, 1969). (Title in English: *The Capital–Output Ratio: A Study in Capital Theory.*)

W. G. Hoffman, *Wachstum und Wachstumsformen der englischen Industriewirtschaft von 1700 bis zur Gegenwart* (Jena, 1940).

L. R. Klein, *An Introduction to Econometrics* (Prentice-Hall: Englewood Cliffs, N.J., 1962) p. 183.

F. A. Lutz and D. C. Hague (eds.), *The Theory of Capital* (London: Macmillan, 1961) pp. x–xi.

J. A. Schumpeter, *Business Cycles*, vol. I, 1st ed. (New York and London, 1939).

Discussion of the Paper by Ernst Helmstädter

Professor Mundlak introduced the paper by saying that it was concerned with the explanation of the empirical phenomenon that the share of wages and the capital–output ratio move in different directions in the long run. The existence of this phenomenon was substantiated by the introduction of free-hand time trends into the data. He thought that Fig. 1.2 was more interesting since it focused on one sector rather than dealing with the economy as a whole.

This paper presented two alternative mechanisms for explaining this phenomenon. With a classical saving function we have $I/K \equiv r = (1-\lambda)/(K/Y)$. This gives us a relationship between three variables r, λ, (K/Y). This relationship should have been checked empirically. Instead r was computed from the data on λ and (K/Y). No data on r were given but it was mentioned that actual rs were 2–3 per cent, whereas the model gives 9–10 per cent.

The second mechanism used a production function. The use of a Cobb–Douglas function was inappropriate, as here labour's share is constant. With a C.E.S. function we can have changes in labour's share with the relationship between the variables under consideration determined by the elasticity of substitution.

He then moved to his criticisms of the paper. He claimed that the relations observed were a property of the production function and did not need an explicit model of the economy. If we used a production function to give an explanation we could then check by estimating a production function from the data. He showed how the relations were a property of the production function:

$Y = F(K, L, t)$ = production function, supposed homogeneous degree one in capital and labour.

$$\hat{X} \equiv \frac{1}{X}\left(\frac{dX}{dt}\right), \quad y = (Y/L), \quad k = (K/L).$$

Then $\hat{y} = \alpha_K \hat{k} + \gamma$ where α_K = elasticity of output with respect to capital and γ is the rate of Hicks-neutral technical change.

$$\widehat{\left(\frac{K}{Y}\right)} = \hat{k} - \hat{y} = \alpha_L \hat{k} - v. \tag{1}$$

Now write

$$\omega = (w/r) = (\alpha_L/\alpha_K)k.$$

Then

$$\sigma = (\hat{k}/\hat{\omega}) \tag{2}$$

and

$$\hat{\omega} = \hat{\alpha}_L - \hat{\alpha}_K + \hat{k}. \tag{3}$$

(2), (3) and $\alpha_L + \alpha_K = 1$ give

$$\hat{\alpha}_L = \frac{(1-\sigma)}{\sigma}\alpha_K \hat{k}. \tag{4}$$

Substituting (1) in (4) shows that the sign of the relationship we are examining ($\dot{\alpha}_L$ and $(\dot{K}/Y)$) is given by the relationship of σ to unity – *provided* $\gamma = 0$.

He concluded by mentioning some problems in the estimation of the production function; for example, we do not know whether we have Hicks-neutral or Harrod-neutral technical progress or whether we are observing population growth or a change of employment. Of course the data may not come from a single production function.

Professor Weizsäcker assumed that the empirical observation being discussed could stand up to more sophisticated tests, for the sake of the discussion. There were two explanations offered – if we use a production function and competitive shares we must assume σ is large. If we use the Kaldorian explanation via the fundamental equation of capital accumulation we have to assume that the distribution of income is determined by that needed to give a rate of accumulation similar to that of other factors (for full employment and with a different savings rate between classes) and we can have a low elasticity of substitution. We should develop an econometric method to distinguish these two explanations.

Professor Hahn interjected that it was nonsense to speak of elasticities of substitution and production functions over the long periods being considered. Big structural changes can occur over hundred-year periods.

Professor Stiglitz asked whether more refined estimation of turning-points had been made and thought he could draw fairly convincing alternative lines through the data shown.

Professor Helmstädter replied that he did not require that σ be constant over the period – only that it be greater than unity. He thought that the only circumstance in which we could look at the economy as a whole using a production function was when we are looking at the economy as a unit of accumulation. The turning-points ought to be explained historically, e.g. the great depression in England.

Professor Patinkin presumed that capital was measured by stock rather than use, in which case the movements in the capital–output ratio would reflect the cycle. We would then expect the two ratios to move together. *Professor Helmstädter* replied that there would be little difference between working with stock and use in the long run.

Professor Rose said that we could think of a different Cobb–Douglas production function at each point of time and so the elasticity parameters would be different. In the paper this had been ruled out by the assumption that α and β were $\geqq 0$. The possibility of $\rho < 0$, i.e. capital saving bias in technical progress, should have been considered. The production function should not be interpreted as giving a choice of technique, but as giving a cost curve for the representative firm. This could shift over time.

Professor Diamond asked if post-1913 data existed for Germany and Britain. *Professor Helmstädter* replied that they did.

Dr Dixit pointed out that agricultural income that should properly be counted as profit or rent is often counted as wages. As agriculture declined, the importance of this spurious element in wages would diminish and thus the decline in wages' share over time may be overstated. Had any adjustment been made to take account of this? *Professor Helmstädter* replied that no such adjustment had been made.

Professor Bruno agreed that profit or rent income was often counted as wages in agriculture, but that this effect might reinforce Professor Helmstädter's conclusions if the share of wages decreased and there were some fluctuations.

Professor Berthomieu said he could not see how you could explain changes in relative shares using production functions with neutral technical progress and constant returns to scale.

Professor Bruno remarked that the explanations using production functions had so far assumed competitive shares. Some time ago he had worked with Israeli data that showed a falling share of wages and a rising rate of profit. A very high elasticity of substitution would have been necessary under the competitive share assumption to explain this. He had dropped the competitive share assumption.

Since this was the only paper at the Conference concerned with data, he posed the more general question of the relevance of the models we are accustomed to using to the facts as we see them.

Professor Mirrlees suggested that a two-sector growth model might provide a more natural explanation of the phenomenon. There could have been a shift to less capital-intensive industries (e.g. perhaps some consumption-goods industries) and then back again. For instance, armaments probably have a high capital–output ratio; thus a shift to armaments before the First World War would explain the increase in the overall capital–output ratio during this period. He wondered whether the facts supported this view.

Mrs Bharadwaj wanted to know what constituted an explanation. Various sets of assumptions could be constructed which suited the facts. Which set ought we to choose? We either have to look at the predictive power of the set of assumptions or look for individual outside validation of the assumptions chosen. No such attempt had been made here, but this was a common shortcoming of our quantitative research.

Professor Spaventa requested evidence on price movements and employment conditions. Such evidence would be necessary to support his hypothesis that an increase in the capital–output ratio would require 'more of current production' for accumulation so that there would be 'less available for immediate consumption by labour'. In general he agreed with Professor Hahn that there is little meaning in questions such as those posed by Professor Helmstädter for the economy as a whole. The Italian experience showed the great influence on aggregate ratios and shares of structural changes.

Professor Uzawa noted that a very drastic change in the savings ratio was used to explain a turning-point (see p. 14). No possible causes of this were offered. It seemed incongruous to assume sharp changes (from 25 per cent to 16 per cent) in savings ratios coupled with production functions stable over a hundred years.

Professor Weizsäcker said we were concerned to explain certain changes in a long time series. We had to decide what had changed and was to be explained, and what was constant and could be considered as parameters. The Kaldorian approach assumed savings behaviour was a long-run constant and explained growth. The neo-classical approach assumed that the technical framework was constant and explained distribution. We had to choose between these theories. If we found a low elasticity of substitution we should drop the neo-classical; if high, we could retain the neo-classical.

Professor Yaari said that the general demands for more data that had been made showed little understanding or concern for the position of the economic historian.

Dr Pasinetti thought that empirical tests as proposed by Professor Weizsäcker would not be very helpful for the reasons indicated by Mrs Bharadwaj. Fitting a neo-classical production function would not be a valid procedure as neither is it then used for prediction nor do we have an indepnedent way of testing the assumptions. He thought that the Keynesian–Kaldorian approach was to be preferred as it was, at least, very simple. The neo-classical approach is more complicated, contains concepts of dubious validity like the neo-classical production function, and does not give us any further insights. If long-run capital–output ratios should be examined at all, a more disaggregated approach should be used in looking at the structural evolution of the composition of production.

Professor Mundlak summed up by saying that acceptance of the production function explanation did not imply a high elasticity of substitution because γ may not be zero.

Present econometric methods could not distinguish the two explanations, since we had one structural equation and two endogenous variables.

All observations are essentially short-run (year by year) and long-run phenomena may well just be chance. He would like to see λ, k plotted against each other – it may show little regularity. If we fail with aggregate explanations we should look at sectoral models. His experience with models with two final consumption goods suggested much richer results. However, directions usually depended on parameters that had to be estimated.

Professor Helmstädter concluded by answering some of the points raised in the discussion and giving the movements of r and the savings ratio over time (cf. Helmstädter [1969]). He noted that r is not constant whereas the stylised r computed (see p. 9) was fairly constant. The stylised r becomes closer to the actual r if we include the savings rates of the two classes (which also are not constant over time). He agreed that equation (1.4A) does not constitute a theory, but it might serve as a framework for understanding long-run movements.

If he had to choose a variable to take as exogenous he would choose the investment ratio – it evokes similar movements in r and thereby influences the capital–output ratio and labour's share.

The purpose of assuming the big jump in the savings rate for Fig. 1.6 was only to show that λ, k movements may be approximated linearly. It was not supposed to be factual. More gradual movements would serve the same purpose. He agreed that price movements are important influences on the capital–output and investment ratios, but could not find series of prices which indicate the turning-points of these ratios. He did not believe that the capital–output ratio was purely technically determined, and emphasised that long-run aggregate production functions should not be interpreted in a purely technical sense but as a tool for understanding the economy as a unit of accumulation.

He saw his paper as an attempt to test neo-classical growth theory which claimed that in the long run certain ratios were constant. He had found that they were not constant but that we could find an explanation inside neo-classical theory provided we assumed certain values of the parameters.

Part 2

Growth and the Short Run

2 Effective Demand in the Long Run*

Hugh Rose
UNIVERSITY OF ROCHESTER, N.Y.

I. INTRODUCTION

The idea of a general macro-dynamic theory of money, growth and fluctuations is appealing but probably chimerical, if only because choice must be made between alternative hypotheses for expectations and speeds of adjustment. But the rather bewildering variety of views about the long run is, I believe, only superficially connected with expectational hypotheses. Most of the theories that have been offered us retain their distinctiveness when recast so as to eliminate differences from this source. Speeds of adjustment, on the other hand, are frequently a defining characteristic.

By adhering to a particular set of expectational assumptions chosen for their convenience, and employing the usual principle of rational micro-economic behaviour, one might hope to construct a reasonably general framework within which the various models, neo-Keynesian, neo-classical and hybrids, can be fitted and brought into relation with one another. In view of the importance of the adjustment speeds, one should resolve to postulate only those lags that are implied by rational conduct, at least when allowance is made for uncertainty and imperfect knowledge.

In this paper I have tried to construct such a framework for the inside-money economy, and have then used it to derive and compare two theories of monetary growth. The first is the 'neo-Swedish' or Wicksellian model which I myself favour [and which I have analysed more fully elsewhere (Rose, 1967, 1969)], and the second an inside-money version of the full-employment monetary growth model proposed by Tobin (1965). They provide a useful illustration of the crucial role of adjustment rates. As a further illustration I give a revision of my previous formalisation (Rose, 1957) of the issue between the liquidity-preference and loanable-funds theories of interest.

* This paper was prepared while the author was receiving support from the National Science Foundation under Research Grant GS-2756 to the University of Rochester. He wishes also to acknowledge many helpful conversations with T. Horst, J. Paunio and E. Sieper.

II. PRODUCTION, INVESTMENT DEMAND AND THE BUSINESS DEMAND FOR MONEY

The aggregate supply function, the demand for labour, investment demand and the business sector's demand for money are to be derived from the intertemporal profit maximisation of the representative firm. We shall exploit recent developments in the intertemporal theory of the firm[1] in combination with convenient assumptions about expectations. In this section the 'state of expectations' is a datum.

(1) *Costs and Profit*

The firm is assumed to maximise the discounted excess of its expected 'proceeds' (= planned net value added) over the factor cost.[2] The factor cost of any period is the lowest expectation of proceeds which would contribute to the firm's survival in the long run. (The decision to survive, however, does not require that expected proceeds cover factor cost at all dates. The long-period supply price of the factors is the discounted integral of factor costs over the whole future.)

Factor cost is the sum of wage cost and normal profit. Define net profit as proceeds minus wage cost. Then the maximand is alternatively expressed as the present value of expected surplus profits (or net revenues), where surplus profit is the excess of net profit over normal profit.

(2) *Expectations*

At time t the firm plans for all times $s \geqslant t$, given its initial command of capital services and its expectations. As t increases the expectations are revised, and a new plan is made at each t, given the new initial capital and the new expectations.

We denote by $X(s, t)$ the value of X planned or expected at t for $s \geqslant t$, and for $X(t, t)$ we write X_t. The dating will, however, be omitted wherever possible. In this section and the following one X stands for $X(s, t)$.

The functions introduced are assumed to be continuously differentiable as many times as the argument requires.

Let $x(s, t)$ be the employment–capital ratio planned for s. Both employment and capital are the amounts commanded by the firm, not the amounts utilised, i.e. they include spare capacity, in so far as it is under contract. Expected real proceeds, or planned net value added, is

$$Y = Kf(x) \tag{2.1}$$

[1] See Arrow (1968) and Treadway (1969) and their references.

[2] Cf. Keynes (1936) pp. 23–5.

and K is planned capital. Y is a flow per unit of time. Technical progress is expected to be labour-augmenting, and will in fact be so, and x is measured in efficiency units. $f(x)$ is positive and increasing. The marginal productivity of labour, $f'(x)$, is eventually diminishing. The marginal productivity of capital, $f(x)-xf'(x)$, may be negative for small x, but it eventually increases with x and is positive. It does not change sign or direction more than once.[1]

Demand at each price is a random variable. The firm's expected demand function is defined as its real expected proceeds at each seelling price. It is (the inverse of)

$$p = Au(Y/B). \tag{2.2}$$

p is selling price, u is a positive, decreasing function, and A and B are expectational parameters. Marginal revenue is positive and strictly decreasing. The firm is a price-maker on its selling side.

The state of demand expectations is given by the positive functions $A(s, t)$ and $B(s, t)$, $s \geqslant t$. B represents the expected trend of demand, the relevance of which disappears as the elasticity of demand, η, approaches infinity. A represents all other influences on demand expectations.

Define the planned ratio of capital to (the trend of) expected demand:

$$k = K/B \tag{2.3}$$

and use it, with (2.1), to write (2.2) in the form

$$p = Au\{kf(x)\}. \tag{2.4}$$

The firm expects a constant exponential growth of B at the rate β,[2] but the trend level at t, B_t, reflects the influence of aggregate wealth at t on expected demand. The simplest assumption is to make B_t proportional to aggregate capital at t, which in turn is a constant multiple of the representative firm's capital at t, K_t. Since the size of the representative firm in relation to the economy is immaterial, we can simply choose to make $B_t = K_t$. Thus

$$B(s, t) = K_t e^{\beta(s-t)} \tag{2.5}$$

and

$$k_t = 1. \tag{2.6}$$

The demand expected for t is then independent of k, being

$$p_t = A_t u\{f(x_t)\}. \tag{2.7}$$

[1] We are allowing for the possibility of constant or falling short-run marginal and average costs. But both are eventually increasing.

[2] β represents Keynes's 'animal spirits'. There is some attractiveness in equating it with the economy's natural growth rate, for in that case the representative firm's expectations of trend will be confirmed on the average.

The other parameter, $A(s, t)$, together with the expected money wage rate of an efficiency unit of labour, $w(s, t)$, the expected general price level of goods, $q(s, t)$, and expected rates of interest, complete the description of the state of expectations. The only non-stationary element affecting A, w and q as functions of s is the expected percentage rate of inflation, λ, which is itself independent of s. Hence

$$q(s, t) = q_t e^{\lambda(s-t)}, \quad A(s, t) = A_t e^{\lambda(s-t)}, \quad w(s, t) = w_t e^{\lambda(s-t)} \tag{2.8}$$

and the ratios A/q, w/q and w/A are independent of s.

w_t and q_t are the actual wage and price levels at t. The firm is a price-taker on the buying side. A_t and λ are also data at t. The behaviour of these variables as functions of t will be described in due course.

Two rates of interest are distinguished, the (real) rate on illiquid claims, r, and the (real) rate on money, ρ. They are data to the firm at t and are independent of s. r is the rate at which real surplus profits are discounted, for we must have $r \geqslant \rho$ if the banks are to supply any money at all.

(3) *Maximum Net Profit, Given k*

The real net profit expected for s, $P = (pY - wxK)/q$, is a function of x and k, by (2.1) and (2.3)–(2.6):

$$P = \frac{A}{q} K_t e^{\beta(s-t)} y\left(x, k; \frac{w}{A}\right) \tag{2.9}$$

where

$$y = \left[u\{kf(x)\} . f(x) - \frac{w}{A} x\right] k. \tag{2.10}$$

We assume that y is bounded above, and that for every positive k and w/A the partial derivative y_x, which is proportional to the excess of labour's marginal revenue productivity over the wage rate, is decreasing,[1] and goes to $-k(w/A)$ as $x \to \infty$ and to infinity as $x \to 0$.

A necessary condition for a maximum of discounted surplus profit is that, whatever k is chosen for s, x should be chosen to maximise $P(s, t)$. The vanishing of y_x, or

$$u\{kf(x)\} f'(x) \left(1 - \frac{1}{\eta}\right) = \frac{w}{A} \tag{2.11}$$

is necessary and sufficient for this.

[1] The condition for this is that $\varepsilon + \mu\theta > 0$, where $\varepsilon = -(xf''(x))/(f'(x))$ is the elasticity of marginal cost with respect to x, μ is the elasticity of marginal revenue, $p[1 - 1/\eta]$, with respect to Y, and $\theta = (xf'(x))/(f(x))$ is the elasticity of Y/K with respect to x. The condition is therefore that marginal cost falls less rapidly as Y/K increases than does marginal revenue.

Particular interest attaches to the short-run plan for t, found by putting $k = 1$ in (2.11):

$$u\{f(x_t)\}f'(x_t)\left(1-\frac{1}{\eta_t}\right) = \frac{w}{A}. \tag{2.12}$$

It gives w/A as a decreasing function of x_t only, the inverse of which is the demand for labour per unit of capital at t.

Equation (2.11) can be solved for x as a function of k and w/A, and therefore, by means of (2.12), as a function of k and x_t. (x decreases with k and increases with x_t.) Hence y in (2.10) becomes a function of k and x_t,

$$\hat{y} = \hat{y}(k, x_t) \tag{2.13}$$

where $\hat{y}$ denotes $\max_x y$.

The partial derivative $\hat{y}_k$ is proportional to the marginal revenue productivity of capital. We assume that it is a decreasing function of k when k is small, and that $\lim_{k\to 0} \hat{y}_k = \infty$ and $\lim_{k\to\infty} \hat{y}_k \leqslant 0$. Thus $\hat{y}_k$ is both positive and decreasing for small k, but our assumptions about $f(x)$ allow it to become, and remain, negative when k is large.[1]

Finally, we assume that capital and labour are 'co-operant',[2] which implies that $\hat{y}_k$ increases with x_t.

Now the general price level at t is simply the price set by the representative firm,

$$q_t = p_t = A_t u\{(x_t)\} \tag{2.14}$$

and so

$$A/q = 1/u\{f(x_t)\}. \tag{2.15}$$

Net profit, P, is therefore a function only of k, x_t and K_t, viz.

$$P(s, t) = e^{\beta(s-t)}K_t\hat{y}(k, x_t)/u\{f(x_t)\}. \tag{2.16}$$

As a function of k and x_t, P has the same qualitative properties as $\hat{y}$.

(4) *Normal Profit:* (i) *Capital Cost and the Business Sector's Demand for Money*

Normal profit consists of three elements: illiquidity cost, forgone interest on capital disposal, and adjustment cost. It is convenient to lump together the first two under the title of capital costs, in contrast to the third, which is an investment cost.

[1] The assumption that $\hat{y}_k$ is positive and decreasing for small k is equivalent to the assumption that, when k is small, x (which rises as k falls) enters the region of increasing marginal and average cost, $\varepsilon > 0$, $\theta < 1$.

[2] Capital is co-operant with labour if a rise in employment with capital constant increases the marginal revenue productivity of capital. The condition is $\varepsilon > \mu(1-\theta)$. In the range where θ is < 1 it can be written as $\mu\sigma < 1$, where σ is the elasticity of substitution; for $\varepsilon = (1-\theta)/\sigma$ when $\theta \neq 1$.

Illiquidity cost measures the trouble and expense of raising and retiring money with every fluctuation in the need for immediate purchasing power, whether in the normal course of transactions or in unknown contingencies. It increases in proportion to the size of the firm, as measured by physical capital. In addition it is a decreasing function of the 'state of confidence', which we shall measure by the parameter A/w: business confidence increases as expected demand rises in relation to cost of production.

Planning a larger average real money balance per unit of capital reduces illiquidity cost per unit of capital, up to a point at least. 'Money' is interpreted broadly as liquid claims. Let $L(s, t)$ be the average real balance (per unit of capital) planned for the receipts–payments interval in which (or at the beginning of which) date s occurs, and let $h(L, A/w) \geqslant 0$ be real illiquidity cost per unit of capital. We assume that h_L is negative for small L, given A/w, but is strictly increasing and eventually becomes positive. (There are diminishing returns to increased liquidity and too much of it is an actual embarrassment.)[1] Also $\lim_{L \to 0} h_L = -\infty$. Both h and h_L are decreasing functions of A/w.

In real terms (and given that $r \geqslant \rho$) the interest forgone on real capital and on the money balance is (per unit of real capital) $r+(r-\rho)L$.

Let $c(s, t)$ be capital cost per unit of planned capital. Then

$$c = r+(r-\rho)L+h(L, A/w). \tag{2.17}$$

Now for maximum discounted surplus profit it is necessary to choose L to minimise c; and since the parameters of c are independent of s, the same L will be chosen for all s. It will be the solution to

$$-h_L(L, A/w) = r-\rho. \tag{2.18}$$

Consequently

$$L = L(x_t, r-\rho) \tag{2.19}$$

for $r \geqslant \rho$ and $x_t > 0$, with both partial derivatives negative. (x_t has been introduced in lieu of A/w, using (2.12) above.) (2.19) is the firm's (average) demand for money.

Write $\hat{c}$ for $\min_L c$. Evidently

[1] The assumption that h_L becomes positive is merely a convenience to avoid the awkwardness of an indeterminate demand for money at $r = \rho$, which would be implied by the alternative (probably more sensible) assumption that h_L is zero for $L \geqslant$ some L^*. But in any case the problem of what happens when $r = \rho$ is really an artificial one, arising only because we intend to abstract from banking costs. If they were included, $r-\rho$ would have to be sufficiently positive to cover them.

$$\hat{c} = \hat{c}(x_t, r, r-\rho). \tag{2.20}$$

It increases with r and decreases with ρ and x_t.

(5) *Normal Profit:* (ii) *Adjustment Cost*

Is investment demand a decreasing function of r? Or is it perfectly elastic at a critical r? The theoretical answer turns on the presence of rising marginal adjustment costs of expansion or contraction. If they exist, they set a margin to investment demand at each r. If not, demand is perfectly elastic. We may capture both cases by assuming either rising marginal adjustment costs or no adjustment costs at all.

We shall confine our attention to subjective adjustment costs,[1] in the spirit of the principle of increasing risk (Kalecki, 1937). There is a risk of marginal loss due to precipitate expansion or contraction, a risk that can be alleviated by circumspection. The marginal expected loss from malinvestment increases when planned investment per unit of capital (which we write I) is above or below the expected growth of demand, β.

Thus if $g(I-\beta)$ is the expected loss from malinvestment, per unit of planned capital, either $g \equiv 0$ (no adjustment cost); or $g(0) = 0$, sign $g'(I-\beta) =$ sign $(I-\beta)$, and $g''(I-\beta)$ is > 0, and remains so as $I-\beta$ approaches the end-points of the interval on which g is defined.

(6) *Investment Demand at t*

Real discounted surplus profits are

$$V_t = K_t \int_t^{\infty} e^{-(r-\beta)(s-t)} \left[\frac{\hat{y}(k, x_t)}{u\{f(x_t)\}} - \{\hat{c}(x_t, r, r-\rho) + g(I-\beta)\}k\right] ds. \tag{2.21}$$

The market will ensure that r exceeds β. The representative firm cannot have infinitely valuable prospects.

(*a*) *Increasing marginal adjustment cost.* V_t is maximised by choosing $I(s, t)$ subject to $\dot{k} = (I-\beta)k$ and the initial condition $k_t = 1$. (The dot means differentiation with respect to s.)

The optimum plan for $k(s, t)$ must, with increasing s, approach the

[1] Many of the objective costs that have been suggested can be circumvented by buying extra (services of) capital already in existence, and hardly any seem to be applicable to contraction. Moreover, the increasing supply price of rapid delivery, which has been suggested as an objective cost, is not really relevant. The requirement of rapid delivery would arise from an *unexpectedly* high rate of planned investment, not from a high rate as such. If plans are laid sufficiently in advance no such costs are incurred, and unless expectations at t differ radically from those of the immediate past, the investment planned at t will consist mainly of projects planned before t.

'desired' capital–demand ratio, k^*, whose marginal revenue productivity equals marginal capital cost, i.e. such that

$$\hat{y}_k(k^*, x_t)/u\{f(x_t)\} = \hat{c}(x_t, r, r-\rho). \tag{2.22}$$

Solving for k^* as a function of the parameters

$$k^* = k^*(x_t, r, r-\rho) \tag{2.23}$$

we could show that k^* must increase with x_t and ρ and decrease with r.

Optimum investment at t is likewise a function of these parameters, and of β. But we can suppress β since we shall not allow it to vary.[1] Thus

$$I_t = I(x_t, r, r-\rho). \tag{2.24}$$

The partials of I_t with respect to x_t and ρ have the signs of the corresponding partials of k^*, i.e. they are positive. But the situation with regard to sign $(\partial I_t/\partial r)$ is slightly more complicated. Given x_t and ρ. I_t must be a decreasing function of r for all r at which k^* is $\geqslant 1$ and, by continuity, for some values of r above this. But for high enough values of r, I_t may begin to increase with r.[2]

(*b*) *No adjustment cost.* The optimum solution is to choose $k(s, t) = k^*$ for all s, jumping initially to it if $k^* \neq k_t \equiv 1$. Thus $I_t = \pm\infty$ according as $k^* \gtrless 1$. When $k^* = 1$, however, I_t is indeterminate. It can be any quantity without penalty of adjustment cost. And although $k(s, t) = k^*$ implies $I(s, t) = \beta$ almost everywhere on s, it does not preclude isolated departures from β, so long as they have a negligible effect on $k(s, t)$, i.e. so long as I is finite. Thus when $k^* = 1$ the firm can be persuaded to take any finite flow of disposal over capital that the market is supplying at t. In short, investment demand is perfectly elastic at the value of $\hat{c}$ which makes $k^* = 1$.

[1] It can be shown that sign $I_t-\beta$ = sign k^*-1. Therefore if β is > 0, planned investment can be positive even when the desired capital–demand ratio is less than the actual ratio at t.

[2] These propositions are based on the elegant proof by Treadway (1969) pp. 237–8, which, however, contains one error. His claim that sign $(\partial I_t)/(\partial r)$ = sign $(\partial k^*)/(\partial r)$ (< 0), regardless of whether desired capital is greater or less than actual capital, is invalid. A rise in r has a twofold effect on I_t. By reducing k^* it tends to reduce $I_t-\beta$. But by lessening the importance of later marginal profits in comparison with earlier marginal profits it tends to reduce the *absolute* value $|I_t-\beta|$. When k^* exceeds k_t both factors pull together, and $(\partial I_t)/(\partial r)$ is < 0, as Treadway shows. But when k_t exceeds k^* the factors are pulling in opposite directions. (There is, however, a limit on the rise in investment that can be induced by high values of r. For with $k^* < 1$ we must have $I_t < \beta$. Cf. note 1 above.)

The critical value of $\hat{c}$ is the marginal revenue productivity of $k^* = 1$, i.e. of initial capital

$$\hat{c}^* = \{f(x_t) - x_t f'(x_t)\}\left(1 - \frac{1}{\eta_t}\right). \tag{2.25}$$

It is an increasing function of x_t. It follows, via (2.20) above, that the critical rate of interest

$$r^* = r^*(x_t, \rho) \tag{2.26}$$

at which I_t is perfectly elastic is an increasing function of x_t and a decreasing function of ρ.[1, 2]

III. CONSUMPTION, SAVING AND THE AGGREGATE DEMAND FOR MONEY

(1) *The Household Plan*

The representative household chooses consumption $C(s, t)$, and wealth, $W(s, t)$ to maximise the integral of utility subject to initial wealth, W_t, and a budget constraint.[3] For brevity we consider only the case of an infinite horizon. Utility depends only on consumption, and marginal utility has a constant elasticity, κ. There is a positive subjective time discount, δ. The real interest rates, r and ρ, are expected to be constant.

The choice of a liquid reserve is decided much as it was by the firm. The average money balance does not enter the utility function, but reduces illiquidity cost. It is chosen to maximise the overall rate of return on wealth. If π is this return,

$$\pi = r - (r - \rho)m - h(m, x_t) \tag{2.27}$$

[1] For the case of zero adjustment cost the marginal revenue productivity of capital must be positive and decreasing at $k = 1$. Thus the short-run plan for t must be characterised by increasing marginal and average costs, and since this must be true for all values of w/A, we are forced to assume uniformly increasing costs for all x, implying that $\hat{y}_k$ is everywhere a positive, decreasing function of k and an increasing function of x_t.

[2] Can we say that *aggregate* investment demand is perfectly elastic at a critical r when this is true for the representative firm? It would seem that those who make this assumption are implicitly assuming that all firms are alike. If they are not alike, it may be possible to justify the notion that aggregate I_t will decrease with r despite investment's being perfectly elastic for some proportion of the firms at every r. (This conjecture was suggested to me in conversation by K. J. Arrow.) However, in what follows we shall take it that r^* is the critical rate for aggregate investment.

[3] The 'public household' is like the private sector, we assume, in choosing rationally public consumption subject to its initial wealth and a budget constraint reflecting the current tax laws. For present purposes the two sectors are consolidated, and the 'representative household' plans total consumption, private and public.

in which m is the ratio of the average balance to wealth and h is illiquidity cost defined analogously to the firm's h, and endowed with the same properties. The inclusion of x_t is to capture the effect of 'confidence', which increases with x_t. m is chosen to maximise π, so that

$$-h_m(m, x_t) = r-\rho \tag{2.28}$$

from which the liquidity ratio is a decreasing function of x_t and $r-\rho$:

$$m = m(x_t, r-\rho). \tag{2.29}$$

$\underset{m}{\text{Max}}\ \pi = \hat{\pi}$ is

$$\hat{\pi} = \hat{\pi}(x_t, r, r-\rho). \tag{2.30}$$

It increases with x_t and with both r and ρ.

Utility is maximised subject to the budget equation

$$\dot{W} = \hat{\pi}W-C. \tag{2.31}$$

The optimum consumption is

$$C = \frac{\delta-(1-\kappa)\hat{\pi}}{\kappa}.W \tag{2.32}$$

provided that $\delta > (1-\kappa)\hat{\pi}$. C/W is a decreasing function of x_t, r and ρ, if κ is < 1, but an increasing function of all three if κ is > 1.[1]

(2) *Aggregate Prospective Wealth at t*

The wealth of the community as a whole is the present value of its expected receipts from work and property. We adopt a simple assumption about these expectations: the ratio, R_t, of aggregate prospective wealth to real capital at cost value (which we may identify with the ratio of the representative household's initial wealth to the initial capital of the representative firm) is an increasing function of current business activity,[2] measured by x_t, and a decreasing function of r.

$$R_t = R(x_t, r) \tag{2.33}$$

$$R_t = W_t/K_t. \tag{2.34}$$

[1] The clear-cut negative interest elasticity when κ is < 1 should not be taken too seriously. If the horizon were finite the commonly recognised ambiguity could emerge.

[2] For (i) employment prospects improve with x_t, and (ii) a rise in x_t (which must be due to a rise in A/w) raises the present value of the representative firm relative to its cost value, K_t.

(3) *Aggregate Consumption and Saving Planned for t*

Substituting (2.33) and (2.34) into (2.32) we obtain C_t/K_t as a function of x_t, r and ρ. If κ is < 1 it is a decreasing function of r and ρ, but the effect of x_t is ambiguous. The liquidity effect, via $\hat{\pi}$, tells against the positive wealth effect. If κ is > 1, C_t/K_t increases with x_t and ρ, but the effect of r is ambiguous.

Define planned saving as the value of the planned increase in wealth. Planned household saving for t is therefore expected cash income ($\hat{\pi}W_t$ minus expected capital gains) less consumption. To this must be added the planned retained profits of business. We assume that households' expected cash income for t is what firms (including the financial sector) are planning to distribute in wages and profits at that time. Let it be D_t. Then planned real saving per unit of capital is

$$S_t = \frac{(Y_t - D_t) + (D_t - C_t)}{K_t} = \frac{Y_t - C_t}{K_t}$$

so that

$$S_t = f(x_t) - C_t/K_t = S(x_t, r, r - \rho). \tag{2.35}$$

If κ is < 1, S increases with r and ρ, and there is a strong presumption that S_{x_t} is > 0 (positive marginal propensity to save). The presumption is weaker if κ is > 1. Moreover, in this case S_ρ is < 0 and sign S_r is ambiguous.

(4) *The Aggregate Demand for Money*

The household sector's demand for money per unit of real capital is mR_t, the product of (2.29) and (2.33). Adding it to business demand (2.19) and letting L now stand for total demand per unit of capital, we get

$$L = L(x_t, r, r - \rho). \tag{2.36}$$

It decreases with r and increases with ρ. But there is now uncertainty about the effect of x_t. The positive wealth effect on household demand could possibly outweigh the negative confidence effect on total demand.

IV. MONEY AND CREDIT FLOWS

From now on we shall be concerned only with the plans and expectations for t and their revision. Accordingly we shall change the notation, using x, A, etc., to stand for x_t, A_t, etc., and letting a dot mean differentiation with respect to t.

(1) *The Flow Excess Supply of Money*

The demand for money, L, is for an average balance over a receipts–payments interval. The real supply (per unit of capital), M, is similarly an average planned over an interval. If there were no uncertainty about cash inflows and outflows, and about the fluctuating recourse to and repayment of bank[1] loans, both demanders and suppliers would adjust instantaneously at t to remove any discrepancy between the planned average and the observed average. But since random flows are anticipated, the rate of adjustment will not be instantaneous. Instead there will be planned hoarding and money creation at a finite rate per unit of time to counter the discrepancy. Therefore the excess flow supply of money, X_M, per unit of capital, is assumed to be

$$X_M = \gamma(M-L) \tag{2.37}$$

with γ a positive constant.[2]

(2) *'Loanable Funds': The Flow Excess Supply of Capital Disposal*

This consists of planned household (including public) and business saving plus the excess flow supply of money, minus investment demand.[3] Per unit of capital it is

$$X_{CD} = \gamma(M-L)+S-I. \tag{2.38}$$

V. THE DYNAMICS OF SUPPLY AND THE PRICE LEVEL

(1) *The Dynamic Multiplier*

In the short-run plan for t:

$$u\{f(x)\}f'(x)\left(1-\frac{1}{\eta}\right) = w/A \tag{2.12}$$

[1] By 'banks' we mean the suppliers of liquid assets generally.

[2] Properly, the flow should be derived from inventory theory, and would be a more general expression, no doubt.

[3] If households expected full employment at t, instead of the employment planned by business, their expected cash income would exceed the planned disbursements of the business sector by the value of the excess supply of labour. If v is the ratio of the supply of labour to the stock of capital, we should have

$$S = (Y-C)/K+\frac{w}{p}(v-x),$$

so that in (2.38):

$$X_{CD} = \gamma(M-L)+\frac{Y-C}{K}-I+\frac{w}{p}(v-x).$$

The excess supply of capital disposal would be the sum of the excess supplies of money, goods and *labour* (Walras's Law *stricto sensu*). Our exclusion of the excess supply of labour seems to be for much the same reason as Clower's (1965). But we are not sure that we can agree with him in the importance he attaches to the omission.

the employment–capital ratio, x, is a decreasing function of w/A. Its percentage rate of change with t is

$$\dot{x}/x = \phi(x)(\dot{A}/A - \dot{w}/w) \tag{2.39}$$

with $\phi > 0$.[1] (2.39) is the basis for the long-run extension of the dynamic multiplier. To complete the picture the determinants of $\dot{A}$ and $\dot{w}$ must be specified.

Expected demand depends on the expected general price level, on the expected prices of the firm's close competitors, and on previous experience of actual demand. (There is also the trend factor, but we have already accounted for that.) Accordingly, we assume for the representative firm

$$\dot{A}/A = \lambda + E(I-S,\ \dot{w}/w) \tag{2.40}$$

in which

$$E(0,0) = 0, \quad \frac{\partial E}{\partial (I-S)} > 0, \quad 0 \leqslant \frac{\partial E}{\partial \dot{w}/w} < 1.$$

The expected demand curve rises over time (a) by the expected rate of inflation, (b) by an amount depending on the excess of actual over expected demand (which for the representative firm is $I-S$), and perhaps on a 'cost push' element, in so far as a rise in w induces the expectation that competitors will raise their prices. Cost push is, however, unlikely to raise demand in proportion to w. For wages do not rise all together, and even if they did the reaction of other firms would be shrouded in uncertainty. In many contexts we may simplify by omitting cost push, writing

$$\dot{A}/A = \lambda + E(I-S). \tag{2.41}$$

With zero excess demand for labour, w rises at the expected rate of inflation.[2] In an imperfect market it is imperfectly flexible in some neighbourhood of zero excess demand, for unemployment and vacancies are each acting as restraints on competition. But both employment and vacancies rise with excess demand. When the unemployment pool becomes negligible, perfect upward flexibility is approached; and similarly perfect downward flexibility as vacancies disappear. Thus

$$\dot{w}/w = \lambda + F(z) \tag{2.42}$$

where z is the ratio of the demand to the supply, $F(1) = 0$, $F'(z) > 0$, and $\lim_{z \to a} F = -\infty$, $\lim_{z \to b} F = +\infty$ $(0 < a < 1 < b < \infty)$. (a and b

[1] ϕ is the reciprocal of $\varepsilon + \mu\theta$.

[2] This means that effort-wages rise with productivity. It need not indicate union power, since the commodity traded is an efficiency unit of labour. The rise with λ reflects the fact that rational bargaining is about the expected *real* wage.

are the values of z at which vacancies and unemployment are respectively zero.)[1]

When (2.41) and (2.42) are substituted into (2.39), we get

$$\dot{x}/x = \phi(x)\{E(I-S)-F(z)\} \tag{2.43}$$

for the long-run dynamic multiplier process.

(2) *The Mechanism of Inflation*

The behaviour of the price level p $(= q)$ follows from the log derivative of

$$p = Au\{f(x)\} \tag{2.7}$$

with respect to t, together with (2.43) to eliminate $\dot{x}/x$:

$$\dot{p}/p = \{1-\xi(x)\}E+\xi(x)F+\lambda. \tag{2.44}$$

ξ must be non-negative.[2] It goes to zero as $\eta \to \infty$, when (unexpected) inflation depends only on the excess demand for goods (and cost push, if any). It is unity when both η and marginal cost are constant, and then (unexpected) inflation depends only on the excess demand for labour. (Under decreasing marginal cost ξ can exceed unity. The influence of E is then deflationary.)

Evidently $E = F = 0$ is insufficient to remove inflation unless λ is always zero in these circumstances.

(3) *The Dynamics of Factor Supply*

(*a*) *Capital.* When there is, for example, an excess demand for goods, firms may respond either by releasing stocks or by working longer hours. In the latter case actual production is greater than planned, and there are unexpected disbursements of cash income or unexpected retained profits. Since consumption depends on prospective wealth only, there is unintended saving. In practice firms are apt to respond in both ways. Let α be the proportion of $I-S$ which is satisfied by unplanned production $(0 \leqslant \alpha \leqslant 1)$. Then $\alpha(I-S)$ is unplanned production = unplanned saving; and *ex-post* accumulation, $\dot{K}/K$, as the sum of planned and unplanned saving, is

$$\dot{K}/K = S+\alpha(I-S). \tag{2.45}$$

We shall assume that α is a constant.

(*b*) *The labour–capital ratio.* Let v be the ratio of the (efficiency) supply of labour to the stock of capital and n the percentage growth

[1] In a perfect market $a = b = 1$, and w is perfectly flexible at $z = 1$.

[2] $\xi = \dfrac{\theta/\eta}{\varepsilon+\mu\theta}$. (It can be shown that $\mu = \dfrac{1}{\eta}$ when η is constant.)

rate of the (efficiency) supply of labour. By definition

$$\dot{v}/v = n - [S + \alpha(I - S)]. \tag{2.46}$$

Finally, also by definition,

$$z = x/v. \tag{2.47}$$

VI. A 'NEO-SWEDISH' THEORY OF GROWTH, INFLATION AND THE CYCLE

(1) *The General Framework*

We have constructed a set of relations referring to time t:

The demand for goods:

Investment demand	(2.24)	$I = I(x, r, r-\rho)$
or I perfectly elastic at	(2.26)	$r = r^*(x, \rho)$
Planned saving	(2.35)	$S = S(x, r, r-\rho)$
The demand for money:	(2.36)	$L = L(x, r, r-\rho)$
Flow excess supplies:		
Money	(2.37)	$X_M = \gamma(M-L)$
Capital disposal	(2.38)	$X_{CD} = \gamma(M-L)+S-I$
Dynamics:		
The multiplier	(2.43)	$\dot{x}/x = \phi(x)\{E(I-S)-F(z)\}$
where	(2.47)	$z = x/v$
Factor supplies	(2.46)	$\dot{v}/v = n-[S+\alpha(I-S)]$
Inflation	(2.44)	$\dot{p}/p = \{1-\xi(x)\}E+\xi(x)F+\lambda.$

To obtain from them a closed dynamic system it is necessary to specify the determinants of the natural rate of growth, n, the expected rate of inflation, λ, the real supply of money per unit of capital, M, and the interest rates, r and ρ.

(2) *The Neo-Swedish Model*

Let n be a constant and λ a non-decreasing function of the level of activity, x. Assume that, given x, r is determined competitively so that $X_{CD} = 0$, but that the nominal rate on money is linked to the discount rate of the central bank, which is a non-decreasing function of x. Wicksell (1936) apparently assumed this to be the only control exerted by the central bank. Consequently, with free entry prevailing in banking, the supply of money would be perfectly elastic at $r = \rho(x)$,[1] and the market rate of interest would always equal the money rate, with M determined passively to satisfy $X_{CD} = 0$. More

[1] We are abstracting from banking costs.

generally, however, we may assume that the central bank determines the banks' (real) cash supply in proportion to the size of the economy, as measured by real capital. If the banks' desired cash–deposit ratio decreases with $r-\rho$ and also with the state of confidence, we shall have M as an increasing function of x and $r-\rho$,

$$M = M(x, r-\rho). \tag{2.48}$$

(Stabilisation policy could be built into (2.48) by assuming that the ratio of cash reserves to total capital determined by the central bank is itself a function of x, etc. This could reduce the magnitude, even alter the signs, of the partials of M.)

With $X_{CD} = 0$ and investment demand subject to adjustment costs, r will be the solution to

$$\begin{aligned} I[x, r, r-\rho(x)] - S[x, r, r-\rho(x)] \\ = \gamma\{M[x, r-\rho(x)] - L[x, r, r-\rho(x)]\}. \end{aligned} \tag{2.49}$$

Thus

$$r = r(x) \quad \text{and} \quad \rho = \rho(x). \tag{2.50}$$

Neither r nor ρ depends on the price level. For (2.48) preserves a distinguishing feature of the Wicksellian assumption, that the suppliers of money have no money illusion.

When (2.50) is substituted into I, S, M and L they become functions of x only, $\hat{I}(x)$, $\hat{S}(x)$, $\hat{M}(x)$ and $\hat{L}(x)$. Moreover $\hat{I}(x) - \hat{S}(x) \equiv \gamma\{\hat{M}(x) - \hat{L}(x)\}$ identically in x. E in (2.43) and (2.44) may therefore be regarded equally as a function of $\hat{I} - \hat{S}$ or of $\gamma(\hat{M} - \hat{L})$. Let this function be

$$H = E(\hat{I} - \hat{S}) = H(x). \tag{2.51}$$

It sums up the influence of 'effective demand' on the economic system. When it is substituted into (2.43) and (2.44) we obtain the dynamic system

$$\left.\begin{aligned} \dot{x}/x &= \phi(x)\{H(x) - F(z)\} \\ \dot{v}/v &= n - G(x) \\ \dot{p}/p &= \{1 - \xi(x)\}H(x) + \xi(x)F(z) + \lambda(x) \end{aligned}\right\} A$$

in which

$$z = x/v \tag{2.47}$$

$$G(x) \equiv \hat{S} + \alpha(\hat{I} - \hat{S}) \equiv \hat{S} + \alpha\gamma(\hat{M} - \hat{L}). \tag{2.52}$$

In the case of zero adjustment costs $r(x)$ in (2.50) is the solution to (2.26) with $\rho = \rho(x)$. The equation $X_{CD} = 0$ then determines $\hat{I}$ as $\hat{S}(x) + \gamma\{\hat{M}(x) - \hat{L}(x)\}$.

The first two equations of system *A* are a self-contained sub-system in x and v, independent of ρ. Having previously examined many of its properties, we shall do no more than summarise them here. It is necessary to assume that there is an $\bar{x} > 0$ such that $G(\bar{x}) = n$, and that $G'(x)$ is > 0; also that the sub-system is twice continuously differentiable and structurally stable.

There is a unique growth equilibrium $(\bar{x}, \bar{z})$, determined by $G(\bar{x}) = n$, $F(\bar{z}) = H(\bar{x})$. Long-run inflation is $H(\bar{x})+\lambda(\bar{x})$. The equilibrium is globally stable if

$$xH'(x) < zF'(z) \tag{2.53}$$

for all $x > 0$ and z in (a, b), but there may be damped oscillations in response to shocks. If, however, $\bar{x}H'(\bar{x}) > \bar{z}F'(\bar{z})$ the equilibrium is unstable, and every motion tends to a limit cycle around it. No shocks are needed to keep a cycle alive.

(3) *Long-Run Inflation and Employment*

Apart from the effects of 'cost push', long-run inflation is independent of the excess demand for labour.[1] The F function determines only the $\bar{z}$ corresponding to $F = H(\bar{x})$, and since, as we shall see, there are practical limits to the variation in $\bar{z}$ achievable by altering the parameters of H, long-run employment depends more on the structure of the labour market than on effective demand.

(4) *Wage Flexibility and the Cycle*

The degree of wage flexibility is of prime importance for the cycle, which could not occur if wages were sufficiently flexible. Given $H'(x)$, with $F'(z)$ large enough, the equilibrium must be stable and non-oscillatory.[2]

(5) *Say's Law and Effective Demand*

The significance of the effective demand factor, $H(x)$, is best appreciated by assuming its absence. Suppose that $\rho(x)$ is determined not by the central bank but by competition,[3] so that $X_M = 0$.

[1] Cost push, whereby $\dot{w}/w$ becomes an argument in the E function (2.40) above, and therefore in H, raises the rate of inflation corresponding to a given $\bar{x}$. Even so, since its partial derivative is < 1, a positive excess demand for labour cannot alone sustain inflation in the long run.

[2] With perfect wage flexibility the path to equilibrium must be monotonic. The system essentially becomes the Solow growth model in that case. See below, section VII.

[3] To ensure a stable adjustment of both interest rates to their market equilibrium, without regard to the relative adjustment rates, it is necessary and sufficient to assume both $S_r > I_r$ and $\dfrac{S_\rho - I_\rho}{S_r - I_r} > \dfrac{M_\rho - L_\rho}{M_r - L_r}$.

Then Say's Law of Markets is established.[1] $\hat{I}(x) \equiv \hat{S}(x)$ and $H(x) \equiv 0$ identically in x.

The equilibrium rate of inflation is then $\lambda(\bar{x})$, the expected rate. Now even though Say's Law is not fulfilled exactly even in the long run, there must be some tendency keeping long-run inflation close to $\lambda(\bar{x})$, i.e. keeping $|H(\bar{x})|$ small. For there is likely to be an adaptive element in λ which will take over if $|H(\bar{x})|$ is large enough. This would induce a cumulative rise (or fall) of the long-run actual rate. System *A* is applicable only if $|H(\bar{x})|$ does not cross the threshold. This is the practical limitation on achieving high long-run employment by means of inflation.

The tendency whereby hyperinflation[2] is avoided may be automatic – market forces may operate, though tardily, on ρ; or monetary policy may move it in the right direction on the average.[3]

Contrary to a popular impression, Say's Law does not necessarily eliminate cycles. As we have shown elsewhere (Rose, 1969), a damped cycle, due, for example, to unsteady technical progress, may be generated if wages are sticky, which has a strong resemblance to those actually observed. Nevertheless the movements of demand in relation to supply greatly enrich the theory. Although the 'over-investment' element of the real cycle must always be present,[4] and the existence of turning-points is ultimately ensured by the behaviour of money wages, yet (i) the actual turning-points can be brought about by non-linearity of $H(x)$, due either to an investment ceiling and floor or to alternations of active and passive monetary control in response to movements of $\lambda(x)$; (ii) the cumulative process may predominantly reflect either the multiplier–accelerator interaction or

[1] If, in addition, there is free entry into private banking, so that M is perfectly elastic at $r = \rho$, it might be thought that money would be completely neutral, in the sense that the configuration of the economy would be exactly like that of an ideal 'barter' system which needs no special monetary assets because it encounters no illiquidity costs. (The ideal system has costless clearing arrangements, and in effect every good and claim is a generally acceptable medium of exchange. It is the world of non-monetary economic theory, not the world of primitive barter.) But in general this is not so. For although with $r = \rho$ *marginal* illiquidity costs are zero, *average* illiquidity costs (h in (2.17) and (2.27) above) may still be positive. (Cf. Friedman and Schwartz (1969) p. 5.) Thus even with Say's Law and $r = \rho$, money is not neutral. The yield on household wealth, $\hat{\pi}$, is $< r$, and r is $< \hat{c}$, the cost of capital to firms, whereas in the ideal system they are all equal. However, neutrality is not necessarily a desideratum, unless the 'barter' configuration is a Pareto optimum.

[2] By hyperinflation we mean not a high rate but an increasing one.

[3] Of course other steps will also normally be taken to guard against a breakdown of the monetary system.

[4] Accumulation (G) in the boom exceeds what can be permanently sustained (n).

the effect of confidence on the excess demand for money, depending on the interest elasticities of the excess demands for goods and money; (iii) shocks, if they are needed, may come from the parameters of effective demand; and finally (iv) the parameters of H provide a lever for stabilisation policy. In fact we have here a very general theory of fluctuations.

We have attributed the failure of Say's Law to inflexibility of p. This is, of course, an oversimplification. The same results can, and no doubt in practice do, flow from rigidity of interest rates on certain illiquid claims,[1] such as bank advances and trade credit.

Should its failure be ascribed in part to the zero nominal yield on currency? Probably not. The supply of currency is usually passively adapted to the demand for it.

VII. STOCKS, FLOWS, AND THE 'NEO-CLASSICAL' THEORY OF MONEY AND GROWTH

The neo-Swedish model takes a large step back from Keynes towards neo-classicism. At the beginning of the *General Theory*[2] Keynes criticised classical economics for supposing that labour can directly influence its employment by accepting reduced money wages, thereby reducing costs. Equation (2.43) tells us that in general the classical supposition is correct.[3]

The problem of the incompatibility of the warranted rate of growth, $\hat{I}(x) = \hat{S}(x)$, with the natural rate, $G(\bar{x}) = n$, which has beset neo-Keynesian growth theory and, in view of its reluctance to rely on real balance effects, necessitated the introduction of v as an argument in $\hat{I}$ or $\hat{S}$ (autonomous investment or consumption), is the direct result either of accepting Keynes's critique or of his other anti-classical postulate, complete wage inflexibility. The problem simply does not arise in the Wicksellian model. A discrepancy (in equilibrium) between the two rates is just a reflection of the inflationary gap.

On the other hand, our theory is obviously at variance with the monetary growth theory of the so-called neo-classical revival.

[1] Cf. Tobin (1969) p. 26.

[2] Keynes (1936) pp. 11–13. But the denial of a direct effect via costs actually dates from the *Treatise*. See Keynes (1930) vol. I, pp. 160, 167.

[3] There are only two assumptions under which Keynes would be right. One is if there is an extreme form of cost push, whereby in (2.40) $(\partial E)/(\partial \dot{w}/w) \equiv 1$. Every wage-change leads the firm to *expect* a proportional change in all prices, hence a proportional change in its own demand curve. The other is if the firm's short-run expectations adjust instantaneously (in the face of excess demand) in relation to the rate of change of money wages. Neither of them has much to recommend it as a foundation for a general theory.

Because the suppliers of money have no money illusion, the price level is 'indeterminate', just as it is in Wicksell. An initial value of it must be stipulated, and if the equilibrium is one with p constant it is, for p, a neutral equilibrium. In contrast, the revivalists have resuscitated (under perfect wage flexibility) an extreme form of the Quantity Theory of Money, in which p is always such as to make the real value of the *given* nominal stock of money equal to the demand for it. In fact, despite its name, their theory is essentially Keynesian: whatever the degree of wage flexibility, wages affect the economy only via real balances, and when they are perfectly flexible the quantity equation determines the price level at each t.

Our comparison of the two theories is confined to the case of perfect wage flexibility. Consider the Wicksellian model under this assumption. The second equation of system A becomes

$$\dot{x}/x = n - G(x) \tag{2.54}$$

and in the first equation $\lambda + E - \dot{w}/w$ must replace $E - F$, by (2.39) and (2.41). Since (2.54) above determines the course of $x = v$, the revised first equation now tells us how w must move to sustain full employment. Together with various substitutions it enables us to derive this expression for the rate of inflation:

$$\dot{p}/p = E\{\gamma[\hat{M}(x) - \hat{L}(x)]\} + \frac{\theta}{\eta}\{\hat{S}(x) + \\ + \alpha\gamma[\hat{M}(x) - \hat{L}(x)] - n\} + \lambda. \tag{2.55}$$

In one variant of the revivalists' theory, at every t there is a stock equilibrium established both for money and for real capital.[1] This would require both that adjustment costs are zero and that $\gamma \to \infty$. There is, in effect, no uncertainty either about investment prospects or about cash flows.

Now our theory can absorb either of these assumptions on its own, but in general not both together.[2] We have already allowed for the case of zero adjustment costs. The case $\gamma \to \infty$ (but increasing marginal adjustment cost) merely implies a 'liquidity preference' theory of interest in place of our 'loanable funds' theory. The flow

[1] It is often assumed for simplicity that money and goods are the only assets. There is no market for capital disposal. This means that every wealth-holder with goods in his portfolio must be an entrepreneur. For if there is a market for the services of capital there is, indeed, a market for loans. To sell a good's services is to lend the good, i.e. to part with its use for a time.

[2] This is true whatever the degree of wage flexibility. There is one exception, namely when ρ is flexible. Under Say's Law the stock-equilibrium postulate presents no problem.

excess supply of money, $\lim_{\gamma\to\infty} \gamma(M-L)$, is perfectly elastic at the r which equates M and L. (It is not zero, however, nor infinite, but equals $I-S$ in market equilibrium; cf. (2.49) above.)[1]

If, however, adjustment costs are zero, r must satisfy equation (2.26), and as γ goes to infinity r is unaffected. Instead $\lim_{\gamma\to\infty} \gamma[\hat{M}(x)-\hat{L}(x)] \equiv \hat{I}(x)-\hat{S}(x)$ will become infinitely positive or negative. Assuming, as seems reasonable, that E goes to $\pm\infty$ when its argument does so, we find that $\dot{p}/p$ in (2.55) must tend to $\pm\infty$, unless by a fluke $\hat{M}(x) = \hat{L}(x)$. The price level is either zero or infinite.

This kind of 'indeterminacy' is, of course, intolerable. It is plausible to say that in these circumstances the nominal money supply would have to be a datum at each t, since it could not be planned to keep pace with the price level. In any case, if it is a datum the indeterminacy is removed. The price level will be instantaneously adjusted to eliminate the infinite flow excess supply, i.e. so that $\lim_{\gamma\to\infty} \gamma[M-\hat{L}(x)] = 0$, where $M = N/pK$ and N is the nominal supply of money. Thus we have

$$\left.\begin{aligned} \hat{L}(x) &= N/pK \\ \dot{x}/x &= n-\hat{S}(x) \end{aligned}\right\} B$$

[for when the supply and demand for money are equal, $G(x)$ $(\equiv \dot{K}/K) = \hat{S}(x)$].

System B is an inside-money version of the 'monetary growth' theory. It can be completed by assuming, e.g., constant exponential growth of N. If the nominal rate of interest on money is constant, $\hat{S}$ will depend on λ, the behaviour of which must also be specified (see Tobin, 1965).

In another variant of the theory, perfect wage flexibility is combined not with stock equilibrium but with the Keynesian postulate of instantaneous adjustment of short-run expectations. There is

[1] The paradox (that with stock equilibrium the flow excess supply is non-zero) is resolved by the consideration that when, e.g., $I > S$, those tending to accumulate unwanted money balances are dishoarding them at a rate, $\lim_{\gamma\to\infty} \gamma(M-L)$; that is, just sufficient to obviate the unplanned hoarding, $I-S$, which would otherwise occur. Thus the tendency is never actualised.

In a previous attempt to formalise the liquidity preference theory (Rose, 1957), I claimed that in it unintended disinvestment ($I-S$) should be subtracted from the demand for funds, so that the flow excess supply of funds equals the flow excess supply of money. I was criticised by Patinkin (1959) for mixing in *ex-post* with *ex-ante* ingredients. Although not convinced of the decisiveness of this criticism, I am now inclined to prefer an explanation that avoids it.

correct anticipation of short-run demand or price, presumably through a Walrasian auction. Here again in (2.55) $\dot{p}/p = \pm\infty$, this time because E is 'perfectly elastic' at $I = S$. In this variant r will depend not only on x but also on M. In general, therefore, so will $\hat{S}$ and $\hat{L}$.

There is, incidentally, one further case in which system B must replace A, namely if, although marginal adjustment costs may be increasing and the derivative of E is finite, (i) neither L nor M depends on interest rates and (ii) $\gamma \to \infty$. [Once again $\lim_{\gamma\to\infty} \gamma[\hat{M}(x) - \hat{L}(x)]$ would be $\pm\infty$.] It establishes the 'crude' quantity theory of money.

The revivalists' monetary recommendations do not, of course, stand or fall with the acceptability of their assumptions. The prima facie attractiveness of the constant-growth-of-money proposal is that it may be easier to guess the natural rate of growth than the natural rate of interest. But if the general framework is completed by this assumption in place of (2.48), the system contains three interlocking differential equations, and if moreover λ is believed to be adaptive whenever it differs from $\dot{p}/p$, a fourth is added. The crucial stability question remains an open one.[1]

REFERENCES

K. J. Arrow, 'Optimal Capital Policy with Irreversible Investment', in *Value, Capital and Growth*, ed. J. N. Wolfe (Edinburgh U.P., 1968).

R. W. Clower, 'The Keynesian Counterrevolution: A Theoretical Appraisal', in *The Theory of Interest Rates*, ed. F. H. Hahn and F. P. R. Brechling (London: Macmillan, 1965).

M. Friedman and A. J. Schwartz, 'The Definition of Money: Net Wealth and Neutrality as Criteria', *Journal of Money, Credit and Banking*, vol. I, no. 1 (Feb 1969).

M. Kalecki, 'The Principle of Increasing Risk', *Economica*, vol. IV (Nov 1937).

J. M. Keynes, *A Treatise on Money* (London: Macmillan, 1930).

—— *The General Theory of Employment, Interest and Money* (London: Macmillan, 1936).

D. Patinkin, 'Reply to R. W. Clower and H. Rose', *Economica*, vol. XXVI (Aug 1959).

H. Rose, 'Liquidity Preference and Loanable Funds', *Review of Economic Studies*, vol. XXIV, no. 1 (Feb 1957).

—— 'On the Non-Linear Theory of the Employment Cycle', *Review of Economic Studies*, vol. XXXIV, no. 2 (Apr 1967).

—— 'Real and Monetary Factors in the Business Cycle', *Journal of Money, Credit and Banking*, vol. I, no. 2 (May 1969).

[1] Stein and Nagatani (1969) have considered a special case, eliminating two equations by assuming instantaneous adjustment of λ and perfect wage flexibility. Personally I doubt whether this throws much light on the general case.

J. L. Stein and K. Nagatani, 'Stabilisation Policies in a Growing Economy', *Review of Economic Studies*, vol. XXXVI, no. 2 (Apr 1969).

J. Tobin, 'Money and Economic Growth', *Econometrica*, vol. XXXIII, no. 4 (Oct 1965).

—— 'A General Equilibrium Approach to Monetary Theory', *Journal of Money, Credit and Banking*, vol. I, no. 1 (Feb 1969).

A. B. Treadway, 'On Rational Entrepreneurial Behaviour and the Demand for Investment', *Review of Economic Studies*, vol. XXXVI, no. 2 (Apr 1969).

K. Wicksell, *Interest and Prices* (London: Macmillan, 1936).

Discussion of the Paper by Hugh Rose

Mr Atkinson introduced the paper by remarking that, because there was so much economics in each equation, it was a hard paper to read. He would adopt a reverse procedure to that of Professor Rose and start with the simplest model with perfect wage flexibility and guaranteed full employment. Professor Rose had constructed a full-scale macro-economic model of a general nature, with a well-developed monetary sector and well-specified behavioural assumptions, and then derived other models as special cases. In the simplest case, the basic equation was (2.54):

$$(\dot{x}/x) = n - G(x).$$

Since x = (effective labour)/capital, this is essentially the Solow equation $(\dot{k}/k) = (sf/k) - n$.

There is, however, an important difference. In the usual Solow-style model we take $G(x) = S(x)$ and assume (often implicitly) that I adjusts through, say, some monetary mechanism (different methods are discussed in the Hahn–Matthews Growth Survey). In the paper, however, the interest rate adjusts to clear the market for capital disposal. (See equation (2.49) for this neo-Wicksellian model.) This does not guarantee that at the steady growth $\bar{x}$, given by $G(x) = n$, we have $I = S$: in long-run 'equilibrium' we may have excess supply or demand in the goods market. He questioned whether such a state of affairs was really plausible. Take one extreme case, $\alpha = 0$ and $\dot{K}/K = S(x)$. Here savings plans are carried out and firms adjust their investment through the absorption or release of stock. If, say, $I(\bar{x}) > S(\bar{x})$, then in long-run equilibrium stocks would always be below their planned level and might even become negative. He would be surprised if this state of affairs did not feed back to firms' investment plans. Similarly, if $I(\bar{x}) > S(\bar{x})$ and $\alpha = 1$, consumers would always be saving more than planned. One expects that such a situation is unlikely to persist in the long run.

He then turned to the employment demand equation and the introduction of unemployment (dropping wage flexibility and keeping the neo-Wicksellian monetary assumptions). The real behaviour of the system is given by the first two equations of system A on p. 40. The first, the employment demand equation, is of critical importance and is based on the profit-maximising behaviour of an imperfectly competitive firm. He had two points about the formulation. (i) Although it is very important to emphasise the imperfectly competitive nature of firms, the resulting form of the equation is, in this case, basically the same as under perfect competition; the only difference is that ϕ is higher in the case of perfect competition. (ii) The assumption that the labour force employed adjusts instantaneously to the desired level is not very acceptable. It appears that the lag in employment adjustment, now between six months and a year, is quite long in relation to the four- to five-year cycle that is to be explained.

The condition for the local stability of long-run equilibrium (whose existence we assume) with Professor Rose's employment demand equation turns out to be $\bar{x}H'(\bar{x}) < \bar{z}F'(\bar{z})$. Without this it is argued that we have a limit cycle round the long-run equilibrium. However, for that conclusion we have to assume a Phillips curve of the shape shown in Fig. 2.1. It is not clear how reasonable this is as we have little knowledge of the curve at the extreme regions. He then wondered how we should feel about the possibility of global instability and thought the problem of our reactions to the instability of a particular model an important one for the Conference to discuss.

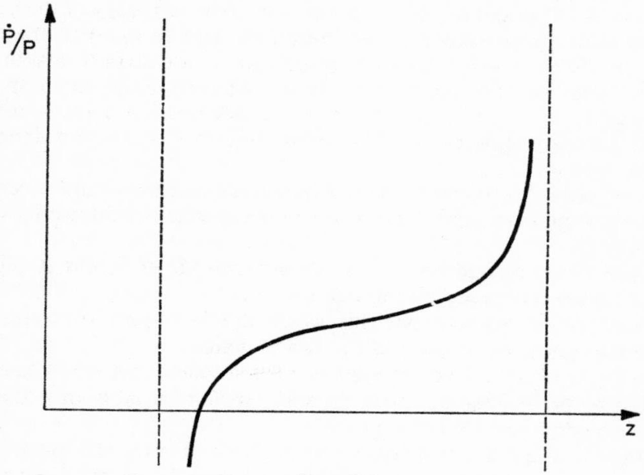

FIG. 2.1

He turned finally to two brief comments on the very important monetary aspects of the model. He thought it would have been interesting to compare the neo-Wicksellian model with a model in which r is assumed constant. For constant r and ρ, $H' = E'(I_x - S_x)$, that is (loosely) the difference between the marginal propensities to invest and save. Suppose we now let r be determined by equation (2.49) with r still constant. He calculated that if $I_x - S_x > 0$, then a sufficient condition for H' to be larger under this policy was $M_x < L_x$. He concluded that instability in the neo-Wicksellian model might be more likely.

He would have liked to have seen the effects on the model of the constant rate of growth of money supply suggested towards the end. An extra differential equation would be much more work, but nevertheless the results might be interesting.

Professor Hahn made a number of comments. He said that he could not understand the role of the representative firm. He asked if it was supposed to be an aggregate concept or descriptive of the behaviour of an average firm. He asked if the production function on p. 26 assumed full capacity.

Professor Rose replied that $f(x)$ gives the expected proceeds of the representative firm. Professor Hahn asked why c was independent of s in equation (2.17). He thought α in equation (2.45) could only be constant over certain ranges of $(I-S)$. He questioned whether human wealth was really a good explanation of savings behaviour. Finally, he suggested that there were two ways of doing economics: (i) using careful axiomatic systems, and (ii) using creative insight into the important elements of a system. The second was the approach used here, but he thought that the informality was overdone when considering the banking system. It was never clear how the central bank decided what it was going to do.

Professor Shell would like to have seen a normative theory of the central bank introduced and asked how it should attempt to dampen the cycle.

Professor Patinkin asked how a firm actually made a profit-maximising decision, including illiquidity costs in its calculation. He said that he could not see any operational difference between using a representative firm and using an aggregate production function so long as distributional effects are ignored.

Professor Hahn questioned whether individual actions would succeed in maximising aggregate profits. He also wondered whether all profits would be distributed.

Professor Rose replied that in a Modigliani–Miller world it did not matter whether profits are distributed or not.

Professor Hahn claimed that this world did not apply over the cycle as people do not take account of the capital gains.

Professor Stiglitz said he believed that Modigliani and Ando had now been able to obtain capital gains as a significant variable in explaining savings behaviour over the cycle.

He asked if illiquidity costs enter into national income accounts.

Professor Rose replied that illiquidity costs may be psychic, but if they occur as real costs to a broker they would be included there.

Professor Stiglitz went on to say that he preferred models in which the demand for capital goods was derived and investment occurred when the demand prices of capital goods were greater than their supply prices. He asked how Professor Rose's approach would be expressed in these terms.

Professor Rose said that the concept of the representative firm was indispensable in macro-economics. We could either assume that all firms are alike or, preferably, that the representative firm depicts the average of a diverse population of firms. He preferred the second assumption for two reasons: (i) It corresponds to the systematic (as opposed to the random) part of the relations in macro-econometrics. The theory of the representative firm is a theory of this systematic component – thus, e.g., we do not assume constancy of relative prices, but rather that the effects of their changes on the index numbers are not systematic. (ii) The concept of macro-equilibrium refers to a state of overall balance without implying equilibrium for all participants. It is not a special case of a Walrasian general equilibrium. This means that we can conceive of a steady state with, for example, overall excess demand. This would not be possible if all firms were experiencing excess demand as they would then accelerate the revision of their expectations. Since, in his theory, overall excess demand does not imply excess demand for all firms nor continuing excess demand for any one firm, the representative firm would not have an incentive to accelerate. A *vis inertiae* could be sustained.

Professor Hahn said that Professor Rose was then anthropomorphising a statistical construct when he said the representative firm maximised discounted present value.

Dr Bliss said that the use of the term 'representative firm' was unfortunate because there is an essential difference from Marshall's concept. For Marshall, the representative firm was associated with industries subject to external economies – thus the cost curve of the representative firm was not the cost curve for any particular firm even if all firms were the same. For Professor Rose, however, the representative firm is just any firm in the special case that all firms are identical.

Professor Uzawa said that α in equation (2.45) should be determined on the basis of rational behaviour. It was not a source of the possibility of a long-run divergence between planned investment and planned saving. α should describe the reactions of a rational entrepreneur to this divergence. If entrepreneurs learn, α should eventually be unity.

Professor Rose replied that α described the reactions to an actual excess demand. Entrepreneurs decide how much to supply out of stocks and how much out of production.

Professor Hahn thought that α was not a rational entrepreneurial parameter but was determined by who was first to the market.

Professor Patinkin said who was first to the market was not random but in the long run we should not have unplanned phenomena.

Professor Stiglitz did not think that the introduction of the idea of many firms, some experiencing excess demand and some not, removed the force of the point concerning the revision of expectations. On the average, with excess demand, firms would revise their expectations and the excess could not persist in the long run.

Professor Uzawa said that if planned investment was not equal to actual investment, then planned consumption would not be equal to actual consumption.

Professor Rose replied that planned saving equals the value of the planned increase in wealth minus planned consumption equals planned value added minus planned consumption. He was assuming that consumption plans were carried out and any difference in planned and actual saving arose from a difference between planned and actual value added.

Professor Stiglitz said that the constancy of the interest rate assumed on p. 45 would require a change in the money supply.

Professor Patinkin said that the existence of a central bank meant the existence of outside money.

Professor Rose replied that money was only outside if we have a difference in wealth effects between the government and individuals. He assumed no difference.

Professor Shell said monetary policy could only work if there was a difference.

Professor Patinkin said that the absence of net portfolio changes was being assumed. Monetary policy could only then affect the price level and not the rate of interest.

Professor Rose concluded the discussion and answered some of the questions that had been raised. The central bank authorities could choose ρ so that Say's Law of Markets was satisfied on the average in the long run. Excess demand in the long run would mean that actual rates of inflation were greater than expected, and this might lead to revision upwards of expected rates and hyperinflation. He therefore thought that Say's Law of Markets held approximately in the long run, although of course hyperinflations do occur. However, planned investment greater than planned saving does not imply that stocks fall to zero. If ρ is determined by the market, Say's Law always holds.

He then explained his assumption of downward flexibility of money wages at low employment rates. We have to incorporate in mathematical models assumptions so that variables stay economically meaningful. Here we must explain why unemployment rates do not become 100 per cent. If we do not make the downward flexibility assumption, we have to assume other factors damp (with no supporting argument) or government intervention (unconvincing, in the pre-Keynesian era at least).

He had eschewed real adjustment costs for investment in the model since most arguments for these are unconvincing. For example, it is sometimes argued that there are high costs to fast expansion; but in that case we should occasionally observe large unplanned investments.

3 Towards a Keynesian Model of Monetary Growth*

Hirofumi Uzawa
UNIVERSITY OF TOKYO

I. INTRODUCTION

Processes of monetary dynamics have been studied in a number of recent papers on growth theory both from the neo-classical and Keynesian points of view. Contributions by Tobin (1955), Sidrauski (1967), Johnson (1966), Levhari and Patinkin (1968) have emphasised the neo-classical approach, while the Keynesian point of view has been adopted by Stein (1966), Rose (1966, 1967, 1969) and Hahn (1960, 1969) among others.

The neo-classical theory assumes that a national economy is composed of homogeneous units, each of which is endowed with certain amounts of factors of production such as labour and capital. Each unit's income is either spent on consumption or on accumulation of real capital, leaving no room for a divergence between investment and saving. Therefore, in neo-classical growth models, as typically illustrated by the contributions of Tobin (1955) and Solow (1956), the processes of capital accumulation are determined by the propensity to save of the community alone.

On the other hand, the basic premises of the Keynesian approach are that the economic units which determine the level of investment are different from those responsible for the determination of savings. In the Keynesian theory, therefore, a crucial emphasis is placed upon the processes by which investment and savings are equilibrated through changes in the level of employment and prices of goods and services.

However, the recent contributions to the Keynesian theory of economic growth seem to have failed, I am afraid, to bring out the crucial difference between the neo-classical and Keynesian approaches. In the present paper I should like to make an attempt to formulate a dynamic model of monetary growth in which the adjustment processes in the various markets of a national economy are

* I am indebted to Koichi Hamada, Ryutaro Komiya and Franklin D. Mills for their comments and suggestions. Financial support was given by the Research Institute of the Japanese Economy at the Faculty of Economics, University of Tokyo.

explicitly described, and some of the more basic characteristics of Keynes's *General Theory* are incorporated. Particular attention will be paid to the role played by the expected long-term rate of interest in the determination of the investment level, as well as to the processes of price adjustment in the goods and services market.

II. THE STRUCTURE OF A CLOSED ECONOMY

The basic premises of the model are similar to those of the two-class model of economic growth model which has been described in Uzawa (1969), except for an explicit introduction of monetary assets, and the Keynesian hypothesis concerning the adjustment mechanism in the labour market. The structure of the model will be briefly outlined in this section.

I shall be concerned with a closed national economy, of which basic units in the private sector are classified into two major categories – households and business corporations. A household is the owner of labour and at the same time possesses, as assets, securities issued by the private sector and money issued by the central bank. A household's income consists of wages paid to the labour services provided by it to the corporate sector, and interest and dividend payments for the monetary assets it possesses. The way the household divides its income between consumption and saving is governed by the intertemporal preference criterion it possesses regarding present and future consumption. On the other hand, the household divides its assets between money and securities in such a manner that the marginal benefits resulting from having a certain quantity of real cash balances are equated to its alternative costs, namely, the market rate of interest prevailing in the securities market.

On the other hand, the corporate sector consists of firms which are engaged in the production of goods and services. A corporate firm is composed of various factors of production which are fixed and specific to the firm. These fixed factors of production include managerial and technological skills as well as physical factors of production such as factories, machinery and equipment. They are integral parts of the firm and cannot be disposed of without incurring significant costs.

To engage in productive activities, the firm has to employ or purchase variable factors of production which are readily obtained in the market. To simplify the analysis below, it is assumed that labour services are the only variable factor of production. The firm at the same time purchases investment goods in order to increase the stock of fixed factors of production. The relationships between the amount of investment and the resulting increase in the firm's productive capacity are specified by the nature and quantity of those factors of production which are limitational to the firm in the processes of expansion.

To finance investment expenditures, the firm issues securities either in the form of shares or bonds. It plans current levels of employment and investment so as to maximise the present value of the stream of expected net cash flows over its time horizon. It is assumed that the rate which the firm uses to discount future net cash flows is not the current market rate of interest, but the expected real rate of interest. When the firm increases the stock of fixed factors of production, it cannot easily dispose of them, and the criterion by which the profitability of various investment programmes is compared depends upon the state of expectations the firm possesses regarding the real rates of interest that will prevail in the future.

The level of labour the firm desires to employ is determined by the current real wage rate and the planned level of production. On the other hand, the desired level of investment depends upon the expected real rate of interest and the expected rate of profit, together with the stock of real capital, and the expected rate of shift in demand. The quantity of real cash balances the firm desires to hold is related to the level of production and rate of interest currently prevailing.

The behaviour of individual households and business corporations outlined above will be adjusted in various markets in the economy. These markets may be classified into the goods and services market, the labour market, the money market and the capital market.

It is assumed that the speed by which prices of goods and services are adjusted to the demand and supply conditions in the market is extremely quick, so that equilibrium always prevails in the goods and services market. In other words, prices are always equated to their marginal prime costs and labour is employed at the level at which the marginal product of labour equals the real wage rate.

On the other hand, adjustment processes in the labour market are not smooth, in particular with respect to downward movements. It is assumed that whenever the demand for labour exceeds its supply, the money wage rate is instantaneously adjusted to restore equilibrium in the labour market, but when supply exceeds demand, the money wage rate remains at the current level, thus resulting in a state of involuntary unemployment.

The money market is the market where money and short-term securities are transacted. It is assumed that the money market is so efficiently organised that, whenever there is a change in the supply of money or securities, the system of prices of securities is instantaneously adjusted to maintain equilibrium in the money market.

Since market rates of interest are inversely related to prices of securities, this assumption amounts to saying that market rates of interest are always equal to equilibrium rates.

In the capital market, newly issued securities or long-term debts in general are transacted. It is assumed that the capital market is not highly competitive, and that adjustments in it tend to lag behind those in other markets, such as the goods and services and money markets. Hence, decisions concerning investment and savings are based upon the expected long-term rate of interest. The expected long-term rate of interest is itself adjusted according to the divergence between the current real rate of interest and the expected rate of interest.

It is assumed that money is issued by the central bank either against fiscal deficits or through open-market operations. The central bank is furthermore assumed to be capable of controlling the rate of increase in the quantity of money independently of the magnitude of fiscal deficits; that is, the central bank may be able to attain any rate of increase in money supply by adjusting the amount of credit extended to the private sector.

To make the analysis simple, deficits in the fiscal budget are assumed to be financed through an issuance of money and the role of tax policy is assumed to be neutral. The following analysis may be easily extended to cover the more general case in which investment and savings are influenced by various tax policies.

III. A KEYNESIAN MODEL OF SHORT-RUN EQUILIBRIUM

Before we proceed with the formulation of an aggregate dynamic model which incorporates the structure outlined above, it may be advisable to discuss briefly the processes by which the short-run equilibrium is attained within the framework of Keynes's *General Theory*.

Let us suppose that there is only one kind of goods and services produced in the economy, so that it is possible to define aggregative real quantities such as real national product, consumption and investment, without ambiguity. The relationships between real net national product Q and the aggregate level of labour employment N are summarised by the aggregate production function

$$Q = F(N) \tag{3.1}$$

where the production function $F(.)$ depends upon the stock of real capital existing in the economy.

The level of employment N which the corporate sector desires to make is determined in such a way that the marginal product of labour is equated to the real wage rate. Let W and P be respectively the money wage rate and price of goods and services. Then, the demand for labour employment N is determined by the equation:

$$F'(N) = W/P. \tag{3.2}$$

In other words, the price level measured in terms of money wage rate, $P_W = P/W$, is equated to the marginal prime costs $1/F'(N)$:

$$P_W = \frac{1}{F'(N)}. \tag{3.3}$$

The aggregate supply price Z corresponding to a certain amount of employment N is by definition the level of output (measured in wage units), the expectation of which just induces the corporate sector as a whole to employ labour at the level N. It is easily calculated from the equations (3.1) and (3.2), namely:

$$Z = P_W Q = F(N)/F'(N). \tag{3.4}$$

The relationship between the amount of employment N and the aggregate supply price Z is illustrated in Fig. 3.1, where employment N is measured along the abscissa, and real output Q is measured along the ordinate. The aggregate supply price Z is then equal to the distance AC.

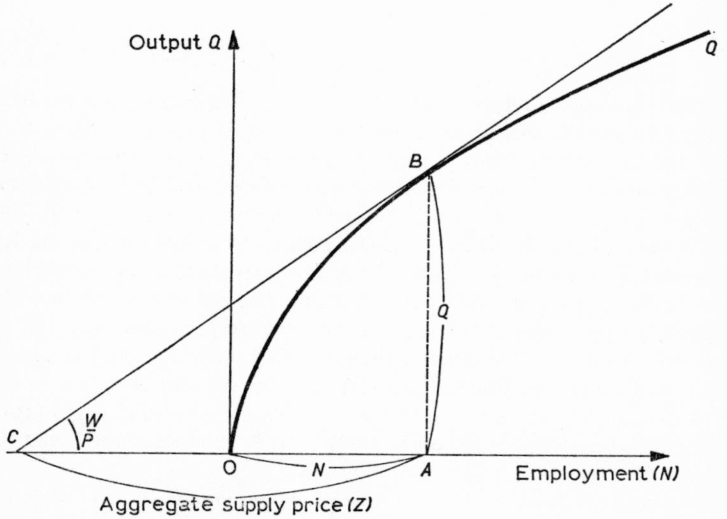

FIG. 3.1

The relationship between employment N and marginal prime costs is described by the curve in the first quadrant in Fig. 3.2, where employment N is measured along the ordinate, and the abscissa measures the price level in wage units.

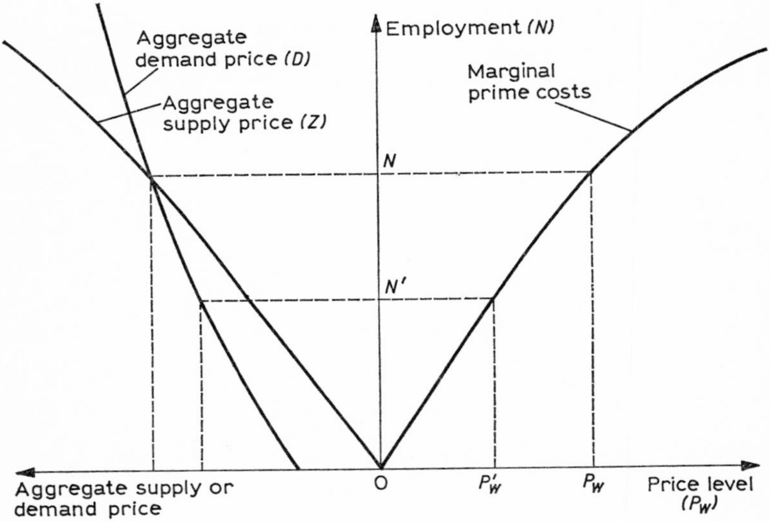

FIG. 3.2

The aggregate demand price D, on the other hand, is equal to the proceeds, again measured in wage units, which the corporate sector expects to receive from a certain amount of employment N. The aggregate demand price D is composed of demand for consumption goods, demand for investment goods and government expenditure.

The consumption demand C_W[1] depends primarily upon the level of national income Y_W. If the representative household decides to divide its income in such a manner that the pattern of the resulting consumption path is optimum with respect to the intertemporal preference ordering it possesses, then both the average propensities to save and consume depend upon the expected real rate of interest ρ^e. As has been shown in detail in Uzawa (1968*a*) and Mills (1969), if the intertemporal preference ordering is homothetic and separable,

[1] C_W indicates that the consumption expenditures are measured in wage units, as is the case with the aggregate demand and supply prices and the following aggregate quantities.

then the resulting consumption and saving functions are both linear homogeneous with respect to income Y_W; and the average propensity to save is therefore independent of the level of income Y_W. The average propensity to save s is solely determined by the expected real rate of interest ρ^e, and it may be assumed that it increases as the expected rate of interest ρ^e is increased. Thus

$$s = s(\rho^e), \quad s'(\rho^e) > 0. \tag{3.5}$$

The saving and consumption functions may then be written:[1]

$$S_W = s(\rho^e)\, Y_W \tag{3.6}$$

$$C_W = [1 - s(\rho^e)]\, Y_W. \tag{3.7}$$

As has been indicated in the previous section, the entrepreneurial decision concerning investment is also based upon the expected real rate of interest rather than the current market rate of interest. The level of investment the corporate sector as a whole desires to make is determined in such a way that the present value, discounted by the expected real rate of interest, of expected future net cash flows in real terms, is maximised. If the goods and services market is perfectly competitive, it may be generally assumed that the desired level of investment is determined by the expected real rate of interest ρ^e, the expected rate of profit r^e, and the existing stock of real capital.

The investment function may be written

$$I = I(\rho^e, r^e) \tag{3.8}$$

where the functional form I depends upon the stock of real capital existing in the economy. The investment level I is increased whenever the expected rate of interest ρ^e is decreased or the expected rate of profit r^e is increased.

The amount of investment measured in wage units, I_W, then, is given by

$$I_W = P_W I. \tag{3.9}$$

If the magnitude of fiscal deficits is assumed to be a certain fraction, say g, of national income Y_W, then the governmental expenditures G_W are given by

$$G_W = g Y_W. \tag{3.10}$$

[1] It would be more desirable and consistent with the Fisherian theory of time preference to adopt permanent income, rather than current income Y_W, as the determining factor for consumption and saving levels. However, to make the analysis of the dynamic structure of the model possible, I have used the more traditional and manageable form for the consumption and saving functions.

The aggregate demand price D is the sum of consumption demand C_W, investment demand I_W and governmental expenditures G_W:

$$D = C_W + I_W + G_W \tag{3.11}$$

which may be written as

$$D = [1 - s(\rho^e) + g] Y_W + I_W(\rho^e, r^e). \tag{3.12}$$

The aggregate supply price Z and the aggregate demand price D are illustrated by the two curves in the second quadrant in Fig. 3.2. These two curves intersect in the way shown in Fig. 3.2, provided that

$$g < s(\rho^e). \tag{3.13}$$

The effective demand is now given by the level of national income Y_W at which the aggregate supply price Z equals the aggregate demand price D. The amount of employment N is determined by the level of effective demand Y_W:

$$Y_W = [1 - s(\rho^e) + g] Y_W + I_W(\rho^e, r^e). \tag{3.14}$$

The processes by which the amount of employment N is determined may be described as follows. If the amount of employment is such that the aggregate supply price Z exceeds the aggregate demand price D (as at N' in Fig. 3.2), demand exceeds supply in the goods and services market. The price of goods and services then rises, and the corporate sector increases the amount of employment, resulting in an increase in both the aggregate supply and demand prices. The processes of price adjustment continue until the amount of employment N corresponding to the effective demand is reached.[1]

The equilibrium condition (3.14) may be rewritten as

$$I_W(\rho^e, r^e) = [s(\rho^e) - g] Y_W \tag{3.15}$$

where the left-hand side indicates the investment expenditures and the right-hand side is the amount of savings. Equation (3.15) means that the goods and services market is in equilibrium when investment is equal to savings.

Equation (3.15) may be written as an equilibrium condition expressed in real terms:

$$I(\rho^e, r^e) = [s(\rho^e) - g] F(N). \tag{3.16}$$

As is seen from equation (3.16), the effective amount of employment N is determined by the expected rate of interest ρ^e and the

[1] Thus Keynes's theory of effective demand may be interpreted as the equilibrium process in the goods and services market through price adjustments, as pointed out by Saito (1962*a*, 1962*b*), Sato (1955) and Fujino (1965).

expected rate of profit r^e. An increase in the expected rate of interest ρ^e decreases the investment demand $I(\rho^e, r^e)$ and increases the average propensity to save $s(\rho^e)$, thus bringing about a decrease in the effective amount of employment N.

The schedule relating the effective amount of employment N to the expected rate of interest ρ^e is illustrated by the *IS* curve in Fig. 3.3, where the ordinate measures the expected rate of interest ρ^e and the abscissa measures the amount of employment N.

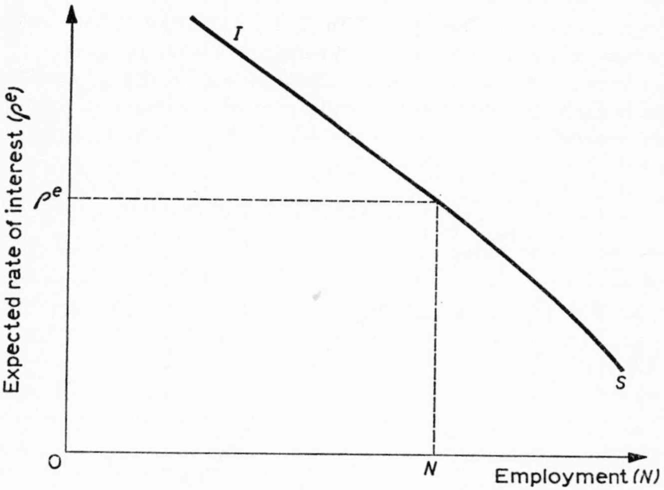

FIG. 3.3

On the other hand, the market rate of interest i is determined in the money market. Let M be the nominal quantity of money issued by the central bank; then the quantity of money measured in wage units is given by:

$$M_W = M/W. \tag{3.17}$$

The quantity of cash balances (measured in wage units) which private economic units in the economy desire to hold is related to the level of national income Y_W and the alternative costs of cash holdings, namely, the market rate of interest i. It is assumed that the demand for cash holdings is primarily for transaction purposes, and proportional to the level of national income Y_W; let $\lambda(i)$ be the quantity of cash holdings which the members of the economy desire to hold, per unit of national income. The desired quantity of cash holdings is then given by $\lambda(i)\,Y_W$. The equilibrium condition in the money market is

$$\lambda(i)\,Y_W = M_W. \tag{3.18}$$

Suppose the equilibrium condition (3.18) is not satisfied, if, e.g., the rate of interest is high so that demand for cash balances is less than the quantity of money supply M_W; then people will shift out of cash holdings by purchasing securities in the money market, thus resulting in an increase in security prices. Hence, the market rate of interest i is decreased until the equilibrium condition (3.18) is obtained. Because of the hypothesis that the money market is efficiently organised, the market rate of interest i may be supposed to equilibrate the money market at each moment of time.

An increase in the amount of employment N shifts the demand curve for cash holdings, thus resulting in an increase in the market rate of interest i.

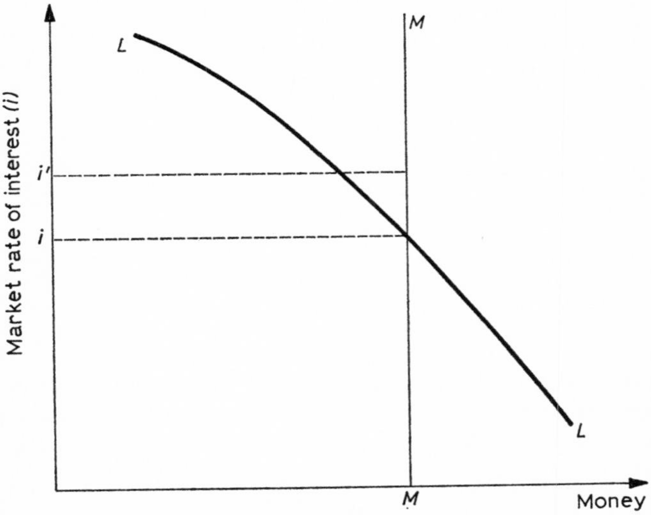

FIG. 3.4

Fig. 3.4 indicates the processes by which the market rate of interest i is determined, while the LM curve in Fig. 3.5 represents the combinations of the market rate of interest i and the amount of employment for which the money market is in equilibrium. It may be noted that an increase in the supply of money M or a decrease in the money wage rate W will shift the MM curve in Fig. 3.4 to the right, resulting in a decrease in the market rate of interest i. Hence, an increase in the stock of money supply M or a decrease in the money wage rate W shifts the LM curve in Fig. 3.5 downward.

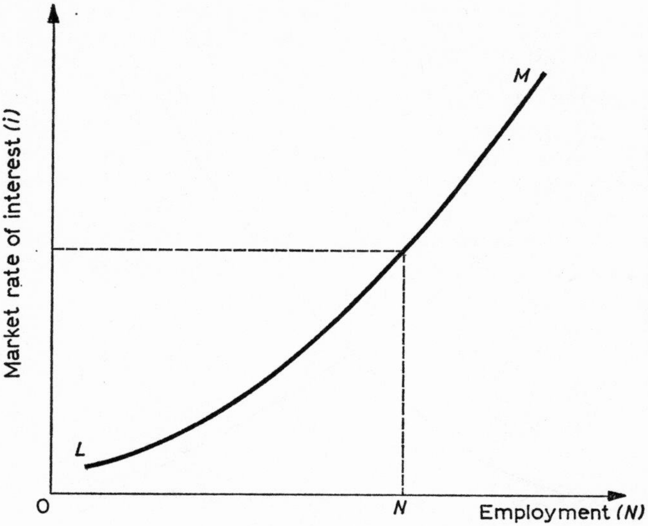

FIG. 3.5

The determination of the amount of employment, N, the market rate of interest, i, and the price level, P, may be summarised by Fig. 3.6. In Fig. 3.6, the abscissa measures the amount of employment N, while the ordinate measures either the expected rate of interest ρ^e or the market rate of interest i in the positive direction. On the other hand, the price level P is measured along the negative ordinate. The IS curve and LM curve are identical with those described above, and the OC curve corresponds to the schedule of marginal prime costs.

The magnitude of the expected real rate of interest ρ^e is determined in the corporate sector based upon past experiences of the market rate of interest and the rate of price increase. The actual amount of employment N is determined in such a manner that the goods and services market is in equilibrium while the expected rate of interest is ρ^e. That is, the amount of employment N is given by the point on the IS curve with the ordinate ρ^e. The market rate of interest i is then determined in the money market: the market rate i is given by the point on the LM curve for which the abscissa is the effective

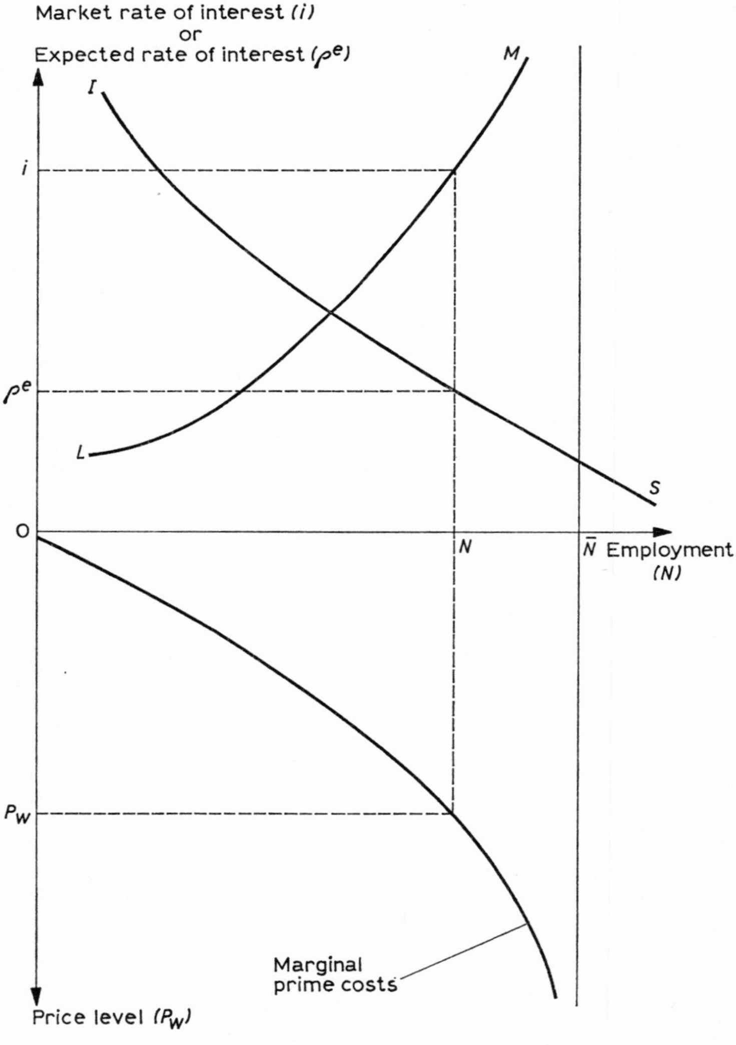
Market rate of interest (i)
or
Expected rate of interest (ρ^e)
I
M
i
ρ^e
L
S
O
N
N̄ Employment
(N)
P_W
Marginal
prime costs
Price level (P_W)

FIG. 3.6

amount of employment N. The price level in wage units, P_W, is determined by the schedule of marginal prime costs.

If the amount of employment N thus determined is less than the amount of full employment $\bar{N}$, the economy is in a state of involuntary unemployment. If employment N exceeds the full employment level $\bar{N}$, the money wage rate W will be instantaneously increased to restore equilibrium in the labour market. In what follows I should like to concentrate on the case of involuntary unemployment, since the analysis is extended to the full-employment case without any difficulty.

The effects of an increase in government expenditure g may be easily analysed. An increase in g results in a shift of the *IS* curve to the right, thus increasing the amount of employment N immediately. The price level and market rate of interest are both instantaneously increased. The effects of a change in the rate of increase in money supply, however, are not necessarily direct. The amount of employment N remains at the same level as before, although the market rate of interest is decreased as the *LM* curve shifts downward. To see the effects which would be exerted by the decrease in the market rate of interest, it will be necessary to examine the dynamic processes by which the expected rate of interest ρ^e is adjusted over time.

IV. A KEYNESIAN MODEL OF MONETARY GROWTH

The expected real rate of interest ρ^e reflects entrepreneurial expectations concerning future real rates of interest. It is formed on the basis of past experience of actual real rates of interest. Therefore, it may be assumed that the expected rate of interest ρ^e is adjusted according to the difference between the current real rate of interest ρ and the expected rate of interest. If β stands for the speed of adjustment of the expected rate ofinterest ρ^e, the adjustment process may be written as[1]

$$\dot{\rho}^e = \beta(\rho - \rho^e) \tag{3.19}$$

where $\dot{\rho}^e = d\rho^e/dt$ and ρ is the current real rate of interest; i.e.

$$\rho = i - \pi \tag{3.20}$$

$$\pi = \frac{\dot{P}}{P}, \tag{3.21}$$

the rate of price increase.

[1] The adjustment process (3.19) is that of adaptive expectations, first introduced by Cagan (1956) in a somewhat different context.

To examine the dynamic processes by which the short-run equilibrium changes as time passes, one has to investigate the way in which the stock of real capital changes over time.

As an index to measure the stock of real capital, I shall use the one which is related to the productive capacity of each business corporation, as introduced in a previous paper (Uzawa, 1969). It is an index linked with the way in which the short-run production curve shifts as real capital is accumulated. Let K_t be the index of real capital defined for the complex of fixed factors of production existing in the corporate sector at time t. Then the short-run production function may be written as

$$Q_t = K_t f(N_t/K_t) \tag{3.22}$$

where $f(.)$ is the short-run production function at time 0 and N_t is the amount of employment at time t.

The rate of increase in K_t is related to the level of investment per unit of real capital, $\varphi_t = I_t/K_t$:

$$I_t/K_t = \varphi(\dot{K}_t/K_t) \tag{3.23}$$

where the function $\varphi(.)$ summarises the nature and quantity of those factors of production within the corporate sector that are limitational to the process of growth and expansion. It is assumed that the function $\varphi(.)$ remains invariant over time.

The dynamic structure of the model may now be completely specified by the three differential equations (3.19), (3.21) and (3.23).

Let us first note that, because of the assumption (3.23), it is possible to rewrite the equilibrium conditions (3.3), (3.16) and (3.18) as

$$\varphi(\rho^e, r) = [s(\rho^e) - g]f(x) \tag{3.24}$$

$$\lambda(i)f(x)/f'(x) = m \tag{3.25}$$

$$P_W = 1/f'(x) \tag{3.26}$$

where

$$x = N/K \tag{3.27}$$

is the level of employment per unit of real capital, and

$$m = M/WK \tag{3.28}$$

is the quantity of money supply in wage units per real capital.

The function $\varphi(\rho^e, r)$ relates the desired level of investment per real capital to the expected rate of interest ρ^e and the rate of profit r, while $s(\rho^e)$ represents the average propensity to save and $\lambda(i)$ is the demand for money function (per national income).

The level of employment per unit of real capital, $x = N/K$, is determined by the equilibrium condition (3.24) in the goods and services market. It is a function of the expected rate of interest ρ^e and the ratio g of fiscal deficit to national income:

$$x = x(\rho^e, g). \tag{3.29}$$

It is easily seen that $x(\rho^e, g)$ is increased whenever the expected rate of interest ρ^e is decreased or the deficit ratio g is increased.

On the other hand, the market rate of interest i is determined so as to satisfy the equilibrium condition (3.25) for the money market. It is uniquely determined by the employment–capital ratio x and the money–capital ratio m:

$$i = i(x, m). \tag{3.30}$$

The foregoing analysis implies that the market rate of interest $i(x, m)$ is increased if x is increased or m is decreased.

The rate of price increase $\pi = \dot{P}/P$ may be obtained by differentiating (3.26) with respect to time t:

$$\pi = \frac{\dot{P}}{P} = \frac{s_K}{\sigma}\frac{\dot{x}}{x} \tag{3.31}$$

where s_K is the relative share of capital and σ is the elasticity of substitution between capital and labour.

The change in the money–capital ratio $m = M/WK$ is given by:

$$\frac{\dot{m}}{m} = \mu - \alpha(\rho^e, g) \tag{3.32}$$

where $\mu = \dot{M}/M$ is the rate of increase in money supply and $\alpha(\rho^e, g)$ is the rate of increase in real capital K corresponding to the investment ratio $\varphi(\rho^e, g)$.

Substituting (3.20) and (3.31) into (3.19), one gets

$$\dot{\rho}^e = \beta\left[i(x, m) - \frac{s_K}{\sigma}\frac{\dot{x}}{x} - \rho^e\right]. \tag{3.33}$$

Differentiating (3.29) with respect to time t, one gets

$$\frac{\dot{x}}{x} = -\gamma\dot{\rho}^e \tag{3.34}$$

where

$$\gamma = -\frac{1}{x}\frac{\partial x}{\partial \rho^e}$$

is the elasticity of the effective employment–capital ratio x with respect to the expected rate of interest ρ^e.

Substitute (3.34) into (3.33) to get

$$\left[\frac{1}{\gamma}-\frac{\beta s_K}{\sigma}\right]\frac{\dot{x}}{x} = \beta[\rho^e(x, g)-i(x, m)] \tag{3.35}$$

where $\rho^e(x, g)$ is the function obtained by solving (3.29) with respect to ρ^e. It is a decreasing function of x and an increasing function of g.

If g is taken to be constant, the dynamics of the model are now described by two differential equations, (3.32) and (3.35). The behaviour of the dynamic system specified by (3.32) and (3.35) is drastically different in the two cases $\beta < \sigma/\eta s_K$ and $\beta > \sigma/\eta s_K$. It will be supposed that one or other of these inequalities always holds. The stationary solution of the system is $x = x^*$, $m = m^*$, where x^* is defined by

$$\alpha[\rho^e(x^*, g), g] = \mu \tag{3.36}$$

and m^* then equates i to the expected rate of interest.

The phase diagram for the case $\beta < \sigma/\eta s_K$ [i.e. slow adjustment in (3.19)] is shown in Fig. 3.7. The typical solution curve shown exhibits a cyclical movement with respect to the employment–capital ratio x and the money–capital ratio m. This cyclical movement may not tend to the stationary solution.

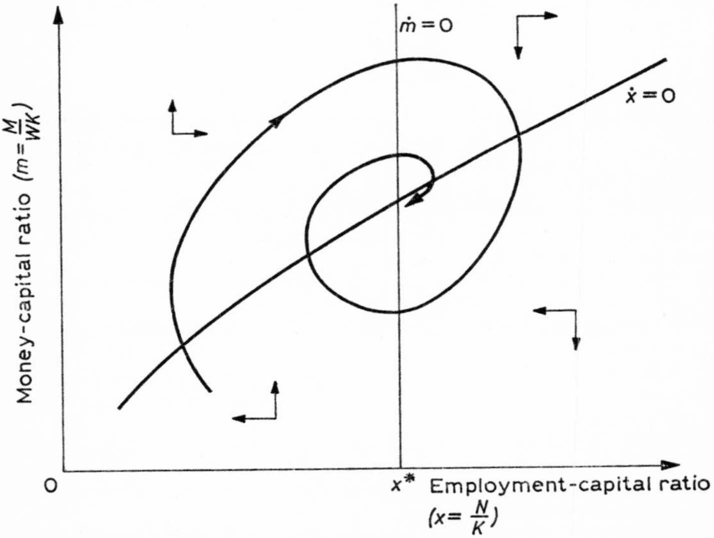

FIG. 3.7

In the opposite case, $\beta > \sigma/\eta s_K$, the long-run equilibrium is a saddle-point and solution paths to the dynamical system show a knife-edge instability. This is illustrated in Fig. 3.8.

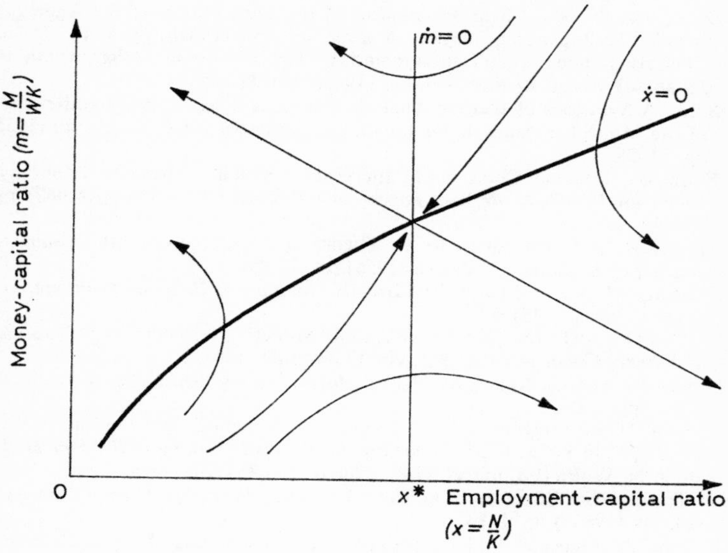

FIG. 3.8

REFERENCES

P. Cagan, 'The Monetary Dynamics of Hyperinflations', in *Studies in the Quantity Theory of Money*, ed. M. Friedman (Chicago U.P., 1956) pp. 25–117.

S. Fujino, *Business Cycles in Japan: Theoretical, Statistical and Historical Analysis of Dynamic Processes of Cyclical Growth* [in Japanese] (Tokyo: Keiso, 1965) esp. chap. 5, pp. 107–27.

F. H. Hahn, 'The Stability of Growth Equilibrium', *Quarterly Journal of Economics*, vol. LXXIV (1960) pp. 206–26.

—— 'On Money and Growth', *Journal of Money, Credit and Banking*, vol. I (1969) pp. 172–87.

H. G. Johnson, 'The Neo-Classical One-Sector Growth Model: A Geometrical Exposition and Extension to a Monetary Economy', *Economica*, vol. XXXIII (1966) pp. 265–87.

J. M. Keynes, *The General Theory of Employment, Interest and Money* (London: Macmillan, 1936).

D. Levhari and D. Patinkin, 'The Role of Money in a Simple Growth Model', *American Economic Review*, vol. LVIII (1968) pp. 713–53.

F. D. Mills, 'Time Preference and Marginal Rates of Substitution', unpublished note (1969).

H. Rose, 'Unemployment in a Theory of Growth', *International Economic Review*, vol. VII (1966).

—— 'On the Non-Linear Theory of the Employment Cycle', *Review of Economic Studies*, vol. XXXIV (1967).

—— 'Real and Monetary Factors in the Business Cycle', *Journal of Money, Credit and Banking*, vol. I (1969) pp. 138–52.

K. Saito, 'On the Short-Run Mechanism of the Distribution of the Aggregate Income' [in Japanese], *Shogaku Ronshu*, vol. XXX (1962*a*) pp. 1–44.

—— 'The Aggregate Supply Function and the Macro-economic Distribution' [in Japanese], *Keizai Kenkyu*, vol. XIII (1962*b*) pp. 314–21.

K. Sato, 'A Synthesis of Income Analysis and Price Theory: A Reconstruction of the Multiplier Analysis [in Japanese], *Keizigaku Kenkyu*, vol. VIII (1955) pp. 51–88.

M. Sidrauski, 'Rational Choice and Pattern of Growth in a Monetary Economy', *American Economic Review, Papers and Proceedings*, vol. LVII (1967) pp. 534–44.

R. M. Solow, 'A Contribution to the Theory of Economic Growth', *Quarterly Journal of Economics*, vol. LXX (1956) pp. 65–95.

J. L. Stein, 'Money and Capacity Growth', *Journal of Political Economy*, vol. LXXIV (1966) pp. 451–65.

——' "Neoclassical" and "Keynes–Wicksell" Monetary Growth Models', *Journal of Money, Credit and Banking*, vol. I (1969) pp. 153–71.

J. Tobin, 'A Dynamic Aggregate Model', *Journal of Political Economy*, vol. LXIII (1955) pp. 103–15.

H. Uzawa, 'Time Preference, the Consumption Function, and Optimum Asset Holdings', in *Value, Capital and Growth: Papers in Honour of Sir John Hicks*, ed. J. N. Wolfe (Edinburgh U.P., 1968*a*) pp. 485–504.

—— 'The Penrose Effect and Optimum Growth', *Economic Studies Quarterly*, vol. XIX (1968*b*) pp. 1–14.

—— 'Time Preference and the Penrose Effect in a Two-Class Model of Economic Growth', *Journal of Political Economy*, vol. LXXVII (1969) pp. 628–52.

Discussion of the Paper by Hirofumi Uzawa

Mrs Bharadwaj gave a summary of the paper and then raised some questions. The capital index used in the short-run production function equation, (3.22), is constructed on the explicit assumption of a constant wage rate. Since a possible question in a Keynesian model is the effect of changes in the wage rate, she wondered how the analysis would be modified if this assumption was relaxed. She asked in what sense it was a short-run production function when there was accumulation going on. She also wondered how the expected rate of profit entering the investment function (equation (3.8)) was determined. She asked whether there was a market for capital goods.

There were two elements an orthodox Keynesian would miss. Firstly, there is no liquidity trap. Perhaps the dependence of investment on the expected real rate of interest (rather than the money rate) allows account to be taken of possible price changes, but she would like to see this further elaborated. Secondly, the average propensity to save is taken as independent of income – she would like to see the effects of relaxing this assumption.

Professor Uzawa said he would like to explain the background of his model formulation. He started from the Hicks–Lange–Samuelson interpretation of Keynes. He referred to Fig. 3.2 on p. 58 of his paper. Adjustment to N^* was assumed. If $N' < N^*$, for example, there was excess demand and employers would increase output until N^* was reached. The demand price D was a decreasing function of the market rate of interest i: if i fell, N^* rose. We thus had the *IS* curve in (i, N) space.

He then referred to Fig. 3.4 from which the *LM* curve (Fig. 3.5) was derived, also in (i, N) space. Effective demand was given by the intersection of these two curves.

This approach had three serious shortcomings. Firstly, a decrease in w meant an increase of M, a shift down in the *LM* curve (Figs. 3.4 and 3.5), and an increase in N. This contradicted the basic Keynesian conclusion. The liquidity trap was introduced to make *LM* insensitive to M. This, however, did not play a significant role in the *General Theory* and some of the important characteristics of the *General Theory* were then lost.

Secondly, empirical findings show investment insensitive to the market rate of interest (i) but sensitive to the expected long-run real rate of interest (ρ^e).

Thirdly, the adjustment process in the goods and services market in the Hicks approach is suspect. If $N' < N^*$ and so $Z > D$ there is no incentive for employers to increase N since N' is their profit-maximising labour force. Keynes had assumed a price mechanism behind this process: excess demand increased the price level and increased the profit-maximising level of employment.

He had tried to produce a consistent theory including these modifications. Shifts in D were brought about by changes in ρ^e: thus the *IS* curve was in (ρ^e, N) space, while the *LM* curve remained in (i, N) space. In other words the division of income between consumption and saving was given by ρ^e and the portfolio division was given by i. A decrease in w shifts *LM* down and decreases i but does not change N. Other such effects were analysed on p. 65.

The dynamics of the system were described by (a) an expectations adjustment process in ρ^e of the type introduced by Cagan, (b) the investment equation, (c) the equation of the rate of inflation with $(i-\rho)$.

The index of capital used was described in his article in the *Journal of Political Economy* of 1969. A business had fixed specific factors of production (those with a large disposal cost) and hired variable factors of production (no hiring or firing costs). In this paper the only variable factor was labour (N). It then had a production function $f(N)$. At time 0 the firm had a fixed stock of specific factors and made a profit π_0; at time 1 the stock and profit (π) had changed. If the wage rate was constant we could take the profit change as an index of the change in the fixed stock, i.e. we could write $K_1 = \pi_1/\pi_0$. In general this index depended on the real wage, but here he had assumed it did not. This was an assumption on the shape of the production function. The change in K would depend on the amount of investment made and $\phi(.)$ gave this relation.

Professor Patinkin said he was unclear about the relationship between the interest rates in the different markets. He thought it was wrong for the only difference between the rates on short- and long-term assets to be the rate of change of the price level. Equilibrium was assumed in the capital market along with a balanced portfolio in holdings. However, it took some time to sell either short- or long-term holdings.

He found the aggregate demand and supply price concepts difficult to understand. This was related to the inconsistency between the general discussion, where the demand for labour was determined by the wage rate and planned level of production, and the model (equation (3.2)), where the demand for labour depended only on the wage rate.

He remarked that the major distinction between this approach and Lange's was that here adjustment of both prices and wages were considered (although there was an asymmetry in the flexibility assumptions), while Lange concentrated on price-level changes. In the usual expenditure–income approach (Fig. 3.9) an excess supply (for example) was supposed to be eliminated by a fall in the price level, an increase in the real wage and a decrease in the input of labour. He thought the expenditure–income diagram in real terms was more useful than talking of YP/W as output, as in the paper.

Professor Uzawa replied that his description of the adjustment process was the same as Professor Patinkin's. The use of aggregate demand and supply prices was an attempt to follow Keynes fairly closely, as was the role he had assigned to the expected rate of interest. In the capital market, money and short-term securities were exchanged, uncertainty about capital gains did not exist, and the market rate of interest was well defined as the inverse of the price of securities. In the market for long-term securities, uncertainty about capital gains played a dominant role and equilibrium might not be instantaneous. He agreed that this was vague, but the relation between the two rates was difficult to understand. Suppose, for example, that i, r are the short- and long-term rates in money terms. Then we might have the current price r determined by i minus the expected capital gains $-(\dot{r}_t/r_t)^e$. We would then need to say how $-(\dot{r}_t/r_t)^e$ was adjusted. Alternatively, we might suppose $\dot{r}/r$ determined by arbitrage with i, r given as $(r-i)$. The first case was stable and the second one was not.

Professor Weizsäcker said that only the former case was operational, as $\dot{r}/r$ was an *ex-post* change. Anyway, the second case was only a special case of the first with perfect foresight, or instantaneous adjustment of $(\dot{r}/r)^e$ to $(\dot{r}/r)$, so how could it be unstable when the first case was not?

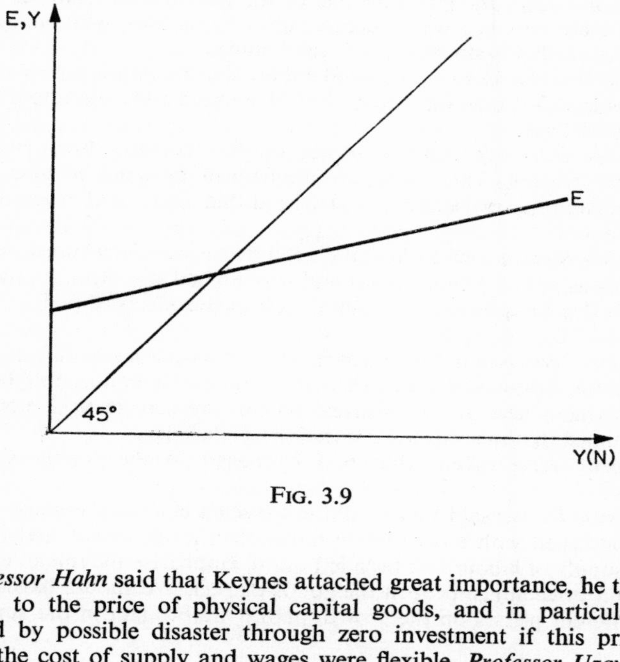

FIG. 3.9

Professor Hahn said that Keynes attached great importance, he thought rightly, to the price of physical capital goods, and in particular was worried by possible disaster through zero investment if this price fell below the cost of supply and wages were flexible. *Professor Uzawa* said that π depended on the price of capital goods.

Professor Hahn said that Leijonhufvud claimed there should be a difference between stock and flow prices. The π in the paper depended on marginal products whereas stock prices were probably determined by future flows. The $w = \bar{w}$ assumption vulgarised Keynes – he was trying to show unemployment was possible even with w downwardly flexible.

Professor Uzawa said that in his model investment goods could not be sold once they had been installed. There was only a market in new investment goods.

Professor Hahn suggested that we should speak of a stock equilibrium and a flow equilibrium. The stock equilibrium was of overwhelming importance in Keynes.

Professor Weizsäcker said that Keynes indicated the stability implications of the relative price of new investment goods when he discussed the inverse relation between the marginal efficiency and volume of investment.

He thought Professor Uzawa's model was unfair to the monetarists – he had no lags in the goods market but lags in the adaptation to the money supply. In fact we know that the multiplier process from the *IS* curve takes some time. This, and the variation of capital-goods prices, should contribute to stability.

Professor Uzawa thought that one of the conclusions from his model was that there were lags for monetary policy but not for fiscal policy. This conformed with Friedman's empirical findings.

Dr Teubal said investment demand did not depend on the cost of obtaining loans in this model (equation (3.8)). He asked what the rate of profit in this model was.

Professor Uzawa replied that ρ^e was the rate at which firms evaluated cash-flow streams. There was no mechanism bringing ρ^e and i into equality. Adaptive expectations guaranteed that actual and expected rates became equal.

Professor Spaventa asked how the fiscal deficit was determined, whether g (p. 59) was given as behavioural and why we had $g < s(\rho^e)$.

Dr Sheshinski suggested we should look at the effects of policy changes in g.

Professor Yaari said that inefficiency in this model manifested itself through unemployment and asked if there was a connection between unemployment here and over-investment in the neo-classical model. *Dr Bliss* claimed that this was not a question of efficiency.

Professor Rose asked what had happened to the supply-of-labour function.

Professor Uzawa said that he did not discuss efficiency because he had been concerned with a descriptive rather than a normative analysis.

The supply of labour had been left out to emphasise the role of expectations and price adjustment in the goods market. We should have to deal with different phases on the growth path if we brought in the supply of labour.

Part 3

Growth of Technology

4 Inventive Activity, Industrial Organisation and Economic Growth*

Karl Shell

UNIVERSITY OF PENNSYLVANIA

Empirical studies by Abramowitz, Denison, Kendrick, Solow and others have made it quite clear that the deepening of capital cannot in itself explain observed increases in productivity. While it is probably incorrect to attribute all the residual (unexplained increases in productivity) to 'technical progress', it is clear that inventive activity contributes importantly to increased productivity. (Although Griliches and Jorgenson in their recent production-function studies have been able to 'sop up' the unexplained residual with quality measures of inputs, hours worked and so forth, their results have not detracted from the importance of 'technical change' – as that expression is commonly understood.)

Spurred by these productivity studies, along with the realisation that *exogenous* theories of technical change are essentially confessions of ignorance, contemporary growth theorists have constructed a variety of models of *endogenous* technical change. Most prominent of these are the learning-by-doing models initiated by Arrow and the 'invention possibility set' models proposed by Hicks and Fellner and more fully elaborated by Kennedy, Samuelson, von Weizsäcker, Phelps and Drandakis, and others. (I shall skip over the planning models, such as Uzawa's study of 'optimal education' and Nordhaus's study of the optimal direction of invention, because my primary concern at this time is with the enterprise – or at least the mixed – economy.)

For the most part, in these contemporary growth models of the mixed or enterprise economy, either perfect competition is assumed or the specification of industrial organisation is vague. The Schumpeterian vision of capitalist development, that the level of inventive[1] activity and in turn growth in productivity are crucially dependent upon the prevailing form of industrial organisation, is

* This investigation was supported in part by National Science Foundation Grant GS 2421 to the University of Pennsylvania.

[1] The distinction between invention and innovation is very important in the Schumpeterian theory. As a first approximation, this distinction is ignored in the present paper. In his paper for this Conference, C. C. von Weizsäcker examines anew the roles of invention and innovation in the growth process.

largely overlooked. In this paper I shall examine three substantially new models of invention and growth. At this writing, while I shall try to be very specific about the role of industrial organisation and growth, these models can only serve as a first step in the taxonomy of models of industrial organisation and inventive activity in the dynamic economy. In the first model, invention is financed solely from monopoly profits in the capital-goods industry. In the second model, inventive activity is financed solely by the government. These two models are in some sense polar cases. My hope is that by studying extreme cases light will be shed on the general problem. In the third model, I begin the analysis of a 'competitive' economy in which invention is primarily financed by the quasi-rents accruing to advanced technology. I shall also attempt to relate the new models to the existing literature on endogenous technical change.

I. MACRO-ECONOMIC MODELS OF GROWTH AND INVENTION: SOME GENERAL COMMENTS

It seems to me that if we are to develop a useful macro-economic theory of technical change, we shall be forced to employ the notion of an (aggregate) stock of technical knowledge. Output of the inventive process is accretion to the stock of technical knowledge. There are strong grounds for objection to this 'capital-theoretic' view of technical knowledge. While in life we can find two pieces of machinery that are essentially alike, if two inventions are very alike they are indeed the same invention. Possession of the first invention is enough; virtually nothing is gained by possession of a second scrap of paper describing an already known invention.[1]

Since there are important distinguishing differences among machines, our models of heterogeneous capital accumulation allow for several different types of machinery. Similarly, we can class technical knowledge by type, e.g. purely capital-augmenting inventions, purely labour-augmenting inventions (Hicks-neutral), output-augmenting inventions and so forth. Perhaps, if our models allowed for heterogeneity of *types* of inventions, then the basic point of Fellner and his followers – that the direction as well as the level of technical change is an endogenous economic variable – would be accounted for without resort to the invention-possibility-set construct.

Many important phenomena of economic development are missed when we study homogeneous (rather than heterogeneous) capital models. None the less, the one-sector growth theory served as an

[1] This point has important qualifications. Because of the costs of transmitting information and uncertainty, it is often socially desirable to pursue 'parallel projects'.

important first step in the study of capital accumulation. Similarly, much of the story of invention and growth will be left out of a model with *homogeneous technical knowledge.* It does seem to me, however, that this is the natural first step to be taken.

This is not to suggest that technical knowledge should be treated as merely another capital good. There are fundamental differences between the processes of invention and investment in physical capital which cannot be overlooked. In the study of the enterprise economy, there are four important facts with which we must contend.

(1) *Appropriability*

The cost of dissemination of technical knowledge is typically very low in comparison with its production cost. Furthermore, technical knowledge can be employed by an economic agent without altering either its quantity or its quality. Thus, we must think of technical knowledge as a public good – primarily a public good in production but also a public good in consumption. In order to promote the production of knowledge (invention), limited property rights (patents) are created, but patents reduce short-run allocational efficiency and enforcement costs are high in many cases.

(2) *Riskiness*

There is no doubt that the return on investment in machinery is substantially less risky than the return on inventive activity. While this is a fact that cannot be ignored, I do not think that it necessarily compels us, at this stage of research, to build models in which the stochastic element is explicitly accounted for. There are, however, important implications of this pervasive uncertainty, notably implications for the financing of R. & D., that must be considered.

(3) *Financial Aspects*

The financing of invention differs in an important way from the financing of more conventional investments, such as plant and equipment expenditure. This difference is only in part due to the greater riskiness of invention. The banker, say, who extends a loan for conventional investment holds a residual claim against tangible assets – buildings, machinery, inventory, accounts receivable and so forth. At each stage, the banker can assure himself that accounts are in order, that plants are being constructed and equipment is being installed. The financier of an inventive activity has far less assurance. Salaries are paid to technicians and scientists, inventories of test tubes and such are on hand, but after a while the main asset of the laboratory is the accumulation of 'experience' and 'intermediate knowledge' that is useful on the route to creating profitable inventions. It is difficult for the financier to judge the quality of the laboratory's 'experience' and 'intermediate knowledge'. If the pay-off is expected to be in the distant future, the financier is likely to worry about whether the laboratory is indeed pursuing its stated objectives. Thus, 'moral hazards' are inherent in the financing of inventive activity. For this reason, the financial markets are less efficient for R. & D. than for plant and equipment. To a greater extent than for conventional investment, we would expect that market R. & D. effort must be financed internally, either through internally generated profits or bankrolling by the inventor-entrepreneur.[1]

(4) *Returns to Scale*

Contemporary growth theory relies heavily on the assumption of constant returns to scale. If technical knowledge is an argument of the production function, then constant returns in *all* factors is not an attractive hypothesis. If the firm doubles its conventional factors, capital and labour, output should be at least doubled since mere replication is always a possibility. Therefore, if the firm doubles its conventional factors and doubles its stock of knowledge (as measured, say, in patents held), then the firm's output must be more than doubled. If the firm does indeed face these increasing returns to scale, then it is glaringly obvious that specification of industrial organisation will not be straightforward. For example, the competitive model with free entry or costless adjustment of inputs will not work. By Euler's Theorem, if factors were rewarded their marginal products, then payments to conventional factors would exhaust output, leaving no room for inventive activity.[2]

II. THE PURE MONOPOLY MODEL

In what follows, I shall study an economy composed of three sectors: (i) consumption, (ii) investment and (iii) inventive sectors.[3] Output of the various sectors is given by

$$Y_j = \Phi_j(K_j, A, L_j) \quad j = I, C, R. \qquad (4.1)$$

[1] The importance of non-market financing of inventive activity should not be forgotten.

[2] This paragraph on increasing returns to scale at the firm level is to be taken as argument by *reductio ad absurdum.* I wish to show the incompatibility of competition and frequently encountered technological assumptions. I do not mean to argue that decreasing returns to scale (especially at the economy level) are impossible.

[3] This section is based on the paper, 'A Schumpeterian Model of Induced Innovation and Capital Accumulation', that I presented to the Winter Meeting of the Econometric Society, San Francisco, December 1966.

The subscripts I, C and R denote respectively the investment, consumption and inventive sectors. At any instant of time the fixed total stock of physical capital, K, can be divided among the three sectors:

$$K \geqslant \sum_j K_j. \tag{4.2}$$

Similarly, the labour force, L, can be divided among the three sectors:

$$L \geqslant \sum_j L_j. \tag{4.3}$$

The parameter A is interpreted as the stock of (homogeneous) technical knowledge. No j subscript is attached to A because the use of knowledge in one sector does not preclude its use in another sector of the economy.

If capital depreciates at the constant rate $\mu > 0$, then

$$\dot{K} = Y_I - \mu K. \tag{4.4}$$

We can also assume that technical knowledge deteriorates at the constant rate $\rho > 0$, so that

$$\dot{A} = Y_R - \rho A. \tag{4.5}$$

Differential equation (4.5) can be interpreted as a crude long-run approximation to fundamental processes not treated in the model. For example, a positive value of ρ reflects the loss to the economy due to retirement of the technically trained members of the labour force.

In what follows, it will be assumed that workers consume all their wages and that the consumption-goods sector is competitive, so that workers' consumption, $Y_C{}^W$, is given by

$$Y_C{}^W = wL = L\frac{\partial \Phi_C}{\partial L_C} \tag{4.6}$$

where w is the market wage rate. It is assumed that the investment-goods sector and the inventive sector are controlled by a single monopolist who sets Y_I and Y_R subject to technological and market constraints in order to optimise his own infinite-lifetime consumption stream.

The monopolist's income is equal to the rentals on machines employed in the consumption-goods sector. Since it is assumed that there is no way to appropriate directly the fruits of inventive activity (no patent system, etc.), inventive activity is pursued by the monopolist in order to lower his own unit costs in machine-goods production and, if possible, to raise the rental rate on physical capital.

The monopolist's expenses are the wages paid (in units of the consumption good) to workers in the research and machine-goods departments. If $Y_C{}^M$ is monopolist consumption, then

$$Y_C = Y_C{}^M + Y_C{}^M \tag{4.7}$$

where

$$rK_C = wL_R + wL_I + Y_C{}^M \tag{4.8}$$

and

$$wL_R + wL_I + wL_C = Y_C{}^W \tag{4.9}$$

where r is the rental on physical capital in terms of consumption.

(1) *Monopoly Capitalism: A Digression*

It is assumed for the purposes of this section that the production functions defined in (4.1) are such that the production-possibility frontier in (Y_C, Y_I, Y_R) space is a plane surface along which all ratios of supply prices are equal to unity. This will simplify the analysis, since by a proper choice of units we can reduce all calculations to those involving a 'single' production function, so that

$$Y \equiv Y_C + Y_I + Y_R = \Phi(K, A, L). \tag{4.10}$$

In order to simplify the analysis further, it is assumed that there is no growth in the labour force, $\dot{L} = 0$. For the purpose of this digression, technical knowledge is assigned no role in production, $(\partial\Phi/\partial A) \equiv 0$ and thus $Y_R = 0$. Under the assumptions made, output per worker y is a function of capital per worker k, written as

$$y = f(k) \tag{4.11}$$

where

$$\left.\begin{array}{l} f(k) > 0, \quad f'(k) > 0 \\ f''(k) < 0, \quad f'''(k) < 0, \quad \text{for} \quad 0 < k < \infty. \end{array}\right\} \tag{4.12}$$

In addition to the usual curvature assumptions, (4.12) implies that the monopolist's profit, $Lkf'(k)$, is a concave function of k. (From here on, assign $L \equiv 1$ for simplicity.)

The capitalist (a *bon vivant*) desires to maximise

$$\int_0^\infty U[(1-s)kf']e^{-\delta t}dt \tag{4.13}$$

where $\delta > 0$ is his subjective rate of time discount. The functional (4.13) is constrained by

$$s(t) \in [0, 1] \tag{4.14}$$

and

$$\dot{k} = skf' - \mu k \tag{4.15}$$

for $0 \leqslant t < \infty$.

Let H be the discounted value of monopolist's profits so that

$$He^{\delta t} = U[(1-s)kf'] + q[skf' - \mu k] \tag{4.16}$$

where $q(t)$ is the capitalist's shadow demand price of investment at time t in terms of utility forgone at time t. We assume that $U' > 0$ and $U'' < 0$ with $U'[0] = \infty$. Therefore, constrained maximisation of (4.13) implies that

$$\dot{q} = (\delta + \mu)q - [f' + kf'']U' \tag{4.17}$$

where s is chosen such that

$$U' \geqslant q, \quad \text{with equality when} \quad s > 0. \tag{4.18}$$

Defining the set N by

$$N = \{(k, q) : U'(kf') \leqslant q\}$$

then in the set N (for non-specialisation)

$$\psi(k, q) \equiv U'[(1-s)kf'] - q = 0. \tag{4.19}$$

Thus, in N,

$$\left.\begin{aligned} &\frac{\partial \psi}{\partial q} = -1, \quad \frac{\partial \psi}{\partial s} = -kf'U'', \\ &\frac{\partial \psi}{\partial k} = (1-s)(f' + kf')U''. \end{aligned}\right\} \tag{4.20}$$

Hence along the capitalist's consumption-optimal trajectory,

$$\left(\frac{\partial s}{\partial q}\right) = \frac{-1}{kf'U''} > 0 \tag{4.21}$$

and

$$\left(\frac{\partial s}{\partial k}\right)_N = \frac{(1-s)(f' + kf'')}{kf'} < 0. \tag{4.22}$$

Stationaries, k^*, q^* and s^*, to the system (4.14), (4.15), (4.17) and (4.18) are given as solutions to

$$\Phi(k) \equiv f' + kf'' = \delta + \dot{\mu} \tag{4.23}$$

where, since $\partial\Phi/\partial k = kf''' + 2f'' < 0$, there exists at most one solution to (4.23). Assume that k^* solves (4.23), then stationarity of k implies that s takes on a value s^* given by

$$0 < s^* = \frac{\mu}{f'(k^*)} < \frac{\mu}{\delta + \mu} < 1. \tag{4.24}$$

And, of course, q is assigned a value q^* given by

$$q^* = U'[(1-s^*)k^*f'(k^*)]. \tag{4.25}$$

Consider, for purposes of exposition, an economy which begins with $k(0) = k^*$. The above shows that, since a programme satisfying (4.14), (4.15), (4.17) and (4.18) is optimal if the transversality condition

$$\lim_{t\to\infty} qe^{-\delta t} = 0 \tag{4.26}$$

holds, the capitalist will strive to maintain k at k^* for ever. Because of monopoly power, long-run accumulation under monopoly capitalism is less than it would have been had wealth been evenly distributed, had everyone's tastes been given as in (4.13), and had they acted upon them. In fact, as $\delta \to 0$, under monopoly capitalism, k^* approaches a value which is bounded below the golden rule capital–labour ratio.

The full-phase diagram in (k, q) space is quite exhausting to treat, especially since there are several qualitatively different cases to examine. Instead of detailing that analysis, I shall limit myself to examination of the 'small vibration' analysis about the point (k^*, q^*). The linear Taylor expansion about (k^*, q^*) is

$$\begin{bmatrix} \dot{k} \\ \\ \dot{q} \end{bmatrix} = \begin{bmatrix} \left(\dfrac{\partial \dot{k}}{\partial k}\right)_* & \left(\dfrac{\partial \dot{k}}{\partial q}\right)_* \\ \\ \left(\dfrac{\partial \dot{q}}{\partial q}\right)_* & \left(\dfrac{\partial \dot{q}}{\partial q}\right)_* \end{bmatrix} \begin{bmatrix} (k-k^*) \\ \\ (q-q^*) \end{bmatrix}. \tag{4.27}$$

But

$$\frac{\partial \dot{k}}{\partial k} = skf''+sf'+kf'\frac{\partial s}{\partial k}-\mu$$

or

$$\frac{\partial \dot{q}}{\partial k} = f'+kf''-\mu$$

so that

$$\left(\frac{\partial \dot{k}}{\partial k}\right)_* = \delta > 0.$$

Also

$$\frac{\partial \dot{k}}{\partial q} = kf'\frac{\partial s}{\partial q} = \frac{-1}{U''} > 0$$

and

$$\frac{\partial \dot{q}}{\partial k} = \delta+\mu-(f'+kf'')$$

so that

$$\left(\frac{\partial \dot{q}}{\partial k}\right)_* = 0.$$

Finally,

$$\frac{\partial \dot{q}}{\partial k} = -q(kf''' + 2f'') > 0.$$

Defining

$$\beta \equiv \left(\frac{-1}{U''}\right)_* > 0 \quad \text{and} \quad \alpha \equiv -q^*[k^*f'''(k^*) + sf''(k^*)] > 0$$

gives the following characteristic equation to the associated linear system (4.18):

$$\begin{vmatrix} \delta - x & \beta \\ \alpha & -x \end{vmatrix} = 0 \tag{4.28}$$

where x is the characteristic root. (4.28) yields two roots and so, by completing the square,

$$x = \frac{-\delta \pm \sqrt{(\delta^2 + 4\alpha\beta)}}{2} \tag{4.29}$$

and thus the characteristic roots are real but of opposite signs. The unique equilibrium point (k^*, q^*) is a saddle-point, and thus we know that except for a finite initial time period the capital–labour ratio will be arbitrarily close to this 'k^* turnpike'.

In the Conference discussion, it was pointed out by Mirrlees and Stiglitz that the capitalist with sufficiently large initial endowments will withhold capital for some initial period of time. Since profits, $kf'(k)$, are concave in k, capital will be withheld if and only if $k > k^{**}$ where k^{**} is defined by $f'(k^{**}) + k^{**}f''(k^{**}) = 0$. Since k^* is defined $f'(k^*) + k^*f''(k^*) = \delta + \mu > 0$, k^{**} is larger than k^*. The capitalist withholds capital, holding investment at zero, until k falls to k^{**}. Thereafter, capital is fully employed and growth is as described above. (At any instant, capital employment will be min (k, k^{**}).) The capital–labour ratio k^* retains the turnpike property.

The Mirrlees–Stiglitz objection causes somewhat more difficulty in the analysis of the model with induced innovation. Because of the interaction of k and A, there may be several isolated episodes in which capital is not fully employed. To do full justice to the calculus of variations problem, one must explicitly allow for unemployment of capital. The added constraint will have an associated shadow price yielding jump conditions for transferring from regimes of unemployment to full employment.

If we allow the capitalist to withhold technological knowledge, then some very interesting cases can occur. Just as critics of the monopolistic invention system have alleged, new technological knowledge adversely affecting current profits would be secreted by the monopolist.

(2) *Monopoly Profits and Induced Innovation*

It is assumed as before that the amount of homogeneous output is dependent upon the size of the labour force and the level of the stock of physical capital. Now we turn to the more interesting case where, in addition, it is assumed that output is an increasing function of the stock of technical knowledge A. For compatibility with the assumptions of non-appropriability of technical knowledge and of competition in the consumption-goods sector, it is assumed that there are constant returns to scale in physical capital and labour and thus increasing returns to scale in all three factors. Output y can be written as

$$y = g(k, A) \tag{4.30}$$

where g is an increasing concave function and profits, $\pi = kg_1$, are also concave in k and A.

The single capitalist maximises the functional

$$\int_0^\infty U[(1-s)kg_1(k, A)]e^{-\delta t}dt \tag{4.31}$$

subject to

$$\dot{k} = \sigma skg_1 - \mu k \tag{4.32}$$

$$\dot{A} = (1-\sigma)skg_1 - \rho A \tag{4.33}$$

$$s \in [0, 1] \quad \text{and} \quad \sigma \in [0, 1] \tag{4.34}$$

where s is the saving fraction and σ is the proportion of saving devoted to capital investment.

Let H be the present value to the capitalist of profits, then

$$He^{\delta t} = U[(1-s)kg_1] + \xi(\sigma skg_1 - \mu k) + \eta[(1-\sigma)skg_1 - \rho A] \tag{4.35}$$

where ξ and η are respectively his demand valuation of a unit of investment and a unit of invention. It is necessary for maximisation of (4.31) that s and σ be chosen such that:

$$U'[(1-s)kg_1] \geqslant \max(\xi, \eta) \equiv \gamma, \quad \text{with equality if} \quad s > 0 \tag{4.36}$$

$$\left.\begin{array}{ll} \sigma = 1, & \text{when} \quad \xi > \eta \\ \sigma \in [1, 0], & \text{when} \quad \xi = \eta \\ \sigma = 0, & \text{when} \quad \xi < \eta \end{array}\right\} \tag{4.37}$$

$$\dot{\xi} = (\delta+\mu)\xi - [kg_{11}+g_1]U' \tag{4.38}$$

$$\dot{\eta} = (\delta+\rho)\eta - kg_{12}U'. \tag{4.39}$$

Conditions (4.38) and (4.39) state that the demand valuation of an asset must change so as to compensate the capitalist for loss due to depreciation plus a reward for 'waiting' less the value (in terms of utility) of the marginal product of that asset.

Defining the set N by

$$N \equiv \{(k, A, \xi, \eta): U'[kg_1(k, A)] \leqslant \gamma\} \tag{4.40}$$

yields from (4.36) that

$$\left(\frac{\partial s}{\partial \gamma}\right)_N = \frac{-1}{kg_1U''} > 0 \tag{4.41}$$

$$\left(\frac{\partial s}{\partial k}\right)_N = \frac{(1-s)[g_1+kg_{11}]}{kg_1} \tag{4.42}$$

$$\left(\frac{\partial s}{\partial A}\right)_N = \frac{(1-s)g_{12}}{g_1} > 0. \tag{4.43}$$

Stationaries to (4.32), (4.33), (4.38) and (4.39) are given by solving the system:

$$kg_{11}+g_1 = \delta+\mu \tag{4.44}$$

$$kg_{12} = \delta+\rho \tag{4.45}$$

$$\sigma skg_1 = \mu k \tag{4.46}$$

$$(1-\sigma)skg_1 = A. \tag{4.47}$$

Defining $D = kg_{11}+g_1-\delta-\mu$, and implicitly differentiating (4.44), yields

$$\left(\frac{dA}{dk}\right)_{D=0} = -\left(\frac{kg_{111}+2g_{11}}{kg_{112}+g_{12}}\right) > 0 \tag{4.48}$$

by the concavity of $g(k, A)$ and $\pi(k, A)$. Defining

$$E = kg_{12}-\delta-\rho$$

and implicitly differentiating (4.45) yields

$$\left(\frac{dA}{dk}\right)_{E=0} = -\frac{kg_{112}+g_{12}}{kg_{122}} > 0 \tag{4.49}$$

by the concavity assumptions. But notice that

$$\frac{\left(\dfrac{dA}{dk}\right)_{E=0}}{\left(\dfrac{dA}{dk}\right)_{D=0}} = \frac{(kg_{112}+g_{12})^2}{kg_{122}(kg_{112}+2g_{11})} < 1 \tag{4.50}$$

by the concavity of $\pi(k, A) = kg_1(k, A)$.

By (4.50) we know that there is at most one solution to the system (4.44) and (4.45) in (k, A) space. Assume that such a solution exists and denote it by (k^*, A^*). Now if $(A^*/k^*) < (\delta/\rho)$, then (4.46) and (4.47) yield

$$s^* = \frac{\mu k^* + \rho A}{k^* g_1(k^*, A^*)} < 1$$

and thus

$$\frac{\sigma^*}{1-\sigma^*} = \frac{\mu k^*}{\rho A^*}$$

ensuring that $\sigma^* \in [0, 1]$.

Also, notice that if development tends to (k^*, A^*), then the transversality conditions

$$\lim_{t\to\infty} \xi e^{-\delta t} = \lim_{t\to\infty} \eta e^{-\delta t} = 0 \tag{4.51}$$

are satisfied. Except for a finite initial time period, growth of the economy is arbitrarily close to the (k^*, A^*) turnpike.

This mathematical argument has been terse and may have led to some confusion. It should be worth while to take some time to elaborate.

I do not mean to say that transversality conditions such as (4.26) and (4.51) are necessary conditions for utility maximisation. The Ramsey optimal-growth problem with zero impatience and zero population growth is a well-known counter-example. We do know that because of the concavity of $U(\cdot)$ and $g(\cdot)$, the utility-maximising programme is unique. Because of the concavity of $U(\cdot)$ and $g(\cdot)$ and because δ is positive, a feasible path satisfying Euler equations (4.36)–(4.39) and transversality conditions (4.51) will be preferred by the monopolist to any other feasible path. In the neighbourhood of (k^*, A^*) a path satisfying the Euler equations and the transversality conditions does indeed exist. I have not shown existence of such a trajectory for all initial endowments vectors, (k, A). Existence could be established by a constructive argument. One would need to show that in (k, A, ξ, η) space the manifold of Euler solutions tending to (k^*, A^*) covers the entire positive orthant of (k, A) plane.

III. TECHNICAL KNOWLEDGE AS A PURE PUBLIC GOOD OF PRODUCTION

Because of space limitations, I was unable in the preceding section to develop many specific conclusions. (Even the concavity assumptions are made more for mathematical convenience than because they are realistic, or the reverse.) While more study is needed before the analysis will lead to definite results (such as the pattern of optimal social control), it is my hope that we have gained some insight into the basic dynamics of a model in which monopoly profits fuel inventive activity.

In this section, we focus on a model in which production of consumption and investment is competitive, with technical knowledge entering each firm's production function as a pure public good. Inventive activity must therefore be supported by non-market institutions. In the present model, the government imposes an excise tax, and the revenue is used to finance government-controlled research.[1]

As before, we simplify by assuming a technology with equal capital intensities, so that we can write

$$Y \equiv Y_C + Y_I + Y_R = \Phi(K, A, L). \tag{4.52}$$

Assume further that for firm i, output, Y^i, is given by

$$Y^i = AF(K^i, L^i) \tag{4.53}$$

where $F(\cdot)$ is positively homogeneous of degree one. In the aggregate,

$$Y = \sum_i Y^i = A \sum_i F(K^i, L^i) \tag{4.54}$$

so that at the economy level the production function under our particular specification is positively homogeneous of degree two in the three factors:

$$A, K = \sum_i K^i, \quad \text{and} \quad L = \sum_i L^i.$$

Since each firm is small, it cannot substantially affect either aggregate A or aggregate Y_R. The competitive price of knowledge is zero although its marginal (and average) social product is equal to $F(\cdot)$.

To repair this market failure, the government imposes an excise tax on the output of consumption and investment. If the tax rate is $0 < \alpha < 1$, then the competitive wage rate, w, and rental rate, r, are given by

$$r = (1-\alpha)AF_K$$
$$w = (1-\alpha)AF_L.$$

[1] The treatment here is condensed since it is based on some earlier work. See Shell (1966, 1967).

Tax revenue, $\alpha(Y_C + Y_I + Y_R) = \alpha Y$, is equal to government production (or purchases) of inventive output, $\alpha Y = Y_R$. If the research department hires factors at competitive prices, then by Euler's Theorem

$$rK + wL = (1-\alpha)AF_K K + (1-\alpha)AF_L L = (1-\alpha)Y.$$

Rewards to capital and labour fully exhaust the output of private goods, $rK + wL = Y_C + Y_I$, while the output of public goods, Y_R, is community property.

If individuals save a constant fraction, $0 < s < 1$, of disposable income, then equation (4.4) can be rewritten as

$$\dot{k} = s(1-\alpha)Af(k) - \mu k \tag{4.55}$$

ignoring labour-force growth. Differential equation (4.5) can be rewritten as

$$\dot{A} = \alpha Af(k) - \rho A. \tag{4.56}$$

Motion of the mixed economy is given by differential equations (4.55) and (4.56). If s and α are constants, and $f(\cdot)$ satisfies the usual regularity conditions, then there exists a unique stationary state (k^*, A^*), which is a saddle-point.

This model – although very primitive – presents two important departures from that of the standard growth paradigm. (i) The rest point (k^*, A^*) is not stable. *The model economy is morphogenetic rather than morphostatic*, i.e. long-run development is very sensitive to initial conditions. (ii) In particular, for the regime of perpetual growth, *the rate of growth in productivity is increasing through time.*[1]

These two basic properties are not independent of the particular forms of the production function, consumption function and so forth. It seems to me, however, that morphogeneticism and the related possibility of an increasing rate of productivity growth are 'likely' for economies exhibiting increasing returns to scale in A, K and L.

[1] See Weizsäcker (1969). The wildly increasing productivity gains that my model predicts may be offset in life by exhaustion of fixed natural resources. This is especially likely if income and consumption are correctly measured to reflect the decreasing quality of the environment that seems to go along with industrial development. (The growth models presented at this Conference assume without exception that $\dot{L}/L = n$, an exogenous constant. It surprises me that, while we study technology so carefully, we have been little interested in demography.)

Notice the important change in the specification of the production function. In the preceding sections the production function is assumed to be concave in k and A, while in this section the function is quasi-concave but not jointly concave in k and A. Even if $f(\cdot)$ is bounded, the analysis of optimal growth based on the technology of this section does not appear to be easy. Without concavity, questions of uniqueness, sensitivity to initial conditions, and so forth, are all open.

IV. A COMPETITIVE MODEL IN WHICH INVENTIVE ACTIVITY IS FINANCED FROM QUASI-RENTS ON ADVANCED TECHNOLOGY

In what we have done so far, invention is either a pure public good financed by government expenditure or is financed by monopoly profits in the production of capital goods. Now we turn our attention to a model which can be thought of as lying between these two extreme models. The present model allows for government intervention in the R. & D. process, but its most salient feature is the financing of R. & D. by competitive firms.[1]

I begin the story with a partial-equilibrium analysis of an industry in which the level of technology may differ over firms. There are several reasons for technological possibilities to be different for two firms in the same industry. While in the long run transmission costs are typically low relative to production costs, it is very costly to transmit information at a rapid *rate*. Firms with advanced technologies have incentives for not revealing their technologies, and employ secrecy to achieve this end. Patents can give some limited legal protection to the 'advanced' firm.

In life there is usually a spectrum of technologies that are employed by the different firms. It will make the story simpler without seriously affecting the basic argument if we assume that there are two types of firms: those capable of operating at the 'advanced' technology (denoted by A_1) and those capable of operating at the 'backward' technology (denoted by A_2). The number of firms (actual and potential) capable of operation at the backward technology is infinite. The number of firms capable of operating at the advanced technology is some finite number, say n. Although finite, n is large enough so that all firms consider themselves to be price-takers.

In order to make things simple, assume that there is only one factor of production, say labour, that the firm can vary in the short run. In Fig. 4.1B, short-run U-shaped average cost curves are drawn for firms of each type. (AC_1 for an advanced firm; AC_2 for a backward firm. Q denotes output of the firm in question.) Also shown in Fig. 4.1B is an advanced firm's marginal cost schedule (MC_1). Ignoring second-order indivisibilities, we can construct from Fig. 4.1B the industry's supply schedule (shown in Fig. 4.1A). If the price of a unit of output is less than the minimum average cost for the advanced firm, $AC_1(Q^*)$, then, of course, supply of output is zero. If the output price is equal to $AC_1(Q^*)$, then supply will be elastic

[1] Some of the fundamental ideas in this section were worked out some time ago in a conversation with Joseph Stiglitz. He bears no responsibility, however, for what I have done with these ideas.

up to the level nQ^*, at which point all firms capable of operating at the advanced technological level will have entered the industry.

If the price of output is slightly greater than the minimum of AC_1, then the n advanced firms will be of equal size and the quantity produced by a representative firm, Q, can be found by solving $MC_1(Q) = P$, where P is the price of output. This regime persists until marginal cost for the advanced firm is equal to minimum average cost for the backward firm, $AC_2(Q^{**})$.

Therefore, if output is less than nQ^{**} (indicated in Fig. 4.1A), then only advanced firms are operating. If industry output is greater than nQ^{**}, then both backward and advanced firms are operating

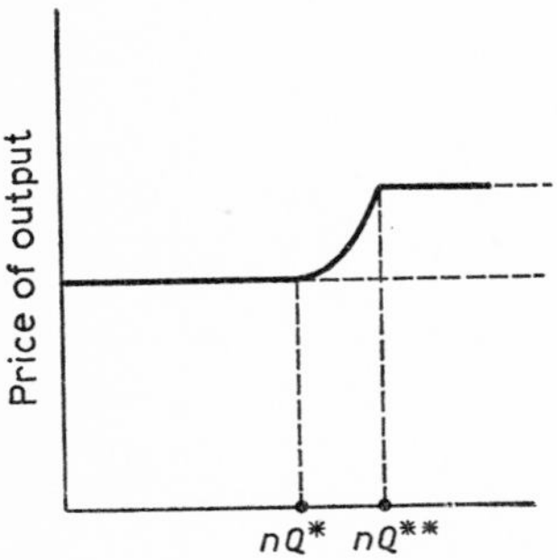

FIG. 4.1A

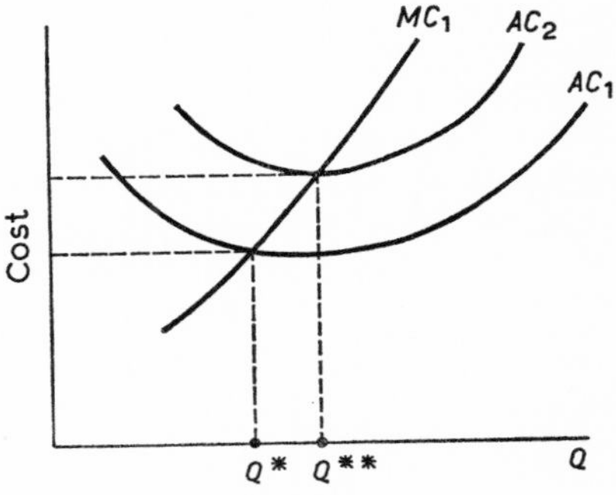

FIG. 4.1B

and the industry supply price of output is equal to the minimum average cost for the backward firms. It is important to observe that *when industry output is greater than nQ^* the advanced firms are reaping positive quasi-rents on advanced technology*. This possibility of positive quasi-rent for an industry in which all producers are price-takers will play a central role in the further analysis of this problem.[1]

We can assume that there are three basic sources of improvement in the ith firm's technology: (i) The firm can devote some of its own resources to the invention of improved technique. (ii) Spillovers from more advanced firms in the same industry. (iii) Spillovers from

[1] It is worth noting that this model is anti-Chamberlinian. One might think of the regime to the right of nQ^* in Fig. 4.1A as imperfectly competitive. But in this imperfectly competitive regime, advanced firms operate to the right of the minimum average cost point – rather than to the left, as in the celebrated case of monopolistic competition.

other industries in the economy, including the socialised sectors. This can be formalised by

$$\dot{A}_i/A_i = \phi^i[R_i, \quad (A_1 - A_i)/A_i, \quad \dot{A}/A] \tag{4.57}$$

where A_i is the index of technology for firm i, A_1 is the index of technology for the most advanced firm in the industry, A is an economy-wide index of accumulated technical knowledge and R_i is the number of man-hours devoted to invention by the ith firm. $\phi^i[\cdot]$ is then an increasing function of its three arguments.

In the long run, because of technological progress, the wage rate, w, and income per head, y, grow at the proportionate rate $\alpha > 0$:

$$\dot{w}/w = \dot{y}/y = \alpha. \tag{4.58}$$

While in the aggregate the economy may tend to some quasi-stationary state, the composition of output is likely to be changing substantially through time. To understand the implications of this point, consider first the 'standard' industry, which in the long run is experiencing factor-augmenting technical progress at the same proportionate rate as the economy-wide rate, α; i.e.

$$\dot{A}_1/A_1 = \alpha = \dot{A}_2/A_2$$

where $A_1 > A_2$. Supply (SS) and demand (DD) schedules for the standard industry are shown in Fig. 4.2. SS does not shift through time since increases in productivity exactly offset increasing factor

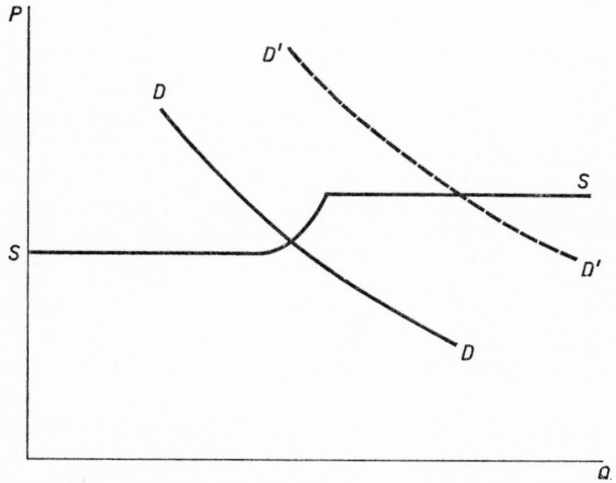

FIG. 4.2 The 'Standard Industry'

costs. But if the industry does not produce an inferior good, then the demand schedule must be shifting rightward through time (to $D'D'$) because of the positive income elasticity of demand. Consequently, quasi-rents are non-decreasing through time, allowing for continuing financing of research, $R_1 > 0$.

If for some industry the previous assumptions hold except that research is even more productive than in the standard industry, so that

$$\dot{A}_1/A_1 = \dot{A}_2/A_2 = \beta > \alpha$$

then the same qualitative conclusion holds, namely, in the long run financing will be available to permit R_1 to be positive.

Consider, on the other hand, the industry in which long-run technical progress for the advanced firm proceeds at a rate slower than the economy average:

$$\dot{A}_1/A_1 = \beta < \alpha$$

even when output is great enough to generate the maximum amount of quasi-rent. This is described in Fig. 4.3. On the vertical axis, we measure $P(t)e^{(\alpha-\beta)t}$, where $P(t)$ is the price of a unit of the industry's output.

Since wages are growing at the rate α while productivity is only increasing at the rate β, the SS schedule will not be shifting in Fig. 4.3. However, the demand schedule (initially DD) will in general shift through time. The direction and manner of shifting will depend on

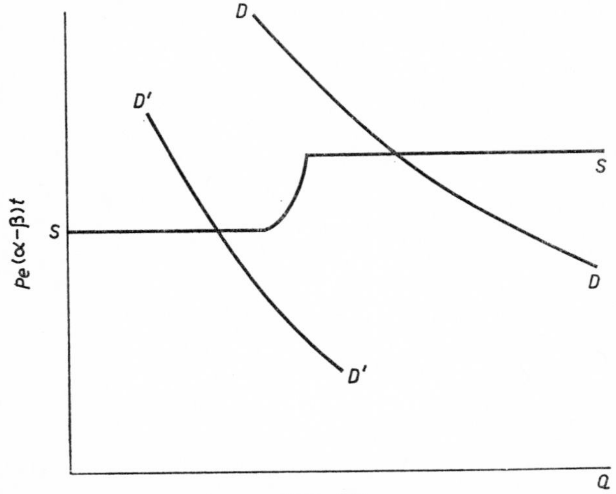

FIG. 4.3

the income elasticity of demand and the price elasticity of demand. If, through time, equilibrium Q is increasing, then positive quasi-rents will be generated and R_1 will be positive. If, however, equilibrium Q is falling, then quasi-rents and research expenditures will fall to zero. With no research expenditures, $R_1 = 0$, the gap between A_1 and A_2 declines so that in the long run the SS schedule becomes everywhere horizontal.

This is the story of a 'sick' industry – an industry with low income elasticity of demand and high price elasticity of demand in relation to the average profitability of research, ϕ^i/R. Such 'sick' industries present a case for social support of industry-related inventive activity. In recent years, the 'sick' industry phenomenon has also provided an opening wedge for expansion of 'conglomerates'. Contrary to the usual view of the conglomerate, 'sick industry' expansion is one important source of growth. The present analysis helps us in understanding this. Financing flows from industries generating high quasi-rents to profitable opportunities, including industries where invention is profitable. An example is the case where quasi-rents from an industry with high income elasticity of demand are invested in technique improvement in a 'sick' (low income elasticity of demand) industry; e.g. from petroleum extraction to coal mining, from the chemical industry to the textile industry.[1]

If A_1 is considered to be an index of the level of economy-wide advanced technology, A_2 an index of economy-wide backward technology, we have from aggregation of equation (4.57) that

$$\frac{\dot{A}_1}{A_1} = G\left[R(\beta), \frac{\dot{A}}{A}\right] \tag{4.59}$$

where $G[\cdot]$ is increasing in both arguments ($G_1 > 0$, $G_2 > 0$) and R is increasing in β where

$$\beta \equiv \frac{A_1 - A_2}{A}. \tag{4.60}$$

Also, from an aggregation based on (4.57),

$$\frac{\dot{A}_2}{A_2} = H\left[\beta, \frac{\dot{A}}{A}\right] \tag{4.61}$$

where $H_1 > 0$ and $H_2 > 0$.

[1] The present framework can be easily employed in the study of a variety of important policy questions concerning invention, industrial organisation and growth, e.g. the question of infant industry protection and so forth. Tempting as such diversions may be, our main task at present is not partial-equilibrium micro-economics but rather general-equilibrium macro-economics.

In the quasi-stationary state

$$\dot{A}_1/A_1 = \dot{A}_2/A_2 = \dot{A}/A \equiv \alpha.$$

Thus stationaries to (4.59) and (4.61) solve

$$\left.\begin{aligned} &G[R(\beta), \alpha] - \alpha = 0 \\ \text{and} \quad & \\ &H(\beta, \alpha) - \alpha = 0 \end{aligned}\right\} \qquad (4.62)$$

two equations in two unknowns (β and α). From (4.57)–(4.62) we know that

$$\text{sign}\left(\frac{d\beta}{d\alpha}\right)_{\dot{A}_1/A_1=\alpha} = \text{sign}\,(1-G_2)$$

and

$$\text{sign}\left(\frac{d\beta}{d\alpha}\right)_{\dot{A}_2/A_2=\alpha} = \text{sign}\,(1-H_2).$$

Without a deeper study of the problem, we can say no more about these two slopes. Consequently, detailed analyses of existence and uniqueness of long-run equilibrium as well as comparative dynamics and stability must be postponed until we know more about the $G(\cdot)$, $H(\cdot)$ and $(R\cdot)$ functions.

REFERENCES

K. Shell, 'Toward a Theory of Inventive Activity and Capital Accumulation', *American Economic Review*, vol. LVI, no. 2 (May 1966) pp. 62–8.

—— 'A Model of Inventive Activity and Capital Accumulation', in *Essays on the Theory of Optimal Economic Growth*, ed. K. Shell (Cambridge, Mass.: M.I.T. Press, 1967) pp. 67–85.

C. C. von Weizsäcker, 'Forschungsinvestitionen und Macroökonomische Modelle: Ein Wirtschaftstheoretisches Dilemma?', *Kyklos*, vol. XXII, pt. 3 (1969) pp. 454–65.

Discussion of the Paper by Karl Shell

Professor Shell said that in order to explain economic development satisfactorily, an endogenous theory of technological progress is required. There seems to be no satisfactory explanation linking inventive activity at the enterprise level with growth in aggregative productivity. Previous studies, while concentrating on constant-returns-to-scale technologies and on competitive markets, have missed the crucial role of industrial organisation in the inventive process.

He offered here three models in which invention is undertaken by 'non-competitive' economic agents. The three cases of industrial organisation may not be realistic, but it is hoped that they are at least internally consistent and that (as polar cases) they may shed light on the more general problem of invention and growth in the enterprise economy.

He emphasised that investment in inventive activity was crucially different from that in machinery for three reasons. Firstly, assumptions concerning returns to scale need to be different. Secondly, the returns to machinery are less risky. Finally, investment in inventions is more difficult to finance since bankers have very little tangible to claim if the investment fails.

Dr Berglas began his discussion of the paper by welcoming the emphasis on industrial organisation and said he would welcome an examination of further cases. He thought that more discussion of the stock of technical progress was needed to clarify its meaning. He did not like the idea of all technical knowledge being produced with a production function with payment to the factors involved exhausting product. Much technical knowledge is not produced in firms but in universities and government establishments. If technical progress was included as a function of time, most of the results (apart from the last model) would disappear.

He pointed to the extreme nature of the assumptions necessary for the most thoroughly analysed case, the first. The consumption-goods sector was competitive – this seemed incongruous with complete monopoly in the capitalist sector. There was a single production function and no growth in the labour force. All wages were saved and the monopolist maximised the present value of a consumption stream.

He thought the assumption in the second model that the government has a constant tax rate to finance inventions inappropriate. It ought to be optimising in some way.

He said that the assumption in the third model of a fixed finite number of advanced firms was inappropriate in the long run. This assumption could be replaced by a pair of assumptions that determine the relative number of advanced and backward firms: (i) research and development units are not perfectly divisible and have an optimum size for an advanced firm; (ii) the cost function of backward firms depends on R. & D. in the industry as a whole, i.e. when research in the advanced sector increases, costs of the backward firms decline. These assumptions ensure that pure profits to the advanced sector imply an increase in the number n of advanced firms, a decrease in the costs of backward firms and therefore a lowering of product prices. n ceases to increase when pure profits to advanced firms are eliminated. In this model inventive activity can continue in a declining industry. As in the paper, n is constant in a growing industry. This feature is eliminated if returns to advanced firms depend on the size of the industry, for then advanced firms may wish to sell patents to backward firms. Without complicating the analysis these assumptions make the model more compatible with long-run competitive equilibrium.

He said the author's policy conclusion that more help for sick industries might be necessary, depended on the fixed number of firms assumption. He did not see why research activities in expanding sectors might not be more helpful to society.

In general he found it difficult to compare the three models since the discussion was not carried on in the same style for each.

Professor Mirrlees noted that different production possibilities for the first two models had been assumed. In the first model, $g(A, k)$ had been assumed concave (p. 86) so that maximisation was made easy. However, the corresponding function in the second model was $Af(k)$. In this model no optimisation was performed, however. If f were Cobb–Douglas and we optimised, we would find that we would get infinite A and k in finite time. This can arise when $g(A, k)$ is not concave. If we assumed f were bounded, however, we would get an interesting steady-state solution.

Professor Shell agreed that the concavity assumptions were made for convenience, but felt that we let in the explosive solutions by abstracting from other constraints such as land.

Dr Bliss said it was unclear to him that investment in innovation *was* more risky than investment in physical capital. Physical capital, if it was very specific, might be worthless on failure of an enterprise. There may well be something left to sell after an innovation project had not produced its intended results – e.g. an alternative product or the knowledge that it is not worth looking further in a particular direction.

Mr Atkinson asked what was meant by a deterioration in technical knowledge (equation (4.5)). *Professor Shell* replied that he was thinking of skilled people dying off. If $\rho = 0$, the model is more likely to be morphogenetic. *Professor Mirrlees* suggested that $\rho > 0$ when we prove more general theorems and discard special cases. *Professor Weizsäcker* pointed out that this would be a net accretion to knowledge, however. *Professor Hahn* said we may lose the processes by which we arrived at theorems, e.g. now that we have replaced the labour theory of value by the non-substitution theorem, we may not be able to see how Marx arrived at the theory. *Professor Weizsäcker* thought that we forgot that which was not useful.

Professor Stiglitz suggested that the two polar cases (monopoly and public sector) had been used to avoid difficulties in specifying how returns from research are captured. We should like to examine a situation where technical knowledge is neither a pure public good nor a pure monopolistic good, e.g. by a patent system where the flow of knowledge is reduced to promote research.

Professor Weizsäcker said Nordhaus had done something like this.

Professor Shell said a difficulty with a competitive model that included a patent system was that we had increasing returns to all factors taken together if we had constant returns to conventional factors. He thought that the importance of patents was low – probably only 5–10 per cent of research and development output passed through the Patent Office; they refuse to handle many types of application, and other people can see filed patents.

Professor Weizsäcker said we should try to develop a theory in which monopolistic rents were returns to investment in invention or special knowledge of some kind. We could then develop an efficiency and equilibrium theory about monopolists.

Mrs Bharadwaj thought there was a danger of implicit theorising if we tried to explain monopolistic rents as returns to an unquantifiable factor like 'knowledge'.

Professor Shell said that the problem was no different from that of the identification of A.

Professor Mirrlees suggested that firms would use patents more if courts did not uphold contracts enforcing secrecy on employees.

Dr Boussard noted that the consumption behaviour assumed in the first two models was different – in the first case we had discounting of utility and in the second a constant propensity to save. He thought this might be the main reason for the different results.

Professor Shell said some sort of optimisation of α might aggravate the morphogenetic problems.

Professor Stiglitz asked whether the monopolist would necessarily maximise his profits by renting out all the capital at his disposal. He also remarked that the $f''' < 0$ assumption was peculiar – if this did not hold, $kf'(k)$ (the monopolist profit) might have several local maxima.

Professor Mirrlees suggested that if k were below the k^* at which long-run consumption was maximised, then the monopolist would want to accumulate until k was equal to k^*. In that case, capital would never be withheld.

Professor Shell said he would look into the question raised by Professor Stiglitz.

Professor Uzawa wondered why the capitalist was a monopolist and why he had the objective function of (4.13).

Professor Shell replied that the monopolistic assumption was made to study a special case. We could think of the monopolist as a good family man or as the committee of the bourgeoisie.

Professor Hahn thought some embodiment ideas were necessary to study the relations between innovations and monopolistic situations. Schumpeter thought innovation would be less in old firms than in new ones. For instance, General Electric tried to suppress the neon light to protect the returns on capital embodied elsewhere, but were eventually forced to invest in it by a small firm carrying out the innovation. More rigorous empirical studies of, for instance, when it paid a monopolist to introduce an innovation were needed in this field.

Professor Shell agreed, but noted that even without enbodiment there are relations $g(\cdot)$ such that with $y = g(k, A)$ inventions do not increase profit.

Professor Stiglitz said that older theories had competitive pressure forcing innovations. Some interaction between firms is needed to capture the flavour of the problem.

Professor Spaventa thought that the author was too quick to jump to conclusions about, for example, conglomerates (p. 95).

Professor Shell said he was not advocating special policies. He was pointing to the possibility that it may in some circumstances be of both social and private benefit that resources be moved from high-growth to low-growth industries.

Professor Weizsäcker said the distinction between sick and other industries depended on there being no switch between the two types of firms.

Professor Shell said he recognised that there was a spectrum of firms in real life. He was pointing out that technical change may not be factor-augmenting. We can allow firms to become advanced by the growth processes of the model: with high quasi-rents a poor firm could improve; with low quasi-rents firms might drift together.

Dr Berglas said that this answer was different from that of the paper – there quasi-rents arose only because of the difference between firms. With the changes he had recommended earlier the number of advanced firms could change.

He said the problem posed by Professor Stiglitz (the withholding of capital) was similar to the contradiction between a monopolistic capital sector and a competitive consumption sector. With the wage equal to the marginal product in the consumption sector, homogeneity gives us $r = f'(k)$. However, a monopolist would be able to make $r > f'(k)$ and thus the wage less than the marginal product of workers.

Professor Shell concluded the discussion and said that a backward firm could become an advanced firm in his model. He agreed that the stark contrast between a monopolised capital sector and a competitive consumption sector was a problem.

He had looked at the optimal control of α. It was not clear whether the model was morphogenetic or morphostatic – it depended on the concavity of the production function. With wildly increasing returns we could have morphogeneticity and the usual criteria for optimality did not apply.

5 Notes on Endogenous Growth of Productivity

C. C. von Weizsäcker
UNIVERSITY OF BIELEFELD, GERMANY

I. INTRODUCTION

Economics is widely understood as the science of the allocation of scarce resources. This definition has been criticised by non-orthodox economists (by Galbraith for instance), who pointed to the phenomena of affluence in developed industrial societies. I do not think that this appearance of affluence should lead economists away from the important fact that basically all societies still have to cope with the problems of scarcity. But I do think that the concept of scarcity has found a one-sided interpretation in most analytical work done in economics. This appears particularly to be the case in the so called neo-classical approach to the phenomenon of economic growth.

Scarcity has been defined by means of the wants of the members of society on the one side and by means of the possibilities to produce goods and services from the given pool of resources on the other side. We talk of the problem of scarce resources when this pool of resources does not suffice to satisfy all wants of all members of society. The limitations to satisfy all wants with given resources come from the limitations to produce goods and services. Economic theory identifies the phenomenon of scarcity with the technological restrictions which nature and the limited pool of knowledge impose on the process of production. Economic growth and progress are then considered to be the result of a growing pool of technological knowledge. Technical progress is thus identified as the main source of economic progress.

If questioned further, economists usually agree that the restrictions imposed on the production process are not purely technological; that it is just a matter of convenience to define any favourable shift in the production functions as being a change in technological know-how. But there remains the paradoxical fact that economists who subscribe to the definition of their field as the science of scarcity are rather uninterested in the precise nature and in the specific cause of that scarcity. Just to give an answer, they identify it with the technological limitations of the process of production.

I think that this attitude imposes a difficulty upon the theory of economic growth. If we identify productivity growth as an alleviation of the limitations put on the production process, a theory of growth should be a theory of the changes in these limitations. As long as we define these limitations as purely technological ones, any such theory must become severely biased. No wonder that until now the theory of endogenous changes in productivity as it has been developed in economics is not at all satisfactory. We can put it in another way. Economics, if understood as the science of allocation of resources under given restrictions on production, is eventually a static theory. In this respect it may be quite useful. But there we should be modest and should not aspire to build a theory of economic growth. Surely this modesty is not what political economists from Adam Smith to John Maynard Keynes wanted to restrict themselves to. I think the theory of growth ought to have the function in economics of initiating a search process for a welfare economics under dynamic conditions from which recommendations for economic policy under dynamic conditions can follow. The questions about market mechanisms versus planning mechanisms, centralisation of decisions, capitalism versus socialism, external economies and diseconomies, distribution of income, efficiency versus equality, etc., might get completely different answers if a theory of endogenous changes of limitations on the production process were available than they get now. Such a theory may be too difficult for it to be obtained in a short period. But I think we have an incomplete view of what function economics should have in society, if we are not aware of the necessity of such a theory.

I would subscribe to the idea that the problem of scarcity remains the central theme of economics. I also think that it is correct to identify the problem of scarcity with the limitations of the production process. But the process of production is essentially a social process. Therefore social as well as technological limitations of the production process are important. A theory of endogenous change of productivity, i.e. a dynamic welfare economics, has to take this into account explicitly.

In the following, I want to try out this idea in two directions. The first tackles the informational aspects of the centralisation/decentralisation problem. The second is concerned with certain aspects of the division of labour.

II. CENTRALISATION AND DECENTRALISATION

In his essay 'The Architecture of Complexity' Herbert Simon develops a theory about the structure of complex systems. His proposition is that a structure of 'near decomposability' into relatively stable sub-systems provides by far the most efficient way of organisation for any complex system. In such a structure, interaction of any given component of the system is concentrated on those other components which are members of the same sub-system, while interaction between elements of different sub-systems is small and is limited to simple and rather 'routine' forms of interaction. If this is the case, interaction between components of different sub-systems can be 'represented' by the interaction between the corresponding sub-systems themselves, where this interaction between sub-systems can be considered not to be more complex than the average interaction of components within a sub-system. In this way the system can afford rather complex forms of direct and indirect interaction between a great number of elementary components without overloading the capacity to interact of any single component. Moreover, such a system has comparatively good chances of further evolution. Changes in the interior structure of any sub-system and the development of new sub-systems can be tried out without endangering the total system too much. For the same reason the system is highly flexible, i.e. it can adapt itself comparatively easily to changes in the environment.

The system of production, consumption and exchange as it is organised in a market economy is a good example of such a nearly decomposable system. Economic theory has shown that the decentralisation of the planning and information processes under certain circumstances does not reduce the efficiency of the economy compared to an 'ideal' centralised system where an omniscient and omnipotent central authority takes all decisions. This reference economy is of course utterly unrealistic and so are the assumptions that have to be made to obtain a model of the market economy which is just as efficient as the 'ideal' centrally planned economy. This 'ideal' market economy is then used as a reference economy for 'real' economies. Deviations of the real economy from the ideal economy are considered to be reasons for state interventions into the market process.

If we compare this kind of reasoning in economics with what I consider to be the essence of Simon's theory (which of course is not restricted to social systems), it becomes obvious that the dimension of communications between the components or the informational aspects of the economic system have been neglected by economic theory. To be sure, the informational aspects have not been left out completely: otherwise there would not have been any reason for preferring the ideal market economy to the ideal centrally planned economy. In accepting that the figure of the omniscient planner is unrealistic, one has made an important proposition about the informational aspects of an economic system. (This proposition and its ramifications have been elaborated by von Mises and others in the famous discussions on central planning in the twenties and thirties.) But beyond this point economic theory did not concern itself very much with the communications aspects in an explicit form. Interactions between individuals of an economy were divided into two classes: market interactions and non-market interactions. The informational aspects of market interaction got some implicit or explicit treatment in the theory of markets. The informational aspects of non-market interactions have been neglected. It looks as though the same assumption of omniscience crept back as a substitute for a more realistic theory. This can be shown by the analysis of the production process or of market failure as it is given in economic theory. The concept of a production function (or its generalisation, the production set) presupposes that the entrepreneurs or the top management have complete knowledge of all relevant details in their firms. The treatment in the theory of market failure of phenomena like indivisibilities, external economies and diseconomies, and public goods presupposes complete knowledge of, or agreement about, the feasible alternatives to a state of *laissez-faire*.

This neglect of the informational aspects of non-market interactions has so far made economics unable to develop a good theory of endogenous economic progress. While most people would probably agree with Simon that decentralisation (in some sense) provides a good environment for social experimentation and innovation, there exists no model in growth economics which investigates this idea by way of a formal and exact analysis.

The present institutional arrangement in capitalist countries probably has a bias in the allocation of resources towards the production of goods and services and against the production of economic innovations, if we consider only the criterion of technological feasibility. Even if innovators and inventors get substantial economic rewards for their activity, there are usually high external economies – much higher than the average external economies in the production of goods and services. This implies that from a purely technological point of view the *status quo* may be inefficient. There have been proposals to change some of these arrangements, for instance with respect to the patent system. Polanyi and others proposed that the monopoly position of the patent holder should be abolished and the patent holder remunerated by the government in proportion to the social benefit of the patent. There is no doubt that under conditions of perfect information (an omniscient government) such a system would be superior to the present one. But otherwise this is not so clear. There are substantial difficulties in ascertaining in practice what the social benefits of an invention are. We have to estimate the demand function for the new product in every period in order to determine the consumers' surplus. Moreover, under oligopolistic conditions the introduction of the new product will induce price changes by producers of competing or complementary commodities. Hence the estimation of the consumers' surplus becomes still more complicated. Demand will be influenced by advertising, and the government will have to measure the effects of advertising for the new product and decide how to interpret these effects in welfare economic terms. In general, several problems in a world of endogenously changing tastes have to be solved theoretically and empirically. The uncertainties of measurement may be quite large. The machinery of administering such a system would have to be complicated. The incentives to distort evidence, keep knowledge secret, etc., may be quite substantial. It is likely that this system, although feasible, would imply such a waste of resources, without accomplishing (due to the uncertainties involved) a substantially improved allocation of incentives for inventors, that the present patent system is superior to it. In other words the present patent system may be efficient if we take into account that any alternative has to meet more restrictions than purely technological ones. I do not see any reason in principle why economic theorists should focus their attention so much on the technological restrictions, if other restrictions are just as important.

III. DIVISION OF LABOUR

The price system serves as a useful instrument for obtaining benefits from the division of labour. This insight, which is at least as old as Adam Smith's *Wealth of Nations*, is one of the best examples of the interdependence of productivity and the social environment. But modern economics by and large has left it to the sociologists to develop theories about the division of labour. It is probably not a very well-defined question if we ask how much the division of labour contributes to our present level of productivity. But there has been very little effort to transform it into a well-defined question and then answer it. (There are of course certain aspects of this theory which are treated in the theory of international trade. There is also the paper of Stigler, 'The Division of Labour is Limited by the Extent of the Market', now in his collection of essays, *The Organisation of Industry*, which treats another aspect of it. But I think this is not sufficient for such an important phenomenon.)

Modern price theory and the theory of general equilibrium have neglected the phenomenon of indivisibility, probably because it is rather difficult to handle in mathematical models. Without assuming the existence of certain indivisibilities it is not possible to understand the advantages of the division of labour. The production of special skills can be easily handled in the modern theory of general equilibrium, if indivisibilities are assumed away. But from the fact that it costs, say, six years of training to produce a skilled physician, it does not follow that two persons with three years of medical training can replace a skilled physician. It should not be very difficult to incorporate this kind of indivisibility into the orthodox theory of the price system, at least as long as we are considering only the static theory. We could then make more precise what the advantages of the division of labour are by measuring the economies of scale for the economy as a whole which follow from the division of labour. We can probably rely on certain results in regional economics in building such a theory.

One could discard this proposal for the static theory by pointing at the huge size of the world economy, which should suffice to meet all reasonable demands for specialisation of human activities in the production process. It is not clear to me whether such an argument would be correct. The supply of specialisation may create its own demand. This possibility I shall discuss below.

But even if the explicit introduction of the division of labour into the static theory may not have high priority, it is surely important in a dynamic theory. The production of new knowledge and of other innovations also is built on the principle of specialisation. The larger is the number of innovators, inventors and research workers, the larger will their output be, and the larger is the potential to raise productivity. Division of knowledge and of labour is the principle which makes possible a higher output of new knowledge when the number of producers of new knowledge increases. I do not see any intrinsic reason why, as the number of other producers of knowledge becomes large, the marginal contribution of a producer should ever fall to zero.

A very simple model can perhaps make this clear. Any given research and development project has a certain period of production. I think we can apply this concept from Austrian capital theory quite usefully in the area of production of knowledge. The more time you are given to finish the project, the fewer resources you need for it. On the other hand, the longer it takes to finish the project, the less relevant it may become. The resources necessary per 'relevance unit' of output will therefore be positively related to the level of knowledge in the society at the moment the project is finished. In the context of economics, we may define the relevance unit of output to be the contribution of the project to raising the logarithm of the productivity level. Thus two projects which are finished at different moments of time have the same quantity of output if they raise the productivity level in the economy by the same percentage.

Let m be the total resources necessary to raise the logarithm of the productivity level by one unit. Let T be the average span of time from the beginning to the end of a project. Let $A(t)$ be the productivity level, at time t, in the economy. Then we assume that the resources required by our project are

$$m = m\left(T, \log \frac{A(t+T)}{A(t)}\right) \tag{5.1}$$

where m_1, the partial derivative with respect to the first argument, is negative and m_2, the partial derivative with respect to the second argument, is positive. We assume that the research and development inputs are evenly distributed through time in my project.

Consider now a steady state of the economy such that T remains constant through time. If γ is the annual growth rate of productivity, we have $\log A(t+T)/A(t) = \gamma T$. It follows that

$$m = m(T, \gamma T). \tag{5.2}$$

The resources spent on a project (which is weighted by its output) per unit of time are m/T. At any one time t all projects are in operation which finish between time t and time $t+T$. There are γT such projects. Given total resources R for all projects, we therefore have the equation

$$R = \gamma T m(T, \gamma T) \frac{1}{T} = \gamma m(T, \gamma T). \tag{5.3}$$

Minimising m with respect to T implies

$$m_1 + \gamma m_2 = 0. \tag{5.4}$$

We seek the effect of changes in R upon the growth rate attained. Given that T has attained its optimal value, we obtain from (5.3) by logarithmic differentiation:

$$\frac{dR}{R} = \frac{d\gamma}{\gamma} + m_2 \frac{\gamma T}{m} \frac{d\gamma}{\gamma}$$

i.e.

$$\frac{d\gamma}{dR} \cdot \frac{R}{\gamma} = \frac{1}{1 + m_2(\gamma T/m)}. \tag{5.5}$$

From the optimality condition for T we get

$$m_1 \frac{T}{m} = -m_2 \frac{\gamma T}{m}$$

and therefore

$$\frac{d\gamma}{dR}\cdot\frac{R}{\gamma} = \frac{1}{1+|m_1(T/m)|}. \tag{5.6}$$

The expression $|m_1(T/m)|$ is the elasticity of research productivity with respect to the 'period of production' in research and development. The influence of additional input for the production of productivity growth on productivity growth $(d\gamma/dR)(R/\gamma)$ is then inversely related to the importance of the period of production on the productivity of research.

This is plausible. If the timing of research inputs is important (and this is equivalent to a high importance for the period of production), then additional resources available now are poor substitutes for resources at a later stage of the project. Then the marginal product of additional resources will be low.

Let us call the production of productivity increases by the name 'meta-production'. We then can describe the economy by a two-sector model, one sector being the production sector, the other one being the meta-production sector. Our argument above gives an interesting implication for the distribution of costs (and hence income) between direct inputs and the costs of 'waiting'. We assume that resources are measured in labour units, hence their price or wage rate w increases with the going wage rate:

$$w = w_0 e^{\gamma t}. \tag{5.7}$$

For a steady state we can assume that the wage rate grows at the same rate as the level of productivity. Given an interest rate r, the costs at time 0 of a project to give a relevance unit of output at time 0 are

$$C = \int_0^T e^{(r-\gamma)v} w_0 \frac{m}{T}\, dv \tag{5.8}$$

$$= \begin{cases} w_0 \dfrac{e^{(r-\gamma)T}-1}{r-\gamma}\dfrac{m(T,\gamma T)}{T} & (r \neq \gamma) \\ w_0 m(T,\gamma T) & (r = \gamma). \end{cases}$$

Here is another golden rule. Suppose the decisions in the meta-production sector are decentralised and that projects are planned in such a way as to minimise costs per relevance unit of output. Then the rate of growth of productivity is maximised, if the rate of interest and the rate of productivity growth are equal (that is, if the labour theory of value is correct). For when T minimises $m(T, \gamma T)$, and resources devoted to meta-production are fixed, (5.3) implies that γ is maximum.

The 'waiting' part of costs and thus the income share of capital in this sector are positively related to the project length T. The project length T is an increasing function of the elasticity of productivity with respect to T, $-Tm_1/m$. This again is immediately plausible. If additional resources have only a small effect on the output in the meta-production sector, their income share should be low.

The optimal 'period of production' in the meta-production sector is closely related to the organisational structure of this sector. I do not know whether precise theorems of this type exist in the management science literature. But my conjecture would be the following. A project with a high degree of substitutability of resources available at different moments of time, and thus with a low period of production, can be organised in a rather decentralised fashion. The role which every sub-project plays and the interdependence of the sub-projects are obvious to all participants. The results to be expected from the sub-projects are clear. Thus the hierarchical superstructure necessary to organise and supervise the project is rather small. A high optimal period of production is an indication that the interdependence between the different parts of the project is complex. It often occurs that the start of some sub-project depends on the availability of results from other sub-projects. Decisions have to be taken in a sequential manner; they depend on intermediate results, which cannot be predicted accurately. The organisational structure of such a project must be much more complex. The principle of decentralisation of decisions can be applied only with more difficulty, if at all.

In meta-production every kind of final output is essentially produced only once. Thus the number of different outputs is closely related to the total quantity of output. And in a similar way, eventually every activity is performed only once. Thus the degree of division of labour is closely related to the total quantity of labour input in the meta-production sector. The marginal product of labour and the marginal product of the division of labour can therefore be identified. By the argument above, there is an inverse relationship between the importance of the division of labour (at the margin) and the length of the 'period of production'. We might take the relative shares in total costs of meta-production of the direct inputs and of 'waiting' as an indicator of the relative importance of Adam Smith's principle (division of labour) and Böhm-Bawerk's principle (roundabout methods of production) in the meta-production sector. The inverse relation between the importance of these two principles appears to be specific to meta-production. I see no reason why it should apply in the realm of conventional production.

If we want to develop a satisfactory theory of meta-production, it appears to be necessary to study the social processes which go under the general name of specialisation and division of labour. I want to mention two other reasons why the division of labour is an object worth studying for growth economists.

I have mentioned earlier one reason why perhaps economists so far have not been very interested in the quantitative aspects of the division of labour. If the economy is very large, any reasonable kind of division of labour in the production of commodities and services appears to be feasible. In such a situation the mistake may not be very large, if one ignores the indivisibilities connected with the division of labour. But this argument may not be valid in the long run, if people have increasingly diversified consumption patterns. It is very likely that with an increasing standard of living people buy more and more different kinds of goods so that through time more and more different activities are necessary to produce them and thus the division of labour becomes finer and finer as time goes on. It may therefore be that in the long run even for large economies division of labour remains an important problem. It is not easy to develop a satisfactory index for the degree of diversification of a person's consumer basket. It is certainly not sufficient to count the number of different goods he buys. Very close substitutes or very close complements should be treated as one good rather than two goods. We are essentially asking for the 'natural' dimension number of the consumer's commodity basket. Our hypothesis would be that the 'natural' dimension increases with an increasing standard of living.

There is another aspect of the phenomenon of division of labour which is neglected in economic theory, but which appears to be quite important in practice. It is today and has always been a fiction to assume that economically relevant decisions in a society are co-ordinated only by the market. No doubt the market mechanism is very important, but other mechanisms of co-ordination are important as well. In particular there are political or quasi-political mechanisms of co-ordination. In the political process division of labour produces special interests of different sub-groups of the population. They will try to influence the political process to increase their share in the national product. They will resist change and progress, if it hurts their particular group. We can observe that the political process has a bias in favour of the demands of interest groups. For any given stratification of the population there may exist an upper bound of the rate of economic progress per unit of time which can be derived from the political and quasi-political limitations to change.

Discussion of the Paper by C. C. von Weizsäcker

Dr Levhari gave a brief summary of the paper and proceeded to his comments. He said Professor Weizsäcker's thoughts on the problem of a model describing the process of generation of technical change were very interesting and challenging, and he joined with the author in calling for more research in this field. The paper was concerned with some ingredients of such a model rather than offering a fully developed model.

He thought that Simon's views on the advantages of decentralised, almost indecomposable, systems were essentially correct, especially if costs of information transfers were counted. Most people arguing for more centralisation in innovational processes exaggerate their point. More flexible and adjustable systems do have advantages in producing and assimilating rapid changes.

Competition between enterprises developing the same innovation frequently accelerates the process; thus there may be social advantages from a decentralised system even when one has allowed for the danger of duplication or the possible advantages from pooling.

In support of his views, he quoted the work of some sociologists of science at the Hebrew University on scientific output in the second half of the nineteenth century (e.g. Ben David, 'Scientific Productivity and Academic Organisation in Nineteenth Century Medicine', *American Sociological Review*, 1960, pp. 828–43). The higher scientific output of Germany (compared with Britain, France and the United States) was attributed to competition between relatively decentralised institutions coupled with a very high mobility.

He then considered the formal part of the paper. He thought that for large T we may have $m_1 > 0$, since we may have problems of divisibility if we try to spread our resources too thinly and more co-ordination would be needed for longer projects.

He said that society should be concerned with the minimisation of C (see p. 108) rather than R (see p. 107). This amounts to the same thing only in the golden-rule situation of $r = \gamma$. r of course is a function of γ or R; thus we have a simultaneous system where we have to find the efficiency growth rate as well as the interest rate.

As the author mentions, his ideas can be embedded in a two-sector model with an ordinary production function and meta-production. We assume that resources devoted to innovations can be measured in terms of the proportion of the labour force. We have the following model:

$$\text{Ordinary output:}\quad x = F(K, (1-R)AL) = \dot{K}+C; \quad L = L_0 e^{nt}$$

$$(\dot{A}/A) = \gamma; \quad R = \gamma m(T, \gamma T).$$

We can then look at this as a descriptive model and see if $dT/ds > 0$ (s savings ratio) or $dT/dR > 0$. Alternatively, we could work at it in terms of an optimal growth model (this has some resemblance to Uzawa's model in the *International Economic Review* of 1966).

He expressed some doubts on whether aggregative models are the right instrument for investigation of the meta-industry. He would like to have seen uncertainty introduced. If non-steady-state situations were examined, we could see if lengthening the period of production meant high capital–labour ratios. He realised that all these extensions would be difficult.

Professor Weizsäcker said he wanted to clarify the calculation of C on p. 108. C had been calculated at $t+T$ in order to compare it with the benefits – since T was variable this seemed the simplest method of approach.

Professor Stiglitz considered a firm which took a constant r and assumed wages would increase at γ. If it controlled T and $A(t+T)$ in order to minimise cost, why should it choose the T and $A(t+T)$ that came from Professor Weizsäcker's optimisation?

Professor Weizsäcker said that γ, r were exogenous for the decentralised unit which only controlled T. However, Professor Stiglitz had raised an important point and he would look into it. We would have to write down the stream of costs and benefits to the firm and find the T that maximised the discounted difference. We should then examine whether this T corresponded to the overall solution he was postulating. (*Professor Stiglitz* pointed out that the private benefits may well differ from the social ones since future costs of production in the research sector are changed.) He had implicitly been assuming that firms would do what everyone else was doing. He introduced the concept of a cost difficulty curve (Fig. 5.1) for projects – m was the resources needed per project and n the number of projects under consideration. In a steady state, society solves the easiest problems first while the number of problems continually increased. If we are solving n problems at time T, then $n = \gamma T$. The second argument of m was really the number of problems under consideration. As the first problem is solved the others become easier to solve, so the curve is stable over time as we solve problems. He said he would further elaborate when he revised the paper.

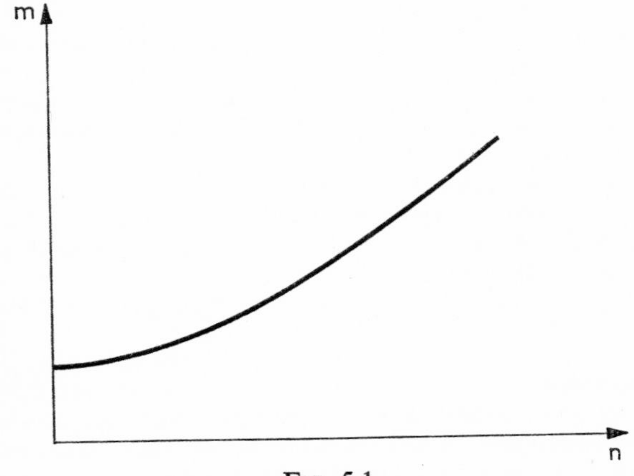

FIG. 5.1

Professor Helmstädter said this was a Barone curve for new production.

Professor Hahn asked when a project was finished. He would like to think of an application curve of a project, e.g. the output of penicillin research was raising A long before the project was completed.

Professor Weizsäcker said that in his model a project was either continuing or finished and it was finished when it made a contribution to A. He thought that difficulty curves for applied projects depended on the level of knowledge in basic research.

Professor Berthomieu said he agreed with Professor Weizsäcker's definition of scarcity, but he asked him whether he would accept a change in his request that the 'theory of growth should be a study of changes in these limitations'. He said the relevant theory of growth in our economic system should be a theory of the production of scarcity. The essence of the capitalist system is the production of profits and the reproduction of scarcity contributes to profits. Then we should explain how new limitations appear.

He asked also whether, during the production period of a project, it could benefit from the increase in A occurring during this period. He asked if a project was macro or micro.

Dr Sheshinski noted that productivity did not increase in the meta-sector.

Professor Weizsäcker replied that by definition its impact was macro although the project itself might be very specific. He thought the increase in general knowledge over time too small to help a specific project.

Professor Garegnani agreed with Professor Berthomieu that economics should look into the 'reproduction of scarcity'. Either we really believe that wants as given at any moment of time are insatiable, or we have to admit that the economic system itself creates new wants.

Professor Weizsäcker said he liked to think of preference structures as exogenous also. He said the phrase 'artificial creation of wants' had unpleasant connotations – the creation of wants may be a good thing. The knowledge of what is technologically feasible can make wants precise (e.g. the invention of the automobile), but he did not want to call this artificial.

Professor Rose said there had probably always existed general classes of wants that are provided for by the particular commodities now available. A clear example is that of transportation.

Professor Weizsäcker said that new wants for transportation are created when new means become available.

Professor Garegnani said that the study of how production and wants interact should be an essential part of the theory of growth.

Dr Bliss emphasised that we must keep separate the concepts of budget constraints and changes in tastes.

Professor Mirrlees said he would like to respond to the enormous stimulation of the paper by more speculation. We should try to define the direction of a research project. The notion of jointness and non-jointness of production might be relevant. We may perhaps observe technological developments reducing the jointness of production. This is what one might expect; for narrowly directed research projects run less risk of being duplicated in part by competing developments. We may therefore from the social point of view have over-concentration in narrowly directed projects.

Professor Stiglitz said that the consequences of duplication in a broadly directed project were less serious since such a project could be more easily redirected.

Professor Hahn said that in general a finer division of labour meant less flexibility. The concept needed formalising. He wondered whether the extent of the division of labour was determined by set-up costs (incurred by the necessity of training more specialised labour) or by the total expenditure on research.

Professor Spaventa asked whether a different complex of interest groups would mean a reordering of the projects on the difficulty curve. *Professor Weizsäcker* said the influence on R. & D. of the distribution of power was important and should be made explicit.

Dr Pasinetti said that the ideas in the second and third section bore a very tenuous relation to those discussed in the first part, where the question of what economics is about was faced. He agreed with Professor Weizsäcker that neither Smith nor Keynes considered the optimum allocation of scarce resources as 'the central theme of economics'. The emphasis on problems of scarcity is relatively recent in the history of economic thought and is responsible for unduly restricting our field of investigations. Interesting ideas, such as those of the last two parts of Professor Weizsäcker's paper, should be pursued without worrying whether they fall inside or outside the received definition of economics.

Professor Weizsäcker concluded the discussion by answering some of the questions that had been raised. He said there was nothing in his paper about the direction of research, but the idea could be handled in terms of his section on decentralisation. We may have over-narrowness because we may need a certain level of integration to obtain broadness of scope – this is suggested by problems of the environment in the United States. It was, however, very difficult to formalise, as were many problems of the interaction of preferences and possibilities – it was possible with an additive utility structure, but this begged the question.

He thought an index of specialisation might be given by the number of independent projects you could set up without any feedback between them. He was not sure whether the division of labour was connected with set-up costs or not. Major differences between meta-production and normal production were, firstly, that we are concerned with a public good, and secondly, that we can index the division of labour by the number of people working. These differences are independent of set-up costs.

He thought a bias in theory had been produced by considering limitations on production as technological. We have not emphasised social limitations which can be very real. We had thrown out many important aspects in the last twenty-five years in order to solve some problems in theory. It was time to bring some of them back.

Part 4

Capital

6 The Badly Behaved Economy with the Well-Behaved Production Function*

Joseph E. Stiglitz

YALE UNIVERSITY

The story of economic growth formalised some fifteen years ago by Solow (1956) and Swan (1956) is a very appealing one; it is a simple model and yet a very rich one, as attested to by the multitude of variations around the central theme to be found in the literature of the last decade and a half. Yet, at least since Professor Robinson's attack against the use of capital aggregates (1953), there have been doubts about the usefulness of the model in describing 'real' economies with heterogeneous capital goods. The doubts have found some substance in the recent discussions of the reswitching of techniques. These discussions have, however, been solely concerned with comparisons of steady states, and not with the growth path of an economy inheriting a particular capital stock, with particular consumption patterns, reproduction rates, etc. It is the latter with which growth theory must ultimately be concerned.

I have been asked to address myself to the implications of the recent discussion of reswitching to truly dynamic economies, i.e. economies out of steady state. I shall attempt to show that (a) although the presence of heterogeneous capital goods does present severe difficulties for the simpler neo-classical stories of capital accumulation, difficulties which are by no means completely resolved at the present time, these difficulties are not those associated with the reswitching phenomenon, and (b) neither the reswitching phenomenon (and the associated valuation perversities) nor the more important difficulties with the conventional growth models presented by heterogeneous capital goods have any bearing on the validity of the more fundamental aspects of neo-classical analysis. What must be altered are our simpler views of the process of accumulation as one of steadily increasing consumption, wage rates and capital intensity of newly constructed machines.

In the present chapter, it will be established that, even in the

* This chapter and the next somewhat expand the paper presented at the Conference. I wish to acknowledge the financial support of the Guggenheim Foundation, the Ford Foundation and the National Science Foundation. My ideas owe much to extended discussions with D. Cass and F. H. Hahn.

limited domain of steady-state analysis, the reswitching phenomenon and the associated valuation perversities are not of great interest. The argument proceeds as follows.

First, I show that reswitching can be ruled out under fairly weak conditions. In section II, five theorems giving sufficient conditions for no reswitching are presented:

1. A process can be used at two interest rates and not at an intervening one only if the process used at the intervening one requires more of some capital goods and less of others (implying, of course, that there must be at least two capital goods).
2. If there are only two capital goods, reswitching can occur only under those conditions in which the factor price equalisation theorem does not obtain, and the process with the higher direct labour requirements is relatively more intensive in the labour intensive capital good.
3. It requires only a limited amount of smooth substitutability to make reswitching impossible:
   (a) if *any* capital good (as an input) is smoothly substitutable (either directly or indirectly) for itself (as an output), then reswitching is impossible;
   (b) if any capital good is smoothly substitutable for every other capital good (either as input or as output), reswitching is impossible;
   (c) if labour is smoothly substitutable for any capital good (either as an output or as an input) which requires a capital good in its production, reswitching is impossible.

   These smooth substitutability relationships need only exist in one industry.

Many of the participants on both sides of the reswitching controversy have suggested that the valuation perversities are more significant than reswitching itself. They always occur when there is reswitching but can occur even without reswitching: a lower level of consumption and value of capital is associated with a lower interest rate (for interest rates greater than the growth rate).

In section III, we show that these perversities – and, indeed, the far more interesting anomaly of a lower level of consumption being associated with a higher value of capital – are not inconsistent with neo-classical economics; indeed, they may occur in a slight modification of the very model Wicksell used to argue against such perversities.

Finally, in section IV, we argue that these perversities have no fundamental significance for neo-classical doctrine; the impression that they do arises from a confusion of the analysis of steady states with true dynamics. For instance, the fact that the value of capital is larger on one steady-state path than on another has nothing to do with the question of whether savings are required if one is to go from the first path to the second, i.e. whether consumption must be forgone, and it is wrong – as some have done – to measure the 'cost' of the transition by the change in the value of capital. Even when reswitching can occur, it is still true that the rate of interest correctly reflects the marginal rates of transformation available to the economy. (In the case of discrete technologies, as usual careful note must be taken of left- and right-hand derivatives, but we should be used to this by now.)

Having argued in this chapter that if reswitching is to have any relevance to capital theory, it must be in the analysis of truly dynamic economies, I shall show in Chapter 7 that there *are* important problems associated with heterogeneous capital goods. But they are not those of reswitching.

I. RESWITCHING

(1) *Definition of Reswitching*

The reswitching phenomenon may be simply described as follows.[1] Consider a competitive economy with a single primary factor (labour), no joint production and constant returns to scale, which is in balanced growth. For such an economy, the dynamic non-substitution theorem obtains (see, e.g., Mirrlees, 1969; Stiglitz, 1970). (This theorem asserts that, for any interest rate, there is a unique set of relative prices, and an associated set of techniques, which will support all competitive equilibria, regardless of preferences). Then there may exist three rates of interest, such that at the highest and lowest the same technology is used, and in between an alternative technology is employed.

(2) *Example of Reswitching*

The possibility of reswitching is illustrated by the following simple example. An economy has a single final good X_1 which can be produced by two alternative technologies, given in the following input–output table, with inputs one period before outputs:

		Technology A	*Technology B*	
Input	*Output*	X_1	X_1	X_2
Labour		a_{01}	b_{01}	b_{02}
X_1		a_{11}	b_{11}	0
X_2		0	b_{21}	0

[1] For references, and a survey of the subject from a viewpoint considerably different from that taken here, see Harcourt (1969).

Technology A requires a_{01} units of labour and a_{11} units of X_1 to produce one unit of X_1. Technology B requires b_{01} units of labour, b_{11} units of X_1 and b_{21} units of X_2 to produce one unit of X_1, while to produce one unit of X_2, b_{02} units of labour are required (and nothing else). Then if the interest rate is r and we let labour be our numeraire, the cost of production of X_1 using technology A is[1] (in long-run equilibrium)

$$p_1 = a_{01}+(1+r)a_{11}p_1 = \frac{a_{01}}{1-(1+r)a_{11}} \tag{6.1}$$

while that using technology B is

$$p_1 = b_{01}+(1+r)(p_1b_{11}+p_2b_{21}) = \frac{b_{01}+b_{21}b_{02}(1+r)}{1-(1+r)b_{11}} \tag{6.2}$$

since the cost of producing X_2 is

$$p_2 = b_{02}. \tag{6.3}$$

The two are equal when

$$\frac{a_{01}}{1-(1+r)a_{11}} = \frac{b_{01}+b_{21}b_{02}(1+r)}{1-(1+r)b_{11}} \tag{6.4}$$

or

$$a_{11}b_{21}b_{02}(1+r)^2+(b_{01}a_{11}-b_{11}a_{01}-b_{21}b_{02})(1+r)+ \\ +(a_{01}-b_{01}) = 0. \tag{6.4$'$}$$

It is clear that if

$$a_{11} > b_{11} \quad \text{and} \quad a_{01} > b_{01} \tag{6.5}$$

then, provided that the B technology does not dominate the A technology at all values of r, there will be, in general, two interest rates at which the two technologies have the same cost of production[2] (see Fig. 6.1). For very low and very high r, the B technology dominates the A, and for intervening interest rates, the A technology dominates the B technology.

(3) *Dated Labour and Multiple Internal Rates Return*

This example also serves to illustrate the following point.

Whenever the non-substitution theorem obtains, we can reduce the costs of production to a (possibly infinite) series of dated labour. That the difference between two such series is zero at a number of rates of interest has been well known for a long time.

[1] In this example we have assumed that wages get paid at the end of the period of production. The results of (6.3) and (6.4) do not depend on this.

[2] This economy is not indecomposable. But it is obvious that this is not a crucial assumption: if we place small $\varepsilon > 0$ in our input–output matrix where before we had zeros, the equations describing the cost of production are altered only infinitesimally.

(4) *Capital Intensities and Reswitching*

The example also suggests two general theorems providing sufficient conditions for the impossibility of reswitching. If we let labour be the numeraire, it is clear that as the rate of interest rises, all prices rise. Since the cost of capital is rising, at higher interest rates the economy should choose the technique with the lower capital costs. Reswitching can then occur only if one process has a higher capital cost than another at two different interest rates, while the second process has a higher capital cost at an intervening interest rate. It immediately follows[1] that if *one process has a higher requirement of*

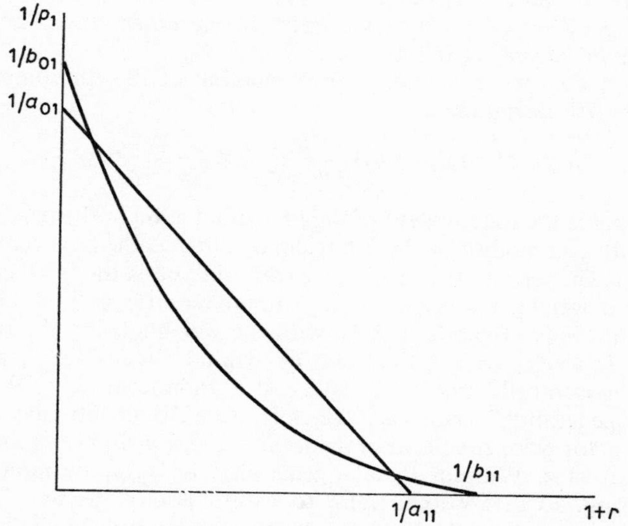

FIG. 6.1 Factor price frontier for simple two-process economy

every capital good than another, then since the capital cost of one will be increasing monotonically relative to the other, *it is impossible for the first process to be used at two different interest rates and the second process at an intervening one*. (Thus, reswitching requires the presence of at least two capital goods.) This theorem says, in other words, that two processes cannot be involved in reswitching if one of them is more 'capital-intensive' than the other regardless of the weights used to form the (additive) capital aggregate. This theorem is helpful

[1] Cf. Bruno, Burmeister and Sheshinski (1966).

in clarifying that it is just those situations where one process requires more of one capital good than another, but less of some other capital good, with which reswitching is concerned.

One might conjecture that if the relative prices of the capital goods move in a systematic way as the interest rate changes, it might be possible to rule out the possibility of reswitching. This is the substance of the theorem presented in the next section.

(5) *Reswitching and the Factor Price Equalisation Theorem*

If there are only two capital goods, reswitching cannot occur if the factor price equalisation theorem obtains, and if the process which has the higher direct labour requirements, i.e. is 'labour intensive', is relatively more intensive in the labour-intensive capital good (the capital good whose price falls relative to the other capital good as the rate of interest increases).

To see this, write the costs of production of the *j*th commodity with the *k*th technique as

$$a_{0j}{}^{k}+(1+r)(p_1+p_2)\left\{\frac{p_1}{p_1+p_2}\,a_{1j}{}^{k}+\frac{p_2}{p_1+p_2}\,a_{2j}{}^{k}\right\}$$

where $a_{ij}{}^{k}$ is the requirement of the *i*th capital good in the production of the *j*th commodity by the *k*th technique ($a_{0j}{}^{k}$ is the requirement of labour). The term in the bracket we can think of as the 'real' capital, and is a weighted average of the capital requirements of the two different kinds of capital goods, with the weights being the relative prices. $(1+r)(p_1+p_2)$ is the 'cost' of 'capital', and since p_1 and p_2 are monotonically increasing with r, it is monotonic in r. Without loss of generality, let $a_{0j}{}^{k}>a_{0j}{}^{l}$: i.e., k is more labour intensive than l. If the factor price equalisation theorem obtains, p_2/p_1 is a monotonic function of r. Without loss of generality, let p_2/p_1 be monotonic increasing, so that we can refer to capital-good 1 as the 'labour-intensive capital good.' Then the relative amount of 'capital' in the two processes k and l will be monotonic in r, if

$$a_{1j}{}^{k}-a_{2j}{}^{k}>a_{1j}{}^{l}-a_{2j}{}^{l}.$$

In the more general model, the connection between the factor price equalisation theorem and the reswitching phenomenon does not obtain; even when all relative prices move monotonically with the rate of interest, the weighted average of capital requirements of one process may be greater than that of another at two interest rates, while the opposite obtains at an intervening interest rate. On the other hand, in a world with free international trade and all economies in balanced growth, we shall never observe the reswitching phenomenon even in a single industry: a technique which is used by a low-interest-rate economy, but discarded by an economy with a higher interest rate, will never be brought back into use at still a third, higher, interest rate. The reason for this is that if there is a single set of international commodity prices, there is a single set of weights by which we can aggregate the various kinds of capital to form the aggregate capital requirements. A process then is either more or less capital-intensive than another (at that particular set of international prices).

(6) *Substitutability and Reswitching*

It was recognised early in the reswitching controversy that if all production functions were differentiable, reswitching could not occur. Indeed, only a limited amount of substitutability is required to rule out the possibility of reswitching. (All the examples of reswitching presented in the literature involve discrete technologies allowing no smooth substitutability in any sector of the economy.) The following three theorems represent extensions and refinements of earlier results of this nature (Solow, 1967, Starrett, 1969).

Consider a transformation schedule, homogeneous of degree zero:

$$\varphi(C_1, \ldots, C_n, \quad X_1, \ldots, X_m, \quad X_{m+1}, \ldots, X_{2m}, L) = 0 \tag{6.6}$$

where $(C_1, \ldots, C_n)$ is the vector of consumption goods (not used in production), $(X_1, \ldots, X_m)$ is the vector of capital inputs, $(X_{m+1}, \ldots, X_{2m})$ is the corresponding vector of capital outputs, and L is the labour input. A 'steady-state technology' is defined by the vector (C, X) (or any scalar multiple of that vector) where $\varphi(C, X, (n+1)X, L) = 0$, n being the growth rate of labour.

(i) *If there is any capital good which is used directly or indirectly in its own production, and it is possible to increase its output by increasing the input of that capital good (leaving all other inputs and outputs unchanged), then there can be no reswitching.* More formally, a technology can be used at only one interest rate if there exists a set of subscripts $i_1, \ldots, i_j, \ldots, i_n$, such that $i_1 \leqslant m$, and

$$\frac{\partial X_{i_{j+1}}}{\partial X_{i_j}} \quad \text{and} \quad \frac{\partial X_{i_1+m}}{\partial X_{i_n}} \quad \text{exist.} \tag{6.7}$$

Indeed, since

$$\frac{\partial X_k}{\partial X_j} = \begin{cases} p_j/p_k & (j-m)(k-m) > 0 \\ p_j(1+r)/p_k & \text{if} \quad j < m, \quad k > m \\ p_j/p_k(1+r) & \qquad j > m, \quad k < m \end{cases} \tag{6.8}$$

$$\frac{\partial X_{i_2}}{\partial X_{i_1}} \times \frac{\partial X_{i_3}}{\partial X_{i_2}} \cdots \frac{\partial X_{i_1+m}}{\partial X_{i_n}} = (1+r). \tag{6.9}$$

(ii) *If there is any capital good which is smoothly substitutable for every other capital good, either as an input or as an output, then reswitching cannot occur*; more formally, a technology cannot be involved in reswitching if for some i and every j, $1 \leqslant i \leqslant m$, $1 \leqslant j \leqslant m$.

$$\text{Either} \quad \frac{\partial X_j}{\partial X_i} \quad \text{or} \quad \frac{\partial X_{j+m}}{\partial X_{i+m}} \quad \text{exists} \tag{6.10A}$$

or

$$\frac{\partial X_i}{\partial X_{j+m}} \quad \text{exists} \tag{6.10B}$$

or

$$\frac{\partial X_{i+m}}{\partial X_j} \quad \text{exists.} \tag{6.10C}$$

The proof follows immediately upon observing that, for instance in the case of (6.10A),

$$\frac{p_i}{p_j} = \frac{\partial X_j}{\partial X_i} \left(\text{or} \quad \frac{\partial X_{j+m}}{\partial X_{i+m}} \right) \tag{6.11}$$

independent of r. Let A denote the input–output matrix for the capital goods corresponding to the given technology. Thus, whenever the given technology is used, the price of the capital goods must be given by

$$p_k = a_0 + p_i(1+r)\left(\frac{p_j}{p_i}A\right)$$

where $\left(\frac{p_j}{p_i}A\right)$ is independent of r. Thus p_k is a linear function of $p_i(1+r)$. Consider any other technology, with its input–output matrix for capital goods B. If we compare the cost of production using the B technology when the prices are those corresponding to the A technology,

$$b_0 + p_i(1+r)\left(\frac{p_j}{p_i}B\right)$$

to the cost of production using the A technology at the same prices, we observe that there is at most one value of r at which they are equal, except in the trivial case where it is profitable to use B whenever it is profitable to use A. The desired result follows immediately.[1]

[1] Since all inputs and outputs are non-negative, when $X_i = 0$ only the right-hand derivative of the expression in (6.7) or (6.10) is defined. But to ensure that the equalities hold in (6.8) or (6.11), we need both left- and right-hand derivatives to be defined (and equal to each other). Hence, in the first theorem, we require $(X_{i_1}, \ldots, X_{i_n}, X_{i_1+m}) > 0$, and similarly for the second theorem.

(iii) *If there is any capital good which is smoothly substitutable for labour, either as an input or as an output* (i.e. if for any i, $\partial X_i/\partial L$ or $\partial X_{i+m}/\partial L$ exists), *and it requires some commodity other than labour in its production, then there can be no reswitching.*

Assume wages are paid at the beginning of the period of production and labour is smoothly substitutable for the ith capital good as a factor of production.[1] Then $\partial X_i/\partial L = 1/p_i$. But p_i is a monotonic function of r if X_{i+m} requires capital in its production; hence the given technology can be used at most at one r. The case of labour being substitutable for capital as an output may be handled similarly.

It is important to observe that in each of the theorems all that we require for the existence of the indicated derivatives of the transformation schedule is that these derivatives be defined for at least one of the sectoral production functions of the economy.[2] Thus, for example, if one capital-goods industry uses its output as an input, and there is a smooth substitutability relationship between the two, reswitching will not be possible, even if all other sectoral production functions have fixed coefficients and that sector itself has a non-differentiable relationship between other of its inputs and output.

III. *WICKSELL'S MODEL*

(1) *Wicksell and Wicksell Effects*

In the previous section we have seen how the changes in the relative prices of the different capital goods (as we change the rate of interest) may lead to the relative 'capital' intensities of two processes changing with the rate of interest; this in turn results in the possibility of the reswitching phenomenon. Wicksell, on the other hand, discussed at great length the consequences of the change in the price of capital goods *relative* to consumption goods as the interest rate changes. Somewhat heuristically, it is now a familiar proposition from the literature on two-sector growth models that if the capital-goods sector is less labour-intensive than the consumption-goods sector, as the wage rate rises and interest rate falls the price of capital goods will accordingly fall. Hence, the value of capital (in consumption numeraire) may increase less rapidly than the 'real capital' stock. This raises the possibility that an increase in the capital stock (number

[1] It is easy to establish that an interest rate is a switch-point between two technologies when wages are paid at the end of the period of production, if and only if it is a switch-point when wages are paid at the beginning of the period.

[2] All three theorems of this section carry over in a straightforward manner to technologies involving joint production. Reswitching is then defined as the existence of a technology that can be chosen at two interest rates, but not at some intervening interest rate.

of machines) may be accompanied by a fall in the total value of capital in consumption numeraire (as we compare steady states), which in turn would imply that an economy with a lower value of capital would have a higher output.

The major thrust of Wicksell's brilliant analysis of Akerman's problem[1] was to argue that 'A growth of capital, as long as it is such as to be profitable, is always accompanied by an increase in the total product'. In establishing his argument, he also shows that the length of life of a machine, the number of machines, the value of capital and the output of consumption goods increase monotonically as the rate of interest falls.

The reswitching phenomenon provides immediate counter-examples to the generality of the last two propositions; for if one technique has a higher consumption (net output) per man than another, at a switch-point it must also have a higher value of capital and profits (since the wages are identical for the two technologies at a switch-point). If, in the stationary state, C is consumption per worker, w is the wage, V_K the value of capital per worker, and r the interest rate, $C = w + rV_K$ or $V_K = (C - w)/r$. If two technologies are competitive at the same w and r, $V_{K1} = (C_1 - w)/r$, $V_{K2} = (C_2 - w)/r$, so $V_{K1} \gtrless V_{K2}$ as $C_1 \gtrless C_2$. Thus the reswitching phenomenon implies that the technology used at an intermediate interest rate has a lower (higher) consumption per man and a lower (higher) value of capital than that used at lower or higher interest rates.[2]

None the less, these models do not contradict the fundamental Wicksellian argument that a 'larger value of capital be associated with an increase in total product'. In the following subsections, we shall show (a) that the Wicksell argument does not hold even for a slight modification of his system and (b) that further slight modifications of the Wicksell model show the same kind of 'perversities' as the discrete heterogeneous capital good model, but (c) none of these perversities are of crucial importance to neo-classical economics.

(2) *A Wicksellian Capital Model*

We follow Wicksell in assuming that there are two sectors in the economy, one producing machines by means of labour alone, and

[1] Akerman's problem, it will be recalled, was the description of the competitive equilibrium for an economy in which the durability of capital was variable: by increasing the labour used to construct a machine, it may be made more durable. See Wicksell (1934).

[2] It should be emphasised, however, that these valuation perversities may occur even when reswitching does not occur, as Champernowne pointed out in his classic paper (1953).

the other producing consumption goods, with labour and machines. All machines are identical except in their durability, a machine lasting T years requiring $N(T)$ man-years to construct. Wicksell assumed that the production function in the consumption-goods sector was Cobb–Douglas; we depart from him here in assuming that it is fixed coefficients – a machine with one unit of labour produces one unit of consumption goods per year. We wish to contrast stationary economies differing in their rate of interest. We shall express all variables in per capita terms.

If the wage is w (in consumption-good numeraire) and the interest rate is r, the present discounted value of the quasi-rents from a machine of durability T is

$$(1-w)\int_0^T e^{-rt}dt = \frac{1-w}{r}(1-e^{-rT}). \qquad (6.12)$$

The competitive firm will choose the technique which maximises returns per dollar invested. T maximises

$$\frac{(1-w)(1-e^{-rT})}{wNr} = R(T, r)\frac{1-w}{wr}. \qquad (6.13)$$

Therefore

$$R_T = 0 \quad \text{and} \quad R_{TT} \leqslant 0.$$

If $v = N'T/N$, the elasticity of N, $R_T = 0$ implies

$$v = \frac{rTe^{-rT}}{1-e^{-rT}}. \qquad (6.14)$$

It is immediate that, as r falls, durability increases:

$$\frac{dT}{dr} = -\frac{R_{Tr}}{R_{TT}} = -\frac{e^{-rT}(1-rT-e^{-rT})}{R_{TT}N(1-e^{-rT})} \leqslant 0. \qquad (6.15)$$

Since per capita consumption, C, is equal to production of consumer goods divided by employment,

$$C = \frac{T}{N+T} \qquad (6.16)$$

and is monotonically increasing with T:

$$\frac{dC}{dT} = \frac{N(1-v)}{(N+T)^2} > 0 \qquad (6.17)$$

(using (6.14) and the fact that $rTe^{-rT}/(1-e^{-rT}) < 1$), C is inversely related to r:

$$\frac{dC}{dr} < 0. \qquad (6.18)$$

We are interested in determining the value of capital, V_K. The value of a machine which has $T-v$ years to live is

$$\frac{(1-w)}{r}(1-e^{-r(T-v)}).$$

Since there are $1/(N+T)$ machines of each age, the total value of capital, V_K, is

$$V_K = \frac{(1-w)(rT-1+e^{-rT})}{(N+T)r^2}. \tag{6.19}$$

The competitive wage is determined to make the present discounted value of the machine of optimal durability equal its cost:

$$\frac{(1-w)}{r}(1-e^{-rT}) = wN(T)$$

or

$$w = \frac{(1-e^{-rT})/r}{[(1-e^{-rT})/r]+N}. \tag{6.20}$$

Substituting (6.20) into (6.19) and simplifying, we obtain

$$V_K = \frac{N}{(N+T)r}\,\frac{rT-1+e^{-rT}}{1-e^{-rT}+rN}. \tag{6.21}$$

That dV_K/dr will be negative if v is constant (i.e. for appropriately chosen units, $N = T^v$) may be seen by rewriting (6.21), letting $rT = x$ (since v is constant, (6.14) implies that x is a constant):

$$V_K = \frac{T^{v+1}(x-1+e^{-x})}{(T^v+T)[1-e^{-x}+xT^{v-1}]x}$$

$$\frac{dV_K}{dT} = \frac{V_K\{(1-e^{-x})(T^{-2}+vT^{-(1+v)})+x[(2-v)T^{v-3}+T^{-2}]\}}{(T^{-v}+T^{-1})(1-e^{-x}+dT^{v-1})} > 0. \tag{6.21'}$$

On the other hand, observing that by making v' arbitrarily large we can make dT/dr arbitrarily small at a point, we can make the sign of dV_K/dr depend on that of $\partial V_K/\partial r$; but consider the case where rT is small (the value of rT depends only on the value of v, not its derivative). Then (6.21) may be approximated by

$$V_K \approx \frac{NT^2}{2(N+T)[N+T-rT^2/2]} \tag{6.21''}$$

which is an increasing function of r.

Thus, we have the possibility that, even in a Wicksellian model, a higher value of capital will be associated with a lower level of net output. The 'paradox' which Wicksell was so concerned to show could not occur in an economy with 'perfectly free competition' – a fall in the national dividend resulting from continued saving and capital accumulation' – may indeed occur.

(3) *Reswitching in a Wicksellian Model*

I think Wicksell would have been equally surprised, and disturbed, to find out that in a slight variant of his model, consumption per man and T^*, the optimal durability, need not be monotonic in r – although I think he needn't have been.

To see this, we depart from Wicksell's formulation, and that presented above in section III (2), by assuming (as seems reasonable) that there are gestation periods for the production of machines. Thus, to produce a machine which will last T years requires an input of labour described by the *function* $N(u, T)$ (i.e. if we normalise by letting $u = 0$ denote the time of the completion of the machine, when it begins to produce output, $N(u, T)$ is the labour required, per machine, in the construction of the machine in the uth year before completion), the total cost of which is, if r is the interest rate and w the wage,

$$w \int N(u, T) e^{-ru} du. \tag{6.22}$$

For simplicity, we shall assume that $N(u, T)$ takes on the simple form

$$N(u, T) = \begin{cases} N_1(T) & 0 \geqslant u \geqslant -1 \\ N_2/b = \text{a constant} & -1 \geqslant u \geqslant -b \\ 0 & \text{otherwise} \end{cases}$$

(where $u = 0$ is the date of completion of the machine).

Then a profit-maximising firm will choose the technique for which the present discounted value of quasi-rents per dollar invested,

$$\frac{(1-w)(1-e^{-rT})}{w\left[\dfrac{N_2}{b}(e^{rb}-e^{r})+N_1(e^{r}-1)\right]} \tag{6.23}$$

is largest. Defining the function

$$\alpha(r) = \frac{e^{rb}-e^{r}}{(e^{r}-1)b} \tag{6.24}$$

which has the property that

$$\alpha'(r) = \frac{be^{rb}(e^r-1)-(e^{rb}-1)}{(e^r-1)^2 b} > 0, \quad \text{since} \quad b > 1, \tag{6.25}$$

we see that a profit-maximising firm will choose T so that

$$\frac{rTe^{-rT}}{1-e^{-rT}} = \frac{-rTh'(rT)}{h(rT)} = \left(\frac{N_1'T}{N_1}\right)\frac{N_1}{N_1+\alpha N_2}, \tag{6.26}$$

where $h(x) = 1-e^{-x}$. The elasticity of h must equal the elasticity of N_1 times the ratio of N_1 to total 'weighted' labour input, where the weight on N_2 is given by (6.24). In the simple Wicksell model, we saw that lower rates of interest are always associated with longer-lived machines. Now, because as the interest rate decreases, the capital costs also decrease, the opposite may also be true, and indeed it is even possible for there to be 'reswitching' of techniques, i.e. a given durability will be optimal for two different interest rates with another durability optimal for an intervening interest rate. Thus, dT/dr has the same sign as

$$\frac{1-rT-e^{-rT}}{1-e^{-rT}}+\frac{rN_2\alpha'}{(N_1+\alpha N_2)}. \tag{6.27}$$

The first term is always negative, the second always positive, and there is an apparent ambiguity in the sign of dT/dr.

Consider, for instance, the following example:

$$N(u, T) = \begin{cases} T & 0 \geqslant u \geqslant -1 \\ 0{\cdot}093 & -1 \geqslant u \geqslant -4. \\ 0 & \text{otherwise.} \end{cases}$$

Then, when $r = 1$, $T = 1$; and since $\alpha = 7{\cdot}6$,

$$\frac{r}{e^{rT}-1} = \frac{1}{1{\cdot}71} = \frac{1}{N_1+\alpha N_2} = \frac{1}{1+0{\cdot}71}.$$

dT/dr is positive. This is shown by calculating, for $rT = 1$,

$$\frac{1-e^{-rT}-rT}{1-e^{-rT}} = \frac{-1}{e^{rT}-1} = -\frac{1}{1{\cdot}71} = -0{\cdot}59$$

and; using $\alpha' = 19{\cdot}8$,

$$\frac{rN_2\alpha'}{N_1+\alpha N_2} = \frac{19{\cdot}8\times 0{\cdot}093}{1{\cdot}71} = 1{\cdot}087 > 0{\cdot}59.$$

It is also apparent that consumption need not be monotonic in T:

$$C = \frac{T}{N_1+N_2+T} \tag{6.28}$$

$$\frac{dC}{dT} = \frac{N_1+N_2-N_1'T}{(N_1+N_2+T)^2}. \tag{6.29}$$

The first-order condition for optimal durability only guarantees that

$$N_1+\alpha N_2 > N_1'T. \tag{6.30}$$

If $\alpha > 1$, then (6.30) can be satisfied and $N_1+N_2 < N_1'T$, so that $dC/dT < 0$. Conversely, a sufficient condition for C to be a monotonically increasing function of T is that[1] $\alpha \leqslant 1$.

This model makes clear why the consumption-per-man 'perversity' is no paradox at all. Consumption per man depends simply on the *total* labour requirements per machine-year,

$$\frac{N_1+N_2}{T} \tag{6.31}$$

while the choice of technique depends on *weighted* labour input (weights given by the intertemporal prices) and the weighted returns; i.e. not T, but $(1-e^{-rT})/r$.

The important point to observe is that the first- and second-order conditions imply constraints on the weighted labour input per unit of value output and its changes, but not necessarily on the unweighted expression (6.31).

IV. RESWITCHING AND NEO-CLASSICAL DOCTRINE

(1) *The Wicksell Effects*

Should Wicksell have been upset if he had discovered that these 'perversities' could in fact occur? Does it have any serious implications for neo-classical doctrine? I think the answer to both of these questions is no. Wicksell made two related errors in attempting to interpret the 'paradox': (i) He confused comparisons of steady states with truly dynamic paths (Mrs Robinson, in spite of her constant warnings to others not to fall into this sinister trap, seems to have fallen into it herself). (ii) He confused savings in value terms with savings in real terms. 'True' neo-classical doctrine asserts the following two propositions: (a) Forgoing consumption today will allow the economy to take increased consumption some time in the

[1] Thus, for example, if $N(T)$ has constant elasticity, and if, for some value of T, $dC/dT < 0$, then $dC/dT < 0$ for all greater values of T.

future, and the marginal rate at which consumption today may be transformed into consumption tomorrow is given, in a competitive economy, by the rate of interest. More formally, consider an economy with an initial endowment vector of capital goods, X; then the consumption possibilities of that economy may be represented by[1] (for simplicity we assume there is a single consumption good):

$$C^0 = \varphi(C^1, \ldots, C^t, \ldots; X) \tag{6.32}$$

where C^t is consumption at time t. Neo-classical doctrine asserts that if r_t is the rate of interest between the t and $t+1$ period, and p_i is the competitive price of the ith capital good, then

$$\begin{aligned} -\frac{\partial C^1}{\partial C^0} &= -\frac{\partial C^1/\partial X_i}{\partial C^0/\partial X_i} = \frac{\partial C^1/\partial X_i}{p_i} = (1+r_0) > 0 \\ -\frac{\partial C^t}{\partial C^0} &= \prod_{i=0}^{t-1} (1+r_i) = \frac{\partial C^t/\partial X_i}{p_i} > 0. \end{aligned} \tag{6.33}$$

The competitive rate of interest is equal to the marginal rate of transformation between consumption (in the relevant periods) and is equal to the marginal physical product of the ith capital good divided by the price of the ith capital good. (b) There is a diminishing marginal rate of transformation:

$$\frac{\partial(\partial C^1/\partial C^0)}{\partial C^0} \leqslant 0, \quad \frac{\partial(\partial C^0/\partial X_i)}{\partial X_i} \leqslant 0. \tag{6.34}$$

These fundamental neo-classical propositions are very different from the propositions with which the reswitching, capital valuation and consumption-per-man perversities are concerned. The latter consider steady states, i.e. situations where $C_0 = C_1 = C_2 = \ldots$, and where $X(r)$ is that endowment of capital goods which will sustain the given steady state. (For a discrete technology with one consumption good, there are only a finite number of such steady states.) If the transformation function is differentiable, each steady state will be characterised by an interest rate, so that we can write unambiguously:

$$C(r) = \varphi[C(r), \ldots, C(r); X(r)]. \tag{6.35}$$

Consider a problem such as that discussed by Wicksell in which V_K and C are continuous functions of r. Wicksell drew attention to the fact that, if we define $V_K(r) = \sum_i p_i(r)X_i(r)$ where $p_i(r)$ is the

[1] Throughout this discussion we shall assume that (6.32) is differentiable. When this is not the case, we must replace the equalities in (6.33) by the appropriate inequalities, but the analysis is essentially unaffected.

equilibrium price of the ith capital good in consumption-good numeraire when the interest rate is r, then

$$\frac{dC(r)/dr}{dV_K(r)/dr} = \frac{dC}{dV_K} \neq r. \tag{6.36}$$

But (6.36) is very different from (6.33), even though it has certain superficial similarities. Indeed, the valuation perversity is just the extreme case of (6.36) where

$$\frac{dC}{dV_K} < 0.$$

It would be foolish to suggest that because the value of capital is lower in one steady state than another, no consumption need be forgone in going from one steady state to another; yet, remarkably enough, Pasinetti, 1969 (among others) has actually suggested that the 'cost' of going from one steady state to another be measured by the change in the value of capital.[1]

The Wicksell effects discussed above are simply a reflection of the fact that in different steady states the price vector and the capital vector are different. To isolate the two effects, we might compare the value of capital in the two steady states at the same price system; a natural price system to use is that at which the two corresponding technologies are equally profitable (i.e. at the switch-point). But at a switch-point, as we have already noted, in a stationary economy,

$$\frac{\partial C}{\partial V_K} = r. \tag{6.37}$$

Yet (6.37) conveys little if any more information than (6.36); it does not tell us whether the transition from one steady state to another is even feasible (as it will not be if the second technology requires a capital good which cannot be produced by the capital goods of the first technology); when it is feasible, it is clear that making the transition may well entail increases in consumption in some periods and decreases in others. Indeed, it would appear that comparing consumptions, values of capital, etc., across steady states conveys little if any information about the true consumption opportunities available to an economy.

[1] Taking proper account of capital which may become redundant in the new steady state. In calculating the rate of return, he compares the values of capital for the two steady states; although in his comparisons he values the capital at the same prices, those corresponding to the switch-point between the two technologies, it is still inappropriate to measure the 'cost' of the transition by the change in the value of capital, as we note below.

It should be noted that in the one-sector Solow–Swan model there can be no Wicksell effects (the price of capital goods in terms of consumption goods is fixed at unity) and hence these valuation perversities cannot occur. But clearly, neo-classical analysis does not depend on this assumption; to suggest that is to suggest that Wicksell, Uzawa, Meade, and indeed Solow and Samuelson in their earlier articles, are not neo-classical. Moreover, in multisectoral models with or without smooth substitutability, but with a single capital good, the amount of this single capital good need not be increasing as the rate of interest falls.

Similarly, the consumption-per-man perversity represents a confusion between steady-state analysis and true dynamics, and between special properties of the simple Solow–Swan model and the properties of more general neo-classical models. Observe that, using (6.33), one can deduce that $\partial r_0/\partial C^1 < 0$, or, somewhat informally,

$$\frac{\partial C^1}{\partial r_0} < 0. \tag{6.38}$$

Higher interest rates between this period and the next correspond to lower values of consumption this period (keeping consumption in periods 2 and after an endowment vector of capital goods constant; other interest rates and prices will, of course, also be changing as r_0 changes). The consumption-per-man perversity is that, along steady states,

$$\frac{dC(r)}{dr} > 0. \tag{6.39}$$

But again, (6.39) is very different from (6.38). In particular, as we change r in one case, we are changing all the capital endowments. Thus (6.39) does not constitute a violation of the law of diminishing returns, as would appear at first sight.

(2) *Differentiability and Reswitching*

In the original examples of reswitching, there were always a finite number of technologies. This led to the conjecture that if there were 'enough' processes in each (or in any) industry, then reswitching could not in fact occur. These results were formalised in the theorems presented in section II (6). Far weaker conditions than differentiability of the transformation surface were required to rule out reswitching. On the other hand, the example of section III (3) showed that reswitching could occur even if there were an infinite number of techniques; 'differentiability' by itself is not sufficient to rule out reswitching.

It should be clear that there is in fact no contradiction between our theorems and our example. Our theorems required, for instance, that when one capital good was substitutable for another, it be substitutable in both directions (i.e. we could increase the first and decrease the second, or decrease the first and increase the second); we required, in other words, that the relevant capital goods be used in the given technology in strictly positive amounts. In our example labour alone produces machines, and machines produce consumption goods with labour. The application of different amounts of labour results in the production of different kinds of machines (for each durability of machine is really a different kind of machine) in a smooth, differentiable manner. But in any technology only one type of machine is employed, and it is not employed in its own construction.

(3) *Reswitching and Rates of Return*

Our example also serves to clarify the relationship between the reswitching phenomenon and neo-classical–marginalist distribution theory. When, as in the case of the propositions just presented, marginal products are well defined, competitive prices will be equal to those marginal products. When there are a discrete number of technologies, or, as in our example, there are an infinite number of technologies, but in each not every (capital) good is produced, there may be several sets of prices which correspond to (i.e. will support) any particular path of the economy. Which price system will be chosen will depend on the preferences of consumers (for instance, on their time preferences).

The lack of smooth substitutability in the economy – even in our example, with an infinite number of technologies, there is only limited substitutability – does have some implications for the concept of the rate of return; for in the absence of such substitutability it may not be possible to reduce consumption this period, increase it next period, keeping consumption in all future periods unchanged and the economy at full employment. Consider, for instance, an economy in steady state with technology A, and consumption $C_A{}^*$, and consider an efficient path which begins with the steady-state endowment corresponding to technology A and eventually reaches steady state using technology B, with steady-state consumption $C_B{}^*$. Let $C_t{}'$ be the consumption in the transition periods $t = 1, \ldots, T$. In general, it will require more than one period to make the transition ($T \geqslant 2$), and $C_t{}' - C_A{}^*$ will be negative in some periods, positive in others.

We can define the internal rate of return as that rate of discount for which

$$\sum_1^{\infty} C_A{}^* \left(\frac{1}{1+\delta}\right)^t = C_A{}^*/\delta = \sum_1^{T} C_t{}' \left(\frac{1}{1+\delta}\right)^t + \sum_{T+1}^{\infty} C_B{}^* \left(\frac{1}{1+\delta}\right)^t. \quad (6.40)$$

(6.40) may have more than one solution. It can be shown that if C_t' is an efficient path along which all capital goods and labour are fully employed, and δ is a solution of (6.40), either (a) the rate of return is equal to the rate of interest at a switch-point, $\delta = r^*$, or (b) at $r^* = \delta$ there is some other technology whose steady-state prices are less than those of A or B (i.e. if A and B were the only technologies, then it would be a switch-point, but there is some other technology D which, at the given interest rate, dominates A and B). Thus, the fact that there may be many switch-points is simply a reflection of the fact that (6.40) may have several solutions (i.e. that $C_t' - C_A^*$ will be negative in some periods, positive in others).[1]

(4) *Other Issues in the Analysis of Steady States*

Much of recent growth literature has focused on issues other than those discussed in the preceding sections. In this subsection, we comment briefly on the relationship between the reswitching phenomenon and two of the more widely discussed issues in growth theory:

(*a*) *Existence of balanced growth with full employment* (equality of warranted and natural rates of growth). The existence of many capital goods (and consumption goods) means that even if there were no substitution of techniques, the ratio of the value of capital to the value of output would change as the rate of interest changes, so that the natural and warranted rates of growth could be brought into equality by price adjustments. The reswitching phenomenon has, of course, nothing to say on this issue, but it does have implications for:

(*b*) *Uniqueness of balanced growth,* since the pseudo-production possibilities schedule of steady states will not be concave and monotone. But neither is it even in the two-sector neo-classical growth model or in the Wicksellian model. Uniqueness of balanced growth equilibrium when a constant fraction of income is saved depends on the value of net output per unit of value capital being a monotone concave function of capital per man (in steady state), and as we have argued above, there is no particular reason why such value constructs should be 'well behaved'.

[1] Pasinetti's (1969) criticism of Solow's (1967) analysis of the relationship between the rate of return and the rate of interest (he argues that they will not in general be equal) is based on two confusions: (a) As we noted above, he used the change in the value of capital to measure the 'cost' of going from one steady state to another; what we should be concerned with, however, is the change in consumption along the transition path. (b) If one steady state requires less of some capital good than another, in going from the second steady state to the first, he assumes capital must become redundant. In fact, Solow establishes the existence of full-employment transition paths under the assumption that all capital goods can also be used for consumption; they probably exist under much weaker assumptions than that.

This means, of course, that the simple parables of *accumulation*, such as those discussed by Solow and Swan, are not likely to be valid in more general models, particularly when there are heterogeneous capital goods. And indeed, this has already been recognised in the works of Hahn, Cass, Shell, Stiglitz and others.

REFERENCES

M. Bruno, E. Burmeister and E. Sheshinski, 'The Nature and Implications of the Reswitching of Techniques', *Quarterly Journal of Economics*, vol. LXXX (Nov 1966) pp. 526–53.

D. G. Champernowne, 'The Production Function and the Theory of Capital: Comment', *Review of Economic Studies*, vol. XXXI (1953–4) pp. 112–35.

G. C. Harcourt, 'Some Cambridge Controversies in the Theory of Capital', *Journal of Economic Literature*, vol. VII (June 1969) pp. 369–405.

J. A. Mirrlees, 'The Dynamic Nonsubstitution Theorem', *Review of Economic Studies*, vol. XXXVI (Jan 1969).

L. L. Pasinetti, 'Switches of Techniques and the "Rate of Return" in Capital Theory', *Economic Journal*, vol. LXXIX (Sep 1969).

J. Robinson, 'The Production Function and the Theory of Capital', *Review of Economic Studies*, vol. XXI (1953–4) pp. 81–106.

R. M. Solow, 'A Contribution to the Theory of Economic Growth', *Quarterly Journal of Economics*, vol. LXX (Feb 1956) pp. 65–94.

—— 'The Interest Rate and Transition between Techniques', in *Socialism, Capitalism and Economic Growth*, ed. C. H. Feinstein (Cambridge U.P., 1967).

D. A. Starrett, 'Switching and Reswitching in a General Production Model', *Quarterly Journal of Economics*, vol. LXXIX (Nov 1969) pp. 673–87.

J. E. Stiglitz, 'Non-Substitution Theorems with Durable Capital Goods', *Review of Economic Studies* (1970).

T. Swan, 'Economic Growth and Capital Accumulation', *Economic Record*, vol. XXXII (Nov 1956).

K. Wicksell, *Lectures on Political Economy* and Appendix 2, 'Real Capital and Interest', trans. E. Classen (London: Routledge, 1934).

7 Recurrence of Techniques in a Dynamic Economy

Joseph E. Stiglitz
YALE UNIVERSITY

I. THE MEANING OF RESWITCHING IN A DYNAMIC ECONOMY

(1) It is apparent that the definition of reswitching given in section II (1) of the previous chapter will not be immediately applicable to truly dynamic situations. This may be viewed in several different ways:

(a) The previous definition required that the choice of technique be independent of preferences among alternative commodities, i.e. that the non-substitution theorem obtain. But out of steady state there is in general no non-substitution theorem. Indeed, each of the *inherited* capital goods and labour in each of the periods may be considered separate primary factors (since they cannot be produced); since there is more than one primary factor, the non-substitution theorem will definitely not obtain.

(b) There is no longer any such animal as 'the interest rate'; since relative prices of different capital goods are changing, there is an own rate of return for each capital good.

(2) What is to be meant then by the reswitching of techniques in a dynamic context? The following two approaches seem to be the interesting ones:

(a) We could ask whether an economy might, on its optimal development trajectory, use (or construct) machines of a particular type over one interval of time, another type over an intervening interval of time, and then return to the earlier technique. Thus, we can address ourselves to the fundamental question – the question which I take it both sides of the Cambridge dispute are really interested in (as opposed to the imaginary question of comparing islands in steady-state equilibrium) – of what sense can we make of the Wicksell–Solow–Robinson neo-classical story of capital accumulation.[1] It need hardly be pointed out, of course, that this reswitching

[1] Readers may wonder at the juxtaposition of 'Robinson' and 'neo-classical'; but it is clear that when Professor Robinson addresses herself to the question of accumulation (as opposed to comparing islands), she tells an essentially Wicksellian story of the deepening of techniques. See, e.g., Robinson (1956, 1960).

in time, which perhaps we should call *recurrence*, is a very different phenomenon from the reswitching of techniques along the factor price frontier. It will be seen that recurrence of techniques may occur in technologies which do not allow reswitching, and in technologies in which there is reswitching there may be no recurrences.

(b) Instead of characterising the evolution of the economy along the optimal path, i.e. a path where savings are chosen optimally and where there is perfect foresight of future prices (of commodities and factors), we could characterise the path for a 'descriptive' model of the competitive economy, e.g. where a constant fraction of income is saved. Again, we can ask whether it is possible for there to be *recurrences* in the choice of technique.

The first topic is pursued in section II, where, using a slight modification of the Wicksell model with *ex-post* fixed co-efficients, I establish that:

1. Along an optimal path of accumulation, there may be recurrences.
2. There may be *discontinuities* in the choices of technique. (The economy goes from technique γ to technique α, skipping technique β.)
3. Consumption may not be a monotonic function of time. (Of course, even in the conventional models, the savings *rate* may not be a monotonic function of time.)
4. The wage rate need not be a monotonic function of time.
5. The consumption rate of interest may not be a monotonic function of time.

Thus, I show that the optimal plan of development may look very different from that suggested by the Ramsey analysis for economies with a single malleable capital good, and that which Wicksell seems to have envisioned. That the corresponding story of development in a descriptive model, as told, for instance, by Solow, runs into difficulties when there are heterogeneous capital goods has been pointed out and extensively discussed by Hahn, 1966, Shell and Stiglitz, 1967, and Samuelson, 1967, among others. Attention has been drawn to a number of particular problems:

(i) In the absence of futures markets extending infinitely far into the future, individuals must form expectations of what prices and rentals will be in the future in order to make their investment decision. These expectations may or may not turn out to be correct. Research has focused on two classes of paths: those in which expectations of prices in the immediate future are fulfilled (short-run perfect foresight), and those in which expectations of prices are based on past experience (adaptive expectations), including, in particular, the case where individuals expect prices next period to be the same as those of this period (static expectations).

(ii) With given expectations, there are a variety of paths which are consistent with short-run perfect foresight (i.e. momentary equilibrium may very well not be uniquely determined).

(iii) The short-run perfect foresight paths may not converge to balanced growth; in other words there is no way of ensuring that the initial prices will be those which lead to convergence.

(iv) Although in the two models which have been perhaps most fully investigated thus far (Shell and Stiglitz, 1967; Cass and Stiglitz, 1969) it has been established that static expectations would ensure that the economy converged to balanced growth, the growth path of the economy, as it converged, might look very different from that described by the Solow–Swan–Meade–Uzawa malleable capital goods models.

The result that static expectations might ensure stability was somewhat disturbing; for static expectations implied that investment decisions were being made (resources allocated) on incorrect expectations, and hence the resulting allocations were likely to be inefficient. This result suggested that the economy might have to sacrifice efficiency for stability, and that it was in fact the 'frictions' and 'imperfections' in the economy which provided the most important forces for stability.

(v) In the same models, it was established that all paths along which expectations were fulfilled for ever must converge to balanced growth; i.e. along those paths which did not converge eventually the perfect foresight assumption would be violated (in finite time).

Unfortunately, it appears that growth equilibrium paths which are consistent with perfect foresight for ever need not converge to balanced growth, and that static expectations need not ensure stability.

In section III, a modified Wicksellian model is used to investigate these and other questions raised by the existence of heterogeneous capital goods. We first consider an economy in which all of profits are saved but none of wages (the Marxian savings assumption) and in which individuals have static expectations. The growth path of the economy is likely to be oscillatory, i.e. there are likely to be recurrences in the type of machine constructed. If the wage is high, this is likely to mean that profits are low and hence savings are low, and that capital-intensive machines will be built. Demand for labour in the consumption-goods sector will decline (as of any given wage). But the excess labour cannot be hired in the investment-goods sector unless savings rise, i.e. unless profits rise. Thus wages fall, enabling more workers to be hired in both the consumption- and investment-goods sector, restoring full employment. But at the lower wage, just the reverse occurs. None the less, it can be established that these capital intensity–distribution cycles are all damped, i.e. the economy converges to balanced growth.

The stability of the balanced growth path turns out to depend, however, on the assumption that capital decays exponentially. If capital has a finite life, the balanced growth path may be unstable, and the economy may converge instead to a limit cycle. This result holds whether there are static expectations or perfect foresight and under a variety of savings assumptions. Indeed, when we attempt to make the model more 'reasonable' by introducing life-cycle savings with overlapping generations, further difficulties arise. The savings (thriftiness) conditions are not sufficient, by themselves, to determine the rate of profit (the dynamic path of the economy); evidently, at least in part, 'the rate of profit is what it is because individuals expect it to be what it is', and had they expected it to be different, it indeed would be different. Moreover, the economy may neither converge to balanced growth, diverge, nor converge to a limit cycle. It simply 'wobbles' along.

These models will serve to illustrate the crucial role which expectations play in the determination not only of the distribution of income today, but also of the entire growth path of the economy. They raise important doubts about the validity of the conventional growth models, which are so structured that expectations play no role at all.

II. THE WICKSELL NEO-CLASSICAL MODEL OF CAPITAL ACCUMULATION

(1) The main features of the neo-classical model of capital accumulation may be summarised as follows:

(a) There is a monotonic increase in consumption per capita accompanied by:

(b) A monotonic increase in the wage rate and fall in the consumption rate of interest.

(c) The increase in capital may take one of several forms:

  (i) machines may be made more durable;

  (ii) more productive machines may be constructed (i.e. machines which have a higher output per worker);

  (iii) workers may move to a more capital-intensive sector.[1]

[1] In the simple Wicksell model there is no ambiguity in defining which is the more capital-intensive sector, since one of the two sectors requires no capital at all.

The first two may be referred to as capital deepening; the third as capital widening. The process of capital accumulation is characterised by steady capital deepening, although not necessarily by capital widening.[1]

The reswitching possibilities alert us to the fact that the introduction of machines having a higher output per worker may not be the appropriate indicator of capital deepening, that indeed no meaning can really be attached to one technique being more capital-intensive than another. But as we have already suggested, the problems with the neo-classical story of capital accumulation are deeper than – and quite separate from – those of reswitching.

(2) *The Two-Sector Putty–Clay Model*[2]

The simplest model in which to examine most of these issues is the two-sector model in which capital is produced by labour alone, and consumption goods are produced by means of machines and labour. We shall focus only on the second kind of capital deepening; i.e. on the question of whether, on an optimal path of accumulation, the output per man on new machines is steadily increased.

We shall assume that a machine of type x requires, when fully manned, x labourers, and produces an output of $b(x)$. All machines require one man-year to be constructed and depreciate exponentially at the rate μ. x may either be a continuous or a discrete variable; in any case, $b(x)$ will be assumed to be a monotonically increasing concave function of x. I shall chiefly consider the case in which b is twice differentiable, so that $b' \geqslant 0$, $b'' \leqslant 0$. This is equivalent to assuming that output per man is a decreasing function of x.

(3) *Steady States*

If the wage rate were w (for ever), then the technique which would minimise costs would be that for which

$$b(x) - wx \tag{7.1}$$

is maximised, i.e.

$$b'(x) = w. \tag{7.2}$$

The competitive interest rate, i.e. that interest rate which would discount quasi-rents back to costs, is given by

[1] In the Solow–Swan one-sector model there is no room for capital widening as defined here; more generally, whether the process of accumulation is accompanied by capital widening will depend, at least in part, on the relative capital intensities of the capital-goods and consumption-goods sectors. If capital goods were more capital-intensive, then there is likely to be capital widening in the early stages of development, but subsequently there may be capital 'narrowing' (cf. Uzawa, 1964).

[2] This form of the Wicksellian model is due to Solow, 1962.

$$r+\mu = \max_x \frac{b(x)-wx}{w} = \frac{b(x)-xb'(x)}{b'(x)} \tag{7.3}$$

which is just the marginal product of capital $b(x)-xb'(x)$ measured in labour numeraire. (7.2) and (7.3) define parametrically the factor price frontier. It is clear that it is 'well behaved', i.e. downward-sloping. Unlike the Samuelson (1962) example, where the capital intensities in the two sectors are identical, the slope of the factor price frontier,

$$-\frac{dw}{dr} = -\frac{dw/dx}{dr/dx} = \frac{w^2}{b} = \frac{w}{r+x+\mu} \tag{7.4}$$

is not equal to the value of the capital stock per capita, V_K, unless the growth rate $n = r$. For

$$V_K = \frac{w}{n+k+\mu} \tag{7.5}$$

since the price of a machine is w, and for each machine x men are operating it, and $n+\mu$ men are engaged on building new machines.

On the other hand, the factor price frontiers corresponding to any two techniques can only intersect once. For a given technique, the factor price frontier is defined by

$$r+\mu = \frac{b(x)}{w} - x. \tag{7.6}$$

r is a linear function of $1/w$.

The pseudo-production function, giving the value of net output corresponding to different values of capital (per capita) in steady state, is given parametrically by (7.5) and

$$Y(x) = w(x) + rV_K(x). \tag{7.7}$$

It is easy to confirm that Y is a monotonically increasing, concave function of V_K, i.e. the pseudo-production function is well behaved.

(3) *Optimal Growth with a Linear Objective Function*

The optimal trajectory of a socialist economy with the technology described in the previous subsections wishing to maximise the discounted value of consumption has been studied by Srinivasan, 1962, Bruno, 1967, and Stiglitz, 1968. A striking feature of the trajectory is that only one type of machine is ever constructed; machines of other capital intensities would be used if they happened to be around – if output per man on these machines were sufficiently high – but they would not be constructed on the optimal trajectory. Although the number of workers working in the consumption-goods sector increases monotonically (capital 'widening' occurs in a smooth way), output of consumption goods need not be monotonically increasing. These results have been shown to hold in Samuelson's slightly more general two-sector model, where even though there is reswitching along the frontier, only one type of machine is ever constructed (Bruno, 1967).

By comparison, in the analogous malleable-capital-good economy, consumption is always monotonic. On the other hand, just as in the *ex-post* fixed-coefficients economy, the wage rate, the price of capital goods in terms of consumption goods and the capital–labour ratio in the consumption-goods sector are constant.

These results depend on two crucial assumptions: (i) the linearity of the utility function and (ii) the assumption that each process uses only one kind of capital good. When either of these are removed, the Wicksellian story begins to look even less plausible. Section II (4) considers the effects of imposing a minimum consumption constraint on the optimal growth trajectory, and section III presents a simple example of reswitching with a linear utility function.

(4) *Minimum Consumption Constraint*

The easiest non-linearity to introduce into the utility function is to assume that there is a minimum consumption constraint. (This also removes the objection raised by Professor Robinson in her note (1969).)

$$\text{Maximise} \int_0^\infty Ce^{-\delta t}dt \tag{7.8}$$

subject to the constraint

$$C \geqslant C_0 \tag{7.8A}$$

where C_0 is the minimum level of consumption and δ is the pure rate of time discount. For simplicity we take $n = 0$.

A similar problem was treated in Cass and Stiglitz (1969). If it has a solution, the solution has two stages (the first of which may not occur): in one the constraint (7.8A) is binding, and in the other it is not. The latter stage is identical to that described above. I shall therefore concentrate on analysis of the former stage.

Consider the shadow prices associated with the optimum path. I use the notation:

- w is the shadow price of labour
- $p(x, t)$ is the shadow price of a machine of type x at time t
- $N(x, t)$ is the number of machines of type $\leqslant x$ existing at t
- M is the number of workers in the investment sector
- μ is the exponential rate of depreciation (the same for all machines).

At t, when the shadow wage is w, a machine of type x is used if $b(x) > wx$, not used if $b(x) < wx$. If $b(x) = wx$ it may or may not be used. Since the value of a machine is the discounted sum of its quasi-rents, discounted by means of consumption rates of interest, we have

$$p(x, t) = \int_t^\infty [b(x) - wx]_+ [1 + \lambda(\tau)] e^{-(\mu+\delta)(\tau - t)} d\tau \tag{7.9}$$

where $\lambda(t)$ is the non-negative shadow price associated with the constraint $C(t) \geqslant C_0$. If $C > C_0$, $\lambda = 0$. The notation $[a]_+$ means a if $a > 0$, and 0 otherwise.

For completeness, note that

$$C(t) = \int_0^z b(x) dN(x, t) \tag{7.10}$$

and

$$1 - M(t) = \int_0^z x dN(x, t) \tag{7.11}$$

where z is such that $b(z) = wz$. If a discrete range of techniques, with $x = x_1, x_2, \ldots$, is possible, we have to write instead

$$C(t) = \sum_{x<z} b(x) N'(x) + \gamma b(z) N'(z) \tag{7.10A}$$

$$1 - M(t) = \sum_{x<z} x N'(x) + \gamma z N'(z) \tag{7.11A}$$

where $N'(x)$ is the number of machines of type x and γ is in the interval [0, 1]. The last term does not occur at times when there is no technique for which $b(z) = wz$.

Machines are constructed only if, at that date, they maximise $p(x, t)$. Unfortunately, there may be more than one value of x that maximises $p(x, t)$ given by (7.9). (Cf. Bliss, 1968; Cass and Stiglitz, 1969.)

In the long run, it is known (Stiglitz, 1968) that the technique being produced is chosen so as to minimise labour costs per unit of output (taking account of depreciation and time preference); i.e. the technique in question, y^*, satisfies

$$\frac{b(y^*) - y^* b'(y^*)}{b'(y^*)} = \mu + \delta. \tag{7.12}$$

The oldest machine in use, of type z^*, satisfies

$$w^* = b'(y^*) = b(z^*)/z^*. \tag{7.13}$$

It can be shown (provided that the initial stage with $C = C_0$ actually occurs) that z will never fall below z^* (i.e. w will never rise above

w^*). It follows (from (7.9)) that $p(x, t)$ has at most one local maximum for $x < z^*$. This information implies that

(i) more than one type of machine may be constructed at any moment of time;
(ii) there may be discontinuities in the choice of technique; that is, machines of type x_1 may be constructed at one time, machines of type x_2 at another, but no machines of types between x_2 and x_1 in the intervening period;
(iii) only one type of machine with $x < z^*$ is constructed at any moment of time, and in the region $x < z^*$ the type of technique chosen varies continuously over time.

To ascertain further properties of the choice of technique, (7.9) is differentiated with respect to t:

$$\frac{\partial}{\partial t}p(x, t) = (\mu+\delta)p(x, t)-(1+\lambda)(b-wx). \tag{7.14}$$

It is clear from this equation that, if w were rising over time, a machine of type x' that is going to be produced in the future must have $b(x')-wx' < b(x)-wx$, since otherwise its price would not be rising as rapidly as the price of the machine of type x. This means that y, the type of machine actually constructed, must be increasing over time. (For it is clear from (7.9) that, if w is increasing with time, the y that maximises p satisfies $b'(y) > w$.) In this case, then, there can be no recurrence of techniques.

But the wage may not rise monotonically along the optimal trajectory. Indeed, the following example illustrates an economy in which wages are not monotonic along the optimum path, and recurrence does occur. There is a discrete set of possible machines. The technology and the initial endowments are set forth in Table 7.1. ($C_0 = 1{\cdot}5$, $\mu = 0{\cdot}2$, $\delta = 0{\cdot}102$.)

Figs. 7.1 and 7.2 show diagrammatically the time paths of prices and capital stocks. In the initial stage type α machine is constructed, while in the next stage type β is constructed, but eventually α is again constructed.

It should also be noted that, in this example, the rate of interest (the own rate of return of consumption or, equivalently, the quasi-rent on newly constructed capital, measured in consumption-goods numeraire) falls (when w rises), rises, and then falls again.

How can we explain these apparent anomalies? Under what circumstances can they occur? As we noted above, we choose our technique so that the marginal productivity of labour along the *ex-ante* production function equals the average wage over the life

TABLE 7.1

Type of machine	*Output per machine* $b(x)$	*Output per man* $b(x)/x$	*Initial endowment of machines*
α	0·50	50	1·22
β	0·625	5	0
γ	0·75	1·5	1·28
ε	0·77	1·0	Not binding constraint

PHASES OF DEVELOPMENT

Phase	*Approximate duration*	*Type of machine constructed*	*Oldest machine in use*
1	0·5	α	γ
2	0·28	β	γ
3	1·35	β	ε
4	3·55	α	ε
5	1·1	α	γ
6	∞	α	β

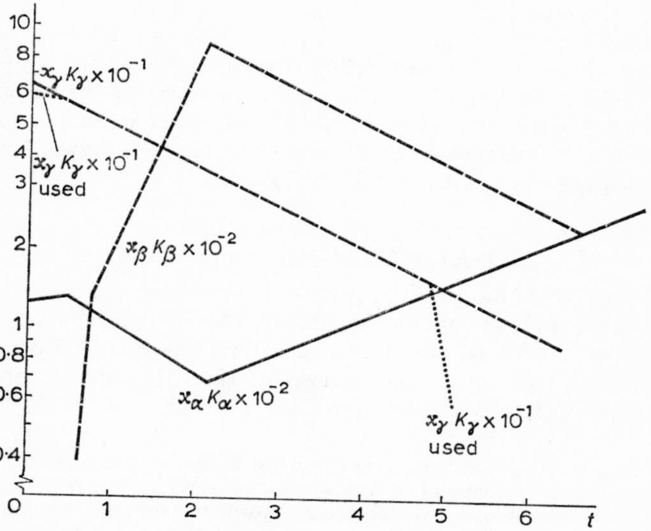

FIG. 7.1 Potential and actual employment on different kinds of machines on optimal path (K_i = number of machines of type i.)

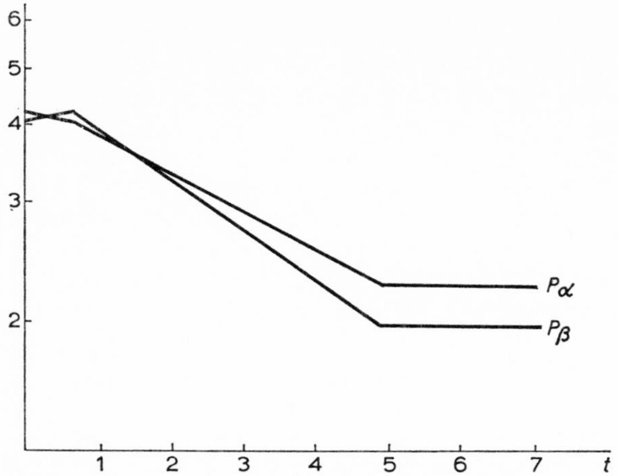

FIG. 7.2 Price of α and β machines along optimal path

of the machine. It is possible that the initial endowment of machines is such that the marginal machine used is sufficiently capital-intensive in relationship to the amount of labour free to work in the capital-goods sector so that, were machines of type $x < b'^{-1}(w)$ constructed, the output on those new machines would be insufficient to replace the output lost from depreciating machines. Hence the wage must fall, and as the wage falls, the capital intensity of the newly constructed machines is reduced; but at the lower capital intensities, the output on the new machines is greater than the output lost from depreciating machines, and the wage rises.[1]

III. ANOTHER EXAMPLE OF RECURRENCE

The example of the previous section showed that recurrences could occur in (a) the type of new machine constructed and (b) some of the machines (processes) used in the consumption-goods industry, i.e. a machine is used over one interval of time, becomes temporarily technologically obsolescent, and then is brought back into use. On

[1] It has been suggested (perhaps somewhat facetiously) that this may be the true economic explanation of China's policy of backyard furnaces. In contrast, the policy of the preceding subsection, of constructing from the beginning of the plan the type of machine which the economy will eventually use exclusively (the very capital-intensive techniques), has some semblance to the policies pursued in the Soviet Union; this policy may be referred to as the 'Stalin Plan', the policy with recurrences as the 'Mao Plan'.

the other hand, some of the processes (machines) continue to be used (if they are available) throughout the development programme (i.e. those with very high output per man). Indeed, whenever capital is not malleable, it seems likely that some processes may be used all along the optimal trajectory. When, however, capital is malleable, it is possible that there be recurrences in the entire input–output matrix of the economy, as the following example illustrates.

There are two sectors in our economy. The first produces capital good 1 by means of labour and capital good 2; there are a number of different processes available. For simplicity, we shall assume that there is a continuum of techniques, described by the production function

$$\dot{K}_1 + \mu K_1 = F(K_2, L) = Lf(k_2) \quad \text{where} \quad k_2 = K_2/L \qquad (7.15)$$

and μ is the exponential rate of depreciation of capital. F has constant returns to scale. For simplicity, we shall assume that the population is constant, and normalised at unity.

The second sector produces capital good 2 and the consumption good and uses only capital good 1:

$$\dot{K}_2 + \mu K_2 + C = \alpha K_1. \qquad (7.16)$$

Thus, the set of input–output matrices available to the economy is summarised by the following table:

Inputs	*Outputs*	*Sector* 1 (*produces* K_1)	*Sector* 2 (*produces* C *and* K_2)
Labour		$\dfrac{L}{F(K_2, L)} = \dfrac{1}{f(k_2)}$	0
K_1		0	$1/\alpha$
K_2		$\dfrac{K_2}{F(K_2, L)} = \dfrac{k_2}{f(k_2)}$	0

Thus specifying k_2 completely specifies the technology used by the economy.

It is easy to show that for this economy there can be no reswitching of techniques along the factor price frontier (i.e. in steady states). None the less, there may be recurrences in techniques even with the linear utility function. The government wishes to maximise

$$\int_0^\infty Ce^{-\delta t} dt$$

where as before δ is the pure rate of time preference. It can be shown that during the initial stages of development $C = 0$. Hence, during this phase, the dynamics of the economy are completely described by

$$\dot{K}_1 = F(K_2, 1) - \mu K_1$$
$$\dot{K}_2 = \alpha K_1 - \mu K_2$$

and are depicted in Fig. 7.3. It is clear that if the initial endowments of K_1 and K_2 are both small and $K_1(0) < \mu K_2(0)/\alpha$, then it is possible that initially K_2 falls and then rises; accordingly, we initially use successively less and less capital-intensive techniques in the first sector ($k_2 = K_2/L$ decreases) and then more and more capital-intensive techniques. It should be clear that similar results hold if the utility function is non-linear (e.g. there is a minimum consumption constraint).

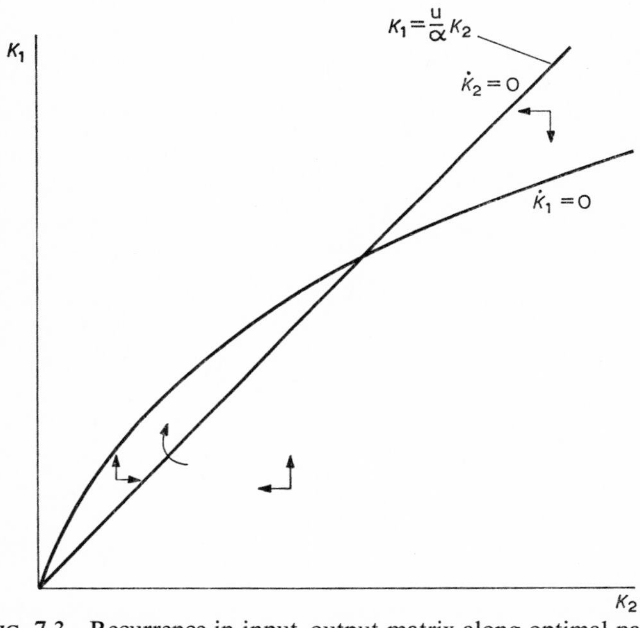

FIG. 7.3 Recurrence in input–output matrix along optimal path

The point of this and the preceding examples is that the reswitching phenomenon has nothing to say about the true dynamic behaviour of the economy out of steady state. Indeed, the fact that the cost of using different kinds of capital goods includes capital gains (losses) as well as rentals makes the occurrence of recurrences all the more likely in a many-capital-good model; even were the real wage in consumption numeraire to increase monotonically, there clearly can be recurrences.[1]

IV. RECURRENCE IN DESCRIPTIVE MODELS

(1) *Introduction*

In this section we continue our investigation of the dynamic behaviour of the Wicksellian model of capital accumulation. We show that if we replace the sophisticated savings behaviour of section II (where the savings rate is chosen to maximise intertemporal utility) by the crude savings functions common in descriptive models of economic growth, and if we replace the assumption of perfect foresight of future prices with alternative, perhaps more reasonable, expectations hypotheses, the economy is still likely to be "badly behaved".

In section IV (2) we assume that there are static expectations and that all of profits are saved but none of wages; although there are likely to be oscillations (in the wage rate, the allocation of labour between the two sectors, the choice of technique, output per man, etc.), all the oscillations are damped.

Sections IV (3) and IV (4) show that the stability observed in the previous subsection depended on the assumption that capital depreciates exponentially. We consider the alternative polar case of capital which lives only one period. Section IV (3) considers two simple savings rules: the Marxian savings assumption and the assumption, common in recent growth theory, that gross savings are a constant fraction of gross output. Section IV (4) considers the life-cycle savings model with overlapping generations.

The assumption of one-period capital goods is clearly unsatisfactory. But Cass and I have been able to show that the qualitative results set forth here hold in more complex models with finitely lived capital goods. Indeed, it can be shown in such models that there also exist efficient oscillations with unemployment of, say, labour in alternate periods.

(2) *The Wicksell–Solow Model with Marxian Savings*

I use the technology and notation described in Section II. Machines can be built with any positive value of x. I introduce the further notation:

$z(t)$ is the marginal machine used at time t
$y(t)$ is the type of machine constructed at time t
$\pi(t)$ is profits at time t.

[1] Das Gupta, 1968, has provided another detailed example of recurrences in an economy in which capital is non-shiftable and in which the investment-goods sector has two processes, one of which requires labour alone.

Then

$$\frac{b(z)}{z} = w. \tag{7.17}$$

Profits are simply the difference between total output and wage payments in the consumption-goods sector:

$$\pi(t) = \int_0^z (b(x) - wx)dN(x, t). \tag{7.18}$$

To close the model we need two further behavioural assumptions (which distinguish it from the optimal growth models presented earlier). Firstly, instead of assuming, as we did earlier, that there is perfect foresight (i.e. the planner knows prices at all times in the future), we shall assume that *individuals have static expectations*: the wage expected to prevail over the future is today's wage. Thus a profit-maximising firm purchases machines at t that will maximise $b(x) - w(t)x$, i.e.

$$b'(y) = w. \tag{7.19}$$

Secondly, instead of assuming that the savings rate is chosen to maximise intertemporal utility, we now assume that all of profits are saved and none of wages. Thus

$$wM = \pi = \int_0^z (b(x) - wx)dN(x, t) \tag{7.20}$$

$$w = C = \int_0^z b(x)dN(x, t). \tag{7.21}$$

The integral equations (7.20) and (7.21) with the associated equations defining w (7.17), and the choice of technique, y, (7.19) completely describe the behaviour of the economy. The analysis of the dynamics is, however, somewhat simpler if we use the difference-differential form of (7.20) and (7.21). To obtain these, we first observe that

$$\frac{\partial N(x, t)}{\partial t} = \begin{cases} -\mu N(x, t) & x < y(t) \\ -\mu N(x, t) + M & x \geqslant y(t). \end{cases} \tag{7.22}$$

The number of machines of any given type decreases exponentially except for the new machines. M machines of type y are constructed at time t. Differentiating (7.20) and (7.21), using (7.22) we obtain

$$\frac{d\pi}{dt} = \frac{d}{dt}(wM) = -\mu wM + [b(y) - wy]M - \dot{w}(1 - M) \tag{7.23}$$

$$\frac{dC}{dt} = \frac{dw}{dt} = -\mu w + b(y)M + \dot{z}b(z)N_x(z, t)$$
$$= \frac{-\mu w + b(y)M}{1-(dz/dw)b(z)N_x(z, t)}. \tag{7.24}$$

The interpretation of these equations is clear. (7.23) says that the change in profits (investment) is equal to the decrease in profits from depreciating machines plus the increase in profits from the new machines, plus the change in production costs from the wage change. (7.24) says that if the wage rate is to be unchanged, the decrease in output of consumption goods from depreciation, $-\mu C$, must be exactly offset by the increased output from new machines, $b(y)M$.

The value of investment, wM, is constant along the curve (when $\dot{w} = 0$)

$$-\mu w + b(y) - wy = -\mu b'(y) + b(y) - b'(y)y = 0.$$

In (wM, w) phase space, this is a vertical straight line. Increasing w decreases y, and hence to the right of the $\dot{\pi} = 0$ curve the value of investment is decreasing, when $\dot{w} \geqslant 0$; to the left investment is increasing, when $\dot{w} \leqslant 0$. w is constant along the curve

$$wM = \frac{\mu w^2}{b(y)} = \frac{\mu b'(y)^2}{b(y)},$$

which is upward-sloping. Since increasing M increases $\dot{w}$, above the curve $\dot{w}$ is positive, below it negative.

It is clear from Fig. 7.4 that oscillations are possible if not likely. To see that these oscillations must be damped, consider the economy at some time t' with wage w' and profit π', where $\dot{w}(t') = 0$, $\ddot{w}(t') > 0$. If the oscillation were periodic or undamped, we must some time later, say at t'', return to the wage w' with $\pi'' = \pi(t'') \leqslant \pi'$. We shall now show that this is impossible.

When $\dot{w} = 0$, $\dot{\pi} > 0$, which implies that

$$b - yb' > Mb$$

or, using (7.19),

$$[1-M(t')]b(y) > w'y \quad \text{for} \quad y = y(t') \tag{7.25}$$

and therefore for all $y \leqslant y(t')$.

Since only machines of types $x < y(t')$ were constructed between t' and t'', $N(x, t'') = aN(x, t')$ for $x \geqslant y(t')$, where

$$a = e^{-\mu(t''-t')}.$$

Therefore, using (7.25), we obtain

$$
\begin{aligned}
0 &< \int_0^{y(t')} \{[1-M(t')]b(x)-w'x\}\,[dN(x,t'')-adN(x,t')] \\
&= \int_0^{z} \{[1-M(t')]b(x)-w'x\}\,[dN(x,t'')-adN(x,t')] \\
&= [1-M(t')]\,(1-a)w'-w'\{[1-M(t'')]-a[1-M(t')]\} \\
&= w'[M(t'')-M(t')],
\end{aligned}
$$

i.e. $$M(t') < M(t'')$$

which implies that $$\pi(t') < \pi(t'').$$

Hence oscillations must be damped.

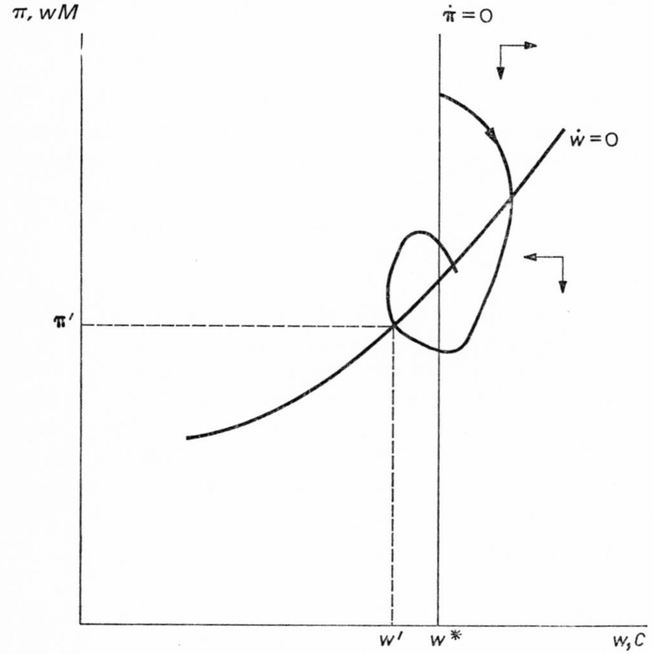

FIG. 7.4 Marxian savings and static expectations

(3) *A One-Period Capital Model*

I shall show that this stability ceases to hold when capital is not infinitely long-lived. For simplicity, suppose capital lives only one period. It is then convenient to make time discrete. All variables are in per capita terms, as of time t. With full employment, output of consumption goods is

$$C(t) = b(x(t))K(t) \tag{7.26}$$

where $x(t)$ is the type of machines used at time t, constructed at time $t-1$; and $K(t)$ is the number of such machines. M being employment in the investment-goods industry,

$$M(t) = 1 - x(t)K(t). \tag{7.27}$$

Since variables are measured per capita, we have

$$M(t-1) = (1+n)K(t). \tag{7.28}$$

The type of machine constructed at $t-1$ is that which maximises expected quasi-rents, i.e. on the assumption of perfect foresight,

$$w(t) = b'(x(t)). \tag{7.29}$$

Finally, we assume, as in the preceding section, that gross investment is equal to gross profits, i.e. wages equal consumption:

$$w(t) = C(t). \tag{7.30}$$

From these equations, we deduce that

$$M(t-1) = (1+n)b'(x)/b(x) \tag{7.31}$$

$$M(t) = 1 - xb'(x)/b(x). \tag{7.32}$$

The stationary state is determined by $M(t-1) = M(t)$:

$$1+n = b(x^*)/b'(x^*) - x^*. \tag{7.33}$$

For this to be a stable equilibrium, it is necessary that $dM(t)/dM(t-1)$ lie between -1 and 1 when $x = x^*$. Using (7.31) and (7.32) it is easily shown that this holds if and only if

$$\sigma > 1 - \tfrac{1}{2}\frac{b(x^*)}{x^*b'(x^*)} \tag{7.34}$$

where σ is the elasticity of substitution along the *ex-ante* production function.

Thus the balanced growth may not be stable. Even if it is locally stable, there may nevertheless be limit cycles.

The explanation of this instability is the following. Consider a situation where initially there are more workers in the consumption-goods sector and less in the capital-goods sector than in long-run equilibrium. This will have two consequences: fewer machines will be constructed and they will be more labour-intensive. If the elasticity of substitution is very small, a large change in the wage rate induces only a very small change in the labour intensity of the machines constructed; hence the number of workers in the consumption-goods sector next period will actually be below the long-run equilibrium value. The economy has 'overshot' equilibrium. If the elasticity of substitution is sufficiently small, these successive oscillations may be (near the balanced growth path) undamped.

It should be clear that these cycles are not replacement cycles of the usual variety, since every period *all* capital is replaced. Rather, they appear to be much more akin to the capital-intensity cycles extensively discussed in the 1930s.

Similar results are readily proved for similar models in which (i) a constant proportion of gross output is saved, (ii) static expectations rather than perfect foresight is assumed.

(4) *Life-Cycle Savings*

Expectations are crucial for determining not only the pattern of investment, but also the level of savings (and hence of investment). Except under very special circumstances, savings will depend on expectations of future rates of return and future wage incomes. These in turn are likely to depend on wages and interest rates prevailing today. On the other hand, the distribution of income – wages and interest rates – *today* will depend on savings today, except in the special case of a one-sector growth model. As a result of these interactions between the present and the future, even when expectations are static, momentary equilibrium need not be unique, and the balanced growth path will not in general be stable. To illustrate these points, we consider the life-cycle model in which individuals live only two periods, working in the first, and living off the proceeds of their savings in the second. For simplicity, we shall assume that the indifference map between consumption in the two periods is homothetic, so that the savings rate, s, may be written simply as a function of the expected rate of return on savings between this period and the next, $r^e(t)$:

$$s(t) = s(r^e(t)). \tag{7.35}$$

Thus if savings are to equal investment at full employment,

$$s(r^e(t)) = M(t). \tag{7.36}$$

Note that full employment cannot be attained through flexibility of the current wage rate, except in so far as changes in current wage rates affect expectations of future rates of return.

What determines the expected rate of return on capital? Clearly, the rate of return on capital depends on expectations of wage rates:

$$1+r^e(t) = \max_x \frac{b(x)-w^e(t+1)x}{w(t)}, \tag{7.37}$$

where $w^e(t+1)$ is the wage expected to prevail at time $t+1$. Thus, if the type of machine constructed for use at time t is $x(t)$,

$$x(t) = b'^{-1}(w^e) \tag{7.38}$$

so

$$1+r^e(t) = \frac{b(x(t+1))-b'(x(t+1))x(t+1)}{w(t)}. \tag{7.39}$$

Consider first the case of static expectations, i.e. where

$$w^e(t) = w(t-1). \tag{7.40}$$

Then the growth of the economy is described by the first-order difference equation

$$s\left(\frac{b-b'(x(t))x(t)}{b'(x(t))}\right) = M(t-1) \tag{7.41}$$

where, along a full-employment path,

$$x(t) = (1+n)\frac{1-M(t)}{M(t-1)}. \tag{7.42}$$

In this model it is quite possible that there be multiple balanced growth paths. A sufficient condition for uniqueness is that

$$(1+n)\frac{s'(1-\alpha)}{\sigma\alpha}+M^2 \tag{7.43}$$

be one-signed, where α is the share of labour along the *ex-ante* production function and σ the elasticity of substitution. Hence, if the savings rate increases as the rate of return increases, there will be at most one balanced growth path. As in the previous model, even when the balanced growth path is unique, it may not be stable. Thus static expectations do not ensure the stability of the economy.

It is more interesting, from our present point of view, that momentary equilibrium may not be uniquely determined. Indeed, it is easy to see that a necessary and sufficient condition for uniqueness of momentary equilibrium is that the savings rate be a monotonic function of the rate of return on capital. Although that will be the case if the utility function is additive and of constant elasticity, this in general will not be true. One might well expect that at low rates of return the substitution effect dominates the income effect, so $s' > 0$ while at higher levels of r (and hence higher levels of utility) the reverse holds, and $s' < 0$.

Similar results hold if, instead of assuming static expectations, we had assumed perfect foresight. The growth path of the economy would then be described by the second-order difference equation:

$$s\left(\frac{b(x(t)) - b'(x(t))x(t)}{b'(x(t-1))}\right) = M(t-1) \qquad (7.44)$$

where now

$$x(t) = b'^{-1}(w(t)) = (1+n)\frac{1-M(t)}{M(t-1)}. \qquad (7.45)$$

As before, even when the balanced growth path is uniquely determined, it may not be stable; rather, it is possible that the economy converges to a limit cycle, thus again illustrating the fact that perfect foresight paths need not converge to balanced growth. And again, momentary equilibrium is uniquely determined if and only if the savings rate is a monotonic function of the rate of return.

Whenever momentary equilibrium is not uniquely determined, the economy may 'wobble'; it may neither converge to balanced growth nor to a limit cycle, simply going from one short-run equilibrium to another. It may well be argued that this model of the 'wobbling' economy is far more descriptive of the behaviour of at least some capitalist economies than the conventional neo-classical models, in which the economy approaches smoothly and steadily the balanced growth path.

This indeterminacy in the growth path is very different from that which arises out of the conventional two-sector growth models. It has nothing to do with the relationship between the distribution of income *today*, the output of capital goods *today* and savings *today*. Indeed, the output of capital goods and consumption goods today is the same in all (full-employment) equilibria. Rather, it has to do with the relationship between the wage rate *today*, expectations of wages *tomorrow*, and the type of machine constructed today for use tomorrow. In the case of static expectations, there is one equilibrium where the wage is low today and hence is expected to be low tomorrow (the rate of return is expected to be high), and another equilibrium where the wage is high today. In the case of perfect foresight, there is one equilibrium where we expect the wage to be low tomorrow, and in fact it will turn out to be low tomorrow, and another in which we expect it to be high and it in fact will be high.

It should be noted that expectations today of the distribution of income tomorrow affect, in general, both the distribution of income today and the distribution of income which will actually prevail tomorrow.

Both static expectations and perfect foresight are polar cases. No matter what expectations formation process is assumed, if there is full employment, (7.36) holds. If for some reason there were a spontaneous increase in the wage rate expected to prevail next period, in order for the rate of return to be such as to ensure full employment (i.e. to satisfy (7.36)), the wage rate today would have to fall. It is in this sense that we can say that the distribution of income today is determined by expectations of the distribution of income tomorrow. Without a theory of expectations, i.e. the determination of the wage expected to prevail next period, there is no theory of the determination of the distribution of income today. This, I take it, is one of the major criticisms of neo-classical theory by the 'Cambridge' economists: the simpler neo-classical models are formulated in such a way that expectations play no role, whereas in the 'real world' they clearly do.

On the other hand, this model is consistent with marginal productivity theory (correctly interpreted): each period, the technique (for the next period) which is chosen, maximises expected quasi-rents, i.e. the marginal productivity of labour (along the *ex-ante* production function) is equal to the expected wage. If the expected wage were equal to the wage that turns out to prevail next period (as it reasonably would if the economy converged to balanced growth), then the wage today would correctly reflect the marginal productivity of labour. On the other hand, in the 'wobbling economy' even with static expectations, although the economy is consistently wrong in its expectations, it does not necessarily consistently underestimate or overestimate the expected wage. In that case the marginal productivity of labour (along the *ex-ante* production function) and the actual wage (as opposed to the expected wage) may have no systematic relationship with one another.

It is by affecting the choice of technique for the capital that will be used tomorrow that expectations today of the wage tomorrow affect the wage tomorrow.

So far, we have assumed that all individuals have the same expectations. In fact, there will undoubtedly be a diversity of expectations of future wages. Since the wage today depends on expectations of what the wage will be tomorrow, estimating what the wage tomorrow will be is equivalent to guessing what individuals tomorrow will expect the wage will be the day after. Hence, individuals who guess better than average what other individuals are guessing the wage rate to be in the future will make better than average returns on their capital: pure profits are simply a return to guessing well.

(5) *Concluding Remarks*

Solow began his classic 1956 paper with the remarks:

> All theory depends on assumptions which are not quite true. That is what makes it theory. The art of successful theorising is to make the inevitable simplifying assumptions in such a way that the final results are not very sensitive. A 'crucial' assumption is one on which the conclusions do depend sensitively, and it is important that crucial assumptions be reasonably realistic. When the results of a theory seem to flow specifically from a special crucial assumption that is dubious, the results are suspect.

It now appears – in the perspective of some fifteen years of subsequent research – that the theory developed by Solow, the picture of an economy smoothly converging to balanced growth in an economy in which expectations play no explicit part, is as suspect in this respect as the earlier theory of Harrod.[1]

Solow's 1956 growth model had three important assumptions which allowed him to ignore completely the role of expectations in the growth process: (a) a single, malleable (shiftable) capital good; (b) constant savings rates; (c) instantaneous adjustment of all markets to equilibrium. If any of these assumptions are dropped, the characteristics of the dynamic path of the economy are significantly altered. Moreover, Solow's assumption that all sectors have identical production functions is necessary for the result that the distribution of income depends only on factor supplies. We have set forth a model in which expectations of future wages and interest rates are crucial for the determination of the distribution of income today.

Thus the difficulties with the conventional neo-classical models of economic growth lie not so much in the capital-theoretic issues of reswitching, as in the questions arising from the heterogeneity of capital goods, from the dependence of savings on the distribution of income and the expectations of future wage and interest rates, and, perhaps most important, from the crucial role of expectations formation in the development of economies without perfect futures markets.

[1] The basic point of Solow's article, that the 'fundamental opposition of warranted and natural rates turns out in the end to flow from the crucial assumption that production takes place under conditions of *fixed proportions*', remains valid. This is a question of balanced growth, rather than of the nature of the dynamic path which an economy might actually follow.

REFERENCES

C. J. Bliss, 'On Putty–Clay', *Review of Economic Studies* 35 (Apr 1968) 105–22.

M. Bruno, 'Optimal Accumulation in Discrete Capital Models', in *Essays on the Theory of Optimal Economic Growth*, ed. K. Shell (Cambridge, Mass.: M.I.T. Press, 1967).

D. Cass and J. E. Stiglitz, 'The Implications of Alternative Saving and Expectations Hypotheses for Choices of Technique and Patterns of Growth', *Journal of Political Economy*, vol. LXXVII (July–Aug 1969).

P. S. Das Gupta, 'On the Optimum Rate of Accumulation in a Labor-Surplus Economy', Carnegie-Mellon University, Oct 1968 (mimeographed).

F. H. Hahn, 'Equilibrium Dynamics with Heterogeneous Capital Goods', *Quarterly Journal of Economics*, vol. LXXX (Nov 1966).

J. Robinson, *The Accumulation of Capital* (London: Macmillan, 1956).

—— *Exercises in Economic Analysis* (London: Macmillan, 1960).

—— 'A Model for Accumulation Proposed by J. E. Stiglitz', *Economic Journal*, vol. LXXIX (June 1969) pp. 412–13.

P. A. Samuelson, 'Indeterminacy of Development in a Heterogeneous Capital Model with Constant Saving Propensity', in *Essays on the Theory of Optimal Growth*, ed. K. Shell (Cambridge, Mass.: M.I.T. Press, 1967).

—— 'Parable and Realism in Capital Theory: the Surrogate Production Function', *Review of Economic Studies* 30 (June 1962) 193–206.

K. Shell and J. E. Stiglitz, 'The Allocation of Investment in a Dynamic Economy', *Quarterly Journal of Economics*, vol. LXXXI (Nov 1967) pp. 592–609.

R. M. Solow, 'A Contribution to the Theory of Economic Growth', *Quarterly Journal of Economics*, vol. LXX (Feb 1956) pp. 65–94.

—— 'Substitution and Fixed Proportions in the Theory of Capital', *Review of Economic Studies* (June 1962) pp. 207–18.

T. N. Srinivasan, 'Investment Criteria and Choice of Technique of Production', *Yale Economic Essays*, vol. II (1962) pp. 59–115.

J. E. Stiglitz, 'A Note on Technical Choice under Full Employment in a Socialist Economy', *Economic Journal*, vol. LXXVIII (Sep 1968) pp. 603–9.

H. Uzawa, 'Optimal Growth in a Two-Sector Model of Capital Accumulation', *Review of Economic Studies*, vol. XXXI (Jan 1964) pp. 1–24.

Discussion of the Paper by Joseph E. Stiglitz (Chapters 6 and 7)

Professor Stiglitz introduced his paper by saying that too many resources had been devoted to the problem of reswitching, and research in this area exhibits sharply diminishing returns. He felt that reswitching had very few implications for anything.

The first part of his paper (Chapter 6) was a review of the results on reswitching in a static situation and contained little that was new. Five conditions in each of which reswitching was not possible were presented:

1. There is some industry such that its process in one technique requires more of every capital good than its process in the other.
2. The factor price equalisation theorem holds in a two-good economy.
3. There exists a capital good smoothly substitutable, directly or indirectly, for itself.
4. There exists a capital good which on the input side is smoothly substitutable for all other capital goods as inputs.
5. Labour is smoothly substitutable for the output or input of any good in the economy.

Cases (3), (4) and (5) show that very little substitutability along the transformation schedule is needed to rule out reswitching (see p. 122 for proofs of these theorems).

Dr Pasinetti had previously pointed out that the valuation perversities that could arise were more interesting than the reswitching phenomenon. It may not be true that the value of capital increases as the rate of interest falls, and it may not be the case that the value of consumption rises as the rate of interest increases towards the rate of growth. A more fundamental perversity concerns the relationship between the value of consumption and the value of capital. In his discussion of the Akerman problem, Wicksell wanted to show that a higher value of capital could not be associated with a lower value of consumption. In fact a simple modification of the Wicksell model can produce the perversity he was trying to avoid (he assumed a constant elasticity durability function to rule it out). The occurrence or not of reswitching says nothing about this perversity. In general, however, these comparisons between steady states are uninteresting and we should be more concerned with paths that proceed from given endowments.

Part II (Chapter 7) begins by examining the concept of reswitching for a dynamic economy. Prices are now changing over time, we have no unique rate of interest and the non-substitution theorem does not apply. We instead introduce the concept of *recurrence*, which occurs when an economy returns to a technique it used in the past. This can occur in a simple putty–clay model (like Solow, *Review of Economic Studies*, 1962) with a maximand $\int ce^{-\delta t}dt$ and a minimum consumption constraint. Professor Mirrlees had also constructed examples of this phenomenon. These paths exhibit very different qualitative properties from those of conventional malleable capital models – all the basic characteristics such as monotonicity of the wage, consumption rate of interest and capital intensity were absent. We should be very careful about the use of such malleable capital models.

More fundamental problems arise, concerned with the formation of expectations, when we consider heterogeneous capital-good models. He uses a simple modification of the Solow 1962 *ex-post* fixed-coefficients model, where, instead of having capital goods with infinite lives, we have the other polar case of one-period capital goods. He had earlier thought that (a) every path consistent with perfect foresight for ever must converge to balanced growth, and (b) static expectations would ensure stability. The model serves to show that both these conjectures are false (Professors Shell and Hahn both have examples showing the same thing).

He then had an example where individuals who expect high wages in the future make investment decisions that lead to high wages. We have an indeterminacy here which is different from the more familiar one where investments and savings behaviour depend on expectations about the future course of the economy. He calls this the wobbly economy since it can wobble along following expectations without any particular teleology.

Finally, he has a model where individuals live for two periods and have life-cycle savings behaviour. Two types of expectation are considered – static and perfect foresight – and it is shown that even though the real side of two economies is the same, the distribution of income differs with different expectations.

The upshot of these examples is the following. In his 1955 article Solow had three assumptions which allowed him to ignore expectations: (i) malleable capital, (ii) constant savings ratio, (iii) instantaneous adjustment of all markets. If any one of these three is dropped, the dynamic paths are drastically changed.

Dr Pasinetti said he was grateful that Professor Stiglitz had given a summary of the paper, since this was really a collection of papers and thus it would have been difficult for a discussant to summarise without being unfair. The title referred only to one of the models – the Wicksellian – which the author shows can exhibit all the non-monotonic relations between the rate of profit on the one hand, and capital, net income and consumption on the other, which have recently been brought to our attention by the reswitching of technique discussion. He listed the many other models dealt with in the paper straight away because he wished to concentrate on the implications of the phenomenon of reswitching.

He said it was difficult to follow some of the arguments, partly because of Professor Stiglitz's frequent affirmation of the irrelevance of reswitching to 'truly dynamic' economies, although some qualification – often using value-loaded words – was usually attached. 'Well-behaved' was one of such words. Just because a production function does not give conclusions about the rate of profit which conform to our traditional expectations, i.e. prejudices, does not mean we should call it badly behaved. The earth probably appeared 'badly behaved' or 'perverse' when it was discovered that it was round and not, as appeared intuitively obvious, flat. Professor Stiglitz was not to be blamed for using much of the terminology. He had, however, introduced some of his own terminology, e.g. that of a 'truly' dynamic system. Surely other dynamical systems are also true. Professor Stiglitz even distinguished between 'true' neo-classical theory and, apparently, 'untrue' neo-classical theory.

When he had stripped these affirmations of their value-loaded words he had been a little disappointed. The theorems ruling out reswitching were very limited compared to the general case (as Bruno, Burmeister and Sheshinski, *Quarterly Journal of Economics*, 1966, had realised). They bring in smooth substitutability and linear homogenous production functions. Reswitching phenomena should have served as a warning to be more critical of assumptions that imply inverse monotonic relations between the rate of profit and other variables.

He said reswitching *per se* was of less general interest than the possibility of non-monotonic relations between the rate of profit and capital, etc. Professor Stiglitz comes to grips with these problems when he discusses his Wicksell model. He distinguishes two notions of marginal products of capital – equation (6.36) expressing the Wicksell notion and (6.33) expressing the 'true' neo-classical notion. The author claims the former fails to hold, but we should not worry since the latter still holds. But (6.33) is a more general expression for the relation Dr Pasinetti had put on the blackboard in the discussion of Professor Spaventa's paper earlier that morning, i.e.

$$r^* \equiv \frac{p^*(Y_\beta - Y_\alpha)}{p^*(K_\beta - K_\alpha)}. \qquad (1)$$

Solow has recently brought this accounting expression to our attention by going back to the idea, suggested by Senior more than a century ago, before marginal productivity theory was invented, that the ratio could be given a meaning for society as a whole by saying that the numerator of a rate of profit expresses the permanent gain and the denominator represents the once-for-all sacrifice. This is only a *description* of what the rate of profit is: it does not explain why a rate of profit is 10 per cent or 20 per cent.

Marginal productivity theory did provide an explanation of the rate of profit by extending to capital the general-equilibrium-analysis notion that each price is an 'index of scarcity'. The monotonic inverse relations between prices and quantities were extended to capital, and the rate of profit was presented as the 'price' of capital, i.e. its index of scarcity. This was a fascinating theory, but we now know, after the reswitching of technique discussion, that it does not hold.

Solow is leaving out this theory and going back to the Senior discussion, by simply relying on ratio (1). But this ratio has an unambiguous meaning only in a one-commodity world. Solow tried to give it an unambiguous meaning for a many-commodity world but needed all his assumptions about technical possibilities and particular prices in the transition from one technique to the other. Professor Spaventa's paper had dealt with some of the difficulties here. Even if society were to consume only one consumption good, we could not give this ratio an unambiguous meaning.

We could not in general evaluate unambiguously what society has given up and what society has gained, since the capital-good structure changes in the transition. Had it been possible to express gains and sacrifices independently of prices, this problem would have been solved at the time of Senior and there would have been no need for marginal productivity theory.

Professor Garegnani said that (6.38) had been derived by considering a *ceteris paribus* increase in K_i. It had been assumed that Pk_i was constant – this was not possible, because the change in K_i changes all prices. Further, if other capital-goods levels are held constant, we no longer have the unique rate of interest r_0 in (6.38). We have to change all capital goods together if we want to keep a unique r_0.

Professor Stiglitz said (6.38) was supposed to be a heuristic explanation of why people might have thought that as r increased past the golden-rule level, steady-state consumption would fall – i.e. diminishing returns on the pseudo-production function. One would normally state diminishing returns assumptions as in (6.34).

Professor Garegnani claimed that the author's criticism of the proposition $(dC(r)/dr) < 0$ applied also to (6.38), which was just as suspect as Wicksell's proposition.

Professor Bruno said that different sorts of difficulties arise in multi-sector models (say with one consumption good and n capital goods). It was important to realise that some problems enter when n goes from 0 to 1, some when n goes from 1 to 2, and so on. We should identify exactly when each problem entered. For instance, valuation perversities crop up when n goes from 0 to 1, Wicksell problems when we go from 1 to 2. Reswitching arises with $n \geqq 2$. Much of the paper was a survey of these known results. He was more interested in the recurrence phenomena, i.e. on an optimum path we choose A at T_0, B at T_1 and A at T_2 (A is a matrix of activities – one activity per good).

Dr Bliss said we should add that technique B does not cover its costs when it is not used, i.e. we are not moving along a facet.

Professor Yaari wondered why anyone should have thought recurrence was not possible. *Professor Stiglitz* agreed with Professor Yaari. He said that he had only spent the time on his paper discussing reswitching as he had been asked to do so by the Programme Committee.

Professor Bruno said it was not true to say that out of steady state there is in general no non-substitution theorem (p. 138). There was one: viz. at a given vector of own rates of return there is only one technique that maximises the real wage. *Professor Stiglitz* pointed out that you had to assume only one consumption good. *Professor Bruno* agreed but said a non-substitution theorem did exist. If our maximand is just an integral of discounted consumption, we know we arrive in finite time at a technique that maximises the real wage at a constant rate of interest.

Professor Hahn said that we have to have as many own rates of interest as there are capital goods.

Returning to a point raised by Dr Pasinetti, he said that it is not true that neo-classical theory says that the price of a good goes up as it becomes scarcer. If we compared two economies in general equilibrium, the only difference being that one had fewer bananas than the other, we could not prove that the price of bananas would be higher in the economy that had less. The two-good case was *the* special case, and even then equilibrium need not be unique. (Of course it is always true that the equilibrium price can act as a shadow price of a constraint.)

Dr Pasinetti said he was considering a *ceteris paribus* change.

Professor Shell said he liked to look at the debate in the following way. Problems such as reswitching and recurrence arise in disaggregated models. Completely aggregated models may therefore be misleading. He wondered, therefore, if theorists might not explore the possibilities of a theory using approximately aggregated functions. *Professor Hahn* thought that such a theory would not be useful. Small deviations from the stringent aggregation conditions (e.g. Champernowne's conditions for his Divisia index) produced large errors if we tried to aggregate.

Professor Rose said that at the bottom of p. 146 it was claimed that there is only one set of expectations consistent with full employment. He said it was peculiar that current wages rates could only change employment through their effects on expectations. *Professor Stiglitz* said that the only way to increase employment was through investment since we had *ex-post* fixed coefficients.

Dr Dixit said that the rate of interest was not necessarily the shadow price of capital in a general-equilibrium model. A dictator would not pay r for a unit of capital, but a price given by the discounted sum of its expected future earnings. *Professor Bruno* said he would pay r for its services.

Professor Weizsäcker said that so long as there was no uncertainty, there was no difference between the capital theory discussed in connection with reswitching, and general-equilibrium theory. You could get all the reswitching phenomena in an atemporal model if you parametrised the rate of interest. Reswitching did not distinguish capital theory from general-equilibrium theory. The notion that the present value of consumption is maximised in equilibrium (introduced by Dr Bliss this morning) was the important one, and this was carried over from general-equilibrium theory. The rate of profit gave the relative price between goods at different dates. Thus Dr Pasinetti's criticisms of neo-classical theory were not valid, as all capital theory under discussion was only a special case of general-equilibrium theory. For instance, no one with experience of general-equilibrium theory should have been surprised that the social rate of return is less than the rate of interest when we have excess capacity.

The main problem connected with capital theory is that we have an asymmetry in the time dimension due to uncertainty and expectations.

Dr Pasinetti said that Professor Weizsäcker was speaking about a different model from himself. He was saying that the marginal productivity theories of Wicksell and Böhm-Bawerk no longer held. *Professor Hahn* said that general-equilibrium theory had been much more than simple macro-models since Hick's *Value and Capital* and Debreu's *Theory of Value*. He agreed with Dr Pasinetti, when pressed, that the previous simplifications had been wrong.

Professor Yaari said that since he had never been based in M.I.T. or Cambridge, England, he could not understand the significance of the reswitching controversy. It has been well known since linear programming was invented that an optimal basis could reappear when we were considering continuous parameter changes. He asked how reswitching was any more than this. He also wondered why fixed coefficients and continous substitutability were considered as different worlds. Surely one could have an 'approximate reswitching' theorem for a technology with smooth substitution possibilities in the sense that it might be possible to get within ε of the original techniques at a different rate of interest.

Professor Stiglitz said that he agreed with Professors Weizsäcker and Yaari. The asymmetry in time due to expectations phenomena and the lack of future markets was the problem that should concern us. He did not think we should be surprised by recurrence and did not think the phenomenon worth any more examples or investigation. He had felt compelled to devote some time to reswitching, but it had nothing to say about the important intertemporal price relations, which explain the sense in which prices can be taken as measures of scarcity.

Dr Pasinetti said it was trivial to say that reswitching had nothing to tell us about these problems. We could just as well say that off-equilibrium analysis was not relevant for reswitching. The interesting point was that the monotonic relations always put into simplified models are not justified. We should keep away from models that are not generalisable: they are misleading, and do not shed any light at all.

8 Notes on Problems of Transition Between Techniques*

Luigi Spaventa

UNIVERSITY OF PERUGIA

I. INTRODUCTION

Recent work has exhaustively treated the properties of linear production models, in which commodities are produced by means of commodities, reswitching may occur and (quite independently of reswitching) justice is done to the tale, of unknown origin,[1] that there is a unique inverse relation between the value of capital and the rate of profit. Outside the case of stationary state, the steady-growth properties of these models can easily be analysed by introducing a savings function.[2] With only one consumer good (or with many goods consumed in fixed proportions), from the savings–investment equality, the price equations and the (dual) quantity equations it is possible to derive the relationship between the growth rate and the rate of profit under different savings hypotheses, so that to each given growth rate there will correspond equilibrium values (not necessarily unique) of all the other variables. More results on steady-state properties can be obtained by allowing for embodied technical progress.[3]

It is to be feared, however, that these exercises will soon yield decreasing returns of knowledge, just as aggregate or one-commodity growth models did. Everybody would agree, I suppose, that the analysis of steady states is, at best, only a beginning; certainly not an end in itself. The study of the problems of transition, or 'traverse', from one steady state to another might on the other hand represent a first step in the right direction.

Multi-commodity production models are, from this point of view, a better tool of analysis than their aggregate ancestors, for they bring fully to light the major problem one has to face out of steady

* I am grateful to Professor Giancarlo Gandolfo for discussing some parts of this paper with me.

[1] Its paternity cannot certainly be attributed to classical economists. In the course of the recent debate, on the other hand, it has been said that it has nothing to do with neo-classical economics. Future history of economic analysis will perhaps clarify the point.

[2] See Morishima (1969), Spaventa (1970).

[3] This has been done by Amendola (1970).

states: the inappropriateness of an old capital stock to a new situation.[1] In this context, an important attempt to study the transition between two equally profitable techniques was made by Professor Robert Solow.[2] Killing two birds with one stone, Professor Solow shows how the transition can take place in a number of cases and arrives at the conclusion that there is a rate of return to society, defined as the ratio of the benefits arising from the change of technique to its costs, which always equals the rate of profit at the point of switch.

It is the purpose of these notes to re-examine these problems. Three issues ought in principle to be distinguished: whether a transition is possible and how it occurs; whether we can derive a meaningful 'rate of return property' of the rate of profit (this was a point challenged by Professor Luigi Pasinetti in a recent article)[3]; whether the kind of approach examined here has any great relevance for understanding the real problems of dynamic economies. The first two issues will have to be treated together; the last will be the object of some final remarks.

At least a part of the treatment offered here is at best work in progress: more than an essay providing an answer to a specific question, this is a collection of notes aimed at clearing the ground for further work.

II. BASIC IDENTITIES

Before examining various cases of transition between different situations, it is useful to write some simple identities which must always hold.

The symbols used here are:

w = the wage rate

r = the rate of profit

m = the rate of growth (at full employment)

h = the value of net output per man

c = the value of consumption per man

v = the value of capital per man.

[1] According to Professor Sir John Hicks, however, an 'Austrian' model, where attention is fixed on time sequence rather than on the horizontal structure of production, is a much better tool than a 'Walrasian' model for dealing with problems of transition. See Hicks (1970).

[2] Solow (1967).

[3] Pasinetti (1969).

Then, from $h \equiv c+mv \equiv w+rv$, it follows that, since

$$v \equiv \frac{h-c}{m} \equiv \frac{h-w}{r} \equiv \frac{c-w}{r-m}$$

$$r \equiv \frac{c-w}{v} + m. \tag{8.1}$$

Compare now two situations, with the same rate of profit, and hence with the same wage rate, and with the same rate of growth, but with different value of capital per man (either because the technique is different or because commodities are consumed in different proportions). Then, from identity (8.1),

$$v_1 - v_2 \equiv \frac{c_1 - c_2}{r-m},$$

so that

$$r \equiv \frac{c_1 - c_2}{v_1 - v_2} + m. \tag{8.2}$$

When the duality property between price and quantity equations[1] holds (which is not always the case, as we shall presently see), these identities provide a straightforward graphical measure on the wage curves of the values of capital per man and output per man in different situations. Let us keep in mind, however, that mere identities, following from the definition of the variables, cannot be given a higher status, and have no heuristic value.

III. CIRCULATING CAPITAL; ALL GOODS CONSUMED

Consider now a linear production system. For simplicity, let there be only two commodities, *A* and *B*. Assume that *both A* and *B* serve as circulating capital and are at the same time consumption goods. We then have

$$y_A = x_A + (1+m)k_A$$

$$y_B = x_B + (1+m)k_B$$

where y_A and y_B are the ratios of the quantities produced of the two commodities to the total labour force in the economy, x_A and x_B *per capita* physical consumption, k_A and k_B the *per capita* quantities of the two commodities necessary as production inputs.

If society decides to pass from situation 2 to situation 1, capital stocks appropriate to the latter, i.e. $(1+m)k_{A1}$ and $(1+m)k_{B1}$, must

[1] On this property, see Bruno (1969), Nuti (1970), Spaventa (1970).

be built up in the transition. Consumption per head of the two commodities in the transition must therefore be

$$\bar{x}_A = x_{A2}+(1+m)(k_{A2}-k_{A1})$$

$$\bar{x}_B = x_{B2}+(1+m)(k_{B2}-k_{B1}).$$

We shall assume that both $\bar{x}_A$ and $\bar{x}_B$ are positive.[1] Thus, the value of consumption per head in the transition is $\bar{c} = \bar{x}_A+p\bar{x}_B = c_2+ +(1+m)(v_2-v_1)$, where prices are measured in terms of A. Hence

$$\frac{c_2-\bar{c}}{1+m} = v_1-v_2. \tag{8.3}$$

By substituting this result into identity (8.2), we obtain

$$r \equiv \frac{c_1-c_2}{c_2-\bar{c}}(1+m)+m. \tag{8.4}$$

It must be noticed that (8.4), being merely another way of writing (8.2) whenever (8.3) holds, is still an identity. In other words, (8.4), far from being defined independently of the rate of profit, *is* by definition the rate of profit. In order better to explore this point, we shall now examine two possibilities: one in which, with only one technique, two situations are different because the composition of output is different; another in which there are two different techniques. Of course, if (8.3) did not hold, identity (8.2) would still remain valid but could not be transformed into (8.4). We shall later consider an important case (see p. 177, below) in which this happens and in which (8.4) therefore acquires a different meaning.[2]

(1) *Changes in the Composition of Consumption*

If both the commodities produced are also consumption goods, given the rate of growth, the quantity equations will preserve one degree of freedom. We can therefore express the other variables as a function of physical consumption per head of one of the two commodities, say commodity B. This of course still applies when there are n commodities, of which $n-1$ are consumed in fixed proportions; this bundle is a function of the quantity consumed of the nth commodity.

We shall first state an interesting result, the proof of which is given in the Appendix, regarding how the duality property, holding

[1] If they were not, transition, as Professor Solow has shown, could be made in more than one period.

[2] Following Professor Solow, on p. 177 we shall obtain an expression similar to (8.4) by discounting the value of the future stream of higher consumption to the value of the present consumption forgone.

in the case of only one consumption good, is transformed when more than one good is consumed.

Let $w = f(r)$ and $p = \varphi(r)$ be the relationships between the wage and the price of B (all measured in terms of A or of a bundle of commodities consumed in fixed proportions), on the one hand, and the rate of profit on the other, for a given technique. It can then be shown that

$$x_A = f(m) - \varphi(m)x_B \tag{8.5}$$

where the coefficients of $f(m)$ and of $\varphi(m)$ are exactly the same as those of $f(r)$ and $\varphi(r)$, with m, the growth rate, in the place of r. It follows that the value of consumption per head is

$$c = x_A + px_B = f(m) + [\varphi(r) - \varphi(m)]x_B. \tag{8.6}$$

It thus appears that the duality relation holds in its original form when either $x_B = 0$ (for then consumption per head consists only of A and its value coincides with its quantity) or the growth rate equals the rate of profit (for then $\varphi(m) = \varphi(r)$).

If we plot x_A and c on the vertical axis of a diagram, (8.5) and (8.6) will have a common intercept, the value of which can be obtained from the corresponding wage curve. The slope of (8.5), however, depends only on the growth rate and is always negative, whereas the slope of (8.6) also depends on the rate of profit and can be positive or negative. In Fig. 8.1, two possible cases are shown: that of a stationary state and that of a positive rate of growth. In the north-west quadrant we plot the wage curve corresponding to the technique in use; (8.5) and (8.6) are shown on the north-east

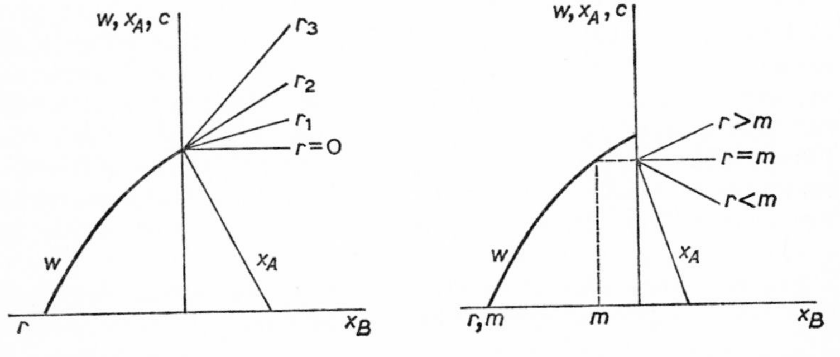

(A) Stationary state: $f(0) = (w)_{r=0}$, $r_3 > r_2 > r_1 > 0$

(B) A positive rate of growth: $f(m) < f(0)$, $\varphi(r) - \varphi(m) \gtreqless 0$ according to whether r $\gtreqless$ m

FIG. 8.1

quadrant, for different values of the rate of profit and a given growth rate, taking into account that, since the wage curve is concave to the origin, $\varphi'(r) > 0$. In the stationary case, $f(m) = (w)_{r=0}$; in the other case, $f(m)$ is obtained from the given value of m plotted on the r-axis.

If the wage curve were convex to the origin, the slope of the c line would be negative and falling with r in Fig. 8.1A; it would be positive for $r < m$, and vice versa in Fig. 8.1B. If, on the other hand, x_A were to denote not a single commodity, but a bundle of commodities, all used as circulating capital, but consumed in fixed proportions, in terms of which prices are measured (so that, say, $x_C = \lambda x_A$ and $p_A + \lambda p_C = 1$), the wage curve may present points of inflection and the price of B may not be a monotonic function of the rate of profit. In this case, the slope of the c-line in both cases would no longer be a monotonic function of the rate of profit: as the rate of profit rises, $\varphi(r) - \varphi(m)$ may change its sign and may moreover be zero also for values of r such that $r \neq m$.

A change in composition with a given technique is the simplest case of transition from one situation to another. The rate of return property of the rate of profit states that the rate of profit at a point of switch equals the rate of return, measured as the ratio between the benefits and the costs of a transition. For this property to be an operationally meaningful proposition, and not merely the result of a definition, the rate of return, and hence the benefits and the costs of a transition, ought to be defined independently of the rate of profit. Our previous analysis confirms that, in the case we are examining, this is not possible (whether the property holds when this is possible will be considered below). The following remarks illustrate the point.

(i) Take a given physical change in the composition of consumption, $-\Delta x_A/\Delta x_B$. In the two-commodity case with stationary state, the 'return to society' of this change, $c_1 - c_2$, rises or falls with the rate of profit according to the curvature of the wage relation (it always remains constant and equal to zero if the latter is linear). The cost of the same change, $v_1 - v_2$, though having *in this case* always the same sign as $c_1 - c_2$, may rise or fall or remain constant with the rate of profit depending not only on the convexity of the wage curve, but also on the relative B/labour intensity in the two sectors. With a linear wage curve, $v_1 - v_2$ would always be equal to zero, so that the ratio $(c_1 - c_2)/(v_1 - v_2)$ would remain undefined.

With a given rate of growth $m > 0$, $c_1 - c_2$, besides rising or falling with the rate of profit, changes its sign as r falls below m, so that the ratio $(c_1 - c_2)/(c_2 - \bar{c})$ becomes negative.

If x_A is a basket of commodities consumed in fixed proportions, and not an individual commodity, the 'return to society' of a given

$-\Delta x_A/\Delta x_B$ may not even be a monotonic function of the rate of profit; it depends on the latter whether a given physical change represents a gain or a loss or is a matter of indifference for the community. In this case, moreover, we may have, as was said above, $c_1 - c_2 = 0$ not only when $r = m$, but also at other values of the rate of profit.

(ii) A given *value* change in consumption per head, on the other hand, implies different costs according to the rate of profit, while, with the same costs, different changes in the value of consumption per head may be obtained according to the value of the rate of profit.

(2) *Different Techniques*

The analysis of the previous section can easily be extended to the case in which two situations differ because the techniques employed are different. Whether or not there is a change in composition, a transition implies here a change in technical coefficients.

Assume that the system is at a point of switch between the two techniques: the rate of profit is such that it is equally profitable to employ one or the other; since the same commodities are used and produced in the two situations, relative prices must be the same. Let then $r = r^0$, equal for the two techniques. Take an arbitrary level m of the rate of growth: that level may correspond to a point of switch of the wage curves – not necessarily that at which $r = r^0$, if there is more than one point of switch – or it may not. If it does not, in correspondence with that rate of growth one wage curve will be superior to the other and, for the corresponding technique, $f(m)$ will be higher and $\varphi(m)$ lower. As a result, both the x_A line and the c line of the technique which is superior at the given level of the growth rate

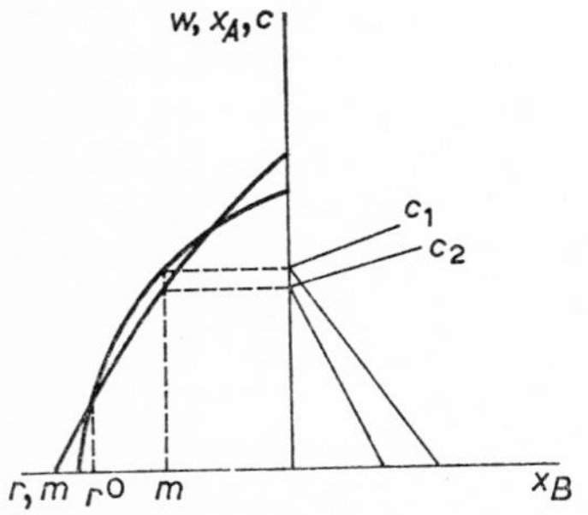

(A) Growth rate not corresponding to point of switch

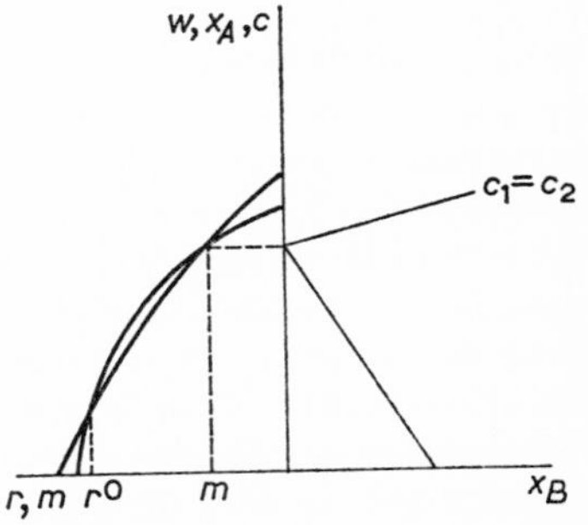

(B) Growth rate corresponding to point of switch

FIG. 8.2

entirely dominate the lines of the other technique. This is the case represented in Fig. 8.2A. If the growth rate is at a point of switch (Fig. 8.2B), both lines will coincide for the two techniques. When the two curves are concave, as in Fig. 8.2, the slope of the c lines is negative if $m > r^0$; when the curves are convex, the reverse happens. If m were equal to r^0, the two c lines would still coincide, but would be parallel to the horizontal axis.

It then follows that, if the wage curves of the two techniques have only one point in common and r is at the corresponding value r^0, $c_1 - c_2 \gtreqless 0$ according to whether $m \lesseqgtr r^0$. With multiple intersections, $c_1 - c_2 = 0$ for all the values of the growth rate corresponding to a switch-point, irrespective of whether it is the switch-point corresponding to the given rate of profit. As the growth rate changes, $c_1 - c_2$ changes its sign after each point of switch.

What happens to $v_1 - v_2$, and hence to $c_2 - c$? The 'cost' of the transition has the same sign as $c_1 - c_2$ whenever $m < r$; it has the opposite sign if $m > r$. When $c_1 - c_2 = 0$, $v_1 - v_2$, and hence $c_2 - \bar{c}$, are equal to zero only if $m \neq r$ – that is, only if the growth rate is at a point of switch different from that corresponding to the ruling value of r. When $m = r$, $c_2 - \bar{c}$ is positive (as could immediately be seen geometrically, since $v_1 - v_2$ equals the difference between the slopes of the tangents to the corresponding wage curves at $r^0 = m$). Hence, the ratio $(c_1 - c_2)/(c_2 - \bar{c})$ is positive for $m < r$, indeterminate at each point of switch not corresponding to the ruling value of r, zero for $m = r$, negative for $m > r$.

Thus the conclusions of the previous subsection also apply in this case.

IV. CIRCULATING CAPITAL; ONE GOOD NOT CONSUMED

We have so far considered a (rather unreal) case in which the goods serving as means of production not only are the same for different techniques but are also all used for consumption. Under these assumptions, (i) it is always possible, at least in principle, to bring the stocks of *all* capital goods to the levels appropriate to a new situation (different composition and/or different technique) by changing today's consumption; (ii) identity (8.2) can always be transformed into identity (8.4) (see section III).

If we remove the assumption that all goods are consumed and introduce the possibility that one or more goods only serve as means of production, (i) it may no longer be possible to fulfil tomorrow's requirements by changing today's consumption; (ii) while identity (8.2) always holds – nor could it be otherwise, for it is merely a definition of the rate of profit – equality (8.3), which allowed the passage to identity (8.4), is no longer valid in general.

We now introduce the hypothesis that only one good, or a fixed bundle of goods, is consumed. It then becomes legitimate, unlike the previous case, to define a notion of rate of return which is independent of the rate of profit. If a transition is at all possible, its costs and benefits are unambiguously measured in terms of homogeneous physical quantities and are unaffected by prices.

The rate of return, ρ, is that rate of discount which makes the flow of future gains in consumption per head arising from a change of technique equal to the present sacrifice entailed by the transition. Hence

$$c_2 - \bar{c} = (c_1 - c_2)\left[\frac{1+m}{1+\rho} + \left(\frac{1+m}{1+\rho}\right)^2 + \left(\frac{1+m}{1+\rho}\right)^3 + \dots\right].$$

If the series in brackets converges, we find a solution for ρ:

$$\rho = \frac{c_1 - c_2}{c_2 - \bar{c}}(1+m) + m. \tag{8.7}$$

For the series to converge, it is necessary that $\rho > m$. It can immediately be seen from (8.7) that the condition for this inequality to be satisfied, and hence for the series to converge, is

$$\frac{c_1 - c_2}{c_2 - \bar{c}} > 0.$$

It must be stressed that this is a necessary condition for (8.7) to hold and for there being a solution for ρ; if the condition were not satisfied, there would be no positive finite value of ρ, at least over an infinite time horizon.[1] Whether and when this condition holds is something that has to be verified; there exists no *a priori* ground to affirm, with Professor Solow,[2] that, 'come what may', $c_1 - c_2$ and $c_2 - \bar{c}$ always have the same sign.

We are thus faced with three problems, into which we must now inquire: (a) when the type of transition considered here is possible with goods which are not consumed, and what other types of transition are possible otherwise; (b) whether and when there exists a rate of return, i.e. whether and when the condition stated above is verified; and (c) if it is, whether the rate of return property of the rate of profit (now no longer an identity, but a meaningful proposition) is valid.

[1] Over a finite time horizon, say of n periods, there would be n solutions for ρ which, however, would have nothing in common with (8.7).

[2] Solow (1967) p. 38.

In order to clarify these points, we shall remain in our two-commodity world in which the same commodities are used by all techniques. We shall assume that *B* is necessary for production but is not consumed, while *A* serves both as means of production and as consumer good. Since there is no possibility of a change in the composition of consumption, we shall consider only the transition from one technique to another.

If a transition of the kind we have been considering is at all possible, we have, in the present case,

$$c_2 - \bar{c} = (1+m)(k_{A1} - k_{A2}) = v_1 - v_2 - p(k_{B1} - k_{B2}).$$

Three cases are conceivable: either $k_{B1} > k_{B2}$, or $k_{B1} = k_{B2}$, or $k_{B1} < k_{B2}$.

The first possibility is incompatible with the kind of transition with which we are dealing. There is not enough *B* to pass to technique 1 and, since *B* is not consumed, the additional quantity of *B* cannot be obtained by squeezing consumption. Hence the economy cannot pass to technique 1 maintaining full employment *and* at the same time with both goods growing at the same rate each period. A different kind of transition may be feasible, but it is outside the present context and will be considered later.

The second possibility has very limited relevance. Not only consumption, but also capital, is homogeneous between the two techniques, so that reswitching, for instance, is ruled out. Here, if a rate of return exists, it coincides with the rate of profit. It can immediately be seen that the condition for (8.7) to be a solution for ρ is that $m < r$. As long as this condition is satisfied, the rate of return coincides with the rate of profit; if the growth rate is equal to or exceeds the rate of profit, the rate of return property of the rate of profit fails simply because there is no finite positive value of the rate of return.

The more general case in which a transition from technique 2 to technique 1 can occur at all is when $k_{B1} < k_{B2}$. We shall now try to show that, in this case: (i) there is a range of values of the growth rate for which there is no finite solution for the rate of return; (ii) when there is a solution, the value of ρ given by (8.7) falls short of or exceeds the rate of profit, depending on the value of the growth rate.

As far as this second point is concerned, we must note that the reason for the divergence of ρ (when it exists) from r resides in the fact that some of today's production of one good (*B* in our case) must run to waste – this being part of the cost of a feasible transition. But then, it may be argued, the price of *B* ought to fall to zero and ρ, if it existed, would therefore coincide with r. This argument, however, leads nowhere. The logic of the exercise we have been performing is the following. We take a *preassigned* value of the rate of profit: the value corresponding to the point of switch between two mutually non-inferior techniques, which, as such, is on the wage, or factor price, frontier. We then consider the transition between the two techniques at the point of switch and see whether a rate of return exists and whether it coincides with the given value of the rate of profit on the frontier. Let now p fall to zero. Evidently, v_1 and v_2 for $p = 0$ are not the equilibrium values appropriate to the two techniques when the system is on the frontier; nor is the value of the rate of profit which can be obtained by putting $p = 0$ the equilibrium value at the point of switch. Thus, whether we allow p to fall to zero in the transition or not is immaterial, for the rate of return would not coincide in any case with the given (equilibrium) value of the rate of profit.

Let us then assume that there is enough B to pass from technique 2 to technique 1 – i.e. that $k_{1B} < k_{2B}$ (thereby implying that transition from technique 1 to technique 2 is impossible). Note that, since we are considering the case of only one consumption good (which may well be a bundle of many goods in fixed proportions), the duality property of the price and quantity equations holds in its entirety. Thus, given a wage curve, we can immediately measure consumption per head for any rate of growth on the w-axis and we can also measure the corresponding value of capital per man, v, as the slope $(c-w)/(r-m)$.

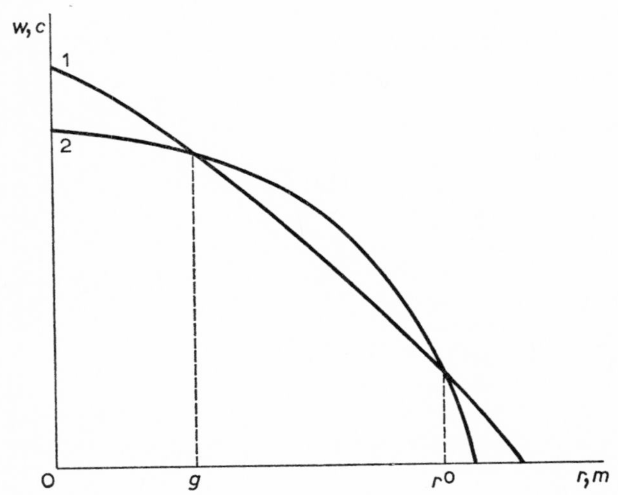

FIG. 8.3

Consider, for the sake of illustration, the case represented in Fig. 8.3. There are two techniques, intersecting each other twice in the relevant range. Let the given rate of profit be r^0, at the lower point of switch, and let g be the value on the r, m-axis corresponding to the higher point of switch. The wage rate and consumption per head are plotted along the vertical axis, the rate of profit and the rate of growth along the horizontal axis.

We can immediately see that:

if $0 \leqq m < g$, $c_1 > c_2$, $v_1 > v_2$; if $m = g$, $c_1 = c_2$, $v_1 = v_2$;
if $g < m < r^0$, $c_1 < c_2$, $v_1 < v_2$; if $m = r^0$, $c_1 = c_2$, $v_1 < v_2$;
if $r^0 < m$, $c_1 > c_2$, $v_1 < v_2$.

Since $k_{B1} < k_{B2}$, by hypothesis,[1] when $v_1 - v_2 \geqq 0$, we must have $k_{A1} > k_{A2}$. When m exceeds g, so that $v_1 - v_2 < 0$, we can still have $k_{A1} > k_{A2}$ for the whole relevant range of the growth rate, as is the case in the numerical example given in the Appendix. Otherwise we may conceivably have an inversion in the inequality sign, as the growth rate rises above a certain value, higher than g.

In the former case, when k_{A1} exceeds k_{A2} over the whole relevant range of m, $c_2 - \bar{c}$ will always be positive. As a result, the ratio $(c_1 - c_2)/(c_2 - \bar{c})$ will be positive only for values of the growth rate lower than g or higher than r^0; it will be zero for $m = g$ and for $m = r$; it will be negative for $g < m < r^0$. Thus, if the growth rate is in the interval between the two switch-points, there is no solution for the rate of return, since the condition of convergence is not satisfied. When a rate of return exists, it is either lower than the rate of profit (if $m < g$) or higher than the rate of profit (if $m > r^0$), so that the rate of return property of the rate of profit is shown not to be valid. As said above, the Appendix contains a numerical example which illustrates these results.

If k_{A2} were to exceed k_{A1} at some value of the growth rate after the first point of switch, $c_2 - \bar{c}$ would become negative. In this case there would be a solution for the rate of return only for $m < g$ and possibly (if the inversion in the sign of $c_2 - \bar{c}$ occurs at a value of m less than r^0) for $t < m < r^0$, where $t > g$. Again, the rate of return property of the rate of profit would not be verified, since ρ, when it exists, is always lower than r^0.

Summing up, we have constructed a case in which the economy can always pass from technique 2 to technique 1. This transition brings about a rise in consumption per head if the growth rate is less than g or higher than r^0. Consumption per head, instead,

[1] In the two-commodity case there can be no inversion of sign of $k_{B2} - k_{B1}$ over the relevant range of m; $k_{A2} - k_{A1}$, instead, can have one change of sign.

remains unchanged when m equals g or r^0, the two switch-points, and falls, as a result of the transition, if the growth rate is lower than r^0 but higher than g. Still, a sacrifice in present consumption is always needed to keep consumption per head unchanged and even, at least for a range of values of m, to pass from a steady state with higher to one with lower consumption per head. In these latter cases it is impossible to find a solution for the rate of return: there is no finite rate of discount making the flow of future benefits equal to present sacrifices. In the other case, when a present sacrifice leads to a gain in consumption per head, the rate of return is either higher or lower than the rate of profit. The one case in which the rate of return equals the rate of profit is that of homogeneous capital.

V. OTHER TYPES OF TRANSITION

We have so far been concerned with a very special and artificial kind of transition between techniques. Society is supposed consciously to perform some (positive or negative) act of saving; owing to very restrictive assumptions (such as the homogeneity of capital goods as between different techniques), the physical change in consumption immediately causes an opposite change in the physical capital stocks. Still, in spite of the assumptions, we have seen that there are cases in which transition from one technique to the other, and hence from a lower to a higher level of consumption per head, becomes impossible as soon as we allow for the possibility of one commodity not being consumed. Since transitions do in fact occur, the latter does not seem to be a very relevant conclusion.

The point is that the approach we have examined in the previous sections made the study of the problems of transition instrumental to the attempt to explain the rate of profit in terms of some notion of rate of return to society. As we have seen, it is an attempt that does not lead very far. If, moreover, we cease to worry about the rate of return, different and perhaps less unrealistic cases of transition can find their place in the analysis.

I do not intend to explore these possibilities in any detail here. I shall first reconsider the problem of what happens when, in terms of our previous example, $k_{B2} < k_{B1}$, so that a transition of the kind examined above is impossible. Another line of research will then be mentioned.

The difficulties encountered when the quantity of a capital good is insufficient for the requirements of a new situation and cannot be increased by squeezing consumption are due to the fact that, in the type of transition examined above, all means of production are made to grow at the same equilibrium rate all the time. This is neither a necessary nor a sufficient condition for the transition to occur. If the stocks available are not the equilibrium ones, quantities of the two goods which are not the equilibrium quantities can be produced while preserving full employment of labour. The problem – a very traditional problem – is then to see whether there is a tendency towards the new equilibrium situation.

If the restriction that all goods should always grow at the same equilibrium rate is removed, a degree of freedom is introduced into the quantity equations. Remember that we are still maintaining the hypothesis that *A* and *B* do not change their physical identity in the passage from one technique to the other. At time 0 we have stocks of the two goods *A* and *B*, which are those produced by means of technique 2 in order to suit the requirements of steady growth with technique 2. These stocks are now going to be used for production with technique 1 (the equilibrium quantities of which are different from those of technique 2), in order to obtain whatever quantities of the two goods and whatever share of *A* devoted to consumption are necessary to preserve full employment.

We shall assume that the amount of *A* necessary for each period's consumption must be produced in the previous period (so that, in each period, the production of *A* must be sufficient to provide not only next period's circulating capital, but also next period's consumption). We can thus write the following system of differential equations:

$$\begin{aligned} L &= l_A(Y_A+\dot{Y}_A)+l_B(K_B+\dot{K}_B) \\ K_A &= a_A(Y_A+\dot{Y}_A)+a_B(K_B+\dot{K}_B) \\ K_B &= b_A(Y_A+\dot{Y}_A)+b_B(K_B+\dot{K}_B) \\ Y_A &= K_A+C \end{aligned}$$

where Y_A is the total production of *A*, *C* is total consumption, and dots indicate derivatives with respect to time. The coefficients are those of technique 1.

Putting $L = L_0e^{mt}$, where *m* is the natural rate of growth of the labour force (so that full employment is ensured), the solution of the system is

$$\begin{aligned} K_B(t) &= Me^{\alpha t}+k_{B1}L_0e^{mt} \\ K_A(t) &= \frac{D_1}{D_2}Me^{\alpha t}+k_{A1}L_0e^{mt} \\ Y_A(t) &= Ee^{-t}-\frac{l_B}{l_A}Me^{\alpha t}+\frac{1}{1+m}y_{A1}L_0e^{mt} \\ C(t) &= Ee^{-t}-\left(\frac{D_1}{D_2}+\frac{l_B}{l_A}\right)Me^{\alpha t}+\frac{1}{1+m}c_1L_0e^{mt}. \end{aligned}$$

Further,

$$\alpha = \frac{l_A}{D_2} - 1.$$

In the above solutions, k_{A1}, k_{B1}, $y_{A1}/(1+m)$, $c_1/(1+m)$ are the equilibrium values of A-capital and B-capital per man, A-production per man and consumption per man appropriate to technique 1.[1] D_1 and D_2 are indicators of the relative intensity of use of labour and each of the two goods in the two industries, for $D_1 = l_A a_B - l_B a_A$ and $D_2 = l_A b_B - l_A b_B$. M is an arbitrary constant, to be set equal to the initial disequilibrium between the B-capital stock available at the beginning of the story (which is that appropriate to technique 2) and that appropriate to technique 1. E is another arbitrary constant, which can be taken to measure the difference between the amount of A available at time 0 (equal to the sum of the equilibrium capital stock and the equilibrium consumption of technique 2) and that necessary for current production with the coefficients of technique 1.

It is easy to see that the condition for convergence to equilibrium is $D_2 < 0$: that is, the B/labour ratio must be higher in the A sector than in the B sector.

We are of course treading well-known paths. Stability conditions of this kind have often been treated in the literature. What is worth noting is that there may be a path from technique 2 to technique 1, at full employment, even when the kind of transition examined in the previous sections is impossible (because $k_{B1} > k_{B2}$). If there is such a path, however, neither the notion of rate of return examined above nor, *a fortiori*, the rate of return property of the rate of profit seem to be applicable. If we look at the solutions of the system of differential equations, we see for instance that the amount of A required as circulating capital at time 0, i.e. K_{A_0}, may well be less than that required in equilibrium by technique 2. In this case, consumption at the beginning of the transition period (being the difference between the given Y_{A_0} and K_{A_0}) will already be higher than the equilibrium level of technique 2, so that no present sacrifice is required to attain the higher consumption per head afforded by technique 1. Many other time profiles are of course possible, but none of them seems liable to a treatment in terms of rate of return.

[1] y_{A1} and c_1 are the steady-state solutions which would obtain if each period's consumption were produced in the same period. The assumption that each period's consumption has to be produced in the previous period only causes the same values to be divided by $(1+m)$. The steady-state quantity equations under this assumption are dual to the equilibrium price equations under the assumption that wages are paid at the beginning of the period. The assumption in question would not change in any way the results obtained in the earlier parts of this paper: the ratio $(c_1-c_2)/(c_2-\bar{c})$ would simply not be multiplied by $(1+m)$.

The real problems, however, still lie ahead. What happens if the two techniques employ fixed capital and if the machines appropriate to each of them are physically different? If this is the case, the stocks left over from technique 2 are not only quantitatively, but also qualitatively, inappropriate to technique 1. These, and not the ones we have so far considered, are the true problems of transition.

Here the question could be approached in the following terms. We must suppose either that the 'old' machines can be used to produce the 'new' ones, or that some commodity produced in the economy can be traded for 'new' machines produced somewhere else. Once the transition begins, the production of old machines will be interrupted: those at the end of their physical life will not be substituted and the old stock will progressively fall to zero. The spare capacity that thus becomes available will be devoted to the construction of new machines or to the production of goods to be traded for them. We shall then have a coexistence of two sub-economies, one expanding, with more and more new machines, the other declining, with fewer and fewer old machines. The duration of this process will depend on the physical life of the old machines and on their capacity to produce new machines. Conditions allowing this process to proceed smoothly may be identified.[1] If these conditions are not satisfied, there will be a point when there is no old machine left in existence but the stock of new machines is not that appropriate to the new equilibrium. In this case we are led back to the stability problem considered in the previous section.

Alternatively, an element of flexibility, which may also be an element of realism, can be introduced, by considering the technical coefficients as 'normal' coefficients.[2] This amounts to assuming that it is possible, within limits, to increase the quantity produced of one commodity by increasing (more than proportionally) some means of productions while leaving some others unchanged. Formally, we thus allow the existence of a third technique, which is inferior to the other two at the ruling rate of profit but which can be used to pass from one to the other. The cost of the transition would then be measured by the fall in profits (or wages) that must be borne in order to build up the appropriate capital stock.

VI. FINAL REMARKS

In the present chapter I shall enter into some enquiry respecting the influence of machinery on the interests of the different classes

[1] The problem is to a certain extent similar to that of introducing embodied technical progress into a model with heterogeneous capital goods.

[2] See Hicks (1965) chap. xvi.

of society, a subject of great importance, and one which appears never to have been investigated in a manner to lead to any certain or satisfactory result.

This is how Ricardo began his chapter, 'On Machinery', of the *Principles.*[1] It can hardly be said that economics has provided 'any certain or satisfactory' treatment of the problems he posed, which are, I submit, the problems which ought to be the proper object of dynamic analysis. Ricardo's argument, whatever its merits, 'failed to become part of the established corpus of economic teaching', as Sir John Hicks observes,[2] and his questions never obtained a proper answer.

From this point of view, a formal treatment of the problems of transition in an economy where full employment must always prevail has, *per se*, very scarce relevance; an economy where those problems are relevant has never existed and will, in all probability, never exist.

In this paper, for instance, we have dealt with the transition from one technique to the other at that rate of profit which makes the two techniques equally profitable. Now, why should there be a transition? The reason given is that society wants to achieve a perpetual gain in consumption per head. But then there is one further question. Since 'society' is an abstraction, whose consumption is going to rise? The answer of course depends on the kind of savings function we are postulating. Every transition to a technique allowing an average higher consumption per head implies a rise in the share of consumption on income, but normally also implies a rise in the share of profits on income. If, say, all wages are consumed, the transition would cause an increase in consumption out of profits as well as in overall profits. (In the case of a socialist economy, the effect would be an increase in public consumption, which is not necessarily consumption for the public's benefit.) In the limiting case in which all profits are saved, a transition may be justified, from the point of view of the owners of capital, by the desire to increase overall profits and their share on national income. What is, in either case, the gain to 'society'?

Consider now a different question. Let there be an economy where part of the population is unemployed; assume that the unemployed live at the expense of the employed, so that consumption per head is the same for everybody. Imagine that the decision is taken to sacrifice part of the present consumption. With the same sacrifice two options are open: either to pass to a technique allowing a higher level of consumption per head with the same level of employment

[1] See Ricardo (1951) p. 386.
[2] Hicks (1970).

(the benefits being shared by employed and unemployed alike), or to increase the stock of capital in order to raise the level of employment, and hence everybody's consumption, with the technique already in use. Here the 'return to society' and the return to capital would be different: the former would be higher with the second option, the latter with the first.

These are merely illustrations of problems which are near to those considered by Ricardo; their treatment, however, is outside the limited scope of this paper.

APPENDIX

(1) *The Relationship between Consumption per Head and the Rate of Growth when More than One Good is Consumed*

Let there be three commodities, A, B and C, all of which are used both for consumption and as circulating capital. The price equations are

$$p_a = l_a w + (a_a p_a + b_a p_b + c_a p_c)(1+r)$$
$$p_b = l_b w + (a_b p_a + b_b p_b + c_b p_c)(1+r)$$
$$p_c = l_c w + (a_c p_a + b_c p_b + c_c p_c)(1+r).$$

The quantity equations are

$$l = l_a[x_a + (1+m)k_a] + l_b[x_b + (1+m)k_b] + l_c[x_c + (1+m)k_c]$$
$$k_a = a_a[x_a + (1+m)k_a] + a_b[x_b + (1+m)k_b] + a_c[x_c + (1+m)k_c]$$
$$k_b = b_a[x_a + (1+m)k_a] + b_b[x_b + (1+m)k_b] + b_c[x_c + (1+m)k_c]$$
$$k_c = c_a[x_a + (1+m)k_a] + c_b[x_b + (1+m)k_b] + c_c[x_c + (1+m)k_c]$$

where x_a, x_b and x_c are the quantities consumed of the three goods.

Let A and C be consumed in fixed proportions, so that, say, $x_c = \lambda x_a$. If the value of one unit of this consumption bundle is taken as the numeraire, $p_a + \lambda p_c = 1$. The value of consumption per head will thus be $p_a x_a + p_b x_b + p_c x_c = x_a + p_b x_b$.

Let

$$D = \begin{vmatrix} a_a & b_a & c_a \\ a_b & b_b & c_b \\ a_c & b_c & c_c \end{vmatrix}$$

and D_a, D_b, D_c be its principal minors. Let $D^{(a)}$, $D^{(b)}$, $D^{(c)}$ be the determinants obtained by replacing respectively the first, the second and the third column of D by (l_a, l_b, l_c), and $D_b^{(a)}$, $D_c^{(a)}$, ..., the principal minors of $D^{(a)}$ ... Put

$$l_a + \lambda l_c - [D_c^{(a)} + D_b^{(a)} + \lambda(D_b^{(c)} + D_a^{(c)})](1+r) + (D^{(a)} + \lambda D^{(c)})(1+r)^2 = S_r$$

and

$$l_a + \lambda l_c - [D_c^{(a)} + D_b^{(a)} + \lambda(D_b^{(c)} + D_a^{(c)})](1+m) + (D^{(a)} + \lambda D^{(c)})(1+m)^2 = S_m.$$

Then

$$w = \frac{1-(a_a+b_b+c_c)(1+r)+(D_a+D_b+D_c)(1+r)^2-D(1+r)^3}{S_r} = f(r)$$

$$p_b = \frac{l_b-(D_c^{(b)}+D_a^{(b)})(1+r)+D^{(b)}(1+r)^2}{S_r} = \varphi_b(r)$$

$$x_a = \frac{1-(a_a+b_b+c_c)(1+m)+(D_a+D_b+D_c)(1+m)^2-D(1+m)^3}{S_m} -$$

$$-\frac{l_b-(D_c^{(b)}+D_a^{(b)})(1+m)+D^{(b)}(1+m)^2}{S_m} x_b = f(m)-\varphi_b(m)x_b.$$

The value of consumption per head is therefore $f(m)+[\varphi_b(r)-\varphi_b(m)]x_b$.

(2) *A Numerical Example for the Case in which One Good is not Consumed*

Let there be two techniques for the production of two commodities, *A* and *B*. Both commodities are means of production, but only *A* is consumed. We take the coefficients characterising the two techniques from a numerical example used by Garegnani (1966). The coefficients are the following:

	Technique 1			*Technique 2*	
	A	*B*		*A*	*B*
Labour	$\frac{89}{10}$	$\frac{9}{50}$	Labour	$\frac{89}{10}$	$\frac{3}{2}$
A	0	$\frac{1}{2}$	*A*	0	$\frac{1}{4}$
B	$\frac{379}{423}$	$\frac{1}{10}$	*B*	$\frac{379}{423}$	$\frac{5}{12}$

These two techniques are equally profitable at two values of the rate of profit: $r_1 = 0{\cdot}1$ and $r_2 = 0{\cdot}2$. Let the given rate of profit in the system be 20 per cent, that is, r_2. At that rate of profit, if $p_A = 1$, $p_B = 0{\cdot}6878$.

From the quantity equations we obtain:

$$c_1 = \frac{42{,}300-4{,}230(1+m)-18{,}950(1+m)^2}{376{,}470-30{,}825(1+m)}$$

$$c_2 = \frac{50{,}760-21{,}150(1+m)-11{,}370(1+m)^2}{451{,}764-120{,}015(1+m)}$$

$$k_{A1} = \frac{18{,}950(1+m)}{376{,}470-30{,}825(1+m)} \quad k_{A2} = \frac{11{,}370(1+m)}{451{,}764-120{,}015(1+m)}$$

$$k_{B1} = \frac{37{,}900}{376{,}470-30{,}825(1+m)} \quad k_{B2} = \frac{45{,}840}{451{,}764-120{,}015(1+m)}.$$

Keeping the rate of profit at 20 per cent, by solving the above expressions for different values of the growth rate, m, we obtain the following results:

m	$k_{B1}-k_{B2}$	$k_{A1}-k_{A2}$	c_1-c_2	$c_2-\bar{c}$	$\dfrac{c_1-c_2}{c_2-\bar{c}}$	ρ
0·00	−0·02852	0·02055	0·00033	0·02055	0·01605	0·01605
0·05	−0·03058	0·02118	0·00014	0·02224	0·00629	0·05629
0·10	−0·03273	0·02174	0·00000	0·02391	0·00000	–
0·15	−0·03497	0·02223	−0·00005	0·02556	−0·00195	–
0·20	−0·03731	0·02265	0·00000	0·02718	0·00000	–
0·25	−0·03976	0·02299	0·00018	0·02874	0·00626	0·25626
0·30	−0·04233	0·02328	0·00050	0·03026	0·01652	0·31652

The rate of return, ρ, is shown not to exist for $0{\cdot}10 \leqq m \leqq 0{\cdot}20$, it is lower than the ruling rate of profit for values of the growth rate lower than 10 per cent, higher than the rate of profit for values of the growth rate higher than 20 per cent.

REFERENCES

M. Amendola, 'Thrift, Economic Life of Capital and Productivity in a Model with Heterogeneous Capital' (1970) unpublished.

M. Bruno, 'Fundamental Duality Relations in the Pure Theory of Capital and Growth', *Review of Economic Studies*, vol. XXXVI (Jan 1969).

P. Garegnani, 'Switching of Techniques', *Quarterly Journal of Economics*, vol. LXXX (Nov 1966).

J. R. Hicks, *Capital and Growth* (Oxford, 1965) chap. XVI.

—— 'A Neo-Austrian Growth Theory', *Economic Journal* (1970).

M. Morishima, *Theory of Economic Growth* (Oxford, 1969).

M. Nuti, 'Capitalism, Socialism and Steady Growth', *Economic Journal* (Mar 1970).

L. L. Pasinetti, 'Switches of Technique and the "Rate of Return" in Capital Theory', *Economic Journal* (1969).

D. Ricardo, *On the Principles of Political Economy and Taxation*, vol. I of *The Works and Correspondence of David Ricardo*, ed. P. Sraffa and M. Dobb (Cambridge, 1951).

R. M. Solow, 'The Interest Rate and Transition between Techniques', in *Socialism, Capitalism and Economic Growth: Essays Presented to Maurice Dobb*, ed. C. H. Feinstein (Cambridge, 1967).

L. Spaventa, 'Rate of Profit, Rate of Growth, and Capital Intensity in a Simple Production Model', *Oxford Economic Papers* (July 1970).

Discussion of the Paper by Luigi Spaventa

Professor Spaventa introduced his paper by saying that he was interested in three issues: (a) when and how a transition in a multi-commodity production model can occur; (b) the examination of a 'rate of return property' of the rate of profit; and (c) whether a study of these questions has any relevance to dynamic economics. These questions had been discussed recently by Solow and Pasinetti. He referred to his paper for specification of models and notation.

We have the identity for the rate of profit $r \equiv (C_1 - C_2)/(V_1 - V_2) + m$. In the case considered by Solow with circulating capital and the consumption of all goods in the system, we have $V_1 - V_2 = (C_2 - \bar{C})/(1+m)$. Substituting this into the expression for r, we have $r \equiv [(C_1 - C_2)/(C_2 - \bar{C})] \times (1+m) + m$, which is the rate of return formula given by Solow. We should then ask what happens if the assumptions giving this identity do not hold, e.g. when one good is not consumed. Continuing with the assumption that two goods are consumed, however, he said the duality property established for one consumption good by Bruno (*Review of Economic Studies*, Jan 1969) can be generalised to two goods. We have

$$X_A = f(m) - \phi(m) X_B$$

$$C = f(m) + [\phi(r) - \phi(m)] X_B.$$

The last term in the second equation is the modification required to generalise to two goods (if $X_B = 0$ the unmodified property holds).

He then considered a physical change in the composition of consumption given by $-(\Delta X_A / \Delta X_B)$. $C_1 - C_2$ is a function, which need not be monotonic, of the rate of profit. $V_1 - V_2$ is also a function of r but has the same sign as $C_1 - C_2$. For a rate of growth $m > 0$ both these expressions change sign as r passes through m.

Similar sorts of results hold when we consider a transition between techniques. $C_1 - C_2$, $V_1 - V_2$ change sign (as functions of the growth rate) at each point of switch, regardless of whether or not this is the ruling rate of profit.

He then turned to situations where one of the commodities is not consumed. We must first see whether and when the kind of transition under consideration is possible. Since we cannot increase the stock of a good that is not consumed by squeezing its consumption, only transitions that reduce the amount of this capital good are possible. We then consider a one-period transition and define a rate of return ρ corresponding to Solow's definition as $\rho \equiv [(C_1 - C_2)/(C_2 - \bar{C})](1+m) + m$. Here ρ is independent of the rate of profit, since only one good is consumed. It can be shown, however, that in this case: (i) there may be no positive finite value for p; (ii) when there is, in general, $p \neq r$; (iii) in the former case, $(C_1 - C_2)/(C_2 - \bar{C}) < 0$, contrary to Solow's claim that this ratio must be positive.

When the stock of the good which is not consumed is insufficient, other kinds of transition may be feasible, even if the one considered by Solow is not. In these cases, however, the rate of return property of the rate of profit does not hold. He summed up by saying that either the rate of return property is not operationally meaningful (since it is true by definition) or it does not hold.

He did not consider that these formal exercises in transitions had any relevance for real problems. They evaded more important issues, such as those indicated by Ricardo in his chapter 'On Machinery'.

Dr Bliss began his discussion of the paper by saying that Professor Spaventa's useful discussion of the problems of transitions between techniques brought out some of the problems of Solow's approach in his paper in the Dobb *Festschrift*. Solow's approach discussed capital stock and consumption changes, arising from capital accumulation, at a price system and rate of interest consistent with the coexistence of two sets of productive techniques (a switch-point) in terms of the internal rate of return and its relation to the rate of interest.

He rearranged equation (8.2) to obtain

$$r = \frac{(C_1 - C_2) + m(V_1 - V_2)}{V_1 - V_2}$$

or the difference in net outputs (including capital accumulation at rate m) divided by the difference in capital per head. He would return to the sense, if any, in which this was an identity. Everything is evaluated at the common price system of the two states. This is the familiar relation between the rate of profit and the marginal product of capital in the special form that relation takes at a switch-point. If the two states can coexist at more than one r, we have a different price system and a different value of the marginal product of capital. This is as it should be, since the relation is not a uni-directional one, in which the marginal product 'determines' the rate of profit. Both are simultaneously determined by the equilibrium conditions of the economic system.

The approach here is comparative dynamic – we compare two economies each in steady state. One economy cannot transform itself into the other (each is constrained by the available capital stock) and we can learn something about the system in equilibrium from the fact that price-taking producers should feel no desire to change their technical practices (they are aware only of prices, not the global constraints). It is interesting to go beyond hypothetical comparative dynamic questions to the study of actual capital stock changes – this was the concern of Solow and the author here.

He thought that the important and fundamental result was the present value maximisation property of equilibrium paths, i.e. for most cases of interest we could show

$$\sum_t p'\Delta C_t \left(\frac{1}{1+r}\right)^t \leqslant 0, \qquad (*)$$

where ΔC_t is a sequence of feasible changes in vectors of net consumption.

Professor Yaari interjected that this was not a general property of optimal growth paths and the sum might not converge.

Dr Bliss said it held in a broad class of cases and he confined himself to these. Defining the rate of return as a root of

$$\sum_t p'\Delta C_t \left(\frac{1}{1+\rho}\right)^t = 0$$

we see immediately that r is a rate of return if we can somehow confine ourselves to cases of equality in (*) – i.e. changes do not introduce activities not profitable at p and r and no scarce good is rendered free. This was Solow's approach; it seemed to the discussant unduly restrictive and obscured the essential property (*). He thought the internal rate of return of little theoretical interest, but it is useful for planning purposes.

He suspected that the elegant two-sector results obtained by Professor Spaventa would not generalise to many commodities.

The word 'identity' was much used here (the author claimed the majority of his relations were identities). To say a relation is an identity can have two meanings: first, it is a definition of a variable, or second, it holds independently of some variation under consideration. He did not believe that relation (8.2) was an identity (he would *define* the rate of profit as P/K). Nor did he accept the related claim by Pasinetti (*Economic Journal*, 1969) that Solow's results are true merely by definition. Although not very profound, these results do embody behavioural postulates, namely cost minimisation. Under different postulates as to what constitutes equilibrium behaviour, the rate of interest at which the contemplated change is equilibrium need *not* be equal to the rate of return. Therefore these results are not just identities or true merely by definition.

He wondered why the author required that benefits and costs be defined independently of the rate of profit for his rate of profit/rate of return result to have meaning. Often there is more than one set of relative prices at which a state is in equilibrium, but it is not true that any set will do. Knowledge of the sets of equilibrium prices tells us something about technology and tastes. He did not find it offensive that different sets gave different rates of return. The rate of return need not be purely a property of technology, any more than the marginal product of capital.

He thought that the question of whether we could have a transition from a given steady state to another which never gave excess supply, given as many periods as we liked, was both interesting and difficult (because of the number of degrees of freedom). It was only academic since we can always allow excess supply.

He welcomed the author's reminder of the great importance of taking into account distributional considerations in actual planning where the distribution of income is not fully controlled independently of the planning decisions.

Dr Pasinetti said that relation (8.2) was precisely the definition $r \equiv (P/K)$ used by Dr Bliss. This could be shown by a few manipulations and so could indeed be called an identity, or rather an accounting expression. Suppose two techniques, α and β, are equally profitable at rate of profit r^* and so have the same wage rate w^* and price vector p^*. We can express the rate of profit either as $(P_\alpha{}^*/p^*K_\alpha)$ or as $(P_\beta{}^*/p^*K_\beta)$ (where $P_i{}^*$ denotes total profits at the switch-point and K_i denotes the capital-goods vector for technique i, $i = \alpha, \beta$) or as $(P_\beta^* - P_\alpha^*)/p^*(K_\beta - K_\alpha)$. When the two systems have the same labour force and therefore at the switch-point the same total wages (the case under consideration), then $P_\beta^* - P_\alpha^* \equiv p^*(Y_\beta - Y_\alpha)$ where Y_i ($i = \alpha, \beta$) is the vector of the physical goods of the two net products. The common rate of profit may then be expressed as

$$\frac{p^*(Y_\beta - Y_\alpha)}{p^*(K_\beta - K_\alpha)} \equiv r^*. \tag{1}$$

No behavioural or maximisation assumptions were implied by (1), contrary to Dr Bliss's assertion – it was merely an accounting expression. It could not but be equal to r^* since *it was* r^*.

Professor Stiglitz emphasised that equality between the rate of interest and the rate of return needed full utilisation of capital stocks. Without this we should not expect equality.

On p. 180 the problem of the stability of a transition was posed, but it was stipulated that the transition occurs immediately. The more interesting case is where we start with A and finish with B and are allowed to mix techniques en route. The stability conditions given in the paper would no longer be applicable.

Professor Bruno said we ought to take two given steady states and consider an optimal change. We could try to maximise $\sum [(C_t)/(1+\rho)^t]$ where ρ was the rate of interest in a steady state. If we change steady state we would have to change the discount rate as we moved. Prices would change continuously.

Professor Stiglitz said we could first take the more narrow question of an optimal transition between states using the switch-point rate of interest. He thought the solution to this problem would not be unique in a wide class of cases and that any efficient change from A to B fully utilising capital would do.

Professor Bruno said we should consider steady states with different interest rates, since the non-substitution theorem tells us that any mix of the two techniques would do for the transition if they are both equally profitable at the common interest rate being considered.

Professor Stiglitz said that the non-substitution theorem was not applicable to such situation, as we were considering a transition between two different capital endowments in which we are trying to maximise a particular integral.

Professor Hahn said that in many discussions the points at issue were virtual changes, as in the controversies concerning the rate of profit and the marginal product of capital. He thought the right question now was what happens when transitions actually occur. However, he asked what we should do if there were no solution to an optimal transition problem and why it was different from any other planning problem. *Professor Stiglitz* said that there may be many solutions.

Professor Shell said we ought to be able to obtain uniqueness with even the smallest amount of curvature to the criterion function.

Dr Dixit said that with the problems of non-linearities and multiple roots we ought to be pleasantly surprised if the internal rate of return did give a good measure of the relation between benefits and costs.

Professor Spaventa concluded the discussion by discussing some of the points that had been raised. Some of his results could be extended to more than two sectors – e.g. if $(n-1)$ goods are consumed in fixed proportions. He felt that $[(P_1-P_2)/(K_1-K_2)]$ is a definition of the rate of profit at the switch-point. He thought that the notion of the internal rate of return might be helpful for planning purposes, but then we would want to know that prices reflected marginal rates of transformation. It was possible to have the same physical rates of transformation with different prices.

He agreed he was allowing capital redundancy in his model. However, in a two-commodity world where only one commodity was consumed we could only have the kind of transition under discussion if we move to a situation needing less of the good not consumed – in these circumstances redundancy arises.

In practice, real transitions need different rates of profit and prices. He thought the more relevant problems from a social point of view were discussed at the end of the paper. Some of them had been treated by Professor Hicks in his forthcoming *Economic Journal* article using an Austrian theory of capital.

9 On Some Equilibrium Paths

F. H. Hahn

LONDON SCHOOL OF ECONOMICS

I. INTRODUCTION

I was asked to discuss the special problems which arise in the analysis of a sequence of equilibria in a neo-classical model of economic growth when there are many capital goods. Some of the results of this kind of investigation are by now well known, but it is the case that it is possible to make considerable simplifications of analysis, and that is one of my tasks.

The constructions which have been most discussed consider cases in which necessary conditions of intertemporal efficiency are satisfied. It is certainly hard to see why they should be. In a world of malleable and freely transferable capital goods, myopia can be justified, but 'correct myopia' has little to recommend it. Accordingly, I shall also be interested in situations where foresight is not correct. This, in part, extends and simplifies an earlier analysis of my own (Hahn, 1970). I shall also take the opportunity to comment on my predecessors in this field.

Everything which follows must be regarded as tentative in one important respect. The conditions for a momentary equilibrium to be uniquely determined, once the resources are known, are in some respects still not properly understood, and at best are only sufficient and never very appealing. But I am not now clear how important this question of uniqueness really is. Certainly, traditional differential equations analysis requires it, and there are some suggestive examples for a simple case, due to Inada, where lack of uniqueness causes serious problems. But I suspect that there may be results on 'differential correspondences' which would have considerable bearing on the problem at hand, but of which, if they yet exist, I am ignorant.

Lastly, I should like to enter the further disclaimer to the effect that I do not believe that these models capture at all accurately the accumulation process of a capitalist economy.

II. BASIC CONSTRUCTION

Let the economy have one consumption good labelled 'O' and m capital goods ($i = 1, \ldots, m$). Write y_i and k_j as the output of the ith good, and the amount of the jth capital good, both per man in the economy. Also $y = (y_1, \ldots, y_m)$, $k = (k_1, \ldots, k_m)$. All prices are taken in unit of account. P_0 is the price of consumption good, and $P = (P_1, \ldots, P_m)$ is the price vector of capital goods.

There are constant returns to scale, and, throughout the analysis, the efficiency frontier of the economy can be represented by a strictly concave, twice differentiable function:

$$F(y_0, y, k) = 0. \tag{9.1}$$

It will also be assumed that

$$\frac{\partial F}{\partial k_i} > 0 \quad \text{for} \quad k_i < +\infty$$

$$\frac{\partial F}{\partial k_i} < +\infty \quad \text{for} \quad k_i > 0.$$

It is convenient to define a set $A(k)$ by

$$A(k) = \{(y_0, y) \mid F(y_0, y, k) \geqq 0\}.$$

Throughout I shall want to examine situations in which the economy is 'momentarily efficient', by which I mean that, with all resources fully used, it is not possible, at that moment, to have more of one good without having less of another. I shall therefore be interested in a function $R(P_0, P, k)$ defined by:

$$R = \max_{A(k)} (Py + P_0 y_0). \tag{9.2}$$

It is clear that R is convex in its price arguments and concave in k. On my assumptions, R will be differentiable everywhere.

Let $R_i = \partial R / \partial P_i$. Then

$$R_i(P_0, P, k) = y_i \quad (i = 0, \ldots, m). \tag{9.3}$$

If one is examining an economy where population is growing at the geometric rate n and capital lives for ever, then

$$R_i(P_0, P, k) - nk_i = \dot{k}_i \quad (i = 1, \ldots, m) \tag{9.4}$$

will be the differential equations one will have to analyse.

Let $R_{m+i} = \partial R / \partial k_i$. The R_{m+i} is the shadow price of the service of capital for the moment under consideration. There are a number of possibilities two of which I take note of now:

(1) *Static Price Expectations*

All agents take it for granted that current prices will persist into the future. In this case I shall be interested in the question whether there exists a scalar $r > 0$, such that

$$R_{m+j}(P_0, P, k) = rP_j \quad (j = 1, \ldots, m). \tag{9.5}$$

The argument behind (9.5) is this. When the economy is in equilibrium, a unit of account invested in any one of the capital goods must have the same rate of return as it has in any other. In the present case this is given by r, since by assumption there are no capital gains or losses. But then the rental of a unit of capital of type j is rP_j and classic duality theory then tells us that this rental should measure the increase in the maximal receipts of the economy which would result from a little more of capital good j.

(2) *Correct Myopic Expectations*

In this case, here at $t = 0$ agents have predetermined expectation $\dot{P}_i(0)$, $i = 1, \ldots, m$. The system evolves so as to justify this. So in this case, by an argument already given, we shall be interested in the solution of

$$R_{m+j}(P_0, P, k) - rP_j = -\dot{P}_j, \quad \dot{P}_j(0) \text{ given}, \quad j = 1, \ldots, m. \tag{9.6}$$

Next, there are two kinds of savings assumptions we can make:

(*a*) *Classical savings*, i.e.

$$R^0(P_0, P, k) - P_0 R_0(P_0, P, k) = 0 \tag{9.7}$$

where

$$R^0 = R - \sum R_{m+j} k_j. \tag{9.8}$$

Note that, by constant returns to scale, R^0 is the shadow price of labour, so that (9.7) demands equality between the wage per man and the value of consumption goods per man.

(*b*) *Proportional savings*, i.e.

$$(1 - S)R(P_0, P, k) = P_0 R_0(P_0, P, k), \quad 0 < S < 1. \tag{9.9}$$

Equation (9.9) is self-explanatory.

III. THE EXISTENCE OF MOMENTARY EQUILIBRIUM

I shall here consider only the case of classical savings and static price expectations. The situation with myopically correct expectations has already been discussed fairly generally in Hahn, 1966.

I shall confine myself to the case $k >> 0$. I want to show that one can solve:

$$R_{m+j}(P_0, P, k) - rP_j = 0, \quad (j = 1, \ldots, m)$$
$$R^0(P_0, P, k) - P_0 R_0(P_0, P, k) = 0.$$

Since all equations are homogeneous of degree zero in the prices, I normalise prices by requiring them to belong to a set $S(k)$:

$$S(k) = \{(P_0, P) | Pk + P_0 = 1, (P_0, P) \geqq 0\}.$$

I shall also make the following assumption:

Assumption A.1. For all $(P_0, P) \in S(k), \sum_{j \neq 0} R_{m+j}(P_0, P)k_j > 0.$

This postulate serves to exclude 'capital satiation' at some prices. I shall also want the following:

Lemma 1: There is a scalar $\lambda > 0$ *such that*

$$Pk + \lambda(P_0 R_0 - R^0) \geqq 0, \quad all \quad (P_0, P) \in S(k).$$

Proof: (a) If $Pk = 0$, $R = P_0 R_0$. By A.1, $R - R^0 > 0$ and so certainly $P_0 R_0 - R^0 > 0$.

(b) Let $g(P_0, P) = R^0 - P_0 R_0$. If $g(\cdot) \leqq 0$ all $(P_0 P) \in S(k)$ there is nothing left to prove. So take it that the set

$$V = \{Pk | g(\cdot) > 0, \quad (P_0 P) \in S(k) |\}$$

is not empty. Let

$$h = \inf_{v} (Pk).$$

By the argument of (a), $h > 0$. Also, since R^0 is bounded, $R_0 \geqq 0$, we may define

$$\hat{g} = \sup_{S(k)} g(P_0, P).$$

By hypothesis $\hat{g} > 0$. Then let

$$\lambda = h/\hat{g}$$

and verify the correctness of the Lemma for this λ.

Lemma 2: (a) $R(P_0, P, k)$ *is differentiable on* $S(k)$ *and on* $0 << k << +\infty$.

(b) *The partial differential coefficients are continuous on* $S(k)$.

Proof: (a) (i) Let $z = y_0, y$, $\tilde{P} = (P_0, P)$, and let $z(\tilde{P}, k)$ be the value of z which maximises R on $A(k)$. By assumption $A(k)$ is strictly convex and so $z(\tilde{P}, k)$ is a vector valued function.

(ii) $R(\tilde{P}+h, k) \geqq (\tilde{P}+h)z(\tilde{P}, k) = R(\tilde{P}, k) + hz(\tilde{P}, k)$

$$R(\tilde{P}, k) \geqq \tilde{P}z(\tilde{P}+h, k) = R(\tilde{P}+h, k) - hz(\tilde{P}+h, k)$$

so

$$\frac{h(z(P+h,k)-z(P,k))}{|h|} \geqq \frac{R(\tilde{P}+h,k)-R(\tilde{P},k)-hz(\tilde{P},k)}{|h|} \geqq 0.$$

Since $h/|h|$ is bounded, the argument of (i) ensures that the left-hand side converges to zero.

(iii) Since $z(\tilde{P}, k)$ maximises $\tilde{P}z+\mu^*F(z)+\lambda^*z$ where μ^* is a positive scalar, λ^* a non-negative vector, $\lambda^*z(\tilde{P}, k) = 0$, the differentiability of $F(\cdot)$ establishes that of $R(\tilde{P}, k)$ with respect to k.

(b) (iv) The continuity of $z(\tilde{P}, k)$ over $S(k)$ is a well-established proposition for our assumptions. But $R_i(\tilde{P}, k) = z_i(\tilde{P}, k)$.

(v) $R_{m+i}(\tilde{P}, k)$ is proportional to

$$\frac{\partial F(z(\tilde{P},k)k).}{\partial k_i}$$

Since F is twice differentiable and $z(\tilde{P}, k)$ continuous on $S(k)$, $R_{m+i}(\tilde{P}, k)$ is continuous on $S(k)$.

One can now prove:

Theorem 1: If A.1, then the system:

$$R_{m+j}(P_0, P, k) = rP_j \quad (j = 1, \ldots, m)$$

$$R^0 - P_0R_0 = 0$$

$$(P_0, P) \in S(k)$$

has a solution, $Pk > 0$, $P_0 < 1$, $r > 0$.

Proof. Consider the mapping

$$T_i(P_0, P) = \min\,[1, Pk+\lambda(P_0R_0-R^0)]\,\frac{R_{m+i}}{R-R^0} \quad (i = 1, \ldots, m)$$

$$T_0(P_0, P) = \max\,[0, P_0+\lambda(R^0-P_0R_0)]$$

where I have omitted the argument of the functions.

By A.1, $R-R^0 > 0$ everywhere on $S(k)$. By Lemma 1, $T_i \geqq 0$ on $S(k)$. Also $\sum R_{m+i}k_i = R-R^0$ everywhere. If on $S(k)$, $Pk+\lambda[P_0R_0-R^0] \geqq 1$, then $P_0+\lambda[R^0-P_0R_0] \leqq 0$. Hence the mapping takes $S(k)$ into itself. By Lemma 2 it is continuous and so has a fixed point.

Let (P_0^*, P^*) be a fixed point. If $P_0^* = 1$, $R_0(P_0^*, P^*, k) = R(P_0^*, P^*, k)$. But by A.1: $R(P_0^*, P^*, k)-R^0(P_0^*, P^*, k) > 0$ and so by the definition of $T_0(\cdot)$, $(1, 0)$ cannot be a fixed point. A similar argument shows $P_0^* = 0$ to be impossible. Therefore $P^*k > 0$, $p_0^* > 0$, and $R^0 = P_0^* R_0$ at the fixed point. Also

$$r^* = \frac{R(P_0^*, P^*, k) - R^0(P_0^*, P^*, k)}{P^*k} > 0$$

$$P_i^* = \frac{1}{r^*} R_{m+i}(P_0^*, P^*, k) \quad (i = 1, \ldots, m).$$

The case of proportional savings and static expectations can be treated in a similar fashion. By an argument similar to that of Lemma 1, one establishes the existence of a scalar, $\mu > 0$, such that everywhere on $S(k)$:

$$Pk + \mu(P_0 R_0 - cR) \geqq 0, \quad 0 < c < 1.$$

The mapping used is that of Th.1. with $\mu(P_0R_0 - cR)$ replacing $\lambda(P_0R_0 - R^0)$ and with the analogous replacement in $T_0(\cdot)$.

IV. UNIQUENESS PROBLEMS

Since I have not assumed the absence of joint production, one cannot expect to find very economically appealing conditions which assure that for $k >> 0$ there is only one equilibrium. But even when joint production is excluded, the multiplicity of capital goods makes such meaningful conditions as there are, very artificial.

Consider the case of classical savings and static expectations. We know that, in any equilibrium, $P_0 > 0$, and we may accordingly, for the moment, change the price normalisation by setting $P_0 = 1$. Under this normalisation, since in the present case *the* rate of profit is well defined, we know that P is uniquely determined by r. (Factor price frontier arguments apply here.) If it were further the case that P is decreasing in r, as it would do if the consumption good used every capital good more intensively than does any other industry, then $R^0 - R_0$ would be monotone in r and uniqueness is assumed. But the story is surely very silly indeed.

For many purposes one is really interested in local uniqueness because the behaviour of the systems in the large is too complicated anyway. Let $\mathbf{B}(r) = [R_{m+j,i}] - r\mathbf{I}$, an $m \times m$ matrix, and let c be an m-vector with elements $R_j^0 - R_{0j}$. (I have here assumed $R(.)$ to be twice differentiable.) Then one wants $\mathbf{E}$ to be non-singular, where

$$\mathbf{E} = \begin{bmatrix} \mathbf{B} & -P \\ c & 0 \end{bmatrix}.$$

Of course **B** and c are evaluated at an equilibrium. Since

$$R_{m+i,j} = R_{j,m+i} \quad \text{and} \quad R_{j,m+i} = \frac{\partial y_j(1, P, k)}{\partial k_i},$$

one has $b = \mathbf{B}P$, where b is the vector with elements

$$\frac{\partial y_0(1, P, k)}{\partial k_j}.$$

If b is not null, one may reasonably argue that $\mathbf{B} = \mathbf{B}x$ has a unique solution $x = P$, so that **B** is not singular. This would certainly ensure that in a small neighbourhood P is uniquely determined by r. But that is not enough for the non-singularity of **E** and I can find no good interpretation other than the very special ones already discussed.

As is well known, the proportional savings assumption with static expectations does ensure a unique momentary equilibrium in the 'two-sector case'. This is so because the economy behaves 'as if' it were maximising a Cobb–Douglas utility function. With many capital goods this argument will no longer do. By the underlying assumptions, this 'as if' utility function would have the sum of investment outlay as an argument, and this is not sufficient for the desired result. In particular, the set of preferred vectors $(y_0(1, P, k), Py(1, P, k))$ will not in general be convex. Once again, in the no joint production case an intensity assumption seems to be required. Recall that in the 'two-sector case' the steady state is generally not unique and that this is due to the lack of one to oneness of the rate of profit and the value capital–output ratio. Intensity assumptions overcome this difficulty. In the present case, if $Py(1, P, k)/Pk$ (which is the value output–capital ratio) is one to one with the rate of profit, as it will be under suitable intensity assumptions, the momentary equilibrium is unique for given k.

I do not pursue these matters simply because I can find no economically interesting conditions for momentary uniqueness.

V. STABILITY

I shall begin by a brief re-examination of the case of correct myopic foresight with classical savings.

Certainly the assumptions ensure the existence of a unique steady state. I denote it by an asterisk and I write R_p and R_k as the vectors (R_i) and (R_{m+i}), evaluated at the steady state. $\mathbf{R}_{pp}$, $\mathbf{R}_{pk}$, etc., are the matrices of second derivatives of R. Also **H** is a $2m \times 2m$ matrix:

$$\begin{pmatrix} \mathbf{R}_{pk} - n\mathbf{I} & \mathbf{R}_{pp} \\ -\mathbf{R}_{kk} & -\mathbf{R}_{kp} + n\mathbf{I} \end{pmatrix}$$

Since $\mathbf{R}_{pp}$ is positive definite, $\mathbf{R}_{kk}$ negative semi-definite, $\mathbf{R}_{pk} = \mathbf{R}_{kp}$, $\mathbf{H}$ has the 'saddle-point property', i.e. if λ is a root, so is $-\lambda$.

I am concerned with linear approximations near the steady state. I may write

$$\dot{r} = c' \begin{pmatrix} k-k^* \\ P-P^* \\ r-n \end{pmatrix}$$

where c' is a $2m+1$ vector, and of course $r^* = n$. The whole system becomes:

$$\begin{pmatrix} \dot{k} \\ \dot{P} \\ \dot{r} \end{pmatrix} = \left(\begin{array}{c|c} \mathbf{H} & \begin{matrix} 0 \\ P^* \end{matrix} \\ \hline \multicolumn{2}{c}{c'} \end{array}\right) \begin{pmatrix} k-k^* \\ P-P^* \\ r-n \end{pmatrix}$$

Let $\mathbf{H}$ have distinct roots, and let $\mathbf{\Lambda}$ be the diagonal matrix of these roots. Then there exists a matrix $\mathbf{T}$ such that

$$\mathbf{T}^{-1}\mathbf{HT} = \mathbf{\Lambda}$$

Define z by

$$\begin{pmatrix} \mathbf{T} & 0 \\ 0 & 1 \end{pmatrix} z = (k-k^*, P-P^*, r-n).$$

Then one finds:

$$\dot{z}_i = \lambda_i z_i \quad (i = 1, \ldots, m)$$

$$\dot{z}_{m+i} = \lambda_{m+i} z_{m+i} - P_i^*(r-n) \quad (i = 1, \ldots, m).$$

Suppose that it is asserted that $z_i(t) \to 0$ for all i, $r(t) \to n$. Then certainly $Rl(\lambda_i) < 0$, $i = 1, \ldots, m$, where $Rl(\cdot)$ stands for 'real part of the root'.

But also then $Rl(\lambda_{m+i}) > 0$, $i = 1, \ldots, m$, and

$$z_{m+i}(t) = e^{(\lambda_{m+i})t} \int_0^t e^{-(\lambda_{m+i})u}(r(u)-n)du + e^{(\lambda_{m+i})t} c_{m+i}.$$

By assumption the integral is bounded. But then in general it will not be the case that $z_{m+i}(t) \to 0$. Hence the system is not in general stable. I do not pursue this further beyond noting how useful the dual formulation is for this case. It is of course closely connected with the Hamiltonian of an appropriate intertemporal efficiency problem.

Let me now turn to the inefficient paths generated by an economy with stationary expectations and classical savings.

I am once again concerned with expansions close to the steady state.

From $rPk = Py$ one obtains easily

$$(r-n) = P^*\dot{k}/P^*k^*.$$

If one could show that

$$P^*(k-k^*)(r-n) < 0$$

everywhere, then one would have enough to deduce stability. From

$$R_k = rP$$

one obtains

$$\mathbf{R}_{kk}(k-k^*)+\mathbf{R}_{kp}(P-P^*)-n(P-P^*) = (r-n)P^*$$

so

$$(k'-k^*)'\mathbf{R}_{kk}(k-k^*)+(k-k^*)'[\mathbf{R}_{kp}-n\mathbf{I}](P-P^*) = (r-n)P^*(k-k^*).$$

Certainly $\mathbf{R}_{kk}$ is negative semi-definite, but we have no information on the second term on the left-hand side. In general, therefore, no easy answer is available and one suspects that there certainly may be cases where the system is unstable.

As an example, let me consider the following stable case. I write

$$F(y_0 y, k) = G(y, k)-y_0 = 0$$

with

$$G(y, k) = y'\mathbf{A}y+\sum \log k_i\alpha_i$$

where $\mathbf{A}$ is a negative definite matrix and $\mathbf{B} = -\mathbf{A}^{-1}$ is positive. Routine calculations give

$$R_p = \mathbf{B}P$$

$$R_k = \{\alpha_i/k_i\}.$$

One notes that R_p is independent of k and R_k independent of P. This is just the sort of situation one would expect to be well behaved.

It is easy to check that momentary equilibrium is unique. Also $\mathbf{R}_{kp} = \mathbf{R}_{pk} = 0$. Also, since $R_k = rP$, one has

$$rP'k = \sum \alpha_i$$

whence $Py = rP'k$ is a constant and

$$(P-P^*)y^*+P^*(y-y^*) = (P-P^*)'\mathbf{B}P^*+P^*\mathbf{B}(P-P^*).$$

But $\mathbf{B}$ is symmetric and so

$$P^*\mathbf{B}(P-P^*) = 0.$$

Now

$$\dot{k} = -\mathbf{I}n(k-k^*)+\mathbf{B}(P-P^*)$$

and

$$P^*\dot{k} = -P^*n(k-k^*)+P^*\mathbf{B}(P-P^*) = -P^*(k-k^*)$$

which is what one wants.

It is plain that this is a very special case indeed. For instance, the relative equilibrium value of capital goods are independent of prices and of endowments. Also, it is easily checked that momentary equilibria are unique. Shell and Stiglitz discuss an even more special situation which in the context of this example would arise if $\sum \alpha_i \log k_i$ were replaced by $\alpha \sum \log k_i$. Then the relative prices of capital goods would be constant and capital goods could be aggregated.

The special cases suggest that the system may do better than it does under myopic expectations, but it is not the case that it *must* do better. Before discussing this, it is instructive to return to the traditional two-sector model with classical savings. Suppose it to be the case that for a small displacement of the capital–labour ratio from its steady-state value, one can always find a momentary equilibrium such that the rate of profit deviates from n in the same direction as the capital–labour ratio does. Then because of the Inada (1963) conditions, momentary equilibrium cannot be unique in the vicinity of the steady state. Although Inada has given an example of instability in this case, the use of ordinary differential equation analysis is difficult. In any event the steady state may be unstable only when momentary equilibrium is not unique.

The question arises whether the same conclusion holds when there are a number of different capital goods. To investigate this, I must first make a small digression.

Suppose there is no joint production anywhere. Suppose $k \neq k'$ (k is again a vector), but let r be the same in both situations. Certainly, from the substitution theorem, P will be the same in both situations. Suppose that it is possible to find a product mix such that all inputs are utilised fully when the endowment is k' or k. Then the rental of each capital good will be the same in both situations and both will be momentarily efficient. By this I mean that with k (or k') it is impossible to produce more of one good without producing less of another. Hence revenue will be at a maximum in both situations, and since the shadow and private rental coincide, $R_k(P, k) = R_k(P, k')$. Hence for certain ranges of the domain of R, R is linear in k. In particular, that will be the case in the vicinity of a steady state where all goods are produced in positive quantities. Note that by the strict concavity of $F(\cdot)$ there is a one to one correspondence between P and product mix. Hence if, because of factor reversal, another r, say r', were also to give the same P, it could not find a product mix which utilised all resources.

With this in mind, one may write the linear expansion of $nP^*-R_k(\cdot)$ about the steady state as

$$(n\mathbf{I}-\mathbf{R}_{kp})(P-P^*)+e(r-n) = 0,$$

where e is the unit vector. One notes that if $\mathbf{R}_{kp}$ were a positive matrix, $(n\mathbf{I}-\mathbf{R}_{kp})$ would not have a positive inverse. To see this, choose units such that $P^* = e$. Since R_k is homogeneous of degree one in all prices, one has for the ith row of $\mathbf{R}_{kp}$:

$$\sum_{j=0} R_{m+i,j} = n-R_{m+i,0}.$$

But $R_{m+i,j} = R_{j,m+i}$. So if $R_{m+i,j} > 0$ all j, $R_{j,m+i} > 0$ all j. That means that there is an increase in the production of every capital good when there is an increase in the amount of the ith capital good and prices are constant. But then there cannot be an increase in the output of consumption good and indeed $R_{0,m+i} = R_{m+i,0} < 0$. But then

$$\sum_{j\neq 0} R_{m+i,j} > n$$

and this is true for all j, whence by a well-known theorem $(n\mathbf{I}-\mathbf{R}_{kp})$ does not have a positive inverse when $\mathbf{R}_{kp}$ is positive. Of course, if $\mathbf{R}_{kp}$ is not positive, this is not necessarily true.

If momentary equilibrium in the vicinity of the steady state is not unique, a local expansion may make no sense. I shall accordingly assume that the production of the consumption good is more intensive in every machine than is the production of any other good. Even so strong an assumption does not take us very far in the present case.

From the requirement that in each momentary equilibrium the demand for consumption goods should equal its supply, I find

$$\begin{pmatrix} 0 \\ -\sum R_{0,m+j}(k_j-k_j^*) \end{pmatrix} = \begin{pmatrix} \mathbf{A} & ne \\ (R_{0j}) & P^*k^*n \end{pmatrix} \begin{pmatrix} P-P^* \\ \dfrac{r-n}{n} \end{pmatrix}$$

where $\mathbf{A} = (n\mathbf{I}-\mathbf{R}_{kp})$ and $\{R_{0j}\}$ is the vector with components R_{0j}. It is clear that even if, say, $\mathbf{A}$ should have a positive inverse, this does not give one very much information. Indeed, suppose that the matrix on the right is a P-matrix. Then it is trivial to show that

$$\text{sign}\,(r-n) = \text{sign}\, -\sum R_{0,m+j}(k_j-k_j^*).$$

But even so, and even taking $R_{0,m+j} > 0$ all j, this is not quite what we require since $\sum P_j^*(k_j-k_j^*)$ need not have the same sign as $\sum R_{0,m+j}(k_j-k_j^*)$. Certainly, in this case if every capital good is increased beyond the steady state, the rate of profit must be lower, but this is a poor result. It would tell us that the system cannot 'explode', but it would not, for instance, exclude the possibility that in the phase space of the capital goods the steady state is a saddle-point. Indeed, elsewhere (Hahn, 1970) I have given an example where this is so.

Let the solution for $(r-n)$ in the above equations be written $y(k-k^*)$. Then the output system becomes

$$\dot{k} = -\mathbf{A}(k-k^*)+\mathbf{BA}^{-1}ey(k-k^*).$$

There is nothing useful one can say about this even if **A** has a positive inverse, and of course **B** is known to be positive definite.

One must conclude that uniqueness of momentary equilibrium with stationary expectations does not, as in the two-sector case, ensure stability. The reasons now seem to me obvious: with many capital goods the uniqueness assumption is not enough to ensure that the rate of profit and the value of the capital–labour ratio are related in any simple way. In the two-sector case one can reduce the system to a miniature general-equilibrium one in labour and capital. It is known that a two-goods general-equilibrium system has a unique equilibrium if and only if the Weak Axiom of Revealed Preference holds. In this context, the Weak Axiom is simply the 'proper' relationship between the rate of profit and the capital stock. When the Weak Axiom holds, stability also is assured. In a many-good world the Weak Axiom is sufficient for uniqueness but not necessary.

It may be instructive to see how far one can get. I choose an example in which production functions are everywhere Cobb–Douglas.

I write α_{ij} as the share of the ith capital good in the receipts of the production of the jth, α_{i0} as its share in the receipts of the consumption sector. Also, the suffix '0' refers both to labour and consumption good and

$$\beta_{ij} = \alpha_{ij}\alpha_{00}-\alpha_{i0}\alpha_{0j}, \;\; \mathbf{B} = [\beta_{ij}]\,\frac{1}{\alpha_{00}}.$$

I suppose the consumption sector to be more intensive in the use of any capital good than is any capital good. (Note the absurdity of this.) This makes **B** a negative matrix which I assume to be non-singular. One calculates at P^*-e that $\mathbf{R}_{kp} = n\mathbf{B}^{-1}$ and

$$(P-P^*) = \frac{r-n}{n}\,e\mathbf{B}(\mathbf{I}-\mathbf{B})^{-1} \tag{9.10}$$

and verifies that $(P-P^*)$ is inversely related to $(r-n)$.

The basic differential equations are

$$\dot{k} = (\mathbf{B}^{-1} - \mathbf{I})(k - k^*)n + \mathbf{R}_{pp}(P - P^*)$$

or

$$-\mathbf{B}\dot{k} = -(\mathbf{I} - \mathbf{B})(k - k^*)n - \mathbf{B}R_{pp}(P - P^*).$$

Let $\mathbf{C} = (\mathbf{I} - \mathbf{B})^{-1}$, then also after substitution from (9.10)

$$-e'\mathbf{CB}\dot{k} = -e'n\mathbf{I}(k - k^*) - e'\mathbf{CBR}_{pp}\mathbf{C}'\mathbf{B}'e\frac{r-n}{n}. \qquad (9.11)$$

Let $v = e'\mathbf{CB}R_{pp}e$. Then, since $\mathbf{R}_{pp}$ is positive definite, $v > 0$. Also, we know that the classical savings assumption gives $e'\dot{k} = (r-n)e'k^*$. Then finally one has

$$e'(w\mathbf{I} - \mathbf{CB})\dot{k} = -ne'(k - k^*) \qquad (9.12)$$

where $w = v/ne'k^*$. The left-hand matrix is positive.

From (9.12) one concludes that in the vicinity of the steady state, if the value, at steady-state prices, of capital per man is higher (lower) than in the steady state, a certain weighted sum of capital per man must be falling (rising).

This seems to be the furthest one can get, and it is not very far, even though the case is a rather favourable one. For instance, (9.12) does not exclude the saddle-point property of the steady state in the phase space of k. Moreover, in the Cobb–Douglas case certainly, the strong intensity assumption is not required to give a unique momentary equilibrium. When it is not used, all is confusion.

VI. SOME CONCLUSIONS

The reason for dwelling so long on the case with static price expectations is this. When I first noted that the case of myopically correct expectations may be ill behaved, I and most others believed that this was simply due to the 'catenary' property of paths that satisfy the necessary condition of intertemporal efficiency. It seemed that the case of static expectations ought to do much better. This belief was reinforced by a misinterpretation of a well-known result due to Morishima: he showed that if the steady-state rate of profit is always expected to rule, then the price system would be stable and the output system might be so. This of course is a different problem and in any case does not claim that outputs must converge on the steady state.

It would now seem to me that all these beliefs were mistaken. Even with static expectations, heterogeneous capital means that we are dealing with many goods, and as students of general equilibrium know, there are no theories which, for instance, ensure a link between uniqueness and stability. The fact that the rate of profit is not simply related to some measure of the capital stock is here the main source of trouble, and this trouble does not arise when there is only one capital good or when the relative prices of capital goods are always constant. The question of whether the economy tends to the steady state has no simple answer at present; I should add again that I doubt that the equilibrium dynamics approach to answering it is the proper one.

REFERENCES

F. H. Hahn, 'Equilibrium Dynamics with Heterogeneous Capital Goods', *Quarterly Journal of Economics* (1966).

—— 'On Some Adjustment Problems', *Econometrica* (Jan 1970).

K. Inada, 'On a Two-Sector Model of Economic Growth', *Review of Economic Studies* (June 1963).

K. Shell and J. E. Stiglitz, 'The Allocation of Investment in a Dynamic Economy', *Quarterly Journal of Economics* (1967).

Discussion of the Paper by F. H. Hahn

Professor Hahn introduced his paper by emphasising that he did not believe that the analysis of equilibrium paths was the appropriate way of understanding the process of capitalist accumulation. He thought the Solow 1956 article and the two-sector models had led us astray.

There was one real point of substance in his paper apart from the dual formulation of growth theory (he found many problems were much more simple to handle in terms of the dual). This point turns on the significance of having many capital goods. We know that with myopic expectations the necessary conditions of intertemporal inefficiency lead normally to equilibrium paths that are errant. In the paper he had shown that there was a further feature of heterogeneous capital goods models which arises even with static expectations and does not arise with a one-capital-good (two-sector) model. In the latter, a necessary and sufficient condition for unique momentary equilibrium is that the Weak Axiom of Revealed Preference holds in comparison with the given equilibrium. This in turn means that 'perverse Wicksell effects' cannot occur when equilibrium is unique. With many capital goods, the Weak Axiom is sufficient but not necessary for uniqueness. Hence, even when equilibrium is unique, 'perverse' Wicksell effects can arise with unpleasant consequences for stability. He then gave a proof that the Weak Axiom is necessary for uniqueness in the two-sector case.

Let there be two goods produced with prices p_1, p_2, and let there be two inputs with prices w_1, w_2 (we could think of w_2 as, say, the 'rental' of capital). From cost minimisation we obtain

$$p = C(w_1, w_2) \tag{1}$$

Assume, since there are constant returns to scale, that at p satisfying (1) producers always try to supply what is demanded. Hence the excess demands in the goods market are zero. Let z_i be the excess demand for input i, $z_i = z_i(p, w_1, w_2)$. Using (1),

$$z_i = z_i(w_1, w_2) \quad i = 1, 2.$$

By Walras's Law, since the two goods markets are in equilibrium,

$$\sum_{i=1}^{2} w_i z_i(w_1, w_2) = 0.$$

We want to show that if $w^* = (w_1^*, w_2^*)$ is a unique equilibrium, then (with some normalisation)

$$\sum w_i^* z_i(w_1, w_2) > 0 \tag{2}$$

when $w \neq w^*$.

Suppose for some $w \neq w^*$ we had

$$\sum_{i=1}^{2} w_i^* z_i(w_1, w_2) \leqq 0. \tag{3}$$

Since w is not an equilibrium, $z_i(w_1, w_2) > 0$ for $i = 1$ or 2. Suppose $z_1(w_1, w_2) > 0$ (so that $z_2(w_1, w_2) \leqq 0$). Then $w_2 > 0$ (for ($w_2 = 0$ implies $z_1 = 0$ from Walras's Law.) We also have $w_2{}^* > 0$ (otherwise $z_1 = 0$ from (3)). Using Walras's Law and (3), we have

$$\frac{w_1}{w_2} = \frac{-z_2}{z_1} \geqq \frac{w_1{}^*}{w_2{}^*};$$

and in fact, since

$$w \neq w^*, \quad \frac{w_1}{w_2} > \frac{w_1{}^*}{w_2{}^*} \quad \text{(in particular } w_1 > 0).$$

Thus we can reduce w_2 towards zero and still have $w \neq w^*$. If $z_1(w_1, w_2{}^1) = 0$ for some $w_2{}^1$, $0 < w_2{}^1 < w_2$, $(w_1, w_2{}^{11})$ is an equilibrium where $w_2{}^{11}$ is the maximum of such $w_2{}^1$. Otherwise $z_1(w_1, 0) \geqq 0$, while $z_2(w_1, 0) \leqq 0$ (since $z_2 \leqq 0$ whenever $z_1 > 0$). By Walras in fact $z_1 = 0$ and $(w_1, 0)$ is an equilibrium. This contradiction establishes (2) – the necessity of the Weak Axiom.

He pointed out that if he could have found a utility function which implied a savings rate of zero (workers) and one which implied a savings rate of unity (capitalists), then his Theorem 1 (existence) would have been easier to prove.

Professor Weizsäcker suggested that, if workers had a utility function which implied a very high time preference rate and they were unable to borrow, then they would consume everything.

Professor Shell said that Professor Hahn had provided a clear explanation of his paper. He thought a brief review of the history of the general problem would be useful.

The trouble began with Hahn's *Quarterly Journal of Economics* (1966) contribution. In a model with m machine goods, one consumption good, myopically correct expectations, classical (i.e. Marxian) saving and Cobb–Douglas production functions, it was found that:

(1) Momentary equilibrium is not necessarily unique. Sufficient conditions for uniqueness of momentary equilibrium have no obvious economic interpretation. He would argue that lack of uniqueness creates no special problems for economic analysis, although it raises some new mathematical difficulties.

(2) The long-run balanced growth equilibrium is unique. In a particular example, the dynamical system $(\dot{k}, \dot{p}) = \phi(k, p)$ is such that the unique rest-point (k^*, p^*) is a saddle-point. k is the m-vector of capital–labour ratios and p is the m-vector of capital-goods prices.

(3) Paths not tending to (k^*, p^*) tend to obviously inefficient oblivion.

Hahn drew the following conclusions:

(i) Real heterogeneous life is apparently unstable and is very different from the Solow story.

(ii) The invisible hand in the infinite horizon sequence economy is not effective – capitalism is doomed – he called it the 'golden nail in the coffin of capitalism'.

(iii) He posed the question of the structure of dynamical system of the capitalist sequence economy.

These questions were investigated in the special model of Shell and Stiglitz, *Quarterly Journal of Economics* (1967).

In the special model, although momentary equilibrium is not unique, this causes no new economic difficulties. If capitalism can cope with the instability of the system it should be able to cope when momentary allocation is set-valued. In Professor Hahn's paper here, since the production set is strictly convex, uniqueness obtains and the needed derivatives exist everywhere.

In the second model the unique rest-point is a generalised saddle-point. It is shown that paths not tending to the unique rest point (k^*, p^*) have some p_i zero (or infinite) in finite time. Such errant trajectories are thus revealed not to be competitive equilibrium paths. With sufficient futures markets and/or long-run foresight, capitalism may be able to steer clear of this dangerous development.

He and Professor Stiglitz had shown that for all initial endowments development tends to (k^*, p^*) with static price expectations. This result holds only for this special model, as Hahn has made clear in his papers here and earlier. Instability can even arise in the Uzawa model where the capital-goods sector is more capital-intensive than the consumption-goods sector. Capital gains play no role in the stability of the Uzawa model. The general point is that the lower the coefficient of adaptation of price expectations, the greater the *tendency* towards stability.

As to the 'general Hahn problem', he conjectured that in a model with myopically correct expectations about capital gains, and unique rest-point (k^*, p^*), the dynamic system can be written as $(\dot{k}, \dot{p}) \in \mathfrak{L}(k, p)$ where $\mathfrak{L}(.)$ is an upper semi-continuous correspondence. Furthermore, the manifold of solutions tending to (k^*, p^*) as $t \to \infty$ is of dimension m (in $2m$-space) as is the manifold of solutions tending to (k^*, p^*) as $t \to -\infty$. Paths not tending to (k^*, p^*) as $t \to \infty$ are revealed as disequilibrium paths in finite time. The study of the above system could follow the general mathematical theory of Bhatia and Szegö or the more particular mathematical analyses of Cellini and Aumann.

He said the basic reason why we had uniqueness of momentary equilibrium in Uzawa's model was that we had convexity of the production set in consumption–investment space and a constant savings ratio could be represented by a utility function $c^{1-s}z^{1-s}$.

Professor Yaari asked if reducing Professor Hahn's theorem to a two-period problem with a simple utility function might not make the proof easier.

Professor Hahn said that we could derive the Weak Axiom of Revealed Preference in comparison with a given equilibrium from the gross substitutes assumption.

(1) In the Hicks case where everyone was alike we had

$$(p'-p)(z(p')-z(p)) < 0, \quad p \neq p'.$$

(2) In the Gross Substitutes case we had if $p^* \in E$, the set of equilibria, and $p \neq p^*$,

$$p^*z(p) > 0.$$

(3) In the Weak Gross Substitutes case we had for $p^* \in E$ and $p \notin E$

$$p^*z(p) > 0.$$

He thought that all discussions of heterogeneous capital goods could be put in a general-equilibrium framework. That serious stability problems can arise is indicated by the demonstration of Hildebrand that if the general equilibrium depends on parameters (say stocks), then small changes in these parameters can lead to large changes in the equilibrium.

He also quoted a theorem of Debreu which (loosely) stated that where we have neither a continuum of agents nor a continuum of goods, the class of economies with an infinity of equilibria has measure zero. *Dr Dixit* added that for Debreu's theorem it was necessary to assume differentiable demand functions.

Professor Bruno said he thought the static expectations model had been over-stressed. Static expectations had to turn out false or we would effectively be in a one-commodity world. We should ask how prices and expectations actually would change.

Professor Hahn agreed that static expectations were unreasonable. He thought, however, that the work on myopia was more relevant to the stock exchange than capital theory. People do not usually buy machines in order to sell them immediately.

Solow thought he was discussing the Harrodian problem when he was considering a series of momentary equilibria. However, Harrod was not considering equilibrium paths but paths where mistakes were being continually made. Our models are all frictionless, but perhaps friction and the mistakes were good for stability.

Professor Uzawa said myopic expectations were most likely to be relevant where transaction costs were small, e.g. for monetary as opposed to real assets.

Professor Shell thought that society usually intervened in financial markets to promote stability: stock exchange trading was suspended if there was a certain amount of excitement. He thought that the absence of certain markets might help to promote stability. He thought the infinite horizon was an important difference between a real and an Arrow–Debreu world.

Professor Uzawa thought that the emphasis on the importance of many capital goods was misleading. The important destabilising assumptions were the liquidity of assets and ease of marketing. Both of these were inapplicable in a wide variety of cases. The number of assets was not the essence of the problem.

Professor Shell agreed that the major driving-force in these models was the asset market.

Professor Rose said that there were no stability problems in a macro-model, provided there were no monetary complications.

Professor Hahn said it was difficult to compare a macro-model with the underlying general-equilibrium one. The macro-behaviour of these many-sector models might not look too bad.

He agreed that the important economic questions centred around the marketability of assets and the non-existence of perfect second-hand markets for machines (where selling costs were very high) rather than the number of goods. Our previous problems arose because we assumed people flipped in and out of assets as in Keynes's chapter 18. The myopic instability theorem was only of mathematical interest. However, it was difficult to provide theoretical constructs such as efficiency definitions when we had transaction, information, and research costs in the model.

Part 5

Optimal Growth

10 Taxation and Public Production in a Growth Setting*

Peter A. Diamond

MASSACHUSETTS INSTITUTE OF TECHNOLOGY

I. INTRODUCTION

The inability of government to achieve full optimality gives interest to the study of the maximisation of social welfare using different sets of control variables. Three growth models will be considered in this paper to examine this maximisation in different settings. The basic model used in all three analyses has several consumer goods (including labour) in each period and a single capital good for affecting future production possibilities. The welfare function is a discounted sum of individual utilities where individuals are assumed to live for two periods, with successive generations overlapping. The first model is of a fully controlled economy where the planners control quantities directly. The model is also considered in a decentralised setting where prices, lump-sum incomes and public debt are controlled by the planners. In the second model the planners are assumed to be unable to affect lump-sum incomes. They have full control, however, over consumer and producer prices (and public debt). In the third model it is assumed that there are taxes only on income and the return to savings, rather than separate taxes on each commodity. Each model is preceded by a discussion of the same policy tools in a static setting. The models are set up to permit use of dynamic programming for derivation of first-order conditions. Neither the existence of an optimum nor the convergence of an optimum path have been proved, although both elements are assumed in the analysis.[1]

Not surprisingly, the analysis of growth repeats the results of static analysis in each of the three models. In addition, there are the asymptotic properties of the models. In the fully controlled and fully taxed economies, aggregate efficiency between public and private production is desired and the marginal product of capital tends to the

* This paper is an outgrowth of my work with James Mirrlees and shows clearly the influence of our discussions. In addition I wish to thank Michael Rothschild and Robert Solow for discussions on this paper, and the National Science Foundation for financial support.

[1] Radner (1967) has used dynamic programming to examine optimal growth and has explored the question of existence of an optimum for a somewhat different model from the one here.

discount rate in both models, satisfying the modified golden rule. However, the equality of asymptotic marginal products in the two models will in general reflect different amounts of capital per worker, for the different tax tools will result in differences in labour per worker. In the partially taxed economy aggregate efficiency is not desired as part of the optimal solution and the marginal product of public capital tends to the discount rate. Unfortunately no progress has been made on relating this to the marginal product of private capital. It is a consequence of constant returns to scale, however, that marginal products in both sectors should have the same weighted average, the weights being the privately supplied quantities.

The presence of overlapping generations in the optimal growth model introduces two concepts of the intertemporal social marginal rate of substitution. It is natural to look at an individual's intertemporal personal marginal rate of substitution and alternatively to consider transferring consumption over time between members of successive generations. In the fully controlled economy, equality of these two rates is part of the optimality conditions. In the fully taxed economy, however, the two concepts will have different values in general. Asymptotically, the second concept will equal the marginal rate of transformation. This reflects the dominance of the stationary nature of the steady state in describing certain intertemporal consumption and production possibilities.

To my knowledge, the problem of public investment criteria in an optimal growth model where full optimality is not achieved has received little attention. Only the work of Arrow and Kurz (1969) has come to my attention. They consider a one-commodity growth model (with labour supplied inelastically) where savings are a fixed fraction of disposable income. The consider income taxation and the public debt as control variables. With just an income tax they find that aggregate efficiency is not desired in general and that the asymptotic return to public capital should equal the consumption rate of interest. With an income tax and borrowing the full optimum is achievable. They also consider several other combinations of available policies. In spirit this analysis is close to theirs except that the problems preventing full optimality in this paper are also problems facing a static economy rather than arising particularly in the growth context.

II. SYMMETRY BETWEEN PUBLIC AND PRIVATE PRODUCTION

There are a number of differences between the positions of publicly and privately controlled production possibilities in an optimal growth model.[1] Under certain sets of assumptions, these differences will vanish and the two production possibilities will enter the model symmetrically. When this is true, the symmetry of the production constraints will lead to symmetry in first-order conditions; that is, equality of marginal rates of transformation in the two sectors will be part of the optimality conditions. The optimal growth problem can then be simplified by considering a single production possibility set rather than two sets.

If planners directly control all quantities, there is symmetry between publicly and privately controlled production assuming bureaucrats and entrepreneurs both follow planners' directives. In such a model, the distinction between the two sectors is not clear and, perhaps, non-existent. If we continue to assume quantity controls for public production, but only price controls for private production, we have several differences between the two. These arise from the constraints on quantities that can be attained by price controls and from the effects on budget constraints of the owners of the private firms. Let us consider the latter question first.

The profits (or losses) of publicly owned firms enter the government's budget constraint, while those of private firms enter the budget of firm owners. If the government has the power to levy lump-sum taxes, differing individual by individual, this difference does not matter, for the pattern of lump-sum taxes can be adjusted for any pattern of profits. If the government does not have lump-sum tax powers, this ceases to be true in general. The ability to levy profits taxes at 100 per cent could eliminate profits, but with just commodity taxes the government cannot change real incomes in the same way as by lowering the profit-tax rate. Thus, in some circumstances the profit tax will be less than 100 per cent and the payment of profits will introduce a difference between public and private production. The assumption of constant returns to scale in privately controlled production implies the absence of profits and thus symmetry from this point of view.

In an economy where there are no lump-sum taxes, the planners will want to use their ability to tax transactions between producers and consumers to improve the distribution of income. This introduces a further difference between public and private in that consumer prices equal private producer prices plus taxes rather than government shadow prices plus taxes. If the government can tax each commodity at an individually chosen rate this difference does

[1] The extremely important question of allocating production possibilities between public and private control will not be considered in this paper. The analysis will be of a given division between public and private without inquiring into the source of the division.

not matter, for the government has full control over consumer prices, with appropriate tax setting, independent of producer prices. Thus in the fully taxed economy there is no asymmetry introduced by this element. If, however, the government's ability to distinguish goods for tax purposes is limited, then we shall have a basic asymmetry. Thus in the partially taxed economy considered below we shall need to distinguish public from private production.

In addition to the asymmetries arising from the different interactions between consumers with public and private producers, there are asymmetries in the relationships between producers and planners. With government-controlled production the planners are usually thought of as able to choose quantities. With private production the planners only choose prices. If private production possibilities are convex, have free disposal and no externalities, and are controlled by price-taking profit maximisers, the planners can select any point on the private production frontier by a suitable choice of prices. (The problem of selecting a particular point in a firm's supply correspondence is ignored.) Thus from the viewpoint of production there is symmetry if conditions are such that planners never choose a point in the interior of the public production possibility set. An interior point might be desired if a consumer has a satiation point or, in the absence of lump-sum taxes, if social preferences are not expressible as a function of individual preferences or if there exists no good whose price change unambiguously increases welfare.[1] In considering the fully controlled and fully taxed economies, we shall assume that production on the frontier is desired. With the other assumptions mentioned above, this permits us to simplify the model and consider a single production set. With the partially taxed economy, we shall consider public and private production separately.

III. FULLY CONTROLLED ECONOMY

As a reference point for later models, it is natural to begin by considering a fully controlled economy. This is the standard optimal growth problem except that the objective function sums individual lifetime utilities, introducing an interdependence between consumption levels at different times. Naturally, this restatement does not lead to unexpected results – we shall obtain the conditions for static and intertemporal Pareto optimality, for optimal income distribution and for the asymptotic capital–labour ratio which satisfies the modified golden rule. We shall also briefly consider the economy in a decentralised setting to examine the role of public debt.

[1] For examples, see Diamond and Mirrlees (1968).

It is assumed that each individual lives for two periods. (The choice of two periods is inessential for the analysis and avoids complicating the problem even further.) Let us denote by

$$a_t = (a_{1t}, \ldots, a_{mt})$$

$$b_t = (b_{1t}, \ldots, b_{mt})$$

the vectors of net consumption and labour by a typical individual in generation t in the two periods of his life.[1] The consumption of a_t and b_t occurs in periods t and $t+1$. We shall denote the utility level of a typical individual in generation t by u_t:

$$u_t = u(a_t, b_t). \tag{10.1}$$

To identify arguments of functions when calculating partial derivatives we shall use just time as the argument of the function. We shall also use subscript letters to denote vectors of partial derivatives. For example:

$$u_a(t) = \left(\frac{\partial u(a_t, b_t)}{\partial a_1}, \ldots, \frac{\partial u(a_t, b_t)}{\partial a_m}\right).$$

We assume that population grows at the rate $n-1$. Denoting the size of generation t by L_t we have

$$L_t = Ln^t. \tag{10.2}$$

We can now express the objective function as the discounted sum of individual utilities

$$\sum_{t=1}^{\infty} n^t \delta^t u_t$$

where it is assumed that the product of the discount and growth factors is less than one ($n\delta < 1$).

To describe production, we shall assume the existence of a single capital good which carries over from one period to the next. The level of capital at the end of period t, K_t, depends on the capital brought into period t, K_{t-1}, and the vector of net outputs in period t, $Y_t = (Y_{1t}, \ldots, Y_{mt})$:

$$K_t = F(K_{t-1}, Y_t). \tag{10.3}$$

Let us measure capital negatively (like firm demands) to make F_y a positive vector. We assume that F displays constant returns to scale. Let us denote by $k_t (= K_t/L_{t+1})$ the amount of capital brought into

[1] By appealing to the aggregation analysis in Samuelson (1956) we can interpret these results as representing an economy with differences among individuals with the numbers of each type of individual growing at the same rate.

period $t+1$ per member of the $t+1$st generation and by $y_t(= Y_t/L_t)$ net output per member of the tth generation. Then we have

$$k_t = n^{-1}F(k_{t-1}, y_t). \tag{10.4}$$

The economy is further constrained in that net output must equal the sum of net consumptions of the two generations alive at any time:

$$y_t = a_t + n^{-1}b_{t-1}. \tag{10.5}$$

To place this problem in a dynamic programming setting it is natural to take the generation rather than the time period as the planning unit. This creates a problem with the level of second-period consumption for the older generation at the start of the planning process (b_0). To fit the stationary nature of the problem we shall assume that b_0 is given; that is, the planners have a commitment to supply a fixed consumption bundle to the older generation. We could introduce further choice into this problem, having calculated the conditions for an optimal path given any level of b_0, by then considering the choice of b_0 either by adding $u(a_0, b_0)$ to the objective function, or, perhaps, by dealing differently with the 0th generation because the earlier part of their lives is part of history, not the planning process. We can now state welfare maximisation as

$$\text{Maximise} \sum_{t=1}^{\infty} n^t \delta^t u_t \tag{10.6}$$

$$\text{subject to (10.1), (10.4) and (10.5)}$$
$$k_0 = \bar{k}_0, \quad b_0 = \bar{b}_0.$$

Let us consider the state valuation function, $w(k_t, b_t)$, which gives the maximal level of welfare from time $t+1$ to infinity discounted back to time $t+1$. Then, by the principle of optimality of dynamic programming[1] and the stationarity of the economy, the state valuation function must satisfy (equations (10.4) and (10.5) have been used to eliminate k_{t+1} and y_{t+1} from this expression)

$$w(k_t, b_t) = \max_{a_{t+1}, b_{t+1}} \{u(a_{t+1}, b_{t+1}) + n\delta w(n^{-1}F(k_t, a_{t+1}+n^{-1}b_t), b_{t+1})\}. \tag{10.7}$$

The first-order conditions for the optimal growth path are obtained by differentiating the fundamental equation (10.7) with respect to the parameters k_t and b_t and by obtaining first-order conditions from the maximand in (10.7). These give us the following equations:

[1] See, e.g., Bellman (1957).

$$w_k(t) = \delta w_k(t+1)F_k(t+1) \tag{10.8}$$

$$w_b(t) = n^{-1}\delta w_k(t+1)F_y(t+1) \tag{10.9}$$

$$u_a(t+1)+\delta w_k(t+1)F_y(t+1) = 0 \tag{10.10}$$

$$u_b(t+1)+n\delta w_b(t+1) = 0. \tag{10.11}$$

Combining these equations we get the standard conditions for welfare maximisation in a static or finite horizon economy. The first set of these conditions is the equality of marginal rates of substitution and transformation in any time period.

$$\frac{\partial u(t+1)/\partial a_i}{\partial u(t+1)/\partial a_j} = \frac{\partial u(t)/\partial b_i}{\partial u(t)/\partial b_j} = \frac{\partial F(t+1)/\partial y_i}{\partial F(t+1)/\partial y_j}. \tag{10.12}$$

Secondly, we have the equality of M.R.S. and M.R.T. intertemporally:

$$\frac{\partial u(t)/\partial a_i}{\partial u(t)/\partial b_j} = \left(\frac{\partial F(t+1)}{\partial k}\right)\left(\frac{\partial F(t)/\partial y_i)}{\partial F(t+1)/\partial y_j}\right). \tag{10.13}$$

Thirdly, there are the static income distribution conditions for allocating consumption among different individuals alive at the same time:

$$\partial u(t)/\partial b_i = \delta \partial u(t+1)/\partial a_i. \tag{10.14}$$

In addition to these we have the asymptotic behaviour of the rate of interest. With convergence to a steady state we have

$$\lim_{t\to\infty} \frac{\partial F(t)}{\partial k} = \delta^{-1} \lim_{t\to\infty} \frac{\partial w(t)/\partial k}{\partial w(t+1)/\partial k} = \delta^{-1}. \tag{10.15}$$

Recalling that δ is the discount factor, we can see that this is the modified golden rule (see, e.g. Cass (1965)).

Thus, as described in section I, the dynamic model yields the first-order conditions for the matching static model. In addition, it gives the asymptotic behaviour of the system which is dominated by the stationary nature of the model.

IV. DECENTRALISATION

The optimal growth path described in the previous section can be achieved by decentralisation by giving each individual the appropriate budget constraint – the budget constraint just sufficient to purchase the net demand bundle allocated to him on the optimal path at prices defined by the marginal rates of transformation. Assuming that the budget allocations are made at the start of a generation's life, it is also necessary to have government debt if we consider markets as clearing period by period rather than once and for all.[1] Alternatively, one could use two transfers to each individual, one in each period of his life, so that it was not necessary to have public debt.[2] Let us illustrate this by considering a single individual. Using marginal products to denote prices, the individual's budget constraint is

$$F_y(t)a' + F_k^{-1}(t+1)F_y(t+1)b' = T \tag{10.16}$$

where T is the lump-sum transfer to this individual and $'$ denotes the transform of a vector. The savings of the individual are then

$$T - F_y(t)a'.$$

If all individuals are the same, this expression times L_t is aggregate savings, since only one generation saves at a time. To clear markets in period t we would need government debt to absorb the difference between desired savings (i.e. wealth) and the optimal capital stock to carry into period $t+1$. (If the necessary debt is negative it would represent government-owned capital.) Thus government debt per member of generation t would equal

$$T - F_y(t)a' + nk_{t+1}.$$

If the consumer is given transfers, T_1 and T_2, in each period of his life, his budget constraint becomes

$$F_y(t)a' + F_k^{-1}(t+1)F_y(t+1)b = T_1 + F_k^{-1}(t+1)T_2 \tag{10.17}$$

with

$$T = T_1 + F_k^{-1}(t+1)T_2 \tag{10.18}$$

to give the consumer the same budget constraint his savings become

$$T_1 - F_y(t)a'$$

which must equal $-nk_{t+1}$ to clear markets without government debt. Thus, the amount of debt to clear markets is equal to the present discounted value of the second-period transfer necessary to achieve the optimal path in the absence of government debt. Thus debt is a device to redistribute income using only one transfer for each individual rather than two. Since debt does not interfere with the equality of marginal rates of substitution and transformation, it would not interfere with the Pareto optimality of the decentralised

[1] Arrow and Kurz (1969) have commented on the role of government debt in controlling an economy.

[2] Bierwag, Grove and Khang (1969) have examined debt and taxes at different times in an individual's life.

economy. A study of the pattern of the quantity of debt that accompanies achieving the optimal path under different circumstances would be interesting.[1]

V. OPTIMAL COMMODITY TAXATION

Before analysing a full set of commodity taxes in a growth setting, we shall review optimal taxation in a static or finite horizon setting.[2] We assume that the planners control prices and production quantities but not consumption quantities. We assume further that the government has no lump-sum redistributive powers and, following the discussion in section II, that there is no other lump-sum income (i.e. constant returns to scale in privately owned production). Let us denote by p the vector of prices, by $v(p)$ the social welfare function, and by $a(p)$ aggregate demand. (In the absence of lump-sum transfers, these functions can be written as functions of prices with considerable generality.) Let y be the vector of net supplies, and $F(y) = 0$ the production constraint. Then we can state welfare maximisation as

$$\begin{aligned} &\underset{p,y}{\text{Maximise}}\ v(p) \\ &\text{s.t. } a(p) = y \\ &F(y) = 0. \end{aligned} \tag{10.19}$$

Forming a Lagrangian expression

$$L(p, y, \lambda, \mu) = v(p) - \lambda[a(p) - y]' - \mu F(y) \tag{10.20}$$

where $'$ denotes the transpose of a vector, we have the first-order conditions

$$v_p - \lambda a_p = 0 \tag{10.21}$$

$$\lambda - \mu F_y = 0 \tag{10.22}$$

where a_p is the matrix of derivatives of aggregate demand functions with respect to individual prices. Eliminating λ from these equations, we have

$$v_p = \mu F_y a_p \tag{10.23}$$

which states that the impact of a price on social welfare is proportional to the cost of meeting the change in demand induced by the price change.[3]

[1] Phelps and Shell (1969) have examined relations between debt and capital for some models of demand formation.

[2] For a full discussion of this model, see Diamond and Mirrlees (1968).

[3] Introducing taxes, as the difference between producer and consumer prices, we can manipulate this expression to show that the impact of a price on social welfare is proportional to the increased tax revenue from the consumer price increase, producer prices held constant.

VI. FULLY TAXED ECONOMY

Let us now examine the same infinite horizon economy as previously, assuming that the planners control all consumer prices rather than consumer quantities and that there are no lump-sum transfers.[1] Let us denote by p_t and q_t the vectors of prices (in present discounted value terms) which a member of the tth generation will face. Individual utility maximisation is then described by

$$\underset{a_t^h, b_t^h}{\text{Maximise}}\ u^h(a_t^h, b_t^h)$$

$$\text{subject to } a_t^h p_t' + b_t^h q_t' = 0. \tag{10.24}$$

Thus we have individual demands a^h and b^h and utility v^h depending only on these two price vectors. Let us denote by a_t and b_t aggregate demand per capita:

$$a_t = a(p_t, q_t) = L_t^{-1} \sum_h a^h(p_t, q_t) \tag{10.25}$$

$$b_t = b(p_t, q_t) = L_t^{-1} \sum_h b^h(p_t, q_t).$$

Given an additive social welfare function, we can describe the per capita contribution of each generation to social welfare:

$$v_t = v(p_t, q_t) = L_t^{-1} \sum_h v^h(p_t, q_t). \tag{10.26}$$

If a generation is composed of k types of individuals and there is equal proportional growth of each of the types, then equation (10.26) can be used for all time periods, since time will not enter explicitly into the definition of v. Thus we can describe the objective function for social welfare maximisation by

$$\sum_{t=1}^{\infty} n^t \delta^t v_t = \sum_{t=1}^{\infty} n^t \delta^t v(p_t, q_t). \tag{10.27}$$

As before, we take the generation as the planning unit. We now have k_0, p_0 and q_0 as initial conditions. Further optimisation over q_0 could also be considered. The fundamental equation now takes the form

$$w(k_t, p_t, q_t) = \text{Max}\ \{v(p_{t+1}, q_{t+1}) + nw(k_{t+1}, p_{t+1}, q_{t+1})\} \tag{10.28}$$

with additional constraints

$$k_{t+1} = n^{-1}F(k_t, y_t) \tag{10.29}$$

$$y_{t+1} = a(p_{t+1}, q_{t+1}) + n^{-1}b(p_t, q_t) \tag{10.30}$$

$$q_t = p_{t+1}. \tag{10.31}$$

[1] The absence of bequests in this model is a serious shortcoming.

The constraints express the technology, market clearance and the fact that only one set of spot prices can occur in the market at any time.[1] Substituting from the constraints we can rewrite the optimality principle as

$$w(k_t, p_t, q_t) = \underset{q_{t+1}}{\text{Max}} \{v(q_t, q_{t+1}) + $$
$$+ n\delta w[n^{-1}F[k_t, a(q_t, q_{t+1}) + n^{-1}b(p_t, q_t)], q_t, q_{t+1}]\}. \qquad (10.32)$$

Differentiating the maximand with respect to q_{t+1} and equating with zero, we have the conditions

$$v_q(t+1) + \delta w_k(t+1)F_y(t+1)a_q(t+1) + n\delta w_q(t+1) = 0. \qquad (10.33)$$

Differentiating the fundamental equation with respect to p_t, q_t and k_t, we obtain the equations

$$w_p(t) = n^{-1}\delta w_k(t+1)F_y(t+1)b_p(t) \qquad (10.34)$$

$$w_q(t) = v_p(t+1) + \delta w_k(t+1)F_y(t+1)[a_p(t+1) +$$
$$+ n^{-1}b_q(t)] + w_p(t+1) \qquad (10.35)$$

$$w_k(t) = \delta w_k(t+1)F_k(t+1). \qquad (10.36)$$

Combining these equations for successive time periods we obtain the same conditions for optimal taxation as in the static case: proportionality of the derivative of welfare to the cost of the derivative of demand with respect to a price. (The equation can be premultiplied by δ^{t+1} to make the same interpretation for taxes in different periods, using (10.36) to complete the comparison.)

$$v_q(t+1) + n\delta v_p(t+2) = -w_k(t+1)\{F_y(t+1)a_q(t+1) +$$
$$+ F_k^{-1}(t+2)F_y(t+2)[a_q(t+1) + na_p(t+2)] +$$
$$+ F_k^{-1}(t+3)F_k^{-1}(t+2)F_y(t+3)[nb_p(t+2)]\}. \qquad (10.37)$$

Thus in the optimal tax formula one must examine both generations which are affected by any price change. From (10.36) we can obtain the asymptotic marginal product of capital, given convergence to a steady state:

$$\lim_{t\to\infty} F_k(t) = \delta^{-1} \lim_{t\to\infty} \frac{w_k(t)}{w_k(t+1)} = \delta^{-1}. \qquad (10.38)$$

[1] Since demands and utility are homogeneous of degree zero in prices, (10.31) also serves as a normalisation equation.

This is the same asymptotic rate of return as in the fully controlled economy.[1] However, this does not necessarily imply the same level of capital per person in the two models since the rate of return also depends on the quantity of other inputs per person $(a+n^{-1}b)$, which will be different, in general, in the two models.

VII. SOCIAL MARGINAL RATES OF SUBSTITUTION

The presence of individuals living more than a single period brings forward two separate concepts of the intertemporal social marginal rate of substitution. The first of these is the intertemporal personal marginal rate of substitution of some individual living over the time periods being considered. Since this concept is internal to a single individual, we shall call it the internal social marginal rate of substitution. The second concept is the social M.R.S. from transferring goods between periods and between identical individuals in successive generations. Since this depends on two individuals, we shall call it the external M.R.S.[2] Naturally, there is a separate measure of each of these two concepts for each good, each pair of time periods and each type of individual. Let us restrict the concept to good one, which we take as numeraire. Then we have the following definitions:

$$\text{internal S.M.R.S.}_t = \frac{\partial u(t)/b_1}{\partial u(t)/a_1} \tag{10.39}$$

$$\text{external S.M.R.S.}_t = \frac{\delta \partial u(t+1)/a_1}{\partial u(t)/a_1}. \tag{10.40}$$

With the fully controlled economy both M.R.S. concepts equal the marginal rate of transformation as part of the necessary conditions for optimal growth [(10.13) and (10.14)]. In the fully taxed economy, the internal M.R.S. is equal to the consumer price ratio, q_{1t}/p_{1t}. In general, if the government has any need to raise money, for expenditures or redistribution, this will not equal the M.R.T. Asymptotically, convergence to a steady state implies that the external M.R.S. does equal the M.R.T. [(10.38) and (10.40)]. Thus the stationary character of a steady-state solution dominates the choice of intertemporal redistribution and the intertemporal margin of production, but it does not determine the intertemporal personal rate of substitution for individuals.

[1] Absolute prices do not converge in this model, but w is homogeneous of degree zero in prices.

[2] The external MRS seems to be the concept that coincides with the MRS in standard optimal growth models.

With two-period lifetimes, the level of second-period prices relative to that of first-year prices affects a single generation. Presumably the need for redistribution among members of that generation will affect the degree of taxation on savings. If high-income persons tend to save more than in proportion to wealth, we would expect savings to be taxed more heavily on this account. In addition, the tax rate will reflect the standard considerations relating deadweight burdens to taxes. To get some notion of these factors, let us consider a special case of the above model, where everyone is identical and there are just two consumer goods (labour and consumption) demanded in the first year and one (consumption) in the second.

Given the assumptions of a two-period individual life, the rate of return on savings is relevant only for members of a single generation. Given the assumption that labour is supplied in only one period, the real wage is relevant only for members of a single generation. Thus we expect the optimal tax structure to coincide with that which is optimal for the problem of taxing an individual in isolation. This is indeed true. Rewriting the first-order conditions (10.37) for this special case, we have:

$$\frac{\partial v(t+1)}{\partial q_1}+n\delta\frac{\partial v(t+2)}{\partial p_1} = -w_k(t+1)\left[\frac{\partial F(t+1)}{\partial y_1}\frac{\partial a_1(t+1)}{\partial q_1}+\right.$$
$$+\frac{\partial F(t+1)}{\partial y_2}\frac{\partial a_2(t+1)}{\partial q_1}+F_k{}^{-1}(t+2)\frac{\partial F(t+2)}{\partial y_1}\frac{\partial b_1(t+1)}{\partial q_1}+$$
$$+nF_k{}^{-1}(t+2)\left(\frac{\partial F(t+2)}{\partial y_1}\frac{\partial a_1(t+2)}{\partial p_1}+\frac{\partial F(t+2)}{\partial y_2}\frac{\partial a_2(t+2)}{\partial p_1}\right)+$$
$$\left.+nF_k{}^{-1}(t+3)F_k{}^{-1}(t+2)\frac{\partial F(t+3)}{\partial y_1}\frac{\partial b_1(t+2)}{\partial p_1}\right]. \qquad (10.41)$$

$$n\delta\frac{\partial v(t+2)}{\partial p_2} = -w_k(t+1)nF_k{}^{-1}(t+2)\left[\frac{\partial F(t+2)}{\partial y_1}\frac{\partial a_1(t+2)}{\partial p_2}+\right.$$
$$+\frac{\partial F(t+2)}{\partial y_2}\frac{\partial a_2(t+2)}{\partial p_2}+$$
$$\left.+F_k{}^{-1}(t+3)\frac{\partial F(t+3)}{\partial y_1}\frac{\partial b_1(t+2)}{\partial p_2}\right]. \qquad (10.42)$$

Consider the optimal taxes for two static, three-good economies (10.23) with μ for the first one equal to $-w_k(t+1)$ and for the second equal to $-w_k(t+2)$. Then (10.42) is satisfied directly. Equation

(10.41) is satisfied by adding equations for successive generations and noting the relationship between multipliers (10.36). Thus we can appeal to what is known about taxes in a three-good economy. Taking labour as numeraire, we are asking whether present or future consumption is taxed at a higher *ad valorem* rate. From the analysis of Corlett and Hague (1953) we know that they will be taxed equally (and thus the internal S.M.R.S. will equal the M.R.T.) only if they are equally complementary to leisure, i.e. if the elasticities of present and future consumption with respect to the wage along the compensated demand curves are equal.

VIII. OPTIMAL PARTIAL TAXATION

The assumption that the government can tax each commodity at a different rate ignores the administrative side of tax collection to such an extent that it seems worth while to examine taxation and public production where there are further restrictions on the tax powers of the planners. We begin with this problem in a static setting before considering growth. To take advantage of the constant returns to scale assumption in private production, we shall single out one good for different notational treatment from the others. (In the growth model, capital will serve the same purpose.) Let us denote by k and g private and public net demand for good zero and by y and z private and public net supply of goods 1 through m. Then we have the production constraints

$$k = F(y) \tag{10.43}$$

$$g = G(z) \tag{10.44}$$

where F displays constant returns to scale. This implies, in particular, that

$$F_{yy}y' = 0 \tag{10.45}$$

by Euler's equation, since F_y is homogeneous of degree zero in y.

Let us denote by q and $p = (p_1, \ldots, p_m)$ the consumer prices of the $m+1$ goods. We assume that there are r tax control variables, $s = (s_1, \ldots, s_r)$ with the *ad valorem* tax rates plus one, $\sigma, \tau_1, \ldots, \tau_m$, being functions of the r controls. A natural restriction would be for given sets of tax rates to have the same value, with the tax control being that value. Let us denote by $\tau(s)$ the diagonal $m \times m$ matrix of tax functions. Then, consumer prices are related to producer prices and taxes by

$$q = \sigma(s) \tag{10.46}$$

$$p = F_y\tau(s). \tag{10.47}$$

Let us denote by $\hat{a}(q, p)$ and $a(q, p)$ the net aggregate demands by consumers for goods 0 and 1 through m respectively. Then we can state the welfare maximisation problem as

$$\text{Max } v[\sigma(s), F_y \tau(s)]$$
$$\text{subject to } \hat{a}[\sigma(s), F_y \tau(s)] = F(y) + G(z) \qquad (10.48)$$
$$a[\sigma(s), F_y \tau(s)] = y + z.$$

Let us denote by μ and λ the Lagrangians associated with these equations. Then we have the following first-order conditions:

$$(v_q - \mu \hat{a}_q - \lambda a_q')\sigma^* + (v_p - \mu \hat{a}_p - \lambda a_p) F_y^* \tau^* = 0 \qquad (10.49)$$

$$(v_p - \mu \hat{a}_p - \lambda a_p)\tau F_{yy} + \mu F_y + \lambda = 0 \qquad (10.50)$$

$$\mu G_z + \lambda = 0 \qquad (10.51)$$

where σ^* is the row vector

$$\left(\frac{\partial \sigma}{\partial s_1}, \ldots, \frac{\partial \sigma}{\partial s_r}\right)$$

and τ is the $m \times r$ matrix of derivatives of τ_i with respect to s_j and F_y^* is the diagonal matrix of elements of F_y.

Comparing (10.49) with the analysis of full taxation (10.20) we see that consumer price effects on welfare are no longer proportional to the cost of the induced change in demand for each individual price. Rather, the proportionality holds on average for groups of prices affected by single tax control variables with the weights being the response of prices to tax controls.[1] The cost of changed demand in this expression is evaluated using government shadow prices, not market prices, and shadow and market prices are different in general:

$$-\mu^{-1}\lambda = G_z = F_y + \mu^{-1}(v_p - \mu \hat{a}_p - \lambda a_p)\tau F_{yy}. \qquad (10.52)$$

The differences in these prices arises from the effect on consumer prices of changing factor proportions in private production. With groups of goods necessarily taxed at the same rate, changes in tax variables are not sufficient to bring consumer prices to any desired configuration independent of producer prices. Thus, by affecting relative quantities in private production, consumer prices can be changed in a way that is different from changes that can be induced by taxation. In general, some such change will be desirable, resulting in different marginal rates of transformation in the two production

[1] Since consumer prices are related to private producer prices, and costs are measured with government shadow prices, the interpretation of the first-order conditions in terms of marginal tax revenues does not carry over to this case.

sectors. However, because of constant returns, a given fraction of private net inputs transferred to public production does not alter consumer prices. As a first-order condition, it must be true therefore that a small transfer of this kind does not alter aggregate output of good one. Postmultiplying (10.52) by y' and using (10.45), we see that this is indeed true:

$$G_z y' = F_y y'. \tag{10.53}$$

Thus, on average, inputs into public and private production have the same productivity. For individual commodities this need not be true because of the price changes from shifting factors between sectors which cannot be imitated by the limited set of tax control variables available.

IX. PARTIALLY TAXED ECONOMY

There are many examples of partially taxed economies which one might explore. As a specific example, let us consider an economy with an annual income tax and a tax on the return to savings. For this analysis we need to distinguish two production functions, one private, one public, with separate net outputs, y and z, and separate capital stocks, k and g (measured negatively). With capital being transferable, we can write the production constraint as[1]

$$k_{t+1}+g_{t+1} = n^{-1}[F(y_{t+1}, k_t)+G(z_{t+1}, g_t)]. \tag{10.54}$$

In addition, we have market clearance

$$y_{t+1}+z_{t+1} = a(p_{t+1}, q_{t+1})+n^{-1}b(p_t, q_t). \tag{10.55}$$

To relate consumer prices to marginal products, we must distinguish commodities which are part of taxable income from those that represent consumption. Let δ_i be 1 or 0 as good i is or is not subject to tax, and let Δ be the $m\times m$ diagonal matrix with terms δ_i. Let s_{t+1} be one minus the income-tax rate and $s(t+1)$ the $m\times m$ diagonal matrix with terms $s^{\delta_i}{}_{t+1}$. Let s'_{t+1} be the inverse of one plus the net rate of return on savings for consumers. Then we can express prices as

$$q_t = s'_{t+1}s(t+1)F_y(t+1). \tag{10.56}$$

There is also the condition that the same prices must hold in the market for both generations trading at the same time:

$$q_{t-1} = p_t. \tag{10.57}$$

[1] Implicit in this set-up is that debt policies permit a difference in quantity between owned capital (or wealth) and capital used in public production.

Taking the same approach as previously, we can consider the prices for a generation as the decision variable. Since these depend on production and tax rates, we can write the fundamental equation as

$$w(k_t, g_t, s_{t+1}, s'_{t+1}, y_{t+1}, p_t) = \max_{\substack{s_{t+2}, s'_{t+2} \\ y_{t+2}, k_{t+1}}} [v(p_{t+1}, q_{t+1}) + \\ + n\delta w(k_{t+1}, g_{t+1}, s_{t+2}, s'_{t+2}, y_{t+2}, p_{t+1})] \qquad (10.58)$$

where equations (10.57), (10.56) and (10.54) can be used to eliminate p_{t+1}, q_{t+1} and g_{t+1} from the equation. Derivation of the conditions which coincide with those of the static analysis given above is straightforward and contained in the Appendix to this section. The conditions can be stated in terms of the vector, Γ, of the excess of the increase in social welfare from a price rise over the cost of meeting the induced change in demand:

$$\Gamma(t+1) = v_q(t+1) + n\delta v_p(t+2) + \delta w_g(t+1)\{G_z(t+1)a_q(t+1) + \\ + G_g^{-1}(t+2)G_z(t+2)[na_p(t+2) + b_q(t+1)] + \\ + G_g^{-1}(t+2)G_g^{-1}(t+3)G_z(t+3)nb_p(t+2)\}. \qquad (10.59)$$

We can now state the first-order conditions corresponding to s', s, k and y as[1]

$$\Gamma(t+1)s(t+2)F_y'(t+2) = 0 \qquad (10.60)$$

$$\Gamma(t+1)s'_{t+2}\Delta F_y'(t+2) = 0 \qquad (10.61)$$

$$\Gamma(t+1)s'_{t+2}s(t+2)F_{yk}'(t+2) + \\ + n\delta^2 w_g(t+1)[F_k(t+2) - G_g(t+2)] = 0 \qquad (10.62)$$

$$\Gamma(t+1)s'_{t+2}s(t+2)F_{yy}(t+2) + \\ + n\delta^2 w_g(t+1)[F_y(t+2) - G_z(t+2)] = 0. \qquad (10.63)$$

As with static analysis, the difference between the gain in welfare from a price rise and the cost of meeting the induced change in demand adds to zero when we consider the prices affected by a tax [(10.60) and (10.61)]. Thus the inner product of gain with producer price is zero for goods subject to income tax. The same is also true for the set of goods not subject to tax:

$$\Gamma(t+1)(I-\Delta)F_y'(t+2) = \Gamma(t+1)[s(t+2) - \\ - s_{t+2}\Delta]F_y'(t+2) = 0. \qquad (10.64)$$

[1] Control of the rate of return on savings implies a zero weight for the change in F_k when k or y change and thus a simplification of these expressions from what they would be with just an income tax.

Again following the static analysis, postmultiplication of (10.62) and (10.63) by k and y respectively and addition gives the equal efficiency, on average, of factors in the two sectors:

$$[F_k(t+2)-G_g(t+2)]k_{t+1}+[F_y(t+2)-G_z(t+2)]y'_{t+2} = 0. \quad (10.65)$$

This implies that in the presence of an optimal income tax a public investment rule which uses a lower discount rate than the private marginal product of capital and uses market prices otherwise cannot be the correct rule. Divergences between marginal products of capital occur to induce relating price changes of consumer goods. Thus, in the unlikely case where capital intensity does not affect relative prices, F_k should equal G_g. This is the case of a separable private production function

$$F(k, y) = \phi[k, \psi(y)] \quad (10.66)$$

implying

$$F_{yk} = \phi_{k\psi}\psi_y = \frac{\phi_{k\psi}}{\phi_\psi} F_y. \quad (10.67)$$

From (10.60) and (10.62) this implies the equality of F_k and G_g at the optimum.

As in the previous models, the shadow price of government capital changes as the inverse of the product of the discount rate and the marginal product of capital in the public (sector Appendix: equation A.7):

$$w_g(t) = \delta G_g(t+1)w_g(t+1). \quad (10.68)$$

Thus, with convergence to a steady state we have the modified golden rule for public capital, but not necessarily for private capital.

X. CONCLUDING REMARKS

The models presented above are only a start towards combining optimal growth considerations with the problems of making the best use of a limited set of policy variables. There are many questions raised by these models. The most obvious is the determination of sufficient conditions to ensure existence of an optimum. It is also necessary to examine whether the optimal path converges to a steady state. Since many examples of optimal growth paths in a fully controlled setting have been calculated, it would be interesting to have some information on the differences in consumption and investment along the optimal paths when there are weaker control variables. The determinants of the quantity of public debt or capital which permits decentralisation could also be examined. There are other examples of partially taxed economies which might be explored;

the case of a country with tariffs but no internal taxation is an obvious candidate. The case of several capital goods, perhaps of different lives, while not very different from that of a single capital good in the fully controlled or taxed economies, may be of greater interest with only partial taxation. Perhaps understanding the dynamics of partially taxed economies would be helped by a better understanding of the statics of the same model.

APPENDIX

We have written the fundamental equation

$$\begin{aligned} w(k_t, g_t, s_{t+1}, s'_{t+1}, y_{t+1}, p_t) = \max_{\substack{k_{t+1}, s_{t+2} \\ s'_{t+2}, y_{t+2}}} [&v(s_{t+1}s'(t+1)F_y(t+1) \\ &s_{t+2}s'(t+2)F_y(t+2)) + n\delta w(k_{t+1}, -k_{t+1} + n^{-1}(F(y_{t+1}, k_t) + \\ &+ G(-y_{t+1} + a(s_{t+1}s'(t+1)F_y(t+1), s_{t+2}s'(t+2)F_y(t+2)) + \\ &+ n^{-1}b(p_t, s_{t+1}s'(t+1)F_y(t+1)), g_t)), s_{t+2}, \\ &s'_{t+2}, y_{t+2}, s_{t+1}s'(t+1)F_y(t+1))]. \qquad (A.1) \end{aligned}$$

Differentiating with respect to the control variables, s', s, k and y, we obtain the first-order conditions

$$\begin{aligned} &v_q(t+1)s(t+2)F'_y(t+2) + n\delta w_{s'}(t+1) + \\ &\qquad + \delta w_g(t+1)G_z(t+1)a_q(t+1)s(t+2)F_y'(t+2) = 0 \qquad (A.2) \end{aligned}$$

$$\begin{aligned} &v_q(t+1)s'_{t+2}\Delta F_y'(t+2) + n\delta w_s(t+1) + \\ &\qquad + \delta w_g(t+1)G_z(t+1)a_q(t+1)s'_{t+2}\Delta F_y'(t+2) = 0 \qquad (A.3) \end{aligned}$$

$$\begin{aligned} &v_q(t+1)s'_{t+2}s(t+2)F_{yk}'(t+2) + n\delta w_k(t+1) + \\ &\qquad + \delta w_g(t+1)(-n + G_z(t+1)a_q(t+1)s'_{t+2}s(t+2)F_{yk}'(t+2) = 0 \qquad (A.4) \end{aligned}$$

$$\begin{aligned} &v_q(t+1)s'_{\ +2}s(t+2)F_{yy}(t+2) + n\delta w_y(t+1) + \\ &\qquad + \delta w_g(t+1)G_z(t+1)a_q(t+1)s'_{t+2}s(t+2)F_{yy}(t+2)) = 0. \qquad (A.5) \end{aligned}$$

Differentiating the fundamental equation with respect to the variables k_t, g_t, s'_{t+1}, s_{t+1}, y_{t+1} and p_t, we have

$$\begin{aligned} w_k(t) = {} &v_p(t+1)s'_{t+1}s(t+1)F_{yk}'(t+1) + \delta w_g(t+1)(F_k(t+1) + \\ &+ G_z(t+1)(a_p(t+1) + n^{-1}b_q(t))s'_{t+1}s(t+1)F_{yk}'(t+1)) + \\ &+ n\delta w_p(t+1)s'_{t+1}s(t+1)F_{yk}'(t+1) \qquad (A.6) \end{aligned}$$

$$w_g(t) = \delta w_g(t+1)G_g(t+1) \qquad (A.7)$$

$$\begin{aligned} w_{s'}(t) = {} &v_p(t+1)s(t+1)F_y'(t+1) + \delta w_g(t+1)G_z(t+1)(a_p(t+1) + \\ &+ n^{-1}b_q(t))s(t+1)F_y'(t+1) + n\delta w_p(t+1)s(t+1)F_y'(t+1) \qquad (A.8) \end{aligned}$$

$$w_s(t) = v_p(t+1)s'_{t+1}\Delta F_y'(t+1)+\delta w_g(t+1)G_z(t+1)(a_p(t+1)+ \\ +n^{-1}b_q(t))s'_{t+1}\Delta F_y'(t+1)+n\delta w_p(t+1)s'_{t+1}\Delta F_y'(t+1) \quad \text{(A.9)}$$

$$w_y(t) = v_p(t+1)s'_{t+1}s(t+1)F_{yy}(t+1)+\delta w_g(t+1)(F_y(t+1)- \\ -G_z(t+1)+G_z(t+1)(a_p(t+1)+ \\ +n^{-1}b_q(t))s'_{t+1}s(t+1)F_{yy}(t+1)+ \\ +n\delta w_p(t+1)s'_{t+1}s(t+1)F_{yy}(t+1) \quad \text{(A.10)}$$

$$w_p(t) = \delta w_g(t+1)G_z(t+1)n^{-1}b_p(t). \quad \text{(A.11)}$$

Substituting from (A.8) for $w_{s'}$ in (A.2), we have

$$((v_q(t+1)+n\delta v_p(t+2))+\delta w_g(t+1)G_z(t+1)a_q(t+1)+ \\ +n\delta^2 w_g(t+2)G_z(t+2)(a_p(t+2)+n^{-1}b_q(t+1))+ \\ +n^2\delta^2 w_p(t+2))s(t+2)F_y'(t+2) = 0. \quad \text{(A.12)}$$

Substituting for $w_g(t+2)$ and $w_p(t+2)$ from (A.7) and (A.11), we have

$$((v_q(t+1)+n\delta v_p(t+2))+\delta w_g(t+1)(G_z(t+1)a_q(t+1)+ \\ +G_g^{-1}(t+2)G_z(t+2)(na_p(t+2)+b_q(t+1))+ \\ +G_g^{-1}(t+3)G_g^{-1}(t+2)G_z(t+3)nb_p(t+2))\times \\ \times s(t+2)F_y'(t+2) = 0. \quad \text{(A.13)}$$

This equation is a direct restatement of the static conditions (10.49) in the context of this model. Let us write it as

$$\Gamma(t+1)s(t+2)F_y'(t+2) = 0. \quad \text{(A.14)}$$

By similar substitution into (A.3)–(A.5) we obtain

$$\Gamma(t+1)s'_{t+2}\Delta F_y'(t+2) = 0 \quad \text{(A.15)}$$

$$\Gamma(t+1)s'_{t+2}s(t+2)F_{yk}'(t+2)+n\delta^2 w_g(t+2)(F_k(t+2)- \\ -G_g(t+2)) = 0 \quad \text{(A.16)}$$

$$\Gamma(t+1)s'_{t+2}s(t+2)F_{yy}(t+2)+n\delta^2 w_g(t+2)(F_y(t+2)- \\ -G_z(t+2)) = 0. \quad \text{(A.17)}$$

REFERENCES

K. Arrow and M. Kurz, 'Optimal Public Investment Policy and Controllability with Fixed Private Savings Ratio', *Journal of Economic Theory*, vol. I, no. 2 (Aug 1969) pp. 119–40.

R. Bellman, *Dynamic Programming* (Princeton U.P., 1957).

G. O. Bierwag, M. A. Grove and C. Khang, 'National Debt in a Neoclassical Growth Model: Comment', *American Economic Review* (Mar 1969) pp. 205–10.

D. Cass, 'Optimum Growth in an Aggregative Model of Capital Accumulation', *Review of Economic Studies*, vol. XXXII (1965) pp. 233–40.

W. J. Corlett and D. C. Hague, 'Complementarity and the Excess Burden of Taxation', *Review of Economic Studies*, vol. XXI, no. 1 (1953).

P. Diamond and J. Mirrlees, 'Optimal Taxation and Public Production', *American Economic Review*, vol. 61, nos. 1 (March 1971) and 3 (June 1971).

E. Phelps and K. Shell, 'Public Debt, Taxation and Capital Intensiveness', *Journal of Economic Theory*, vol. I, no. 3 (Oct 1969) pp. 330–46.

R. Radner, 'Dynamic Programming of Economic Growth', in *Activity Analysis in the Theory of Growth and Planning*, ed. E. Malinvaud and M. O. L. Bacharach (London: Macmillan, 1967).

P. Samuelson, 'Social Indifference Curves', *Quarterly Journal of Economics*, vol. LXX (1956) pp. 1–22.

Discussion of the Paper by Peter A. Diamond

Dr Sheshinski summarised the paper and then raised some questions. The problem of existence had been omitted. He would like to see this tackled – especially for a decentralised setting – but he realised this would be formidable given the difficulties in more simple models. We should also like to know whether the optimal plan converged to a steady state. It had been shown in the partially taxed case that the asymptotic marginal product of private-sector capital should not equal the long-run discount rate. We should like to know the appropriate relation between the marginal private- and public-sector products for use in cost–benefit analysis. He asked when the assumption that we should be on the production possibility frontier was warranted.

He had two specific suggestions for further analysis. Firstly, the implicit assumption behind assuming a restricted set of possible taxes was that there exist collection costs. A more economic (as opposed to mechanical) approach would make this assumption explicit with a collection cost function.

Secondly, we could examine the open convergence and existence questions in more simple models. This would also guide us as to the characteristics of the optimal paths. In order to try some of these questions, he had looked at a model where people decayed exponentially (as opposed to falling apart after two periods), and had iso-elastic utility functions, while the number of families was growing and there was constant elasticity of substitution in production.

Professor Diamond said he had been asked to take the static theory of taxation and public investment and consider it in the setting of an optimal growth problem. He thought there were two reasons for attempting such an exercise. Firstly, one often learns something from considering a familiar problem in a somewhat unfamiliar setting. The second relates to the purpose of optimal growth analysis which, he felt, was to obtain some notion of the savings rates that ought to obtain – the detailed aspects of optimal growth being merely repetitions of the finite horizon optimality conditions. The question of the degree of complexity we want to consider in optimal growth analysis then hinges on the importance of different complications for the level of optimal savings. It is natural to ask whether a limitation in tax powers of the government is a significant complication in this sense. This is a question of numerical analysis which he had not undertaken.

In line with the first purpose, there were several things which he had learned as a result of this analysis, although he thought they might not be new to everyone. The consideration of optimality in an overlapping generation setting had raised two different concepts of the intertemporal social marginal rates of substitution. In the first, one considers transferring the consumption of a single consumer over time; in the second, commodities are transferred between members of successive generations. The latter concept fitted with the discount rates that arise in standard optimal growth models, while the former is the concept which we can observe by watching individuals lend or borrow. The constant returns to scale assumption in the setting of partial taxation (where the government is unable to tax each commodity at a different rate) was seen to imply the desirability of equal efficiency, on the average, between public and private production, even though aggregate efficiency (identical marginal rates of transformation) is not desired.

The models also pointed up the importance of the steady-state (or stationary) character of the long-run solution in determining the first-order conditions. He did not know whether this increased or decreased the significance of the analysis, although he inclined towards the latter.

Dr Bliss wondered how to formalise the view that the number of taxes is limited. He thought that analysis by means of the cost functions involved in collecting taxes would be impossibly difficult to handle. The cost function would have a big leap at zero and then would probably decline. The problem would be hopelessly intractable.

Professor Shell said we might simplify the problem by excluding *a priori* some taxes that were clearly very difficult to collect or enforce. The problem would still be very difficult, however.

Professor Stiglitz said that one of the problems limiting the tax tools was the difficulty in distinguishing commodities, e.g. wage and rent income in the unincorporated sector. This would be a reason for having to tax commodities at the same rate.

Mr Atkinson said we should also consider the choice of groups of commodities to be taxed at the same rates rather than choosing tax rates for particular pre-selected groups of commodities.

Professor Diamond said two groups bore the costs of taxation: the Treasury and private individuals or companies involved in administering the tax. For example, we might have to tax all goods that were sold in certain types of stores at the same rate.

We might consider a general sales tax and exempt some commodities, e.g. necessities or those bought by lower income groups. This would be using the method suggested by Mr Atkinson. It would be difficult to decide which method was the better as we would have to compare sets of optima that were not adjacent.

Professor Hahn said the spirit of these models was to raise taxes to redistribute income. We should extend this to distribution between generations, as in the case of tree-planting in Israel. However, taxes were also imposed to supply public goods and he asked if this consideration modified the results.

Professor Diamond said that if we had no income distribution problems, i.e. we were only interested in achieving Pareto optimality, we could finance public goods with a head tax. Worries about income distribution were the reason for not doing this, and the financing of public goods was in principle no different from the general problems discussed here.

Dr Sheshinski said we would have to choose between different Pareto optima.

Professor Hahn considered an extreme example where the present generation was identical to future generations except that it was very effort-elastic with respect to wages. In this case a competitive equilibrium might not be Pareto-efficient. *Professor Diamond* said that this result would be due to the open-endedness of the problem. *Professor Hahn* agreed. He asked whether a mixture of the two marginal rates of substitution introduced in the paper was appropriate for distribution problems between generations a long way apart.

Professor Diamond said if they were a long way apart we should just want the external marginal rate of substitution. For a point-input, point-output project with a forty-year life, a mixture would be appropriate. *Dr Bliss* asked why point-input point-output was relevant here. Partially grown trees were a bequest. *Professor Bruno* said trees were a bad example as private individuals were happy to pay for the planting.

Professor Weizsäcker asked what was the static equivalent of the two concepts of the marginal rate of substitution. *Professor Diamond* said it was similar to the difference between giving one man oranges instead of apples and taking an apple from one man and giving an orange to the next numbered man. *Professor Mirrlees* suggested that an example using different locations would do.

Professor Weizsäcker said that if people lived for more periods, many more marginal rates of substitution would be needed. He asked whether there was a multiplicative rule similar to the one which gave us the new marginal rates of substitution which arose when a third good was considered where previously only two had been. *Professor Diamond* replied that this rule was valid for external rates (e.g. man–son–grandson) but there was no multiplicative rule between internal and external rates.

Professor Shell asked what was meant by saying that the modified golden-rule interest rate might help us in policy–should this guide us for all interest rates? We should be very uncertain what the rate should be, for taking the asymptotic steady state as an approximation was a bad over-simplification.

Professor Diamond said it might be interesting that the long-run consumption rate of interest was less than 5 per cent (many thought we should not want a high discount rate on utilities) when in production we might discount at present marginal products of capital which were 15–20 per cent. He said the asymptotic steady state *was* badly over-simplified, but we had to choose between various *ad hoc* models. It made life very easy to look at steady states, since outside these the models were complicated to deal with.

Professor Hahn said there was no general answer to whether or not the steady state was good enough as an approximation. For the U.K. or U.S.A. it might be all right, but certainly not for India. *Professor Bruno* remarked that long-run consumption rates of interest were higher if we brought in technical progress and population growth.

Professor Mirrlees said the problem of deciding whether or not a simplification was good enough was an important general one. In a simple one-sector Solow-type model, with technical progress you could precisely work out the optimal path and utility integral starting from given initial conditions. This framework allows us to compare policies, simplifications and sensitivity to initial conditions. There is more insensitivity than one would have expected. The general question is whether experience obtained from a simple model was relevant evidence. He believed, in the absence of anything more helpful, that it was.

Professor Hahn said that we were likely to meet more sensitivity to initial conditions with a many-sector model, especially in an open economy.

Professor Stiglitz said that qualitative properties of paths were fairly sensitive to initial conditions even in closed-economy models.

Dr Bliss said that the Mirrlees–Stern paper ('Fairly Good Plans', J.E.T., 1972) had given a criterion for these problems.

Professor Mirrlees said that we should look at the aggregate figures obtained from these models, e.g. savings rates and interest rates.

Professor Diamond thought that the savings rate was more relevant, as interest rates served many different purposes. For example, the discount rate for cost–benefit analysis may be different from the interest rate that determined savings.

He said that Newbery had shown that the gains from income redistribution could be very large. *Professor Mirrlees* said that this redistribution conclusion assumed the possibility of lump-sum transfers. *Professor Shell* pointed out that this raised the question of taxation costs introduced by Dr Sheshinski.

Professor Bruno claimed that nothing could be said in general about the tax cost and sensitivity questions in empirical planning models. Open linear models were, in aggregate, insensitive to discount rates, but sectoral shifts could be very sensitive although utility changes were small. We thus had a link between optimum growth models and empirical planning models. He felt that although costs of taxation problems would be difficult, this did not mean we should not try them.

Dr Bliss said he would be prepared to accept the judgement of civil servants. *Professor Bruno* said that certain commodities in Israel had initially been fairly easy to tax. Each time more revenue was needed these taxes were increased, although the *a priori* optimal policy might have looked very different. *Dr Bliss* said this mistake was due to narrowness of view. The kinds of models being proposed would not eliminate such mistakes.

Professor Hahn said that determination of the optimal savings rate was only important for the Communist countries. In the U.S.A. and Israel it did not matter very much, and India and Pakistan should be more concerned with discount rates.

Professor Bruno said foreign exchange constraints were much more important in open economies, although in closed economies optimal savings rates were very important.

Professor Mirrlees said it came to the same thing: because of foreign trade difficulties the marginal rate of transformation between consumption and saving might vary very much with consumption. *Professor Bruno* said it was not always possible to increase exports, and so earn foreign exchange for capital imports, by decreasing consumption.

Professor Mirrlees said that it was often argued that there was a relation between saving and income redistribution: redistributing income to the poor might decrease saving. Thus it had been argued that we should build up capital first and redistribute later. This was the cost of taxation question again.

Professor Weizsäcker said that it was necessary to know the utility functions of individuals in order to determine tax policy both in this model and in the Diamond–Mirrlees formulation. It would be difficult to obtain this information as there was an incentive to distort.

Professor Diamond said that we could look at demand elasticities classified by income bracket if we were looking only for a local formulation of the welfare function to check that first-order conditions were satisfied. We would just need to know that people were price-takers and were not colluding to distort the evidence. We needed information on utility functions only if we were looking for a global maximum.

Professor Shell said that we could observe only fairly general demand curves generated by people with very different utility functions. The information we needed was more specific. *Dr Sheshinski* asked how we could test that people were price-takers.

Dr Bliss saw the main use of Diamond–Mirrlees-type analysis in knocking down rules of thumb for second-best situations.

Professor Mirrlees said that in formulating utility functions we used both value judgements and evidence. He felt there was a possibility of distortion of the evidence because it did not pay individuals and groups to convey such evidence (on their relative marginal utility of income, say) honestly.

Professor Diamond said that the market information would be unlikely to be distorted to any great extent. The procedure in practice would probably be fairly casual – using a classification of luxuries and necessities, for example.

11 Intertemporal National Optimality and Temporal Social Preferences*

M. Inagaki

SIR GEORGE WILLIAMS UNIVERSITY, MONTREAL

I. INTRODUCTION

During the past decade the problem of optimal growth has attracted considerable attention from theoretical economists. However, the discussion has essentially centred around the mathematical implications of Ramsey's principle. Little progress has been made in the way of formulating alternative definitions of optimality: from the point of view of economics, the theory of optimal growth has remained in a state of relative stagnation ever since Ramsey's pioneering contribution (Ramsey, 1928).

It seems to me that the main reason for this unsatisfactory state of affairs is the formal identification of the problem of optimal growth with an individual decision-making problem. The result is an over-simplification of the problem of optimal growth which neglects one of its most fundamental and fascinating aspects: *the intertemporal conflict of interest between populations living at different periods of time*.

Indeed, the identification of a nation with a single decision-maker can hardly be considered as realistic. Only at a given point of time can a (centrally governed) nation be conceivably identified with a single (central) government, i.e. with a single decision-maker. This is no longer possible over the whole lifetime of a nation. The life of a nation extends over a long sequence of governments each of which has a finite time horizon and, generally, a still shorter political mandate. Even at the highest level of abstraction, a nation can only be identified with an infinite sequence of such 'finite' (central) governments.

I have therefore attempted to reformulate the problem of optimal economic growth as a group-decision problem over time. The members of the group are the above-mentioned governments. The problem is no longer to maximise a unique national utility index, but to find a group-decision rule which is acceptable to all successive governments. Each of such rules or strategies, including Ramsey's principle, can be considered as an *a priori* admissible definition of optimal economic growth.

* The author is indebted to the Canada Council for the financial contribution it made to the study.

A rational way to proceed is first to specify the properties which a growth strategy must satisfy in order to be *a priori* admissible from the national point of view. For instance, one may want to reject any growth strategy which implies a monotonically declining savings ratio in a situation where technological progress ensures an ever-rising level of income per capita: why should the present and poorer generations of a nation make relatively higher sacrifices than the future and richer generations? If retained, this argument would generally rule out Ramsey's principle as a nationally admissible growth strategy.

There are many other conditions which could conceivably be included in the concept of national admissibility. They all tend to introduce some minimum degree of 'fairness' in the long-term intertemporal distribution of consumption. It may be noted that this problem of a 'fair' intertemporal distribution of consumption is very similar to the static problem of income distribution within a given nation. Indeed, the first can be viewed as the dynamic analogue of the second. In both cases, the concept of 'fairness' is subject to various interpretations.

It is thus clear that a number of alternative sets of *a priori* desirable properties can be considered as an appropriate definition of national admissibility. It follows, furthermore, that the choice of the *optimal* strategy can only be made relatively to a given set of admissible strategies.

This choice requires an intertemporal national preference pattern with respect to the set of admissible strategies. This preference pattern need not establish a complete ordering of all members of the set; it only has to establish the superiority of one member over all others. It may not establish any ordering at all among the non-optimal admissible strategies. Formally, all we need is a utility index which associates the value 1 to one of the admissible strategies (i.e. to the optimal strategy) and the value 0 to all others.

Even so, the construction of such an index is generally not a simple matter. It is only in the case of *unanimous preference* that the choice of the optimal strategy becomes simple and obvious. If a given member of the set of admissible strategies is preferred to all others by all successive governments, it is clearly *optimal* with respect to the set.

Whether or not a unanimously preferred strategy exists will depend on the particular properties of the strategies included in the admissible set. This raises the problem as to under what conditions a set of admissible strategies contains a unanimously preferred member. The theory set forth in this paper[1] considers that this is the central problem of optimal economic growth.

[1] First introduced in Inagaki (1970).

II. THE ELEMENTS OF THE THEORY

(1) *The Instantaneous Governments*

We shall begin by the definition of the actors which participate in the process of optimal planning. In a discrete (yearly) time description of the growth process, these are what I have called the yearly governments or YGs. A YG acts for and according to the preferences of the population of a nation living in a given year. Thus Optiland's YG in 1970 represents the citizens of Optiland alive in 1970. This YG is entirely characterised by the two following properties:

(i) It completely[1] controls the national consumption level in, but only in, 1970.

(ii) It has a well-defined preference pattern with respect to all feasible consumption programmes extending from 1970 to, say, 2000.

Generally speaking, the YG in year t controls the national consumption level in the year t only, even though it is directly interested in the consumption levels of the years t to, say, $t+\omega$.

In order to define the preference pattern of a YG, we assume the existence of an instantaneous and time-invariant utility function $U(c)$ which, at any given point of time, expresses the instantaneous preference pattern of the population with respect to all levels of per capita consumption c. We further assume that all YGs have the same finite time horizon ω. For the sake of simplicity, we do not consider any time discounting in this paper. Finally, we assume that, given any two feasible consumption programmes, a YG prefers the programme which gives the greater value to the index

$$I\{c_t^{t+\omega}\} = \sum_{n=t}^{t+\omega} U(c_n). \qquad (11.1)$$

In a continuous time description, this index becomes

$$I\{c_t^{t+\omega}\} = \int_t^{t+\omega} U[c(\tau)] \qquad (11.2)$$

and the YGs become *instantaneous governments* or IGs.

It is important to realise that the YGs differ from each other with respect to their positions in historical time only. *They are different decision-makers*, only *because they represent people living at different periods of time*. This fact is, however, crucial. *It causes a fundamental conflict of interests among the successive YGs*, i.e. among the successive populations they represent. The theory set forth in this

[1] Within the limits of economic feasibility.

paper[1] considers the solution of this conflict as the central problem of optimal economic growth.

(2) *The Set of Admissible Growth Strategies*

In order to formulate the problem of optimal growth as a decision problem in terms of the YGs, we have to define the *set of feasible acts* among which a YG has to make its choice. The first idea which comes to mind is to identify the set of feasible acts of the YG in year t with the set of programmes which are feasible over the period t to $t+\omega$, given the initial conditions prevailing at time t. Such an identification introduces, however, an unnecessary theoretical complication: by making the set of feasible acts dependent on the initial conditions at time t, every YG will generally be endowed with a different set of feasible acts. Fortunately this complication can be avoided by defining the set of feasible acts in terms of feasible growth *strategies*, and not in terms of feasible growth *programmes*.

The concept of growth strategy is explained and defined in Inagaki (1970),[2] with respect to a general class of neo-classical macro-economic growth models. Among other things, these models are characterised by the fact that, given the initial capital–output ratio κ_0, the time path of the savings ratio s completely determines the time paths of all endogenous variables of the model, i.e. of capital K, production Y and consumption C.[3]

With respect to growth models which have this property, a growth strategy can roughly be defined as a *rule* which associates, at every given point of time, a unique value of the savings ratio $s = \dot{K}/Y$ to every given value of the capital–output ratio $\kappa(\tau)$, $0 \leqslant \tau < +\infty$. The continuous function $S(\kappa, \tau)$ is[4] a *feasible growth strategy* for the constraints $0 \leqslant G(\tau) < \kappa(\tau) < H(\tau)$,[5] $0 \leqslant \tau < +\infty$, if the differential equation

$$s = S(\kappa, \tau) \tag{11.3}$$

determines an indefinitely feasible growth programme[6] $\kappa(\tau)$, $t \leqslant \tau < +\infty$, whenever

$$G(t) < \kappa(t) < H(t), \quad 0 \leqslant t < +\infty.$$

[1] See note 1, p. 242 above.

[2] Op. cit., section 1.6.

[3] Capital and lower-case letters denote respectively national and per capita values.

[4] The following concept of growth strategy is more general than that given in Inagaki (1970) section 2.3.

[5] $G(t)$ and $H(t)$ are assumed to be continuous over $t_0 \leqq t < +\infty$.

[6] An indefinitely feasible growth programme is, in terms of $\kappa \equiv K/Y$, a continuously differentiable positive function $\kappa(t)$, $t_0 \leqslant t < +\infty$, which satisfies both the initial condition at t_0, and the given growth model over $t_0 < t \leqslant +\infty$.

Ramsey's principle provides an instance of a feasible growth strategy in the above sense.[1] In its continuous time version, this principle prescribes[2, 3] that

$$\frac{dU}{dc}(t) = \int_{t}^{t+\omega} \frac{\partial Y}{\partial K}(\tau)\frac{dU}{dc}(\tau)e^{-\lambda(\tau-t)}d\tau, \quad 0 \leqslant t < +\infty. \quad (11.4)$$

where K, Y and λ respectively denote capital, production and the demographic rate of growth.

In words, it postulates that at any instant t the marginal utility of per capita consumption should be equal to the marginal utility of the sum over infinite time of per capita returns resulting from investments made at time t. We shall therefore refer to Ramsey's principle as *marginal utility equilibrium over infinite time* or MUEIT.

Another instance of a feasible growth strategy is provided by the principle of *marginal utility equilibrium over finite time* or MUEFT:[4]

$$\frac{dU}{dc}(t) = \int_{t}^{t+\omega} \frac{\partial Y}{\partial K}(\tau)\frac{dU}{dc}(\tau)e^{-\lambda(\tau-t)}d\tau, \quad 0 \leqslant t < +\infty.^{5} \quad (11.5)$$

Both MUEIT and MUEFT can be considered as ethical principles. MUEFT is, however, more realistic. It requires only that, in terms of utility, the people of a nation should always invest exactly as much as the returns they expect from their investments over their common social time horizon ω.[6] This social time horizon may be defined as follows:

$$\omega = \frac{\sum_{\eta=1}^{100} y_\eta e_\eta p_\eta}{\sum_{\eta=1}^{100} y_\eta p_\eta} \quad (11.6)$$

where p_η denotes the income-earning population of age n, e_η the life expectancy of the population p_η and y_η the income per capita of the population p_η.

The definitions of the MUEIT and MUEFT strategies are both

[1] For some $G(\tau)$ and $H(\tau)$, and granted that certain existence conditions are satisfied. See Inagaki (1970) subsection 3.1.1.

[2] Inagaki (1970) subsection 4.2.1.

[3] It also prescribes that, given κ_0, (11.4) must be applied in such a way that the resulting programme is efficient. An indefinitely feasible programme is efficient if there is no other which yields always as much and sometimes more consumption.

[4] For some $G(\tau)$ and $H(\tau)$, and granted that certain existence conditions are satisfied. See Inagaki (1970) subsection 2.5.2, and chap. 4.

[5] As in the case of (11.4), (11.5) must be applied in an efficient way. See note 3, p. 245 above.

[6] This is the same ω as in (11.1) and (11.2).

implicit and relatively complicated. There are much simpler strategies. The simplest of all are the constant and positive savings ratio or CPS strategies:

$$S(\kappa, \tau) = s, \quad 0 < s = \text{constant} < 1. \tag{11.7}$$

These strategies are all feasible in $0 < \kappa(\tau) < +\infty$, $0 \leqslant \tau \leqslant +\infty$.

Let us now return to our problem of identifying the set of feasible acts of a YG with a set of feasible growth strategies. As already said, we want this set to be the same for all YGs. Moreover, for reasons which will become clear in the next section, we also require that all strategies of the set be feasible in a given common region $\bar{G}(\tau) < \kappa(\tau) < \bar{H}(\tau)$, $0 \leqslant \tau < +\infty$, where $\bar{G}(\tau)$ and $\bar{H}(\tau)$ are the same for all strategies.

Accordingly, we endow the YGs with a feeling of *national allegiance*,[1] by virtue of which they are willing to restrict their choice to a set of *admissible* strategies which satisfy the above requirements.[2] The definition of this set expresses the nature and degree of the national allegiance of the YGs, and varies from case to case. In a certain sense, *the concept of national allegiance introduces an ethical factor* in the solution of the problem of optimal economic growth. It does so, however, in a much more flexible way than the Ramsey theory. In fact, the latter can be considered as an extreme case of national allegiance, where the set of admissible strategies contains one member only, namely the MUEIT strategy.

(3) *The Concept of Unanimous Preference*

The fact that the set of feasible acts is the same for all YGs does not automatically solve the conflict of interest which opposes the different YGs in their respective choice of the 'optimal' strategy. Of any two admissible strategies, a YG prefers the one which gives a greater value to its utility index $I\{c_t^{t+\omega}\}$. Now, the value of this index does not only depend on the selected strategy, but also on the historically given capital stock at t. Which of the two admissible strategies S_1 and S_2 is preferred by the YG of year t may very well depend on the historically given capital–output ratio $\kappa(t)$, even within their common interval of feasibility $\bar{G}(t) < \kappa(t) < \bar{H}(t)$.

Fortunately, it sometimes happens that there exists a sub-region of common feasibility, throughout which all YGs prefer one strategy to the other. More precisely, we say that the admissible strategy S_1 is *unanimously preferred*[3] to the admissible strategy S_2 in $G^*(\tau) < \kappa(\tau) < H^*(\tau)$, $\bar{G}(\tau) \leqslant G^*(\tau) < H^*(\tau) \leqslant \bar{H}(\tau)$, $0 \leqslant \tau < +\infty$, if:

[1] Inagaki (1970) section 2.3.
[2] This definition is more general than the one in Inagaki (1970) section 2.3.
[3] This definition is more general than that in Inagaki (1970) section 2.4.

(i) It defines a growth programme $\kappa_1(\tau)$ which satisfies

$$G^*(\tau) < \kappa_1(\tau) < H^*(\tau) \tag{11.8}$$

over $t \leqslant \tau < +\infty$, provided only it satisfies (11.8) at $\tau = t \geqslant 0$.

(ii) Whatever $t \geqslant 0$, and an 'initial' capital–output ratio κ_t such that $G^*(t) < \kappa_t < H^*(t)$, the index $I\{c_t^{t+\omega}\}$ takes on a greater value along $\kappa_1(\tau)$ than along $\kappa_2(\tau)$.

Now it is sometimes possible to define the set of admissible strategies in such a way that it contains a member $\hat{S}$ which is *unanimously preferred to all others* in some region $G^*(\tau) < \kappa(\tau) < H^*(\tau)$, $\bar{G}(\tau) \leqslant G^*(\tau) < H^*(\tau) \leqslant \bar{H}(\tau)$, $0 \leqslant \tau < +\infty$.[1] *The conflict of interest among the different YGs can then be considered as solved in this region.* Accordingly, we shall say that *the admissible strategy* $\hat{S}$ is optimal in the region $G^*(\tau) < \kappa(\tau) < H^*(\tau)$, $0 \leqslant \tau < +\infty$, if it is unanimously preferred to all other admissible strategies in this region.

The concept of unanimous preference is of fundamental importance. It is therefore very important that no confusion arises with regard to this concept. In particular, it should be clear that the choice of the *IG* at t only depends on what happens over the time interval t to $t+\omega$. For the *IG* at t, bygones are bygones. The initial conditions at time t must be accepted as historically given. This does not mean, however, that the IG at t would not have preferred that the preceding IGs had applied a more investment-oriented strategy. It obviously would have preferred to be provided with the highest possible capital stock at time t. History is irreversible, however, and the IG at t can only base its choice of a growth strategy on the latter's implications for the future, more precisely for the period t to $t+\omega$.

Another aspect of the concept of unanimous preference which should be stressed is that it introduces the possibility of ordering strategies, and not only specific programmes. It thus permits the establishment of a partial hierarchy among ethical principles; in particular, it permits the comparison of the MUEIT and MUEFT principles.[2]

III. CONSTANT AND POSITIVE SAVINGS RATIO

(1) *Preference and Growth Assumptions*

The form of the utility index of the instantaneous government or IGs has already been specified by (11.2). In what follows we shall

[1] One can extend the definition of feasible and admissible strategies to include the case where this region reduces to a line $G^*(\tau) = H^*(\tau)$, which may even be independent of τ.

[2] Inagaki (1970) section 4.4.

assume that the instantaneous utility function of per capita consumption c is a Bernoulli function

$$U(c) = -c^{-(\nu-1)}, \quad \nu > 1 \tag{11.9}$$

which has a Bliss level, and an elasticity of marginal utility greater than 1 (see Frisch, 1964).

The utility index of the IGs thus becomes

$$I\{c_t^{t+\omega}\} = -\int_t^{t+\omega} c^{-(\nu-1)}(\tau)d\tau. \tag{11.10}$$

The growth model is characterised by

$$Y = F(K, L, \tau) \quad \text{(production function)} \tag{11.11}$$

$$C = Y - \dot{K} \quad \text{(closed economy)} \tag{11.12}$$

$$L = e^{\lambda\tau} \quad \text{(labour supply)} \tag{11.13}$$

where $\lambda \geqslant 0$ is the demographic growth rate. (For the sake of simplicity we let $L_0 = 1$ and identify labour with population.)

Three different production functions will be considered. They will be respectively specified in the following subsections.

(2) *The Case of a Constant Capital–Output Ratio*

For the rest of this paper we restrict our discussion to the case where the set of admissible strategies is the set of all savings ratios

$$0 < s = \text{const.} \leqslant 1. \tag{11.14}$$

To begin with, we consider the simple constant capital–output or CCO production function

$$Y = \frac{1}{\kappa}K, \quad \kappa = \text{const.}^{1} \tag{11.15}$$

Given the initial condition $K(0) = K_0 > 0$ and the constant savings ratio $s > 0$, it follows from our general growth assumptions (11.11), (11.12) and (11.13), that

$$C = (1-s)\frac{K_0}{\kappa}e^{(s/\kappa)\tau} \tag{11.16}$$

and, consequently,

$$c = \frac{C}{L}$$

$$= (1-s)\frac{K_0}{\kappa}e^{((s/\kappa)-\lambda)\tau}. \tag{11.17}$$

[1] The concept of a growth strategy should be defined here in terms of K and not κ. This can easily be done, but leads to a somewhat more cumbersome formulation.

Accordingly,

$$I\{c(\tau)_0{}^\omega\} = -\frac{\kappa}{K_0}\frac{1}{(1-s)^{\nu-1}}\int_0^\omega e^{-(s-\lambda\kappa)(\nu-1)\tau/\kappa}d\tau$$

$$= -\frac{\kappa}{K_0}\frac{\kappa}{(1-s)^{\nu-1}(s-\lambda\kappa)(\nu-1)}\{1-e^{-(s-\lambda\kappa)(\nu-1)\omega/\kappa}\}. \quad (11.18)$$

The maximum of $I\{c(\tau)_0{}^\omega\}$ is obtained for the s which satisfies

$$\frac{d}{ds}I\{c(\tau)_0{}^\omega\} = 0 \quad (11.19)$$

i.e.

$$\frac{1}{s-\lambda\kappa}-\frac{\nu-1}{1-s} = \frac{\omega}{\kappa}\frac{(\nu-1)}{e^{(s-\lambda\kappa)(\nu-1)\omega/\kappa}-1}. \quad (11.20)$$

Now (11.20) does not depend on K_0. It follows that the s defined by (11.20) is the optimal CPS strategy whatever K_0. In the case of the CCO model this optimal constant and positive savings ratio $\hat{s}$ or CPS strategy does only depend on $\lambda\kappa$, ω/κ and $(\nu-1)$.

$$\hat{s} = \hat{s}(\lambda\kappa, \omega/\kappa, \nu-1). \quad (11.21)$$

Table 11.1 gives the values of $\hat{s}$ for $\lambda = 0{\cdot}02$, $\kappa = 3$, and different values of ω and ν.

TABLE 11.1

VALUES OF $\hat{s}$

ν \ ω	10	15	20	25	30
2	0·30	0·43	0·48	0·51	0·52
3	0·25	0·33	0·36	0·37	0·37
4	0·21	0·27	0·29	0·29	0·30
5	0·18	0·23	0·24	0·25	0·25

It is seen that the utility-maximising savings ratio $\hat{s}$ increases with the time horizon ω and decreases with the elasticity of marginal utility ν. Over the range of values considered, $\hat{s}$ depends more on ν than ω. For $\nu \geqslant 4$, and $\omega \leqslant 30$, one finds that $\hat{s} \leqslant 0{\cdot}30$. In general, the values of the optimal savings ratio $\hat{s}$ are not too unrealistic, especially if one takes into account that they have been derived without introducing any time discounting.

However, they should be considered with caution. Indeed, a CCO model generally assumes a labour surplus and a fixed capital–labour ratio. Now these assumptions make little sense in a theory which assumes that the growth model holds true over infinite time.

Given a fixed capital–labour ratio, only an infinite labour supply can maintain a labour surplus along a capital path which grows faster than the population. Now, under the above assumptions, the 'optimal' growth rate of capital

$$\frac{\dot{K}}{K} = \frac{\hat{s}}{\kappa} \tag{11.22}$$

varies between 6 per cent and 17 per cent. This is much higher than the highest demographic growth rate ever recorded. The above exercise should therefore be merely considered as a 'logical experiment'.

(3) *The Cobb–Douglas Case with Autonomous Technology*

The next production function we consider is the well-known Cobb–Douglas function with autonomously and exponentially growing technology:

$$Y = e^{\rho\tau} K^{\alpha} L^{1-\alpha} \tag{11.23}$$

where ρ = constant $\geqslant 0$ is the rate of technological progress and $0 < \alpha$ = constant < 1 is the elasticity of production with respect to capital.

Under assumptions (11.23), (11.12) and (11.13), a constant and positive savings ratio defines, for any given initial capital–output ratio $\kappa_0 > 0$, the κ-path

$$\kappa(\tau) = \frac{s}{g} + \left(\kappa_0 - \frac{s}{g}\right) e^{-(1-\alpha)g\tau}, \quad 0 \leqslant \tau < +\infty \tag{11.24}$$

where

$$g < \frac{\rho}{1-\alpha} + \lambda.$$

The corresponding per capita consumption path is

$$\begin{aligned} c(\tau) &= (1-s)\kappa(\tau)^{\alpha/(1-\alpha)} e^{(g-\lambda)\tau} \\ &= (1-s)\left\{\frac{s}{g} + \left(\kappa_0 - \frac{s}{g}\right) e^{-(1-\alpha)g\tau}\right\}^{\alpha/(1-\alpha)} e^{(g-\lambda)\tau}. \end{aligned} \tag{11.25}$$

Under our preference assumption (11.10), it follows that

$$\begin{aligned} I\{c(\tau)_0{}^{\omega}\} &= -\int_0^{\omega} c^{-\nu-1}(\tau) d\tau \\ &= -\frac{1}{(1-s)^{\nu-1}} \int_0^{\omega} \frac{d\tau}{\left\{\frac{s}{g} + \left(\kappa_0 - \frac{s}{g}\right) e^{-(1-\alpha)g\tau}\right\}^{(\alpha(\nu-1))/(1-\alpha)} e^{(g-\lambda)(\nu-1)\tau}}. \end{aligned} \tag{11.26}$$

Except for particular values of the parameters (for instance, $g = 0{\cdot}04$, $\lambda = 0{\cdot}02$, $\alpha = 0{\cdot}5$), this integral cannot be integrated in closed form. Moreover, even when it can be integrated, its differentiation with respect to s leads to a rather complicated equation. It is therefore more convenient to study numerically the dependence of the optimal s on κ_0.

For this purpose, we have used values of the parameters which are believed to describe approximately the United States economy: $\alpha = 1/3$; $g = 3/100$; $\lambda = 1/100$; $\omega = 30$. For $\nu = 2$,[1] $\omega = 30$ years, and different values of κ_0, Table 11.2 gives the value $s = \hat{s}(\kappa_0)$ which maximises $I\{c(\tau)_0{}^\omega\}$ under the initial condition $\kappa(0) = \kappa_0$.

TABLE 11.2

κ_0	2·3–2·8	2·9	3·0–3·1	3·2–3·3	3·4–4·0
$\hat{s}(\kappa_0)$	0·15	0·13	0·12	0·11	0·10
$\dfrac{\hat{s}(\kappa_0)}{g}$	5·00	4·33	4·00	3·67	3·33

It is seen that $\hat{s}(\kappa_0)$ varies only between 10 per cent and 12 per cent for initial values of the capital–output ranging between three and four years. Moreover, a more detailed numerical analysis shows that

$$\hat{s}(3{\cdot}4) = 0{\cdot}101$$

i.e.

$$\frac{\hat{s}(3{\cdot}4)}{g} = 3{\cdot}4.$$

It follows that there exists an initial value $\hat{\kappa}$ of the capital–output ratio, such that $\hat{s}(\hat{\kappa}_0)$ is unanimously preferred at the point $\hat{\kappa}_0$ and, consequently, $\hat{s}(\hat{\kappa}_0)$ is the optimal CPS strategy over $0 \leqslant \tau < +\infty$. Under the above numerical assumptions, $\hat{\kappa}_0 = 3{\cdot}4$ and $\hat{s}(\hat{\kappa}_0) = 10{\cdot}1$ per cent; this strategy defines the golden age programme

$$\kappa(\tau) = \hat{\kappa}_0, \quad 0 \leqslant \tau < +\infty \tag{11.27}$$

$$c(\tau) = [1 - \hat{s}(\hat{\kappa}_0)]\hat{\kappa}_0{}^{\alpha/(1-\alpha)}e^{(g-\lambda)\tau}, \quad 0 \leqslant \tau < +\infty. \tag{11.28}$$

This is a rather remarkable result, since it roughly corresponds to the actual behaviour of the United States economy. It is also noteworthy that in terms of the value of s the conflict of interest among the different IGs is not 'very great', even if $\kappa_0 \neq 3{\cdot}4$, provided only that $3 \leqslant \kappa_0 \leqslant 4$.

[1] See Frisch (1964).

(4) *The Cobb–Douglas Case with Non-Autonomous Technology*

Even though the numerical results of the last section are very satisfactory, they are based on a growth model which is not very appropriate for optimal growth analysis. Indeed, one of the properties of this model is that, given any CPS value s and intial value κ_0, $\kappa(\tau)$ tends monotonically to the value s/g (see (11.24)). Table 11.3

TABLE 11.3

s	0·1	0·2	0·3	0·4	0·5	0·6
s/g	3·33	6·67	10·00	13·33	16·67	20·00

gives s/g for $g = 0{\cdot}03$ and different values of s. It means that the United States economy would end up with a capital–output ratio of ten years, if it decided to apply hereafter a savings ratio such as that prevailing in Japan. This seems hard to believe.

In my opinion, the problem resides in the assumption of a completely autonomous rate of technological progress (ρ = const. > 0). It seems to me that, in the long run, a higher savings ratio must lead to a higher rate of growth, i.e. to a higher rate of technological progress. For the sake of a logical experiment, let us therefore assume

$$g(t)-\lambda = \frac{1}{\delta}\int_{t-\delta}^{t} G[s(\tau)]d\tau. \tag{11.29}$$

If the savings ratio remains constant over time, (11.29) implies

$$g = G(s)+\lambda. \tag{11.30}$$

Let us furthermore set

$$G(s) = \tfrac{25}{100}s-\tfrac{30}{100}s^2.$$

This leads to the following values of g for $\lambda = 1$ per cent (Table 11.4).

TABLE 11.4

s	0·10	0·20	0·30	0·40	0·50	0·60	0·70
g	0·035	0·048	0·058	0·062	0·060	0·052	0·038
s/g	2·85	4·17	5·17	6·45	8·33	11·54	18·42

It is seen that g has a maximum for s = 40 per cent (exactly for s = 41·67 per cent). However, over the actually observed range of the savings ratio, i.e. over s = 10–30 per cent, the order of magnitude of the g values is by no means unrealistic. Over the range in question, the increase of the long-term (asymptotic) capital–output ratio is greater than what one would generally expect to observe; it is, however, much smaller than in the case of autonomous technological progress (see Table 11.3).

Table 11.5 gives the values of $\hat{s}(\kappa_0)$ in the case where the constant $g = (\rho/1-\alpha)+\lambda$ in the model of the last section is replaced by $\{G(s)+(1/100)\}$. As before, the time horizon ω is 30 years and $v = 2$.

TABLE 11.5

κ_0	2–4·1	4·2–4·4	4·5–6·0
$\hat{s}(\kappa_0)$	0·30	0·28	0·27
$\dfrac{\hat{s}(\kappa_0)}{g(\hat{s}(\kappa_0))}$	5·8	5·0	4·85

As in the case of autonomous technology, there is a value of $\hat{\kappa}_0 = 4{\cdot}85$ years. The corresponding $\hat{s}(\hat{\kappa}_0)$ is 27·05 per cent. It is higher than before. This was to be expected, because of the positive influence of s on g in the range $0 < s < 41{\cdot}67$ per cent. However, the range of κ_0 values for which the conflict of interest among the different IGs remains, in terms of $\hat{s}(\kappa_0)$, within narrow limits (± 10 per cent of $\hat{s}$) is much greater ($2 \leqslant \kappa_0 \leqslant 6$).

From the point of view of the theory of optimal growth, the above growth model seems more realistic than the preceding one. The form of $G(s)$ and the parameters of $G(s)$ could be further studied. As to the values of $\hat{s}(\kappa_0)$, they can probably be decreased with the help of a suitable time discount rate.

IV. CONCLUSION

The main objective of section III was to indicate the potentialities of the conceptual framework set forth in section II. In order to keep our exposition free from side-issues, we have purposely restricted our analysis to the case of the simple CPS strategies. Nevertheless, the results we have obtained are rather interesting.

For three different growth models we have found that the constant savings ratio which maximises utility over finite time is very insensitive to the initial capital stock, at least over the range of values which are usually observed. In the case of the CCO model, there is complete insensitivity. In the case of the two Cobb–Douglas models, it was further found that there was a utility-maximising savings ratio which satisfied the condition of golden age growth ($s = g\kappa$). Finally, it was found that the numerical results we obtained were relatively realistic, at least much more so than most numerical results which have been derived from Ramsey's principle.

Specifically, we always found at least one value of the initial capital stock for which the set of constant and positive savings ratios contains a unanimously preferred member. This initial capital stock corresponds to a capital–output ratio which lies well within the range of actually observed values. Moreover, at least over the central part of this range, the conflict of interest between the IGs seems very small. For all practical purposes, it may be somewhat loosely said that a 'quasi-optimal' constant savings ratio always appears to exist.

The CPS ratios constitute only one possible set of admissible strategies. The concepts of *instantaneous government*, *national allegiance* and *unanimous preference* can be used to analyse other sets of admissible strategies or, more simply, to compare any two given strategies such as MUEIT and MUEFT.[1] It is hoped that the discussion of these concepts will open up a new line of approach to the problem of optimal economic growth.

[1] Inagaki (1970) section 4.4.

REFERENCES

R. Frisch, 'Dynamic Utility', *Econometrica*, vol. XXXII, no. 3 (1964).

M. Inagaki, *Optical Economic Growth: Finite Shifting Versus Infinite Time Horizon. Contributions to Economic Analysis* (North-Holland Publishing Company, 1970).

F. P. Ramsey, 'A Mathematical Theory of Saving', *Economic Journal*, vol. XXXVIII (Dec 1928).

Discussion of the Paper by M. Inagaki

Professor Inagaki introduced his paper by saying that about four years ago he decided to reconsider the basic nature of the problem of optimal growth. He pointed out that Ramsey's principle implied the 'marginal utility equilibrium over infinite time' or MUEIT condition:

$$u(c(t)) = \int_t^\infty \frac{\partial Y}{\partial K}(\tau) u(c(\tau)) \frac{L(t)}{L(\tau)} e^{-i(\tau - t)} d\tau$$

where $u(c)$ was the marginal utility of consumption per head c, and Y, K and L were production, capital and labour; differentiated with respect to t, MUEIT yields Euler's condition. In terms of discounted utility units, MUEIT means that the people investing at time t will never get back the value of their investments over their own lifetime. Moreover, under the usual assumptions regarding $u(c)$ and the initial conditions, Ramsey's principle generally implies a greater savings ratio for the poorer generations. He found these implications of the Ramsey principle unacceptable.

He also disagreed with the identification of the problem of optimal economic growth with an individual decision-making problem. He argued that the problem of optimal economic growth was essentially a problem of the conflict of interest between present and future generations.

Accordingly, he introduced the concept of yearly governments (YG) which controlled the level of savings in a single year t, but had preferences over the period t to $t+\omega$ where ω could be interpreted as the mean life expectancy of the population living at time t. If $\omega = 30$ years, each YG knows that there are 29 other yearly governments in the decisions of which it is interested, but over which it has no direct control.

The problem for the YG of year t was therefore to find a rational way to choose the savings ratio in year t. He considered this problem as the central problem of optimal growth. In order to solve it he introduced two further assumptions.

Firstly, he assumed that each YG determined its savings ratio by selecting a growth strategy (i.e. rule of capital accumulation) which it would like to see enforced by all later YGs. Secondly, he assumed that all YGs had a feeling of national allegiance by virtue of which they were willing to restrict their choice to a set of admissible strategies. If this set was properly restricted, he found that it would contain a unanimously preferred strategy, i.e. one which every successive YG would prefer to see enforced over the next ω years. Whenever a unanimously preferred strategy existed, he considered the resulting growth path as optimal and the problem of optimal growth as solved.

In the present paper he deals with the case of the strategies defined by a constant savings ratio. He referred those who were interested in more complicated instances of unanimous preference to his book *Optimal Economic Growth: Finite Shifting versus Infinite Time Horizon.* There, he showed that the 'marginal utility equilibrium over finite time' or MUEFT condition, derived from MUEIT by replacing the infinite upper limit of the MUEIT integral by the finite time horizon ω of the YGs, was unanimously preferred to MUEIT in all cases which he was able to investigate.

Dr Bliss said that his comments consisted of several questions to the author.

1. He asked what we meant by optimal growth. To characterise a path as 'optimal' is to recommend it within some model according to an ethical principle. This is Ramsey's approach and is what Meade has called 'perfect altruism'; no generation holds its own welfare in special regard relative to any other generation's welfare. Anyone who wants to propose another ethical principle should be prepared to defend it as an ethical principle. Economics throws up some very interesting problems in applied ethics and he thought economists should discuss these as part of their subject, bringing in ethics as a tool. It was not clear that the economists' comparative advantage for solving these problems fell below that of the philosophers.

The author had introduced the principle of perfect selfishness (i.e. each generation cares only for its own welfare) which he calls the MUEFT principle. The author had claimed that the discussion of the outcome of the application of this principle was 'the central problem of optimal economic growth'. He therefore asked the author what ethical arguments he would use to defend this principle. Without such arguments it was not a theory of optimal growth but a theory of equilibrium growth under perfect selfishness.

2. He asked for clarification of the concept of 'national allegiance'. It seemed to mean that perfect selfishness was modified by an ethical principle constraining a nation's set of actions. This gave rise to a characteristic ethical problem. We may want to know what ethical principle is being applied when an ethical statement prohibits something. In other words, one did not establish an ethic by a list of prohibited acts. 'National allegiance' should be analysed down to the fundamental intertemporal distributional values which gave rise to it.

3. The author largely confined his attention to 'unanimous preference'. He asked how the author reconciled his early claim that the conflict between generations was the central problem of economic growth with the exclusion of that conflict from his analysis.

4. In section III (2) of the paper the class of cases considered was drastically restricted by the assumption (11.14) (constancy of s). He asked what was the meaning of this assumption as a restriction on any particular generation's actions.

5. Finally, he offered another interpretation of what the author had actually done in the final section of his paper. Consider a rolling plan (each generation of planners has the same finite horizon) where each generation of planners prepares a complete plan for the horizon (and hence an immediate rate of consumption). We look for an equilibrium development in the sense of a development such that each new generation of planners will not wish to revise the plans prepared by their predecessors but will merely extend them.

The author had considered the solutions to a number of such problems for particular cases. The utility function is always isoelastic and the production function is fixed coefficient, Cobb–Douglas or C.E.S. He wondered why the author had not considered the problem unconstrained by the arbitrary requirement that the saving ratio be constant for each plan and then examined the path the economy would follow. If his earlier claim that the problem outlined was the fundamental problem of optimal economic growth were correct, then this seems the right case to tackle. Problems of this type had been analysed by Goldman, Phelps and Pollak, and Meade.

Professor Berthomieu said the mechanism for defining the time horizon (on p. 245) replaced the traditional wage earner–profit earner opposition by a new kind of political agreement procedure even if limited to the time horizon. He asked how sensitive ω was to the weighting procedure used. He felt the assumption of a constant ω was difficult to accept for a long-run growth process, using the given weighting procedure, since the proportion of young people in the population was growing. He asked whether the assumption of a constant coupled with constancy of relative income shares did not furnish a sufficient condition for the existence of a unanimously preferred strategy.

Professor Inagaki said that other weighting procedures could equally well have been used to determine ω as the one here. In fact it made little difference – e.g. in a wide class of procedures for the United States the answer had varied between 28 and 32 years. He agreed a constant age structure had been used here, but an exogenously changing structure would have been difficult to specify. He pointed out that there was obviously an upper limit to ω.

He was mainly concerned with a framework for discussion, and felt that criticisms such as the one on the assumption of a constant ω applied also to Ramsey.

Professor Rose said that in order to draw up a finite horizon plan each set of planners had to decide on a terminal capital stock. If we then consider why they wanted to leave a capital stock – for the benefit of future generations – we saw that ω should be infinite. *Professor Inagaki* replied that a group forming a finite horizon plan (the period being the mean life expectancy) would strictly want nothing left at the end. However, in order to admit the possibility of agreement we restricted the strategies under consideration to those that gave indefinitely feasible paths.

Professor Uzawa asked why only the conflict between populations over time had been considered. There was no reason to suppose we could obtain agreement on a savings ratio inside a population as people might just choose to carry out their own consumption plans. *Professor Inagaki* said the grand solution would solve both problems together and agreed that the problem posed by Professor Uzawa was important. As a first step he had started with the intertemporal problem.

Professor Hahn strongly disagreed with Dr Bliss's view of optimal growth as a moral calculus. Optimal growth was about having a language for discussion of the savings rate – it was unfair to criticise Professor Inagaki's procedure for having no general moral foundations.

Dr Bliss said he did not understand Professor Hahn's argument and completely disagreed. He had been asking why something should be called optimal.

Dr Dixit asked why we should be interested in unanimously preferred policies. Each YG would have no guarantee the path would be followed: for example, ω might change. If a YG thought its successors would not follow the strategy, they might do something different. *Professor Inagaki* said he was considering honest people who expect others to follow their preferred path.

Professor Berthomieu said there would not exist a sufficient condition for a unanimously preferred path if income distribution and thus ω changed.

Professor Yaari said the Phelps–Pollak work had been continued by Peleg. The position where no one had an incentive to move if they assumed others would not was called a Nash equilibrium. The trouble with this approach is that a Nash equilibrium is not necessarily Pareto optimal.

Professor Inagaki said that if we had a unanimously preferred strategy, everyone would be worse off if someone switched. It was impossible to find a strategy which was preferred by everyone to a unanimously preferred strategy. He drew a diagram showing the consumption profile for a Ramsey path (R) and a MUEFT path with a given $\omega(M_\omega)$. Whether or not we could get everyone to prefer M_ω to R depended on the relation between ω and the crossing-point of M_ω and R.

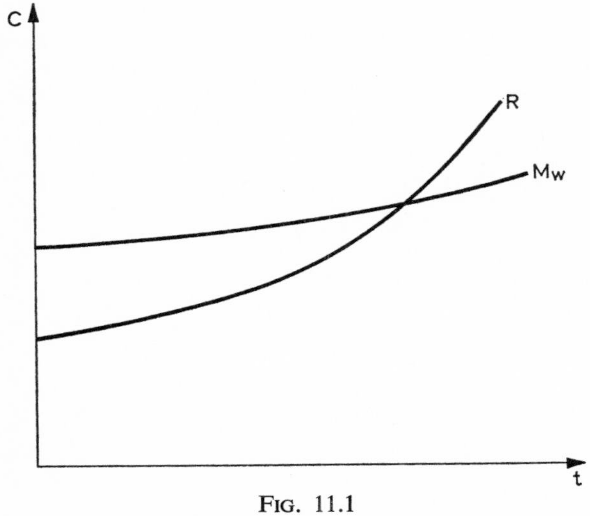

FIG. 11.1

Professor Hahn said that Professor Yaari's point had not been answered. He considered a game-theoretic situation where we had coalitions. He asked whether there was a coalition of governments that could improve themselves no matter what any of the others did, i.e. was there a core in strategy space?

Professor Yaari said his point was stronger. He knew there did not exist a feasible path uniformly above R. He asked if this was true of M_{ω}. *Professor Weizsäcker* said there did not exist an efficient MUEFT path.

Professor Inagaki said that we would need an infinite series of coalitions between YGs if we allowed coalitions, as a final one would have no one to collaborate with. He said the MUEFT path was not Eulerian (as could be seen by differentiating equation (11.4) with respect to time), so the integral of utilities from t to $t+\omega$ was not maximised by a MUEFT path.

Professor Weizsäcker said in that case a MUEFT path was not Pareto optimal. *Professor Inagaki* said that he had proved that the MUEFT path (whatever ω) is unanimously preferred to the Ramsey path, provided $d\phi/dc > 0$ – where $\phi(c)$ is the elasticity of marginal utility with respect to consumption.

Professor Mirrlees said that this theorem said nothing about Pareto optimality. If a MUEFT path did not maximise the integral from t to $t+\omega$ of utilities, he asked how the different generations could agree to it. In fact in the paper a unanimously preferred path had existed only in a special case. He thought the concept uninteresting if such paths existed only in special cases.

Professor Shell said that Phelps–Koopmans inefficiency (over-saving) was possible on the MUEFT path. *Professor Hahn* asked why the MUEFT path should be Pareto optimal.

Professor Inagaki said he was not exclusively interested in MUEFT. He had been interested in comparing rules for accumulation. He had proved in a wide class of cases that wherever a Ramsey-optimal path exists, MUEFT exists, and he conjectured this was true in general. Furthermore, MUEFT was always unanimously preferred to Ramsey.

Dr Bliss said we should be thinking of a sequence of generations rather than a conference of generations. In these circumstances the stability of the Nash equilibrium was important. Since we could neither arrive at nor enforce such an equilibrium, he was dubious about the usefulness of the concept. *Dr Pasinetti* said the problems of agreement arose with Ramsey's principle. *Dr Bliss* replied that no agreement was necessary with Ramsey. *Dr Pasinetti* said that the most interesting aspect of Professor Inagaki's paper was represented by his attempt to bring into the open one conflict of interests: the conflict between successive generations. He would like to see more of these conflicts of interests brought into open discussion, rather than see them ignored and covered up by assuming a chimerical social utility function which we cannot construct. *Dr Bliss* said the utility function is the outcome of our moral calculus. *Professor Weizsäcker* said the only way to defend Ramsey was altruism. We have to predict future utility functions and adopt them as our own.

Professor Inagaki concluded by remarking that Ramsey could be fitted into his framework if we specified national allegiance so strong that only the Ramsey strategy was included.

12 On the Existence of Optimal Development Programmes in Infinite-Horizon Economies*

Daniel McFadden

UNIVERSITY OF CALIFORNIA, BERKELEY

I. INTRODUCTION

1.1. An economic development programme is a description, over the lifetime of an economy, of the commodity vectors which resource holders, firms and consumer units are required to supply and demand. The objective of development planning is to choose from the set of programmes which are feasible for an economy the one that is best in terms of the planner's imputation of social preferences. In practice, programmes are chosen to maximise an objective function over a relatively short horizon, with terminal conditions established to make this optimisation consistent with optimisation over the full lifetime of the economy.

An important problem in the theory of development planning is to establish the logical relationships which hold among the structure of the social preference ordering, the properties of lifetime optimisation, and the terminal conditions in the practical planning computation.[1] In particular, it is necessary to determine the conditions on social preferences which guarantee the existence of a lifetime optimal development programme.

When the lifetime of an economy is finite and time can be considered as a sequence of short periods, the existence of optimal programmes follows from the mild condition that the set of feasible plans be closed and bounded and that the social preferences be continuous over this set.[2] However, when an economy has an infinite lifetime,

* This research has been supported in part by National Science Foundation Grant GS-2345. The author has benefited from discussions with William Brock, David Gale and Alan Manne, and the assistance of Eytan Sheshinski, but claims sole responsibility for errors. Professor McFadden was prevented from attending the conference, although his paper had been circulated. Because of its technical character, no discussion session was devoted to it.

[1] Important contributions to this problem have been made by Strotz (1956) and Goldman (1969).

[2] When time can be treated as a sequence of short periods, all the results of classical theory of value apply to this problem (Debreu, 1957, 1962). In a continuous time formulation of the problem, the mathematical analysis is more complex, but essentially the same conclusions hold (Yaari, 1964; Bewley, 1969).

existence of an optimal programme will depend on structural properties of its social preferences and technology.[1] Koopmans (1966) has argued for the desirability of conducting 'logical experiments' to establish existence criteria for such economies, and has reviewed in Koopmans (1967) most of the results obtained on this topic through 1966.[2] This paper summarises more recent results of Brock (1970), Brock and Gale (1970) and the author (McFadden (1970)), and provides several multi-sector generalisations.

1.2. We begin by considering Ramsey's classical one-commodity growth model in which aggregate output y_t in period t is divided into consumption c_t and an input x_t to production of the following period's output. The technology is defined by a production function $y_{t+1} = f(x_t)$, where f is assumed to be non-negative, non-decreasing, continuous and concave.[3] The economy begins with a positive endowment y_0. A programme (x_t, y_t, c_t) is *feasible* if it is non-negative and satisfies $x_t + c_t \leqslant y_t$ and $y_{t+1} \leqslant f(x_t)$ for $t = 0, 1, \ldots$.

1.3. It is frequently assumed that the relative social desirability of two feasible programmes (x_t, y_t, c_t) and (x_t', y_t', c_t') can be determined by computing a discounted sum of utility differences

$$\sum_{t=1}^{H} \delta^t [U(c_t) - U(c_t')] \tag{12.1}$$

where $U(c_t)$ is an atemporal utility of consumption in period t and δ is a discount factor. The stream (c_t) is said to be *no worse than* [resp., *better than*] the stream (c_t') if, as H approaches infinity in (12.1), all the limit points of the partial sums are non-negative [resp., positive]. (Note that if the partial sums have both positive and negative limit points, then the two streams are not comparable.)

[1] A fundamental difficulty in the infinite-horizon economy is that reasonable axioms on social preferences which are consistent for a finite horizon may be inconsistent for an infinite horizon (Koopmans (1960); Diamond (1965)). Moreover, reasonable preference orderings will frequently fail to admit a continuous numerical representation in any topology in which the set of feasible programmes is closed and bounded (McFadden (1967)).

[2] Several authors, including this one, have argued rather unconvincingly that infinite-horizon models are a reasonable representation of reality, and are thus worthy of a scholastic examination of internal consistency. A better case is this: to the extent that infinite-horizon models allow one to simplify the description of an economy by eliminating terminal conditions, such models will be useful approximations to reality (in the spirit of frictionless planes and point masses). It is then important to know the internal logical structure of these approximations.

[3] In growth theory, the one-commodity model is usually given the formulation $c_t + i_t = g(k_{t-1})$ and $k_t = i_t + (1-d)k_{t-1}$, where c_t, i_t, k_t are consumption, gross investment and capital stock, respectively, and d is a depreciation rate for capital stock. In the terminology of this paper, $x_{t-1} = k_{t-1}$, $y_t = c_t + k_t$ and $f(x_{t-1}) = g(x_{t-1}) + (1-d)x_{t-1}$. Hence, $f'(+\infty) = g'(+\infty) + (1-d) = 1-d$ is positive if capital is not completely perishable.

This is called the overtaking criterion for optimality, introduced by Weizsäcker (1965) as a generalisation of Ramsey's notion of a 'bliss' comparison utility level.[1]

A feasible programme is *optimal* if it is comparable to and no worse than any other feasible programme, and is *maximal* if it is no worse than any other feasible programme to which it is comparable. Any programme which is optimal is also maximal, but an economy may have many non-comparable maximal programmes (one example is given by Brock (1970), and a second is given in section 2.13 below).

We assume that the atemporal utility function U is concave and twice continuously differentiable for positive c, with $U'(c)$ positive and $U(0) = \lim_{c \to 0} U(c)$.

1.4. We wish to discover the conditions on the production function, atemporal utility function and discount rate which imply the existence or non-existence of an optimal programme. An elementary result due to Ramsey (1928) provides a prototype existence criterion for a much broader class of economies.

1.5. *Lemma. In the one-commodity Ramsey growth model, assume a linear production function* $y_{t+1} = f(x_t) = \rho_0 x_t$ *with* $\rho_0 > 0$, *and a constant elasticity utility function* $U(c) = c^{1-\alpha}/(1-\alpha)$ *with* $\alpha > 0$, $\alpha \neq 1$. *Then, an optimal programme exists if and only if*

$$\delta \rho_0^{1-\alpha} < 1. \tag{12.2}$$

Further, an optimal programme has c_t *decreasing* [*resp., constant, increasing*] *if* $\delta\rho_0 < 1$ [*resp.,* $\delta\rho_0 = 1$, $\delta\rho_0 > 1$].

1.6. Note that the constant elasticity utility function is bounded below for $0 < \alpha < 1$ and bounded above for $\alpha > 1$. Hence in the no-discounting case $\delta = 1$, the inequality (12.2) holds if and only if the constant elasticity utility stream is bounded for all feasible programmes. This property again generalises to a broader class of economies.

1.7. Several generalisations of the existence criterion (12.2) can be made for the one-commodity model. Retaining the assumption of a linear production function, but removing the assumption of a constant elasticity utility function, the author (McFadden (1967), Theorem 4 and Lemma 10) has established the following result.

1.8. *Lemma. In the one-commodity Ramsey growth model, assume a linear production function* $y_{t+1} = f(x_t) = \rho_0 x_t$ *with* $\rho_0 > 0$. *Then the following existence conditions hold* (*Note: the remarks relate these conditions to the criterion* (*12.2*) *for the constant elasticity case*):

[1] The use of this formulation of social preferences is discussed by Gale (1967) and McFadden (1967).

(i) *Suppose* $\delta = 1$, $\rho_0 > 1$. *An optimal programme exists if and only if* $U(c)$ *is bounded above.* [*Remark:* $\delta\rho_0^{1-\alpha} < 1$ *if and only if* $\alpha > 1$.]

(ii) *Suppose* $\delta = 1$, $\rho_0 < 1$. *An optimal programme exists if and only if* $U(c)$ *is bounded below.* [*Remark:* $\delta\rho_0^{1-\alpha} < 1$ *if and only if* $\alpha < 1$.]

(iii) *Suppose* $\delta\rho_0 \leqslant 1$, $\rho_0 > 1$. *An optimal programme exists for any* $U(c)$. [*Remark:* $\delta\rho_0^{1-\alpha} < 1$ *if* $\alpha > 0$.]

(iv) *Suppose* $\delta\rho_0 > 1$, $\rho_0 > 1$, $\delta \leqslant 1$. $U(c)$ *bounded above implies an optimal programme exists.* [*Remark:* $\delta\rho_0^{1-\alpha} < 1$ *if* $\alpha > 1$.]

(v) *Suppose* $\rho_0 > 1$, $\delta \geqslant 1$. *The existence of an optimal programme implies* $U(c)$ *bounded above.* [*Remark:* $\delta\rho_0^{1-\alpha} > 1$ *if* $\alpha < 1$.]

(vi) *Suppose* $\delta\rho_0 \geqslant 1$, $\rho_0 \leqslant 1$. *No optimal programme exists for any* $U(c)$, *unless* $\delta = \rho_0 = 1$ *and* $U(c)$ *is linear.* [*Remark:* $\delta\rho_0^{1-\alpha} \geqslant 1$ *if* $\alpha \geqslant 0$.]

(vii) *Suppose* $\delta\rho_0 < 1$, $\rho_0 < 1$, $\delta \geqslant 1$. *The existence of an optimal programme implies* $U(c)$ *bounded below.* [*Remark:* $\delta\rho_0^{1-\alpha} > 1$ *if* $\alpha > 1$.]

(viii) *Suppose* $\delta\rho_0 < 1$, $\rho_0 \leqslant 1$, $\delta \leqslant 1$. $U(c)$ *bounded below implies the existence of an optimal programme.* [*Remark:* $\delta\rho_0^{1-\alpha} < 1$ *if* $\alpha < 1$.]

1.9. A second generalisation of the criterion (12.2) to the case where both the production function f and the utility function U are arbitrary has been made by Brock and Gale (1970). This result introduces two concepts, the *asymptotic elasticity* of the utility function $U(c)$, and the *asymptotic average productivity* of the production function $f(x)$. Define an elasticity of marginal utility with respect to consumption at any $c > 0$ by

$$\alpha(c) = -d \log U'(c)/d \log c = -cU''(c)/U'(c). \qquad (12.3)$$

(Note that in the case of the constant elasticity utility function in 1.5, one has $\alpha(c) = \alpha$.) Define asymptotic elasticities,

$$\alpha_0 = \lim_{c \to 0} \alpha(c) \quad \text{and} \quad \alpha_1 = \lim_{c \to +\infty} \alpha(c) \qquad (12.4)$$

assuming that these limits exist.[1] The average productivity of a production function $f(x)$ at a positive input level x is equal to $\rho(x) = f(x)/x$. Define asymptotic average productivities

$$\rho_0 = \lim_{x \to 0} \rho(x) \quad \text{and} \quad \rho_1 = \lim_{x \to +\infty} \rho(x). \qquad (12.5)$$

[1] When these limits fail to exist, the existence conditions given below continue to hold with appropriate lim inf and lim sup operations replacing lim operations. Note that the elasticity α_1 in the terminology of this paper is equal to $1-\alpha$ in the terminology of Brock and Gale.

Because the production function is concave and non-decreasing, these limits will always exist, and for a non-trivial technology (i.e. $f \neq 0$) satisfy $0 < \rho_0 \leqslant +\infty$, $0 \leqslant \rho_1 < +\infty$, and $\rho_1 \leqslant \rho_0$. The results obtained by Brock and Gale can readily be shown to imply the following.[1]

1.10. *Lemma. In the one-commodity Ramsey growth model, assume that the asymptotic elasticities of the utility function (12.4) and the asymptotic average productivities of the production function (12.5) are given. Then, any one of the following three conditions is sufficient for the existence of an optimal programme:*

(a) $\rho_1 > 1$ *and* $\delta \rho_1{}^{1-\alpha_1} < 1$;

(b) $\rho_0 < 1$ *and* $\delta \rho_0{}^{1-\alpha_0} < 1$;

(c) $\rho_0 > 1 > \rho_1$ *and* $\delta < 1$.

Further, any one of the following three conditions is sufficient for the non-existence of a maximal programme:

(d) $\rho_1 > 1$ *and* $\delta \rho_1{}^{1-\alpha_1} > 1$;

(e) $\rho_0 < 1$ *and* $\delta \rho_0{}^{1-\alpha_0} > 1$;

(f) $\rho_0 > 1 > \rho_1$ *and* $\delta \rho_1 > 1$.

[1] The existence criteria in Brock and Gale (1970) formulae (I) and (II)) are defined only for the special case of completely perishable capital, $\rho_1 = 0$, but allow commodity-augmenting technical change. This lemma is an easy modification of their result in the case of no technical change. Alternately, one can generalise the Brock–Gale model in the case technical change is present as follows. Suppose one has $c_{t+1}+i_{t+1} = A^t g((B/A)^t k_t)$ and $k_{t+1} = i_{t+1}+(1-d)k_t$, with $g'(+\infty) = \rho \geqslant 0$, where A and B are interpreted as rates of 'labour' and 'capital' augmentation, respectively. Define $h(x) = g(x)-\rho x$. Then, $h'(+\infty) = 0$. Suppose $\beta = \lim_{x \to +\infty} xh'(x)/h(x)$, termed the asymptotic elasticity of h, exists and satisfies $\beta < 1$, and suppose α_1 is defined as in the text of this paper. The gross production of the economy then satisfies $y_{t+1} = A^t h((B/A)^t x_t)+(\rho B^t+1-d)x_t$ with $x_t = k_t$ and $y_t = k_t+c_t$. If $\rho = 0$, one finds that an optimal programme exists for $\delta < \bar{\delta}$, and fails to exist for $\delta > \bar{\delta}$, where $\bar{\delta} g^{1-\alpha_1} = 1$ and $g = AB^{\beta/(1-\beta)} > 1$, and finds further that an optimal programme grows asymptotically at rate g. (This is precisely the Brock–Gale result. Hence, that conclusion derived under the assumption $d = 1$ actually holds under the more general depreciation condition $0 < d \leqslant 1$.) If $\rho > 0$ and $B = 1$, the critical discount rate again satisfies $\bar{\delta} g^{1-\alpha_1} = 1$, but $g = \text{Max}\,\{A^\beta, 1+\rho-d\}$. (The optimal programme will grow asymptotically at the rate g only if $A^\beta > 1+\rho-d$.) Finally, if $\rho > 0$ and $B > 1$, an optimal programme exists for $\alpha_1 > 1$ and any δ, and grows asymptotically at a faster than geometric rate, whereas no optimal programme exists for $0 < \alpha_1 < 1$.

One final generalisation of these formulae may deserve a note. If the partial utility sums in (12.1) have the form $\sum_{t=0}^{\nu} \delta^t U(\lambda^t c_t)$, where λ is a discount factor 'inside' the utility function, then the critical discount rate is given by $\bar{\delta}(\lambda g)^{1-\alpha_1} = 1$.

1.11. An interpretation of conditions (a)–(c) in this lemma is that they establish critical levels of the discount factor below which the distant future is insignificant and optimal programmes exist, and above which no maximal programmes exist. Note that this lemma is exhaustive except for 'borderline' cases. Unfortunately, two of these cases, which require a detailed analysis of the structure of the economy to establish existence criteria, correspond to commonly used economic models. The first is a model arising in neo-classical growth theory of a productive, primary resource-limited economy with no discounting or with some negative discounting (i.e. $\rho_0 > 1 > \rho_1$ with $\delta = 1$ or with $\delta > 1$, $\delta\rho_1 \leqslant 1$). With mild additional differentiability assumptions, Koopmans (1966) has established that optimal programmes exist in the no-discounting case, and that maximal programmes fail to exist in the case of negative discounting. The second borderline case, arising in the study of Leontief and von Neumann models, is a productive linear economy without resource constraints and with no discounting (i.e. $\rho_1 > 1$ and $\delta = 1$). Existence criteria sharpening 1.10 (a) and (d) have been established for this case by the author (1967), (1970).

1.12. The non-triviality of the question of existence in the borderline cases above can be illustrated with several examples. For the resource-limited, no-discounting economy with $\delta = 1$, $U(c) = \log c$, and $y = f(x) = x^\beta$, $1/2 < \beta < 1$, and with $y_0 = 1/2$, one has $\rho_0 = +\infty$, $\rho_1 = 0$, and the existence of an optimal programme satisfying $c_t = (1-\beta)2^{-\beta^t}\beta^{\beta(1-\beta^t)/(1-\beta)}$. However, in the limit $\beta = 1$, one has the case in 1.8 (vi) in which no optimal programme exists.

In the next example, consider a productive linear technology $y = f(x) = \rho_0 x$, $\rho_0 > 1$, with no discounting ($\delta = 1$), and consider the utility functions $U(c) = \log(1+c)$ and $U(c) = -1/\log(1+c)$. The first of these functions is unbounded above, and no optimal programme exists, by 1.8 (i), while the second function is bounded above and an optimal programme exists. However, both functions have the asymptotic elasticity $\alpha_1 = 1$, and 1.10 (a) or (d) do not apply. Further, one can show that for $U(c) = -1/\log(1+c)$, the sum $\sum_{t=0}^{\infty} [U(c_t) - \bar{u}]$, where (c_t) is the optimal programme, diverges for every constant $\bar{u}$. This is in contrast to any economy satisfying (a), (b) or (c) in 1.10, for which the sum $\sum_{t=0}^{\infty} \delta^t U(c_t)$ converges for the optimal programme when the zero level of U is defined appropriately. This convergence property plays a crucial role in the proof of 1.10. Hence, this example shows that the Brock–Gale approach cannot be extended directly to all the borderline cases. This example also shows that the overtaking criterion applies to a broader class of economies than the Ramsey comparison with bliss.

For a final example, consider an economy with the linear utility function $U(c) = c$ and a discount factor $\delta > 1$. In the first case, suppose the economy has a production function

$$y = f(x) = \begin{cases} \rho_0 x & \text{for} \quad x \leqslant 1 \\ \rho_0 + \rho_1 x & \text{for} \quad x > 1 \end{cases}$$

with $\rho_0 > 1 > \delta\rho_1$, and has $y_0 = \rho_0$. Then, the programme $x_t = 1$, $c_t = \rho_0 - 1$ can be shown to be optimal. This example shows that differentiability is essential to Koopman's conclusion that no maximal programmes will exist in the resource-limited economy with negative discounting.

1.13. Result 1.10 and the two major borderline cases discussed in 1.11 provide a useful taxonomy of existence criteria: (1) the case in which the distant future is insignificant and one of the conditions 1.10 (a)–(c) is satisfied; (2) the resource-limited economy with no discounting; and (3) the productive linear economy with no discounting and no resource limits. The following sections of this paper will discuss each of these cases in turn for multi-commodity economies.

II. A MODEL OF A MULTI-COMMODITY ECONOMY

2.1. Consider time as an infinite sequence of short periods $t = 0, 1, \ldots$, and assume that there are a finite number of commodities N in each period. Let $\mathbf{x}_t$, $\mathbf{y}_t$ and $\mathbf{c}_t$ denote commodity vectors specifying the inputs to production, outputs from production, and consumption, respectively, in period t. Assume that the production possibilities of the economy are defined by a set $\mathbf{T}$ of non-negative input–output vectors $(\mathbf{x}_t, \mathbf{y}_{t+1})$ with the property that the output vector $\mathbf{y}_{t+1}$ can be attained when the input vector $\mathbf{x}_t$ is utilised in the preceding period.[1] Define an output correspondence $\mathbf{Q}(\mathbf{x}) = \{\mathbf{y} \mid (\mathbf{x}, \mathbf{y}) \epsilon \mathbf{T}\}$. A feasible programme will be a non-negative sequence $(\mathbf{x}_t, \mathbf{y}_t, \mathbf{c}_t)$ satisfying $\mathbf{x}_t + \mathbf{c}_t = \mathbf{y}_t$ and $\mathbf{y}_{t+1} \epsilon \mathbf{Q}(\mathbf{x}_t)$ for $t = 0, 1, \ldots$, where $\mathbf{y}_0$ is a given initial endowment.

[1] Hereafter we ignore the possibility of technical change, either via the introduction of new commodities or improvement in the technique of making old ones. There is no difficulty in principle in modifying the existence criteria below when technical change is present. However, there seems to be no consensus on the most appropriate way to introduce a structure on technical change in the multi-commodity model.

2.2. The following assumptions will be imposed on the production possibility set $\mathbf{T}$ and its output correspondence $\mathbf{Q}(\mathbf{x})$:

A.1. $\mathbf{T}$ is a closed convex set in the non-negative orthant of a $2N$-dimensional Euclidean space.

A.2. $\mathbf{T}$ allows free disposal of inputs and outputs $[(\mathbf{x}, \mathbf{y})\epsilon\mathbf{T}, \mathbf{x}' \geqslant \mathbf{x}, \mathbf{0} \leqslant \mathbf{y}' \leqslant \mathbf{y}$ imply $(\mathbf{x}', \mathbf{y}')\epsilon\mathbf{T}]$.

A.3. $\mathbf{Q}(\mathbf{0})$ is bounded.

A.4. Every commodity is producible [there exists $(\mathbf{x}, \mathbf{y})\epsilon\mathbf{T}$ with $\mathbf{y}$ positive].

These assumptions encompass both von Neumann and neo-classical models of the technology, provided in the latter case that endowments of primary and non-producible commodities grow at a common geometric rate, and the production possibility set is defined only over producible commodities, deflated by the growth rate of primary resources. In the case of a von Neumann technology, assumptions A.1 to A.4 are imposed directly on the production possibility set, along with the requirement that $\mathbf{T}$ be a cone and that $\mathbf{Q}(\mathbf{0}) = \{\mathbf{0}\}$. In the case of a neo-classical technology, we may think of an underlying production possibility cone $\mathbf{T}'$ containing triples $(\mathbf{z}_t, \mathbf{x}_t', \mathbf{y}'_{t+1})$ composed of a vector of endowments of commodities $\mathbf{z}_t$, including possibly both producible and primary commodities, a vector of inputs $\mathbf{x}_t$ attained from the output just produced, and a vector of outputs $\mathbf{y}_{t+1}$ in the following period. If $\mathbf{z}_t$ grows at a geometric rate g, so that $\mathbf{z}_t = \mathbf{z}_0 g^t$, define deflated commodity vectors $\mathbf{x}_t = \mathbf{x}_t'/g^t$, $\mathbf{y}_t = \mathbf{y}_t'/g^t$, and a stationary technology $\mathbf{T} = \{\mathbf{x}, \mathbf{y})\,|\,(\mathbf{z}_0, \mathbf{x}, g\mathbf{y})\epsilon\mathbf{T}'\}$ expressed in 'per unit of primary commodity' terms. This technology will satisfy A.1 to A.4.[1]

2.3. It is convenient to summarise the asymptotic structure of the technology by defining the following two sets (illustrated in Fig. 12.1). Let $\mathbf{T}_0$ denote the closed cone spanned by the production possibility set $\mathbf{T}$, i.e.

$$\mathbf{T}_0 = \text{Closure}\,(\{\lambda(\mathbf{x}, \mathbf{y})\,|\,(\mathbf{x}, \mathbf{y})\epsilon\mathbf{T}, \quad \lambda \geqslant 0\}). \tag{12.6}$$

Let $\mathbf{T}_1$ denote the asymptotic cone of $\mathbf{T}$, i.e.

$$\mathbf{T}_1 = \{(\mathbf{x}, \mathbf{y})\,|\,\lambda(\mathbf{x}, \mathbf{y})\epsilon\mathbf{T} \quad \text{for all} \quad \lambda \geqslant 0\}. \tag{12.7}$$

Clearly $\mathbf{T}_1 \subseteq \mathbf{T} \subseteq \mathbf{T}_0$, with $\mathbf{T}_1 = \mathbf{T}_0$ if and only if $\mathbf{T}$ is a cone. We shall employ the following standard result on a *linear* technology.

2.4. *Theorem.*[2] *If* $\mathbf{T}^*$ *is a cone satisfying A.1, A.2, A.4 and* $\mathbf{Q}(\mathbf{0}) = \{\mathbf{0}\}$, *then there exist semi-positive vectors* $\hat{\mathbf{x}}$ *and* $\hat{\mathbf{p}}$ *and a positive scalar* ρ *(termed the maximal expansion rate or von Neumann growth rate of the technology) such that* $\hat{\mathbf{x}}$ *can be expanded at the*

[1] Gale (1967) gives the details of this construction, and discusses its properties.
[2] Karlin (1959) or Gale (1956).

rate ρ [*i.e.* $(\hat{\mathbf{x}}, \rho\hat{\mathbf{x}}) \epsilon \mathbf{T}^*$], *profits* $\hat{\mathbf{p}}.\mathbf{y} - \rho\hat{\mathbf{p}}.\mathbf{x}$ *are non-positive for all* $(\mathbf{x}, \mathbf{y}) \epsilon \mathbf{T}^*$, *and for all* $(\mathbf{x}, \mathbf{y}) \epsilon \mathbf{T}^*$, $\mathbf{x} \neq \mathbf{0}$, ρ *is at least as great as any scalar* λ *satisfying* $\mathbf{y} \geqslant \lambda\mathbf{x}$.

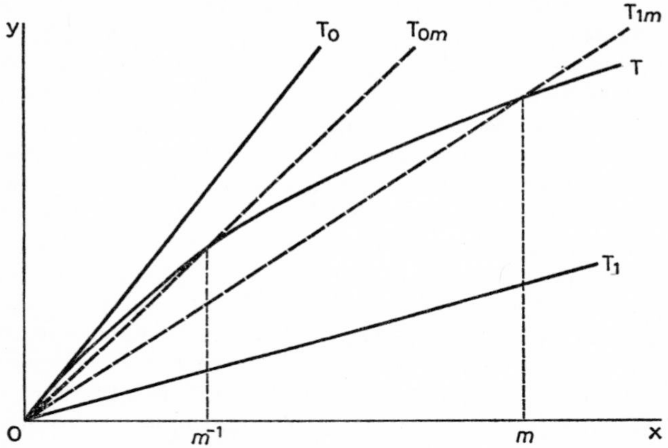

FIG. 12.1

2.5. The cone $\mathbf{T}_0$ either satisfies 2.4 and has a maximal expansion rate $\rho_0 < +\infty$, or contains a point $(\mathbf{0}, \mathbf{y})$ with $\mathbf{y} \neq \mathbf{0}$ and can be defined to have a maximal expansion rate $\rho_0 = +\infty$. Similarly, the cone $\mathbf{T}_1$ either satisfies 2.4 and has a maximal expansion rate $\rho_1 > 0$, or has some non-producible commodity which is essential to production and can be defined to have a maximal expansion rate $\rho_1 = 0$. The expansion rates ρ_0 and ρ_1 will play the same role as did the asymptotic average productivities in the one-commodity model.

2.6. If maximal expansion in a linear technology $\mathbf{T}^*$ is achieved at an input vector $\hat{\mathbf{x}}$ which is not strictly positive, it may be impossible to produce a positive output vector starting from $\hat{\mathbf{x}}$. Alternately, if there exists a sequence $(\hat{\mathbf{x}}, \mathbf{x}_1, \ldots, \mathbf{x}_{N-1})$ with $(\mathbf{x}_n, \mathbf{x}_{n+1}) \epsilon \mathbf{T}^*$ and $\mathbf{x}_{N-1}$ positive, the technology is said to have the *recovery property*. This property will be required on the cones $\mathbf{T}_0$ or $\mathbf{T}_1$ of the general technology $\mathbf{T}$ for some existence criteria.

2.7. We shall assume that the overtaking criterion defined in section 1.3 is used to order feasible programmes, with the atemporal utility function $U(\mathbf{c})$ now assumed to have the following properties:

B.1. $U(\mathbf{c})$ is a continuous, concave, non-decreasing function of positive $\mathbf{c}$.

B.2. $U(\mathbf{c})$ is closed; i.e. if $\mathbf{c}$ is non-negative with some zero components, then

$$\overline{\lim_{\substack{\mathbf{c}'>0\\ \mathbf{c}'\to\mathbf{c}}}}\; U(\mathbf{c}') = U(\mathbf{c}) \geqslant -\infty.$$

B.3. $U(\mathbf{c})$ is non-satiated; i.e. $\mathbf{c}'-\mathbf{c}$ positive implies $U(\mathbf{c}') > U(\mathbf{c})$.

2.8. We now define asymptotic elasticities for the utility function $U(\mathbf{c})$, following rather closely the construction of Brock and Gale. Define a scalar $\bar{u}$ equal to the least upper bound of $U(\mathbf{c})$ provided this bound is finite, and equal to zero otherwise. For any positive vector $\mathbf{c}$ and scalar γ with $U(\gamma\mathbf{c}) \neq \bar{u}$ and $\gamma \neq 1$, define the *exponent* of $|U(\gamma\mathbf{c})-\bar{u}|$ as

$$1-\alpha(\mathbf{c},\gamma) = \log_\gamma |U(\gamma\mathbf{c})-\bar{u}|. \tag{12.8}$$

Then, one has

$$|U(\gamma\mathbf{c})-\bar{u}| = \gamma^{1-\alpha(\mathbf{c},\gamma)} \tag{12.9}$$

revealing the relation of the exponent to the parameter α in the one-commodity, constant elasticity utility function. On the ray through a positive $\mathbf{c}$, define an asymptotic elasticity $\bar{\alpha}_1(\mathbf{c}) = \overline{\lim}_{\gamma\to+\infty} \alpha(\mathbf{c},\gamma)$. We next show that $\bar{\alpha}_1 = \bar{\alpha}_1(\mathbf{c})$ is independent of $\mathbf{c}$.

For a positive scalar λ and a large positive scalar γ, one has from (12.8) the relation $1-\alpha(\mathbf{c},\lambda\gamma) = [1-\alpha(\lambda\mathbf{c},\gamma)](1-\log_{\lambda\gamma}\lambda)$ and $\lim_{\gamma\to+\infty} \log_{\lambda\gamma}\lambda = 0$. Hence, $\bar{\alpha}_1(\mathbf{c})$ is homogeneous of degree zero in $\mathbf{c}$. Consider two positive vectors $\mathbf{c}'$ and $\mathbf{c}''$, and positive scalars λ, μ such that $\lambda\mathbf{c}' \leqslant \mathbf{c}'' \leqslant \mu\mathbf{c}'$. By B.3, we have $U(\gamma\lambda\mathbf{c}') \leqslant U(\gamma\mathbf{c}'') \leqslant U(\gamma\mu\mathbf{c}')$, implying that $\alpha(\mathbf{c}'',\gamma)$ is bracketed by $\alpha(\lambda\mathbf{c}',\gamma)$ and $\alpha(\mu\mathbf{c}',\gamma)$. Hence, $\bar{\alpha}_1(\mathbf{c}'')$ is bracketed by $\bar{\alpha}_1(\lambda\mathbf{c}') = \bar{\alpha}_1(\mathbf{c}')$ and $\bar{\alpha}_1(\mu\mathbf{c}') = \bar{\alpha}_1(\mathbf{c}')$, implying $\bar{\alpha}_1(\mathbf{c}'') = \bar{\alpha}_1(\mathbf{c}')$. Hence, $\bar{\alpha}_1(\mathbf{c})$ is independent of $\mathbf{c}$. Similarly, $\bar{\alpha}_1 = \underline{\alpha}_1(\mathbf{c}) = \underline{\lim}_{\gamma\to+\infty} \alpha(\mathbf{c},\gamma)$ is independent of $\mathbf{c}$.

With this result, we define the asymptotic elasticity of the utility function

$$\alpha_1 = \lim_{\gamma\to+\infty} \alpha(\mathbf{c},\gamma) \quad \text{(for any positive } \mathbf{c}) \tag{12.10A}$$

where we impose the assumption

B.4A. The limit defining α_1 exists (i.e. $\bar{\alpha}_1 = \alpha_1$).

A similar construction will give an asymptotic elasticity α_0. Define $\bar{u}$ in (12.8) to be the greatest lower bound of $U(\mathbf{c})$ provided this bound is finite, and set $\bar{u}$ equal to zero otherwise. Then define the asymptotic elasticity of the utility function

$$\alpha_0 = \lim_{\gamma\to 0} \alpha(\mathbf{c},\gamma) \quad \text{(for any positive } \mathbf{c}) \tag{12.10B}$$

where this limit is again independent of $\mathbf{c}$, and exists under the assumption

B.4B. The limit defining α_0 exists (i.e. $\bar{\alpha}_0 = \alpha_0$).

Note that the following implications hold between the asymptotic elasticities and boundedness of the utility function:

$$\begin{aligned}
\alpha_1 > 1 &\rightarrow U(\mathbf{c}) \text{ bounded above} &&\rightarrow \alpha_1 \geqslant 1\\
0 \leqslant \alpha_1 < 1 &\rightarrow U(\mathbf{c}) \text{ unbounded above} &&\rightarrow 0 \leqslant \alpha_1 \leqslant 1\\
0 \leqslant \alpha_0 < 1 &\rightarrow U(\mathbf{c}) \text{ bounded below} &&\rightarrow 0 \leqslant \alpha_0 \leqslant 1\\
\alpha_0 > 1 &\rightarrow U(\mathbf{c}) \text{ unbounded below} &&\rightarrow \alpha_0 \geqslant 1
\end{aligned}$$

2.9. An important property of a maximal programme $(\bar{\mathbf{x}}_t, \bar{\mathbf{y}}_t, \bar{\mathbf{c}}_t)$ in an economy is that it can normally be sustained by a 'decentralised' price system $(\bar{\mathbf{p}}_t)$ satisfying

$$\delta^t[U(\mathbf{c}) - U(\bar{\mathbf{c}}_t)] \leqslant \bar{\mathbf{p}}_t.(\mathbf{c} - \bar{\mathbf{c}}_t) \quad \text{for all positive } \mathbf{c} \tag{12.11}$$

and

$$\bar{\mathbf{p}}_{t+1}.\bar{\mathbf{y}}_{t+1} - \bar{\mathbf{p}}_t.\bar{\mathbf{x}}_t \geqslant \bar{\mathbf{p}}_{t+1}.\mathbf{y} - \bar{\mathbf{p}}_t.\mathbf{x} \quad \text{for all} \quad (\mathbf{x}, \mathbf{y})\varepsilon\mathbf{T}. \tag{12.12}$$

A price system for which (12.12) is satisfied has been shown to exist under very general conditions (see Malinvaud, 1953; Radner, 1967). Price systems satisfying both (12.11) and (12.12) have been shown by Gale (1967) to exist for the resource-limited economy with no discounting, and by McFadden (1967) to exist for the non-resource-limited linear economy with no discounting. These constructions hold for much more general economies. We have the following result, in which the hypotheses are still unnecessarily strong:

2.10. *Theorem. Suppose an economy has a technology satisfying A.1 to A.4 and social preference satisfying B.1 to B.3. Suppose that the asymptotic cone of the technology,* $\mathbf{T}_1$, *has the recovery property. If* $(\bar{\mathbf{x}}_t, \bar{\mathbf{y}}_t, \bar{\mathbf{c}}_t)$ *is a maximal programme, then there exists a price system* $(\bar{\mathbf{p}}_t)$, *not identically zero, such that* (12.12) *holds, and*

$$U(\mathbf{c}) \geqslant U(\bar{\mathbf{c}}_t) \quad \text{implies} \quad \bar{\mathbf{p}}_t.\mathbf{c} \geqslant \bar{\mathbf{p}}_t.\mathbf{c}_t. \tag{12.13}$$

If $\bar{\mathbf{p}}_t.\bar{\mathbf{c}}_t > 0$ *for any t, then the price system* $(\bar{\mathbf{p}}_t)$ *can be scaled so that both* (12.11) *and* (12.12) *hold.*

Proof: Define $\mathbf{c}^\nu = (\mathbf{c}_0, \ldots, \mathbf{c}_\nu)$, and define the set

$$\mathbf{C}^\nu = \{\mathbf{c}^\nu \,|\, \mathbf{c}_t = \mathbf{y}_t - \mathbf{x}_t, \quad (\mathbf{x}_t, \mathbf{y}_{t+1})\varepsilon\mathbf{T}, \quad \mathbf{y}_0 = \bar{\mathbf{y}}_0, \quad \mathbf{x}_\nu = \bar{\mathbf{x}}_\nu\}$$

and the function

$$W^\nu(\mathbf{c}^\nu) = \sum_{t=0}^{\nu} \delta^t U(\mathbf{c}_t).$$

Define the set

$$\mathbf{A} = \{(\mu, \mathbf{c}^\nu) \,|\, \mathbf{c}^\nu \geqslant \mathbf{c}'^\nu - \mathbf{c}''^\nu, \quad \mu \leqslant W^\nu(\mathbf{c}'^\nu), \quad \mathbf{c}''^\nu \epsilon \mathbf{C}^\nu\}.$$

One can show that $\mathbf{A}$ is closed and convex, with a non-empty interior, and that $[W^{\nu}(\bar{\mathbf{c}}^{\nu}), 0]$ is a boundary point of $\mathbf{A}$. Then, there exists a vector $(\lambda, -\mathbf{p}^{\nu}) \neq 0$ such that

$$\lambda W^{\nu}(\bar{\mathbf{c}}^{\nu}) \geqslant \lambda\mu - \mathbf{p}^{\nu}.\mathbf{c}^{\nu}$$

for all $(\mu, \mathbf{c}^{\nu})\varepsilon\mathbf{A}$. From the construction of $\mathbf{A}$, one has $\lambda \geqslant 0$ and $\mathbf{p}^{\nu} \geqslant 0$. If one had $\lambda = 0$, then one would obtain the inequality $\mathbf{p}^{\nu}.\mathbf{c}^{\nu} \geqslant 0$, which is contradicted for some negative $\mathbf{c}^{\nu}$. Hence, one can normalise $\lambda = 1$. Taking $\mathbf{c}'^{\nu} = \bar{\mathbf{c}}^{\nu}$, $\mathbf{c}''^{\nu} = \mathbf{y}^{\nu} - \mathbf{x}^{\nu}$, $\mathbf{x}^{\nu} = (\bar{\mathbf{x}}_1, \ldots, \bar{\mathbf{x}}_{t-2}, \mathbf{x}, \bar{\mathbf{x}}_t, \ldots, \bar{\mathbf{x}}_{\nu})$ and $\mathbf{y}^{\nu} = (\bar{\mathbf{y}}_0, \ldots, \bar{\mathbf{y}}_{t-1}, \mathbf{y}, \bar{\mathbf{y}}_{t+1}, \ldots, \bar{\mathbf{y}}_{\nu})$ with $(\mathbf{x}, \mathbf{y})\varepsilon\mathbf{T}$, one obtains the condition

$$\mathbf{p}^{\nu}{}_{t+1}.\bar{\mathbf{y}}_{t+1} - \mathbf{p}_t{}^{\nu}.\bar{\mathbf{x}}_t \geqslant \mathbf{p}^{\nu}{}_{t+1}.\mathbf{y} - \mathbf{p}_t{}^{\nu}.\mathbf{x} \quad \text{for all} \quad (\mathbf{x}, \mathbf{y})\epsilon\mathbf{T}.$$

Since $\mathbf{T}_1$ has the recovery property, one has $(\mathbf{x}^*, \theta\mathbf{x}^*)\epsilon\mathbf{T}_1$ for some positive θ and $\mathbf{x}^*$, and hence $(\bar{\mathbf{x}}_t + \mathbf{x}^*, \bar{\mathbf{y}}_{t+1} + \theta\mathbf{x}^*)\epsilon\mathbf{T}$ implies in the inequality above that $\mathbf{p}_t{}^{\nu}.\mathbf{x}^* \leqslant \theta^{-t}\mathbf{p}_0{}^{\nu}.\mathbf{x}^*$. Next, letting $\mathbf{c}'^{\nu} = (\bar{\mathbf{c}}_1, \ldots, \bar{\mathbf{c}}_{t-1}, \mathbf{c}, \bar{\mathbf{c}}_{t+1}, \ldots, \bar{\mathbf{c}}_{\nu})$ and $\mathbf{c}''^{\nu} = \bar{\mathbf{c}}^{\nu}$ define a point in $\mathbf{A}$, one obtains the condition $\delta^t[U(\mathbf{c}) - U(\bar{\mathbf{c}}_t)] \leqslant \mathbf{p}_t{}^{\nu}.(\mathbf{c} - \bar{\mathbf{c}}_t)$. Now consider the sequence $\{\mathbf{p}_0{}^{\nu}\}$ as $\nu \to +\infty$. By B.3 and the last inequality, $\mathbf{p}_0{}^{\nu}$ is bounded positive as $\nu \to +\infty$. If $\{\mathbf{p}_0\}$ has a bounded sequence converging to a point $\bar{\mathbf{p}}_0$, then one can construct by the diagonal process and the bound $\mathbf{p}_t{}^{\nu}.\mathbf{x}^* \leqslant \theta^{-t}\mathbf{p}_0{}^{\nu}.\mathbf{x}^*$ a subsequence of $\mathbf{p}^{\nu}$ as $\nu \to +\infty$ converging pointwise to a sequence $(\bar{\mathbf{p}}_t)$ satisfying (12.11) and (12.12). Alternately, if $\{\mathbf{p}_0{}^{\nu}\}$ is unbounded, then a diagonal subsequence of $\{\mathbf{p}^{\nu}/|\mathbf{p}_0{}^{\nu}|\}$ converges to a sequence $(\bar{\mathbf{p}}_t)$ satisfying (12.12). Further, $U(\mathbf{c}) \geqslant U(\bar{\mathbf{c}}_t)$ implies $\mathbf{p}_t{}^{\nu}.(\mathbf{c} - \bar{\mathbf{c}}_t) \geqslant 0$, and hence $(\bar{\mathbf{p}}_t)$ satisfies (12.13). Taking $\mathbf{c} = \bar{\mathbf{c}}_t/2$ implies $\mathbf{p}_t{}^{\nu}.\bar{\mathbf{c}}_t \leqslant 2\delta^t[U(\bar{\mathbf{c}}_t) - U(\bar{\mathbf{c}}_t/2)]$, and hence in this case one has $\bar{\mathbf{p}}_t.\bar{\mathbf{c}}_t = 0$ for all t.

2.11. A feasible programme $(\bar{\mathbf{x}}_t, \bar{\mathbf{y}}_t, \bar{\mathbf{c}}_t)$ satisfying (12.11) and (12.12) is termed a *finitely competitive programme*. It would be most useful if every finitely competitive programme could be shown to be optimal, or even maximal. Combining (12.11) and (12.12), one can show that a finitely competitive programme satisfies

$$\sum_{t=0}^{\nu} \delta^t[U(\mathbf{c}_t) - U(\bar{\mathbf{c}}_t)] \leqslant \bar{\mathbf{p}}_{\nu}.(\bar{\mathbf{x}}_{\nu} - \mathbf{x}_{\nu}) \tag{12.14}$$

for any feasible programme $(\mathbf{x}_t, \mathbf{y}_t, \mathbf{c}_t)$. If one can establish that $\bar{\mathbf{p}}_{\nu}.\bar{\mathbf{x}}_{\nu} \to 0$, or that $|\bar{\mathbf{p}}_{\nu}(\bar{\mathbf{x}}_{\nu} - \mathbf{x}_{\nu})| \to 0$ for any programme that is not 'infinitely worse' than the finitely competitive programme, then one can attain this desired conclusion. This is the case, for example, in some models studied by Gale (1967) and the author (1967). However, in general, a finitely competitive programme need not be maximal, and a maximal programme need not be optimal. We give two examples:

2.12. First, consider a one-commodity economy with a production function $y_{t+1} = f(x_t) = x_t$, a utility function $U(c) = c/(1+c)$, a discount factor $\delta = 1$, and an initial endowment $y_0 = 1$. Then, $\bar{x}_t = \bar{y}_t = 1$, $\bar{c}_t = 0$, $\bar{p}_t = 1$ is a finitely competitive programme satisfying (12.11) and (12.12), but is clearly not maximal. (In this example, due to Gale, no maximal programme exists.)

2.13. Second, consider a six-commodity economy with a utility function $U(\mathbf{c}) = c_6$ which is linear in the sixth commodity and independent of the remaining commodities, a discount factor $\delta = 1$, and a von Neumann technology of the form $\mathbf{T} = \{(\mathbf{x}, \mathbf{y}) | \mathbf{x} \geqslant \mathbf{A}\mathbf{v}, \mathbf{y} \leqslant \mathbf{B}\mathbf{v}, \mathbf{v} \geqslant \mathbf{0}\}$, where $\mathbf{A}$ and $\mathbf{B}$ are matrices satisfying

$$\mathbf{A} = \begin{bmatrix} 1 & 0 & 0 & 1 & 0 & 0 \\ 0 & 1 & 0 & 0 & 0 & 0 \\ 0 & 0 & 1 & 0 & 0 & 0 \\ 0 & 0 & 0 & 0 & 1 & 0 \\ 0 & 0 & 0 & 0 & 0 & 1 \\ 0 & 0 & 0 & 0 & 0 & 0 \end{bmatrix}, \quad \mathbf{B} = \begin{bmatrix} 0 & 0 & 0 & 0 & 0 & 0 \\ 2 & 0 & 2 & 0 & 0 & 0 \\ 0 & 2 & 0 & 0 & 0 & 0 \\ 0 & 0 & 0 & 2 & 0 & 2 \\ 0 & 0 & 0 & 0 & 2 & 0 \\ 2 & 0 & 2 & 0 & 2 & 0 \end{bmatrix}.$$

Suppose the economy has the initial endowment $\mathbf{y}_0 = (1, 0, 0, 0, 0, 0)$. A pure accumulation programme using activity 1 in period zero, followed by activities 2 and 3 alternated in succeeding periods, yields a consumption stream $(c_{6t}') = (0, 2, 0, 8, 0, 32, \ldots)$. Alternately, a pure accumulation programme using activity 4 in period zero, followed by activities 5 and 6 alternated in succeeding periods, yields a consumption stream $(c_{6t}'') = (0, 0, 4, 0, 16, 0, \ldots)$. These two streams and their convex combinations are the only efficient consumption programmes. However, one has for $\nu > 1$:

$$\sum_{t=0}^{\nu} [U(\mathbf{c}_t') - U(\mathbf{c}_t'')] = \begin{cases} 2(2^\nu - 1)/3 & \text{for } \nu \text{ even} \\ -2(2^\nu + 1)/3 & \text{for } \nu \text{ odd.} \end{cases}$$

Hence, for any $0 \leqslant \theta \leqslant 1$, the programme $(\theta \mathbf{c}_t' + (1-\theta)\mathbf{c}_t'')$ is maximal, but none of these maximal programmes are optimal.

III. *EXISTENCE CRITERIA FOR ECONOMIES WITH AN INSIGNIFICANT FUTURE*

3.1. We are now prepared to state a multi-sector generalisation of the existence criteria for that 'insignificant future' case treated by Brock and Gale.

3.2. *Theorem. Suppose a multi-sector economy has a technology satisfying A.1 to A.4 and social preferences satisfying B.1 to B.4. Suppose that the overtaking criterion (1) is used to define optimal programmes. Suppose further that the initial endowment* $\mathbf{y}_0$ *is positive. Then, any one of the following three conditions is sufficient for the existence of an optimal programme:*

(a) $\rho_1 > 1$, $\delta\rho_1^{1-\alpha_1} < 1$, *and* $\mathbf{T}_1$ *has the recovery property.*

(b) $\rho_0 < 1$, $\delta\rho_0^{1-\alpha_0} < 1$, *and* $\mathbf{T}_0$ *has the recovery property.*

(c) $\rho_0 > 1 > \rho_1$ *and* $\delta < 1$.

3.3. The remainder of this section will be taken up with the proof of this theorem and the statement and proof of the converse non-existence theorem. We begin with a series of preliminary lemmas.

3.4. *Lemma. If A.1 to A.4 hold, then, given* $\varepsilon > 0$, *there exists* $m > 0$ *such that the cones*

$$\mathbf{T}_{0m} = \{\lambda(\mathbf{x}, \mathbf{y}) \,|\, (\mathbf{x}, \mathbf{y}) \epsilon \mathbf{T},\ |\mathbf{x}| \geqslant m^{-1},\quad \lambda \geqslant 0\}$$
$$\mathbf{T}_{1m} = \{\lambda(\mathbf{x}, \mathbf{y}) \,|\, (\mathbf{x}, \mathbf{y}) \epsilon \mathbf{T},\ |\mathbf{x}| \geqslant m,\quad \lambda \geqslant 0\}$$

satisfy $|\rho_{0m}{}^{-1} - \rho_0{}^{-1}| < \varepsilon$ *and* $|\rho_{1m} - \rho_1| < \varepsilon$, *where* ρ_{im} *is the maximal expansion rate for* $\mathbf{T}_{im}$, $i = 0, 1$ *(see Fig. 12.1).*

3.5. *Lemma.*[1] *Suppose* $\mathbf{T}^*$ *is a linear technology with a maximal expansion rate* ρ'. *Then, for any* $\rho > \rho'$, *there exists* $\eta > 1$ *such that for any sequence* $(\mathbf{x}_0, \ldots, \mathbf{x}_t)$ *with* $(\mathbf{x}_{\tau-1}, \mathbf{x}_\tau) \epsilon \mathbf{T}^*$, $\tau = 1, \ldots, t$, *it follows that* $|\mathbf{x}_t|/\rho^t \leqslant \eta|\mathbf{x}_0|$.

3.6. *Lemma. If* $\mathbf{T}$ *satisfies A.1 to A.4 and has* $\rho_1 \geqslant 1$, *then for any* $\rho > \rho_1$, *there exists* $\eta_2 > 0$ *such that* $|\mathbf{c}_t|/\rho^t \leqslant \eta_2$ *for any feasible programme* $(\mathbf{x}_t, \mathbf{y}_t, \mathbf{c}_t)$.

Proof: Given ρ, choose $\varepsilon = (\rho - \rho_1)/2$ in 3.4. Consider the cone $\mathbf{T}_{1m}$, and let η be the bound given by 3.5. Note that $(\mathbf{x}, \mathbf{y}) \epsilon \mathbf{T}$, $|\mathbf{x}| \leqslant m$ implies $|\mathbf{y}| \leqslant m\eta$. Consider any $\mathbf{y}_t$. If $|\mathbf{x}_{t-1}| \leqslant m$, then $|\mathbf{y}_t| \leqslant m\eta \leqslant m\eta\rho^t$. Alternately, if one has $|\mathbf{x}_s| \leqslant m$ and $|\mathbf{x}_\tau| > m$ for $s < \tau < t$, then 3.5 implies $|\mathbf{y}_t|/\rho^{t-s} \leqslant \eta m \leqslant \eta m\rho^s$. Finally, if one has $|\mathbf{x}_\tau| > m$ for $0 \leqslant \tau < t$, then 3.5 implies $|\mathbf{y}_t|/\rho^t \leqslant \eta|\mathbf{y}_0|$. Hence, taking $\eta_2 = \eta \max(m, |\mathbf{y}_0|)$ yields the result.

3.7. *Lemma. If* $\mathbf{T}$ *satisfies A.1 to A.4 and has* $\rho_1 < 1$, *then there exists* $\eta_2 > 0$ *such that* $|\mathbf{c}_t| \leqslant \eta_2$ *for any feasible programme* $(\mathbf{x}_t, \mathbf{y}_t, \mathbf{c}_t)$.

Proof: In the proof of 3.6, choose $\varepsilon = (1 - \rho_1)/2$. Then, that argument implies $|\mathbf{y}_t| \leqslant \eta \max(m, |\mathbf{y}_0|) = \eta_2$.

3.8. *Lemma. If* $\mathbf{T}$ *satisfies A.1 to A.4 and has* $\rho_0 \leqslant 1$, *then for any* $\rho > \rho_0$ *there exists* $\eta > 0$ *such that* $|\mathbf{c}_t|/\rho^t \leqslant \eta$ *for any feasible programme* $(\mathbf{x}_t, \mathbf{y}_t, \mathbf{c}_t)$.

Proof: Since $(\mathbf{x}_t, \mathbf{y}_{t+1}) \epsilon \mathbf{T}_0$, 3.5 implies the result.

3.9. *Lemma. Suppose* $\mathbf{T}^*$ *is a linear technology with a maximal*

[1] Winter (1965) theorem 2.

expansion rate ρ' which has the recovery property. Then, for any $\rho'' < \rho'$, there exists a feasible programme $(\mathbf{x}_t, \mathbf{y}_t, \mathbf{c}_t)$ for $\mathbf{y}_0$ positive such that $\lim_{t\to+\infty} \mathbf{c}_t/(\rho'')^t = +\infty$.

Proof: Let $(\hat{\mathbf{x}}, \hat{\mathbf{x}}_1, \ldots, \hat{\mathbf{x}}_{N-1})$ be the sequence defined in the recovery property which has $\hat{\mathbf{x}}_{N-1}$ positive. Choose $\theta > 0$ such that $\theta^{-1}\mathbf{y}_0 \geqslant 2\hat{\mathbf{x}} + \sum_{i=1}^{N-1} \hat{\mathbf{x}}_i$. Computation shows that a programme based on accumulation at the maximal rate can yield $\mathbf{c}_t = \theta\hat{\mathbf{x}}_{N-1}$ for $t = 0, \ldots, N-1$ and $c_t = \theta(\rho' - \rho)\rho^{t-N}\hat{\mathbf{x}}_{N-1}$ for $t = N, N+1, \ldots$, and $\rho'' < \rho < \rho'$, establishing the result.

3.10. *Lemma. Consider a utility function $U(\mathbf{c})$ satisfying B.1 to B.4 with asymptotic elasticities α_0 and α_1. Given $\varepsilon > 0$ and a closed, bounded set $\mathbf{C}$ of positive vectors $\mathbf{c}$, there exists $\gamma_1 > 0$ such that*

$$\gamma^{1-\alpha_1-\epsilon} < |U(\gamma\mathbf{c}) - \bar{u}| < \gamma^{1-\alpha_1+\epsilon} \tag{12.14A}$$

for $\mathbf{c}\in\mathbf{C}$ and $\gamma \geqslant \gamma_1$, where $\bar{u}$ is defined as in equation (12.8). Similarly, there exists $\gamma_0 > 0$ such that

$$\gamma^{1-\alpha_0-\epsilon} > |U(\gamma\mathbf{c}) - \bar{u}| > \gamma^{1-\alpha_0+\epsilon} \tag{12.14B}$$

for $\mathbf{c}\in\mathbf{C}$ and $\gamma \leqslant \gamma_0$.

Proof: Given $\mathbf{C}$, choose any $\mathbf{c}'\in\mathbf{C}$ and positive scalars λ, μ such that $\lambda\mathbf{c}' \leqslant \mathbf{c}'' \leqslant \mu\mathbf{c}'$ for all $\mathbf{c}''\in\mathbf{C}$. From the definition of α_1, there exists γ_1 such that (12.14A) holds for $\mathbf{c} = \lambda\mathbf{c}'$ and $\mathbf{c} = \mu\mathbf{c}'$, and such that $U(\gamma\lambda\mathbf{c}')$ is univalent for $\gamma \geqslant \gamma_1$. Then $|U(\gamma\mathbf{c}) - \bar{u}|$ defined on $\mathbf{C}$ is bracketed by the values of this expression for $\mathbf{c} = \lambda\mathbf{c}'$ and $\mathbf{c} = \mu\mathbf{c}'$, implying the stated result. A similar argument establishes (12.14B).

3.11. *Lemma.*[1] *Let $\mathbf{U}$ be a family of non-negative sequences (u_t) which is closed under pointwise convergence and such that $\sum_{t=0}^{+\infty} u_t < +\infty$ for at least one member of $\mathbf{U}$. Then, there is a member $(\bar{u}_t)$ such that $\sum_{t=0}^{+\infty} \bar{u}_t$ is a minimum.*

3.12. We are now prepared to prove the theorem 3.2. The argument follows closely that of Brock and Gale.

(a) Suppose $\rho_1 > 1$ and $\delta\rho_1^{1-\alpha_1} < 1$. Choose $1 < \underline{\rho} < \rho_1 < \bar{\rho}$ and $\underline{\alpha} < \alpha_1 < \bar{\alpha}$ such that $\delta\underline{\rho}^{1-\underline{\alpha}} < 1$ and $\delta\bar{\rho}^{1-\underline{\alpha}} < 1$. First consider the case of $U(\mathbf{c})$ unbounded above, implying $0 \leqslant \alpha_1 \leqslant 1$. By 3.6 and 3.10, $U(\mathbf{c}_t) = U[\bar{\rho}^t(\mathbf{c}_t/\bar{\rho}^t)] \leqslant U(\bar{\rho}^t\eta_2\hat{\mathbf{c}}) < (\bar{\rho}^t)^{1-\underline{\alpha}}$ for sufficiently large t, where $\hat{\mathbf{c}}$ is a vector of ones and $(\mathbf{c}_t)$ is any feasible programme. Hence, for η_5 sufficiently large, the sequence $\{\eta_5(\delta\bar{\rho}^{1-\underline{\alpha}})^t - \delta^t U(\mathbf{c}_t)\}$

[1] Brock and Gale (1970).

is non-negative for any feasible programme $(\mathbf{c}_t)$. By 3.9, there exists a feasible programme $(\tilde{\mathbf{c}}_t)$ with $\tilde{\mathbf{c}}_t/\underline{\rho}^t \to +\infty$. For t large, $\tilde{\mathbf{c}}_t/\underline{\rho}^t \geqslant \hat{\mathbf{c}}$, and 3.10 implies $U(\tilde{\mathbf{c}}_t) \geqslant U(\underline{\rho}^t\hat{\mathbf{c}}) \geqslant (\underline{\rho}^t)^{1-\bar{\alpha}}$. Hence, $\sum_{t=0}^{\infty} \delta^t U(\tilde{\mathbf{c}}_t)$ is bounded below. Since U is continuous and the set of feasible programmes is pointwise closed and bounded, the family of sequences $\{\eta_5(\delta\bar{\rho}^{1-\underline{\alpha}})^t - \delta^t U(\mathbf{c}_t)\}$ satisfies 3.11. This result then establishes that an optimal utility stream exists and is achieved by some feasible programme which is consequently optimal.

Next consider the case of $U(\mathbf{c})$ bounded above, implying $\alpha_1 \geqslant 1$. Without loss of generality, take $\bar{u} = 0$. Then, $-\sum_{t=0}^{+\infty} \delta^t U(\mathbf{c}_t)$ is non-negative, and by 3.9 and 3.10 there exists a programme $(\tilde{\mathbf{c}}_t)$ such that for large t, $-U(\tilde{\mathbf{c}}_t) \leqslant (\underline{\rho}^{1-\underline{\alpha}})^t$, or $-\sum_{t=0}^{+\infty} \delta^t U(\tilde{\mathbf{c}}_t) \leqslant \eta_6/(1-\delta\underline{\rho}^{1-\underline{\alpha}})$, for some η_6. Then 3.11 implies the existence of an optimal programme.

(b) and (c). Suppose $\rho_1 < 1$. By 3.7, there exists a bound η_2 such that $|\mathbf{c}_t| \leqslant \eta_2$ for any feasible programme $(\mathbf{c}_t)$. Hence, without loss of generality, we can define the zero level of $U(\mathbf{c})$ so that $\{-U(\mathbf{c}_t)\}$ is a non-negative sequence for all feasible programmes. Consider any $\underline{\rho}$ satisfying $0 < \underline{\rho} < \rho_0$. By 3.4, there exists $m > 0$ such that $\mathbf{T}_{0m}$ has the recovery property, and has a maximum expansion rate ρ with $\underline{\rho} < \rho < \rho_0$. Further, $(\mathbf{x}, \mathbf{y}) \epsilon \mathbf{T}_{0m}$ and $|\mathbf{x}| < m^{-1}$ implies $(\mathbf{x}, \mathbf{y}) \epsilon \mathbf{T}$. In case (b) with $\delta\rho_0^{1-\alpha_0} < 1$, choose $\underline{\rho} < \rho_0$ and $\bar{\alpha} > \alpha_0$ such that $\delta\underline{\rho}^{1-\bar{\alpha}} < 1$. We can apply 3.9 to $\mathbf{T}_{0m}$ to establish the existence of a feasible programme $(\tilde{\mathbf{c}}_t)$ with $\tilde{\mathbf{c}}_t/\underline{\rho}^t \to +\infty$. Then, using 3.10, one has $-U(\tilde{\mathbf{c}}_t) \leqslant (\underline{\rho}^{1-\bar{\alpha}})^t$ for t large, and $-\sum_{t=0}^{\infty} \delta^t U(\tilde{\mathbf{c}}_t)$ is bounded. Then, 3.11 can be applied to establish the existence of an optimal programme. In case (c) with $\rho_0 > 1$, choose $\underline{\rho} = 1$. Then using the same arguments as in the proof of 3.9, we can establish the existence of $(\tilde{\mathbf{x}}, \tilde{\mathbf{y}}) \epsilon \mathbf{T}_{0m}$ with $|\tilde{\mathbf{x}}| < m^{-1}$ and $\tilde{\mathbf{c}} = \tilde{\mathbf{y}} - \tilde{\mathbf{x}}$ positive. Then, $(\tilde{\mathbf{x}}, \tilde{\mathbf{y}}) \epsilon \mathbf{T}$, and we can assume $\tilde{\mathbf{y}} \leqslant \mathbf{y}_0$. Hence, the steady-state programme $(\tilde{\mathbf{c}})$ is feasible, and $-\sum_{t=0}^{\infty} \delta^t U(\tilde{\mathbf{c}})$ is bounded. The existence of an optimal programme is then established using 3.11.

3.13. One would like to establish a multi-commodity analogue of the non-existence criteria (d)–(f) in 1.10, corresponding to the result 3.2. That some further assumption is required to establish such a theorem is shown by the following example. Consider a two-commodity economy with a constant elasticity utility function $U(c_1, c_2) = c_2^{1-\alpha}/(1-\alpha)$ and a linear technology with a single efficient activity $(\mathbf{x}, \mathbf{y}) \epsilon \mathbf{T}$ satisfying $\mathbf{x} = (1, 0)$ and $\mathbf{y} = (\rho, \rho)$ with

$\rho > 0$. Then, given $\mathbf{y}_0 = (1, 1)$, the programme $\mathbf{c}_t = (0, \rho^t)$ is optimal for any values of the parameters δ, ρ and α. We next introduce several conditions which will be sufficient to establish criteria for non-existence.

We shall call a utility function $U(\mathbf{c})$ which satisfies B.1 to B.4 *asymptotically homothetic* at infinity (resp., at zero) if it can be written as the sum of two functions $U(\mathbf{c}) = u[H(\mathbf{c})] + V(\mathbf{c})$, where H and V are concave non-decreasing functions of positive $\mathbf{c}$, with H linear homogeneous and u a concave increasing function on the positive real line, and where $U(\mathbf{c})$ and $u[H(\mathbf{c})]$ have the same asymptotic elasticity α_1 (resp., α_0).[1] Without loss of generality, one can assume in the definition of an asymptotically homothetic utility function that

$$\operatorname*{Max}_{|\mathbf{c}|=1} H(\mathbf{c}) = 1.$$

Then,

$$\operatorname*{Max}_{|\mathbf{c}|=\gamma} u[H(\mathbf{c})] = u(\gamma).$$

If $U(\mathbf{c})$ is asymptotically homothetic at infinity, $u(\gamma)$ and $H(\mathbf{c})$ are continuously differentiable, and

$$\lim_{\gamma \to +\infty} \log_\gamma u'(\gamma)$$

exists, then $U(\mathbf{c})$ will be called *asymptotically smooth*. For this case, one has

$$\alpha_1 = -\lim_{\gamma \to +\infty} \log_\gamma u'(\gamma).^{2}$$

A similar definition can be made at zero. The following condition guarantees that maximal programmes will be strictly positive:

B.5. $U(\mathbf{c})$ is continuously differentiable for $\mathbf{c}$ positive, and if a non-negative $\mathbf{c}'$ has some zero components, then the corresponding components of $U'(\mathbf{c})$ are unbounded for positive $\mathbf{c}$ converging to $\mathbf{c}'$.

We are now prepared to state criteria for non-existence of maximal programmes.

3.16. *Theorem. Suppose a multi-commodity economy has a technology satisfying A.1 to A.4, and social preferences satisfying B.1 to B.5. Suppose that the initial endowment* $\mathbf{y}_0$ *is positive. Then, any one of the following three conditions is sufficient for the non-existence of a maximal programme:*

[1] Suppose the function $u(\gamma)$ on the positive real line has an asymptotic elasticity α_1' defined as in (12.10A), and that the function $V(\mathbf{c})$ has asymptotic elasticities α_1'' and $\bar{\alpha}_1''$ defined as in the argument preceding (12.10A). If $\alpha_1' \leqslant \underline{\alpha}_1''$ and $H(c)$ is not identically zero, then $U(c)$ has the same asymptotic elasticity $\alpha_1 = \alpha_1'$ as $u(H(c))$. Analogously, if $\alpha_0' \geqslant \bar{\alpha}_0''$ and $H(c)$ is not identically zero, then $\alpha_0 = \alpha_0'$.

[2] Brock and Gale (1970) Appendix.

(d) $\rho_1 > 1$, $\delta\rho_1{}^{1-\alpha_1} > 1$, $\mathbf{T}_1$ *has the recovery property, and* $U(\mathbf{c})$ *is asymptotically homothetic and smooth at infinity.*

(e) $\rho_0 < 1$, $\delta\rho_0{}^{1-\alpha_0} > 1$, $\mathbf{T}_0$ *contains a point* $(\hat{\mathbf{x}}, \rho_0\hat{\mathbf{x}})$ *with* $\hat{\mathbf{x}}$ *positive, and* $U(\mathbf{c})$ *is asymptotically homothetic and smooth at zero.*

(f) $\rho_0 > 1 > \rho_1$, $\delta\rho_1 > 1$, *and* $\mathbf{T}_1$ *contains a point* $(\hat{\mathbf{x}}, \rho_1\hat{\mathbf{x}})$ *with* $\hat{\mathbf{x}}$ *positive.*

Proof: (d) Suppose $\rho_1 > 1$ and $\delta\rho_1{}^{1-\alpha_1} > 1$, but suppose that a maximal programme $(\bar{\mathbf{c}}_t)$ exists. By B.5, $\bar{\mathbf{c}}_0$ is positive. Choose $\theta > 0$ such that $\bar{\mathbf{c}}_0 - \theta\hat{\mathbf{x}}$ is positive, where $\hat{\mathbf{x}}$ is a semi-positive vector with $(\hat{\mathbf{x}}, \rho_1\hat{\mathbf{x}}) \epsilon \mathbf{T}_1$. Since $\mathbf{T} = \mathbf{T} + \mathbf{T}_1$, a programme $(\tilde{\mathbf{c}}_t)$ with $\tilde{\mathbf{c}}_0 = \bar{\mathbf{c}}_0 - \theta\hat{\mathbf{x}}$, $\tilde{\mathbf{c}}_\tau = \bar{\mathbf{c}}_\tau + \theta\rho_1{}^{\tau-N}\mathbf{x}_{N-1}$, and $\tilde{\mathbf{c}}_t = \bar{\mathbf{c}}_t$ for $t \neq 0$, τ is feasible for $\tau > N$, where $\mathbf{x}_{N-1}$ is a positive vector which can be produced from $\hat{\mathbf{x}}$ in N periods. Let $\lambda = U(\bar{\mathbf{c}}_0) - U(\tilde{\mathbf{c}}_0)$. Note that $0 < H(\mathbf{x}_{N-1}) \leqslant H'(\mathbf{c}).\mathbf{x}_{N-1}$ for all positive $\mathbf{c}$, and hence that

$$u[H(\mathbf{c}+\mathbf{c}')] - u[H(\mathbf{c})] \geqslant u'[H(\mathbf{c}+\mathbf{c}')]H'(\mathbf{c}).\mathbf{c}' \geqslant u'[H(\mathbf{c}+\mathbf{c}')]H(\mathbf{c}').$$

Then,

$$\sum_{t=0}^{+\infty} \delta^t[U(\tilde{\mathbf{c}}_t) - U(\bar{\mathbf{c}}_t)] \geqslant -\lambda + \delta^\tau\{u[H(\tilde{\mathbf{c}}_\tau)] - u[H(\bar{\mathbf{c}}_\tau)]\}$$
$$\geqslant -\lambda + \delta^\tau u'[H(\tilde{\mathbf{c}}_\tau)]H(\theta\rho_1{}^{\tau-N}\mathbf{x}_{N-1}).$$

Choose $\underline{\alpha} < \alpha_1$ and $\bar{\rho} > \rho_1$ such that $\delta\rho_1\bar{\rho}^{-\underline{\alpha}} > 1$. From the properties of the asymptotic elasticity, one has $u'(\gamma) > \gamma^{-\bar{\alpha}}$ for γ sufficiently large. By 3.6, one has $|\tilde{\mathbf{c}}_t|/\rho^{-t} \leqslant \eta$. Hence,

$$H(\tilde{\mathbf{c}}_\tau) \leqslant \eta\rho^{-\tau} \quad \text{and} \quad u'[H(\tilde{\mathbf{c}}_\tau)] > (\eta)^{-\bar{\alpha}}\bar{\rho}^{-\bar{\alpha}\tau}.$$

Let

$$\lambda' = (\eta)^{-\bar{\alpha}}\theta\rho_1{}^{-N}H(\mathbf{x}_{N-1}).$$

Then,

$$\sum_{t=0}^{+\infty} \delta^t[U(\tilde{\mathbf{c}}_t) - U(\bar{\mathbf{c}}_t)] \geqslant -\lambda + \lambda'(\delta\rho_1\bar{\rho}^{-\underline{\alpha}})^\tau.$$

For τ sufficiently large, the right-hand side of this expression is positive, contradicting the supposition that $(\bar{\mathbf{c}}_t)$ was maximal.

(e) Suppose $\rho_0 < 1$ and $\delta\rho_0{}^{1-\alpha_0} > 1$, but suppose that a maximal programme $(\bar{\mathbf{c}}_t)$ exists. Choose $\rho < \rho_0$ such that $\delta\rho^{1-\alpha_0} > 1$. From the construction of $\mathbf{T}_0$, there exists a positive scalar γ such that $\gamma(\hat{\mathbf{x}}, \rho\hat{\mathbf{x}})$ is the interior of $\mathbf{T}$. Then, there exists $\eta > 0$ such that $(\mathbf{x}, \mathbf{y}) \epsilon \mathbf{T}$ and $|\mathbf{x}| \leqslant \eta$ imply $\gamma(\hat{\mathbf{x}}, \rho\hat{\mathbf{x}}) + (\mathbf{x}, \mathbf{y}) \epsilon \mathbf{T}$. By 3.8, the maximal programme $(\bar{\mathbf{x}}_t, \bar{\mathbf{y}}_t, \bar{\mathbf{c}}_t)$ has $|\bar{\mathbf{x}}_t| \leqslant \eta/2$ for $t \geqslant \nu$, some $\nu > 0$. Choose $\theta > 0$ such that $\bar{\mathbf{c}}_\nu - \theta\hat{\mathbf{x}}$ is positive. Then, the programme $(\tilde{\mathbf{c}}_t)$ with $\tilde{\mathbf{c}}_\nu = \bar{\mathbf{c}}_\nu - \theta\hat{\mathbf{x}}$, $\tilde{\mathbf{c}}_\tau = \bar{\mathbf{c}}_\tau + \theta\rho^{\tau-\nu}\hat{\mathbf{x}}$, and $\tilde{\mathbf{c}}_t = \bar{\mathbf{c}}_t$ for $t \neq \nu$, τ is feasible, and can be shown by an argument paralleling that of (d) to be better than $(\bar{\mathbf{c}}_t)$ for τ sufficiently large. Hence, $(\bar{\mathbf{c}}_t)$ cannot be maximal.

(f) Suppose $\rho_0 > 1 > \rho_1$ and $\delta\rho_1 > 1$, but suppose that a maximal programme $(\bar{\mathbf{c}}_t)$ exists. Since $(\bar{\mathbf{x}}_t+\hat{\mathbf{x}}, \bar{\mathbf{y}}_{t+1}+\rho_1\hat{\mathbf{x}})\epsilon\mathbf{T}$ for all t, one must have $U(\bar{\mathbf{c}}_t)+\delta U(\bar{\mathbf{c}}_{t+1}) \geqslant U(\bar{\mathbf{c}}_t-\theta\hat{\mathbf{x}})+\delta U(\bar{\mathbf{c}}_{t+1}+\theta\rho_1\hat{\mathbf{x}})$ for small θ, implying $0 \geqslant -\delta^t U'(\bar{\mathbf{c}}_t).\hat{\mathbf{x}}+\delta^{t+1}\rho_1 U'(\bar{\mathbf{c}}_{t+1}).\hat{\mathbf{x}}$. Hence, $U'(\bar{\mathbf{c}}_t).\hat{\mathbf{x}} \leqslant U'(\bar{\mathbf{c}}_0).\hat{\mathbf{x}}/(\delta\rho_1)^t$. But the right-hand side of this expression converges to zero, implying that $\bar{\mathbf{c}}_t$ is unbounded, and contradicting 3.7. Hence, $(\bar{\mathbf{c}}_t)$ cannot be maximal.

IV. EXISTENCE CRITERIA FOR THE RESOURCE-LIMITED, NO-DISCOUNTING ECONOMY

4.1. We next summarise existence criteria for an important 'borderline' case, the economy with no discounting in which outputs of produced commodities are limited by the availability of primary resources. This problem has been solved for the multi-commodity case by Gale (1967). A slight weakening of Gale's assumptions and a considerable simplification in analysis have been made by Brock (1970). In stating this result, we require one additional assumption (a somewhat weaker condition is used by Brock):

B.6. $U(\mathbf{c})$ is strictly concave and continuously differentiable, with $U'(\mathbf{c})$ bounded, for all positive $\mathbf{c}$.

Note that assumption B.6 is inconsistent with assumption B.5.

4.2. *Theorem. Suppose a multi-commodity economy has a technology satisfying A.1 to A.4, with* $\rho_0 > 1 > \rho_1$, *and social preferences satisfying B.1 to B.3 and B.6, and* $\delta = 1$. *Suppose that the initial endowment vector* $\mathbf{y}_0$ *is positive. Then, an optimal programme exists.*

Proof: By 3.7, if $\rho_1 < 1$, then all feasible programmes are bounded. Hence, replacing the original technology $\mathbf{T}$ with the technology $\mathbf{T}' = \{(\mathbf{x}, \mathbf{y})\epsilon\mathbf{T}\,|\,|\mathbf{x}| \leqslant \eta\}$ for a large scalar η leaves the problem unchanged except that the technology $\mathbf{T}'$ is closed and bounded. Then, Brock's proof applies.

V. EXISTENCE CRITERIA FOR THE NON-RESOURCE-LIMITED NO-DISCOUNTING ECONOMY

5.1. The final 'borderline' case we shall consider is a productive linear technology (i.e. $\mathbf{T}$ is a cone with $\rho_0 = \rho_1 > 1$) in which outputs are not limited by the availability of primary resources, for the case of no discounting. For this case, results 3.2 (a) and 3.16 (d) establish (1) if the asymptotic elasticity α_1 is greater than one (implying $U(\mathbf{c})$ bounded above), then an optimal programme exists; and (2) if α_1 is less than one and $U(\mathbf{c})$ is asymptotically homothetic and smooth (implying $U(\mathbf{c})$ unbounded above), then no optimal programme exists. With several additional restrictions on the technology, the author

(1970) has sharpened this result to establish that $U(\mathbf{c})$ bounded above is necessary and sufficient to imply the existence of an optimal programme. To the assumptions A.1 to A.4, we first add the condition:

A.5. The technology $\mathbf{T}$ is a cone with $\rho_1 > 1$, and the vectors $\hat{\mathbf{x}}$ and $\hat{\mathbf{p}}$ in 2.4, satisfying $(\hat{\mathbf{x}}, \rho_0\hat{\mathbf{x}})\epsilon\mathbf{T}$ and $\hat{\mathbf{p}}.\mathbf{y} \leqslant \rho_0\hat{\mathbf{p}}.\mathbf{x}$ for all $(\mathbf{x}, \mathbf{y})\epsilon\mathbf{T}$, can be taken to be positive.

This assumption will be satisfied if the economy is irreducible (i.e. all commodities are needed, directly or indirectly, to produce any given commodity) and has sufficient output substitutability to avoid 'over-production' of some commodities in attaining maximal growth.

A feasible programme $(\tilde{\mathbf{x}}_t, \tilde{\mathbf{y}}_t, \tilde{\mathbf{c}}_t)$ is *good* if there is a scalar $M > 0$ such that for any other feasible programme $(\mathbf{x}_t, \mathbf{y}_t, \mathbf{c}_t)$, one has

$$\sum_{t=0}^{\nu} [U(\mathbf{c}_t) - U(\tilde{\mathbf{c}}_t)] \leqslant M, \quad \nu = 1, 2, \ldots.$$

The first result is a condition for the existence of good programmes:

5.2. *Theorem. Suppose a multi-commodity economy has a linear technology satisfying A.1 to A.5. Suppose that social preferences satisfy B.1 to B.3 and* $\delta = 1$. *Suppose that the initial endowment* $\mathbf{y}_0$ *is positive. Then, a good programme exists if and only if* $U(\mathbf{c})$ *is bounded above.*

Proof: McFadden (1967), Theorem 6.

5.3. A sequence of programmes $(\mathbf{x}_t^j, \mathbf{y}_t^j, \mathbf{c}_t^j)$ for $j = 1, 2, \ldots$, is termed an *optimising sequence* if each of these programmes is comparable to all other feasible programmes; i.e.

$$\lim_{\nu\to\infty} \sum_{t=0}^{\nu} [U(\mathbf{c}_t) - U(\mathbf{c}_t^j)]$$

exists for all feasible programmes $(\mathbf{c}_t)$, and one has

$$\lim_{j\to+\infty} \sum_{t=0}^{\infty} [U(\mathbf{c}_t) - U(\mathbf{c}_t^j)] \leqslant 0.$$

A result established by the author for a very general class of economies with linear technologies can be specialised to give a relationship between good programmes and optimising sequences of programmes:

5.4. *Theorem. Suppose an economy satisfies A.1 to A.5, B.1 to B.3, and* $\delta = 1$. *Suppose that* $\mathbf{y}_0$ *is positive, and that a good programme* $(\tilde{\mathbf{x}}_t, \tilde{\mathbf{y}}_t, \tilde{\mathbf{c}}_t)$ *exists. Then, the following results hold:*

(1) *All good feasible plans are comparable, and if a programme* $(\mathbf{x}_t, \mathbf{y}_t, \mathbf{c}_t)$ *is not good, then*

$$\lim_{\nu\to\infty} \sum_{t=0}^{\nu} [U(\mathbf{c}_t) - U(\tilde{\mathbf{c}}_t)] = -\infty.$$

(2) *There exists an optimising sequence* $(\mathbf{x}_t^j, \mathbf{y}_t^j, \mathbf{c}_t^j)$, $j = 1, 2, \ldots$.

(3) *The optimising sequence has a subsequence converging pointwise to a programme* $(\bar{\mathbf{x}}_t, \bar{\mathbf{y}}_t, \bar{\mathbf{c}}_t)$, *which is good.*

(4) *There exists a price system* $(\bar{\mathbf{p}}_t)$, *not identically zero, such that* $(\bar{\mathbf{x}}_t, \bar{\mathbf{y}}_t, \bar{\mathbf{c}}_t)$ *is a finitely competitive programme* (*i.e.* (*12.11*) *and* (*12.12*) *hold*). *Further,*

$$\sum_{t=0}^{\infty} \bar{\mathbf{p}}_t \cdot \mathbf{c}_t$$

exists for all feasible $(\mathbf{c}_t)$, *and one has*

$$\sum_{t=0}^{\infty} [U(\mathbf{c}_t) - U(\tilde{\mathbf{c}}_t)] - \overline{M} \leqslant \sum_{t=0}^{\infty} \bar{\mathbf{p}}_t \cdot (\mathbf{c}_t - \mathbf{c}_t^j),$$

where

$$\overline{M} = \sup \{ \sum_{t=0}^{\infty} [U(\mathbf{c}_t') - U(\tilde{\mathbf{c}}_t)] \,|\, (\mathbf{c}_t') \textit{ feasible} \}$$

and $(\mathbf{c}_t^j)$ *is any member of the optimising sequence.*

(5) *If*

$$\sum_{t=0}^{\infty} \bar{\mathbf{p}}_t \cdot (\bar{\mathbf{c}}_t - \mathbf{c}_t) \geqslant 0$$

for all feasible $(\mathbf{c}_t)$, *then* $(\bar{\mathbf{c}}_t)$ *is optimal.*

(6) *If*

$$\lim_{j \to \infty} \sum_{t=1}^{\infty} |\mathbf{c}_t^j - \bar{\mathbf{c}}_t| / \rho_0^{\,t} = 0,$$

then $(\bar{\mathbf{c}}_t)$ *is optimal.*

(7) *If*

$$\lim_{\nu \to = \infty} \sup \{ \sum_{t=\nu}^{\infty} \bar{\mathbf{p}}_t \cdot \mathbf{c}_t \,|\, (\mathbf{c}_t) \textit{ feasible} \} = 0,$$

then $(\bar{\mathbf{c}}_t)$ *is optimal.*

Proof: McFadden (1970), Theorem 3.

5.5. The technology **T** will admit one or more supporting planes at each point $(\mathbf{x}, \mathbf{y})$ in its boundary. The technology is *smooth* at $(\mathbf{x}, \mathbf{y})$ if the supporting plane there is unique. We make one additional assumption:

A.6. The technology is smooth at the maximal expansion path $(\hat{\mathbf{x}}, \rho_0\hat{\mathbf{x}})$.

This condition is satisfied if production possibilities are representable by a collection of production and transformation functions which are differentiable at the maximal expansion path, or is satisfied by a finite von Neumann technology in which $2N-1$ linearly independent activities are operated at non-zero levels at the maximal expansion path.[1] Under this assumption, the price system $(\bar{\mathbf{p}}_t)$ given in 5.4 (4) has a 'turnpike' property that $[\bar{\mathbf{p}}_{t+1}(1+\varepsilon)-\bar{\mathbf{p}}_t].\hat{\mathbf{x}} \leqslant 0$ when the angle between $(\bar{\mathbf{p}}_t, \bar{\mathbf{p}}_{t+1})$ and $(\rho_0\hat{\mathbf{p}}, \hat{\mathbf{p}})$ is sufficiently large (McFadden, 1970, Lemma 5). Hence, one has

$$\lim_{t\to+\infty} \rho_0{}^t\bar{\mathbf{p}}_t = \theta\hat{\mathbf{p}}$$

for some non-negative scalar θ (McFadden, 1970, Lemma 6). We are now able to state the main result:

5.6. *Theorem. Suppose a multi-commodity economy has a linear technology satisfying A.1 to A.6. Suppose that social preferences satisfy B.1 to B.3 and* $\delta = 1$. *Suppose that the initial endowment* $\mathbf{y}_0$ *is positive. Then, an optimal programme exists if and only if* $U(\mathbf{c})$ *is bounded above.*

Proof: McFadden (1970), Theorem 5.

[1] Since A.6 allows non-joint production, it is less objectionable economically than the dual proposition frequently assumed in turnpike theory that the maximal expansion path is the only 'break-even' programme at von Neumann prices.

REFERENCES

T. Bewley, 'A Theorem on the Existence of Competitive Equilibria in a Market with a Finite Number of Agents and Whole Commodity Space is L_∞', CORE Discussion Paper (Louvain, 1969).

W. Brock, 'On Existence of Weakly Maximal Programs in von Neumann Growth Models', *Review of Economic Studies* (1970).

—— and D. Gale, 'Optimal Growth under Factor-Augmenting Progress', *Journal of Economic Theory* (1970).

G. Debreu, *Theory of Value* (Wiley, 1957).

—— 'New Concepts and Techniques for Equilibrium Analysis', *International Economic Review* (1962).

P. Diamond, 'On the Evaluation of Infinite Utility Streams', *Econometrica* (1965).

D. Gale, 'The Closed Linear Model of Production', in Kuhn and Tucker (eds.), *Linear Inequalities and Related Systems, Annals of Mathematical Study*, no. 38 (1956).

—— 'On Optimal Development in a Multi-Sector Economy', *Review of Economic Studies* (1967).

S. Goldman, 'Sequential Planning and Continual Planning Revision', *Journal of Political Economy* (1969).

S. Karlin, *Mathematical Methods and Theory in Games, Programming and Economics*, vol. I (Addison-Wesley, 1959).

T. Koopmans, 'Stationary Ordinal Utility and Impatience', *Econometrica* (1960).

—— 'On the Concept of Optimal Growth', in *The Econometric Approach to Development Planning* (Rand McNally, 1966).

—— 'Objectives, Constraints, and Outcomes in Optimal Growth Models', *Econometrica* (1967).

D. McFadden, 'The Evaluation of Development Programs', *Review of Economic Studies* (1967).

—— 'On the Existence of Optimal Development Plans', in Harold W. Kuhn (ed.), *Sixth Princeton Symposium on Mathematical Programming*, vol. I (Princeton U.P., 1970).

E. Malinvaud, 'Efficient Capital Accumulation', *Econometrica* (1953, 1962).

R. Radner, 'Efficiency Prices for Infinite Horizon Production Programs', *Review of Economic Studies* (1967).

F. Ramsey, 'A Mathematical Theory of Savings', *Economic Journal* (1928).

R. Strotz, 'Myopia and Inconsistency in Dynamic Utility Maximisation', *Review of Economic Studies* (1956).

C. von Weizsäcker, 'Existence of Optimal Programs of Accumulation for an Infinite Time Horizon', *Review of Economic Studies* (1965).

S. Winter, 'Some Properties of the Closed Linear Model of Production', *International Economic Review* (1965).

M. Yaari, 'On the Existence of an Optimal Plan in a Continuous-Time Allocation Process', *Econometrica* (1964).

13 Agreeable Plans

Peter J. Hammond and James A. Mirrlees
NUFFIELD COLLEGE, OXFORD

I. THE NON-EXISTENCE OF OPTIMUM GROWTH

Consider a one-good growth model (with exogenous labour):

$$c_t + \dot{k}_t = y_t = f(k_t, t), \quad k_t \geqslant 0, \quad c_t \geqslant 0. \tag{13.1}$$

Granted an instantaneous utility function, $u(c, t)$, one says that a path (c_t^*, k_t^*) is optimum if for any other (c_t, k_t) satisfying (13.1) with the same initial capital,

$$\int_0^T [u(c_t^*, t) - u(c_t, t)]dt \geqslant 0 \tag{13.2}$$

for all sufficiently large T. This 'overtaking' criterion seems to be rather natural. Unfortunately there are many quite plausible and appealing specifications of f and u for which no optimum path exists, as the following examples illustrate.[1]

(1) *Constant Rate of Return, Logarithmic Utility, No Impatience*

$$f(k, t) = ak, \quad u(c, t) = \log c. \tag{13.3}$$

In this case, if (c_t, k_t) is feasible,

$$\int_0^T e^{-at} c_t dt = k_0 - e^{-aT} k_T \tag{13.4}$$

and

$$\int_0^T \log c_t dt = \int_0^T \log (e^{-at} c_t) dt + \tfrac{1}{2} a T^2$$

$$< T \log \left[\frac{1}{T} \int_0^T e^{-at} c_t dt \right] + \tfrac{1}{2} a T^2 \tag{13.5}$$

[1] Numerous examples of the non-existence of optimum growth have been given. The first discussions were Tinbergen (1959) and Chakravarty (1962). Rigorous analysis of particular cases can be found in Weizsäcker (1965), Koopmans (1966) and Mirrlees (1967). Gale, McFadden, McKenzie and others have extended the discussion to many-commodity models.

The first two examples given here are well known. (The proof of the first may be new.) The third example gives a case of non-existence which we have not noticed elsewhere in the literature. It is, of course, a particular case of a general class of non-existence examples for bounded production.

unless $e^{-at}c_t$ is constant for t in $[0, T]$. It is clear from (13.4) that $e^{-at}c_t$ can be constant for all t only if $c_t = 0$. In that case we can certainly improve upon the proposed path. Otherwise we can choose T_0 so large that

$$\int_0^{T_0} \log c_t dt < T_0 \log \left[\frac{1}{T_0}(k_0 - e^{-aT_0}k_{T_0})\right] + \\ + \tfrac{1}{2}T_0^2 = \int_0^{T_0} \log c_t' dt \qquad (13.6)$$

where c_t' is defined to be $e^{at}(1/T_0)(k_0 - e^{-aT_0}k_{T_0})$ $(t \leqslant T_0)$, and $c_t' = c_t$ $(t \geqslant T_0)$. Clearly, (c_t') is feasible, and

$$\int_0^T \log c_t dt < \int_0^T \log c_t' dt \qquad (13.7)$$

for all $T \geqslant T_0$. This shows that no consumption path can satisfy (13.2) for all sufficiently large T. Therefore no optimum path exists.

(2) *Cobb–Douglas Production with Technical Change, Constant Elasticity Utility Function, Constant Rate of Impatience*

$$\left.\begin{aligned} f(k, t) &= k^b e^{m(1-b)t}, \quad (0 < b < 1, \quad m > 0) \\ u(c, t) &= \frac{1}{\gamma} c^\gamma e^{-\rho t} \quad (1 > \gamma \neq 0) \quad (c \geqslant 0) \end{aligned}\right\} \qquad (13.8)$$

Define

$$x = ke^{-mt}, \quad z = ce^{-mt}. \qquad (13.9)$$

It is a necessary condition for an optimum path that

$$\frac{1}{u_c(c_t, t)} \frac{d}{dt} u_c(c_t, t) = -f_k(k_t, t) \quad (t \geqslant 0). \qquad (13.10)$$

As is well known, this follows from the fact that the optimum path is better than any other with the same T-finale for any $T > 0$.[1] We shall refer to (13.10) as a *local optimality condition.* Using the notation (13.9), (13.10) becomes

$$(\gamma - 1)\left(\frac{\dot{z}}{z} + m\right) - \rho = -bx^{b-1}$$

or

$$(1-\gamma)\dot{z} = z[bx^{b-1} - \rho(1-\gamma)m]. \qquad (13.11)$$

At the same time, (13.1) implies that

$$\dot{x} = x^b - mx - z. \qquad (13.12)$$

[1] We call consumption in the first T years of a path its *T-overture*. Consumption after time T is referred to as its *T-finale*.

The usual phase diagram (Fig. 13.1) shows the various solutions of (13.11) and (13.12).

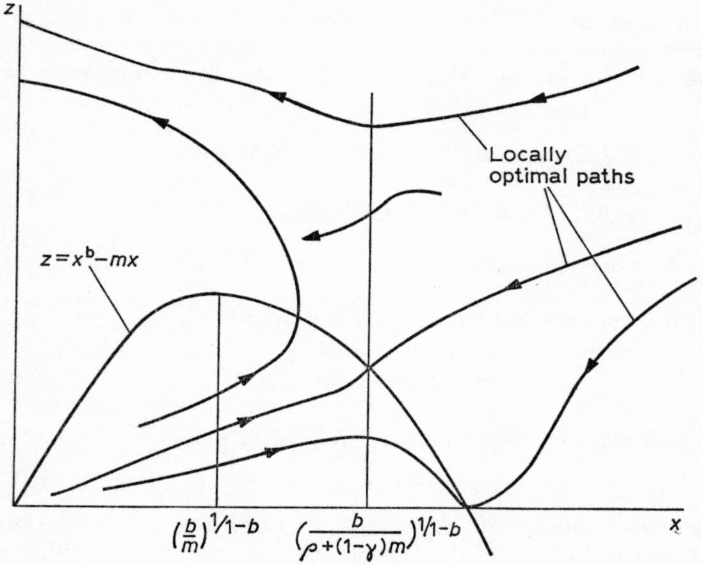

FIG. 13.1

If $\rho < (\gamma - 1 + b)m$, none of the paths satisfying (13.11) and (13.12) remain feasible for all time: sooner or later, x becomes negative. *Proof:* under the stated inequality, (13.1) implies that $(1-\gamma)\dot{z} > bz(x^{b-1} - m)$; so that if $\dot{x} \geqslant 0$ and therefore $x^b \geqslant mx$, z is increasing, and eventually becomes so large that $\dot{x} < 0$. After that, $\dot{x}$ remains negative, and x must eventually become negative also. Therefore no optimum path exists.

In fact, no optimum exists if only

$$\rho < \gamma m. \tag{13.13}$$

To prove this, one notes that when $(\gamma - 1 + b)m \leqslant \rho < \gamma m$, any feasible path satisfying (13.11) and (13.12) has the property that

$$\lim_{t \to \infty} x_t > \bar{x} = \left(\frac{b}{m}\right)^{1/(1-b)} \tag{13.14}$$

where $\bar{x}$ is the 'golden rule' level of capital per efficiency unit of labour, defined by $f_k = m$. At the same time

$$\lim_{t \to \infty} z_t < \bar{z} = (1-b)\left(\frac{b}{m}\right)^{b/(1-b)} \tag{13.15}$$

where $\bar{z} = \bar{x}^b - m\bar{x}$. These facts are clear from the diagram, whose main features are easily verified. If $x_t > \bar{x}$, $z_t < \bar{z}$ $(t \geqslant T_0)$, we can do better by defining a new path identical to (x_t, z_t) for $t < T_0$, but constant at $(\bar{x}, \bar{z})$ for $t \geqslant T_0$. This is clearly feasible, and gives greater consumption at all $t \geqslant T_0$. Therefore any feasible path satisfying (13.11) and (13.12) can be bettered: no optimum path exists.

(3) *Bounded, Increasing Production, No-Impatience*

$$\left.\begin{aligned} f(k,t) &= a^{-d} - (a+k)^{-d} \quad && (d > 0, \quad a > 0) \\ u(c,t) &= u(c) && (u' > 0, \quad u'' < 0) \end{aligned}\right\} \tag{13.16}$$

In this case the local optimality conditions

$$\frac{1}{u'}\frac{d}{dt}u' = -d(a+k)^{-d-1} \tag{13.17}$$

can be integrated. The locally optimal paths satisfy

$$u(c) + (f-c)u'(c) = \text{constant}. \tag{13.18}$$

It is easily verified that this formula, due to Ramsey, provides paths that satisfy (13.17). On the feasible paths, $c < f$. We show that any such path can be bettered. More precisely, we show that the consumption (c_t) provided can be obtained with less initial capital.

Notice first that we can restrict our attention to paths on which $c_t \to a^{-d} \equiv b$. Any path on which $\lim c_t < b$ is clearly worse, and $\lim c_t$ exists for all locally optimal paths, and is equal to b for one of them, namely that for which

$$u(c) + (f-c)u'(c) = u(b). \tag{13.19}$$

Let (c_t, k_t) be the path defined by (13.19) and (13.1).

Suppose (h_t) has the property that

$$\dot{h}_t = f(h_t) - c_t. \tag{13.20}$$

Let μ be a number such that $0 < \mu < 1$, and suppose that at some particular t,

$$h_t \geqslant \mu k_t. \tag{13.21}$$

Then

$$\begin{aligned} \dot{h}_t - \mu\dot{k}_t &= f(h_t) - \mu f(k_t) - (1-\mu)c_t \\ &\geqslant f(\mu k_t) - \mu f(k_t) - (1-\mu)c_t \\ &= \mu(a+k_t)^{-d} - (a+\mu k_t)^{-d} + (1-\mu)(b-c_t). \end{aligned} \tag{13.22}$$

If we write $y = b-c$, (13.19) can be written in the form

$$\frac{u(b)-u(b-y)}{yu'(b-y)} = 1-\frac{(a+k)^{-d}}{y}. \tag{13.23}$$

Now $y_t \to 0$ as $t \to \infty$; and then the left-hand side of (13.23) tends to 1. Hence

$$\frac{(a+k_t)^{-d}}{y_t} \to 0 \quad (t \to \infty). \tag{13.24}$$

Therefore there exists t_0 such that

$$y_t \geqslant \frac{\mu^{-d}-\mu}{1-\mu}(a+k_t)^{-d} \quad (t \geqslant t_0). \tag{13.25}$$

Applying this inequality to (13.22), we obtain

$$\begin{aligned} h_t-\mu\dot{k}_t &\geqslant \mu^{-d}(a+k_t)^{-d}-(a+\mu k_t)^{-d} \\ &> 0 \end{aligned} \tag{13.26}$$

since $\mu < 1$.

We have shown that there exists t_0 such that we can at t_0 reduce the capital stock to a fraction $(1-\mu)$ of itself, and yet continue the same consumption after that date as on the path we started with. That path is therefore inefficient, and consequently not optimal. Therefore no optimum path exists.

It may be asked whether production is likely to be bounded above, without the upper bound ever being achieved for a finite capital stock. In fact, the following gives an indication of how such a production function might arise.

Suppose that there is a fixed quantity of labour L. Suppose that, in addition to the labour needed to operate each machine, l, there is also lg more labour needed to repair and maintain each machine. Suppose that there is learning by doing, whenever a new machine is built, which reduces the maintenance costs on each machine – i.e. this technical progress is entirely disembodied. Then, when the capital stock is k machines, the number of men needed to operate each machine is $l[1+g(k)]$. Clearly, $g(k)$ will decrease with k. Suppose that $g(k) \to G$, as $k \to \infty$. G can be interpreted as the theoretical number of men needed to maintain each machine – it may be zero, of course. For simplicity, assume that output is just equal to the number of machines operated. (That is, assume a linear production relationship, and choose units.) As k increases, there will eventually be more machines than there are men able to operate and maintain them. Nevertheless, it may still be worth building machines, because this is the only way of saving the amount of labour which is needed for maintenance. Once there are enough machines to employ all the labour force (other cases are not important, when the economy is productive, and optimal or agreeable paths are being considered for their asymptotic properties as $k \to \infty$), the production function is $f(k) = L/l[1+g(k)]$, and

$$f(k) < b = L/l(1+G) = \lim_{k\to\infty} f(k), \quad \text{for all} \quad k.$$

These examples show that the non-existence of an optimum may not be very obvious. No restriction on the class of utility functions will ensure existence; nor can one claim that realistic production assumptions by themselves are enough to exclude the problem. It must be wrong to change the specification of the problem merely to ensure that it has a solution. That a solution does not exist perhaps indicates that something is wrong with the specification; but it does not tell us what is wrong. If no persuasive method of reformulating these growth problems can be found, we may have to accept that in certain situations there is no answer to the questions one wants to ask: no optimum rate of growth, for example.

We do not believe that all interesting questions of choice have answers. But we do think that there is a way of reformulating the choice among alternative paths of economic growth that greatly extends the class of situations in which answers can be given, without resorting to arbitrary modifications of the problem (such as 'suitable' utility discounting). In the next section we introduce a definition of 'agreeable' plans: such a plan is one upon which it would be sensible to agree. The definition we propose is based upon an analysis of the reasons that lead economists to use an infinite time horizon in the formulation of growth problems. In later sections, we demonstrate that the definition has most of the properties one can reasonably wish for. The discussion is restricted to the one-good model.[1]

II. DEFINITION

If we were willing to specify a particular date after which events are certain to be without any significance for us, we could regard the optimum growth problem as a finite-horizon problem. Clearly this could happen only when human beings, and beings about which they care, had ceased to exist; since, at least, respect for a man's preferences implies concern for his children, and so on until the last generation. Few are quite certain about an upper bound to the end

[1] One of us (Hammond) is preparing a paper analysing the concept of agreeable plans in many-commodity models.

of mankind. Few can believe such knowledge would have any significance for us. Even those who would willingly accept a finite time horizon will usually accept an infinite time horizon, on the grounds that it cannot matter. The technical convenience, for clear and quantitative results, of using an infinite time horizon is rather great.

Unfortunately, the use of an infinite time horizon does make a difference, as we have seen. If it were at all probable that mankind, or beings for whom we should have concern, would exist for ever, we should have to accept the fact that sometimes no sensible decision is possible. But there is evidence – such as that represented by the second law of thermodynamics – which leads us to reject that view. The appropriate time horizon is presumably always very long; but we do not care to consider exactly how long. If we would choose more or less the same policy whatever particular long time horizon we used, there is no need for further thought on the matter: people with diverse views about the time horizon should be able to agree, more or less, about a policy, so long as they agree that the time horizon should be far away. More precisely, we should expect agreement about the desirability of a particular policy if, whatever the (long) time horizon postulated, no great improvement upon that policy is possible. We call such a policy, and the growth path generated by it, *agreeable*, and introduce the formal definition:

Definition. A feasible consumption path (c_t^*) is *agreeable* if, for all positive numbers ε and T_0, there exists $T_1 > T_0$ such that for any feasible consumption path (c_t) and any time horizon $T \geqslant T_1$ we can find a consumption path (c_t') such that

$$c_t' = c_t^* \quad (0 \leqslant t \leqslant T_0) \tag{13.27}$$

and

$$\int_0^T u(c_t')dt > \int_0^T u(c_t)dt - \varepsilon. \tag{13.28}$$

The idea of the definition is that, given a particular sensitivity to utility differences, measured by ε, and a particular 'planning period' over which the chosen policy is to operate, everyone who agrees that the appropriate time horizon is at least as great as T_1 can agree on the desirability of the policy (c_t^*), for the time being. One could imagine making c^* depend upon ε and T_0; but it is all the more appealing if c^* does not depend upon them, and is then unique. We shall prove that, in a wide class of cases, this is so.

It may be felt that, in any particular case, it would be desirable to obtain numerical information about the relationship between T_1 and the standards of sensitivity, T_0 and ε (measured, no doubt, by equivalent consumption differences). While such information would indeed be interesting, we suspect that it would be hard to upset the 'agreeability' of such a consumption path. Men are accustomed to allow the extent of probable disagreement to affect their estimates of the deviation from optimum policies that they will be prepared to regard as tolerable.

We suggest that it is more important to establish the extent to which the notion of agreeability may help to resolve the non-existence of optimum policies. As a check on the reasonableness of the definition, it must be shown that, when an optimum path exists, it is (usually) agreeable; and that agreeable paths are usually unique. It must also be shown that agreeable paths exist in many cases where optimum paths do not exist. In addition, we have to seek ways of characterising the agreeable path in cases where the known methods of characterising optimum paths cannot apply.

We are prepared to claim more for the agreeableness of agreeable plans than the definition suggests. Although the idea of an optimum plan is clearly fundamental, it seems to us that one might, if there were any choice in the matter, prefer an agreeable plan to an optimum plan in a simple, deterministic model.

If we knew that we had a perfect and certain specification of the economy and of preferences, we should want the optimum plan. (If none existed, we could have no recourse to any alternative definition.) In fact, we are very uncertain about many aspects of the specification given in any model. For example – to mention the most common point made in this connection – we do not know what form of utility function we should use if we lived a hundred years later. Planners must expect to change their minds. One possible way of dealing with this problem is to specify more exactly the nature of our uncertainty, most conveniently by introducing a stochastic model. Numerical solution of even the simplest plausible models of this type seems to be rather hard, at least when technological uncertainty is allowed for.[1] Beyond such an improved specification, yet more sophisticated and complicated models lie.

Much of economics is concerned, however, with avoiding over-complex models. Excessively profound thought and empirical research about the assumptions and structure of a model is to be avoided, not only because it is costly, but because, like some medical treatment, it is not, beyond a point, likely to lead to any improvement. The reason that economists have not troubled to develop models that specify in detail the various possible technological and perceptual developments of the next century is not so much that they are rather

[1] As one of us found in an as yet imperfect and unpublished paper: Mirrlees, 'Optimum Accumulation under Uncertainty'.

uncertain about precisely which developments will happen – after all, we have the language of probabilities with which to describe uncertainty among many possible developments. It is rather that, on intuitive grounds, they do not expect any worth-while improvement in current policy recommendations to follow from a more careful specification of the future.

The property of agreeability makes a precise claim of this kind. If a plan is agreeable, no more careful specification of the time horizon can lead to a significant improvement in policy, provided that that horizon is known to be at least as great as some particular number. Uncertainty about the time horizon is only one, very special, source of uncertainty; but it may plausibly be taken to stand for the much larger class of uncertainties that have to do with the far distant future. If an agreeable plan exists, and parameters ε and T_0 are specified, and time horizons greater than T_1 are accepted, clearly we must have some reason for giving considerable weight to consumption in the years beyond T_1 before we should be prepared to argue in favour of a different plan. We should have to believe that greater weight ought to be given to this distant part of the consumption plan that would be given by someone who believed that the presently specified valuation of consumption paths should be maintained beyond T_1 and that the economy will continue for a finite period beyond T_1 – even an extremely long finite period. Although future generations will surely see the value and possibilities of consumption differently from ourselves, and therefore do something different from what we should work out for them now if we choose to, few would be prepared to insist that the weight to be given to their consumption should be much greater than is implied by simply projecting the present into the future.

In that case, we can surely expect the agreement of those who think that the specified utility function will not be appropriate in the distant future, as well as of those who think it probably will be, but disagree with us about the time horizon. To put the conclusion less metaphorically, but more meta-economically, an agreeable plan is one that cannot be significantly improved upon by further research into and meditation about the nature of the far distant economy of the future. No precise theorem can fully capture the nature of that assertion, which is therefore not capable of precise proof. But we find the argument convincing. Let us remark, finally, that this more general argument suggests that numerical calculations of T_1 for various ε and T_0 may be more interesting than one would suppose if one thought of T_1 as merely the ultimate time horizon, rather than a date beyond which serious disagreement about the shape and preferences of the economy is of negligible importance.

III. THE MAXIMAL LOCALLY OPTIMAL PATH

In this section and the following one we shall proceed rather formally. The model is specified at the beginning of the paper. We assume that

f is twice continuously differentiable, defined for all $k \geqslant 0$ and t

$f_k > 0, f_{kk} \leqslant 0, f(0, t) = 0$

u is three times continuously differentiable, defined for all $c > 0$ and t

$u_c > 0, u_{cc} < 0, u(0, t) = -\infty.$

The last assumption is made for convenience, to avoid special consideration of zero consumption levels.

A path is *locally optimal* in $[0, T]$ if it is feasible for $0 \leqslant t \leqslant T$ (i.e. $k_t \geqslant 0$, $c_t > 0$ in this interval) and

$$\frac{d}{dt} u_c = -u_c f_k \quad (0 \leqslant t \leqslant T). \tag{13.29}$$

Weizsäcker has shown, in his 1965 paper, that if a path exists which is locally optimal for all $t \geqslant 0$, there exists a *maximal locally optimal* path, defined by the property that consumption at any time is greater on it than on any other locally optimal path feasible for all $t \geqslant 0$.[1] It is reasonably clear why this is so. Given two alternative levels of initial consumption, it is easily seen from (13.29) and the production relationship (13.1) that the magnitude of the difference between $\log u_c$ on the two paths never becomes smaller. Thus if consumption is ever greater on one than on the other, it is always greater. It is then fairly clear that the least upper bound of initial consumption levels for which the solution of (13.29) is feasible for all $t \geqslant 0$ itself leads to a perpetually feasible locally optimal path: if it did not, neither would a slightly smaller initial consumption level.

It is quite possible that no locally optimal path exists. This is the case in the first example discussed in section I of the paper. If $c_0 > 0$, $c_t = c_0 e^{at}$ on a locally optimal path. This implies, by solution of the differential equation $\dot{k} = f - c$, that $k_t = (k_0 - c_0 t)e^{at}$, which becomes negative in time. Therefore no locally optimal path exists. If such a path does exist, we have the following result:

Proposition 1. If an optimal path exists, it is the maximal locally optimal path (*and so is unique*).

Proof. A path is optimal according to the overtaking criterion

[1] Op. cit., pp. 97, 103. The proof given refers only to the case in which u is independent of time, but can be extended without difficulty.

(13.2) if and only if it is not overtaken by any other path. In particular, it must be locally optimal, because if a path is not locally optimal up to time T, it is overtaken by one with a better T-overture and the same T-finale. Moreover, it must be the maximal locally optimal path, since otherwise it is overtaken by the maximal locally optimal path.

We have already seen that the maximal locally optimal path is not necessarily optimal. In particular, it may not be efficient: it may be possible to find another path that provides more consumption at all times.

Proposition 2. If an agreeable path exists, then it is the maximal locally optimal path.

Proof. (i) Let (c_t^*, k_t^*) be agreeable. We shall show that it is locally optimal. If it is not locally optimal, there is some T_0 such that it is not locally optimal in $[0, T_0]$. Therefore it does not maximise $\int_0^{T_0} u(c, t)dt$ subject to $k_{T_0} = k_{T_0}^*$. Therefore we can find a path (c_t, k_t) such that, for a positive number ε,

$$\int_0^{T_0} u(c, t)dt \geqslant \int_0^{T_0} u(c^*, t)dt + \varepsilon$$

and

$$k_{T_0} = k_{T_0}^*.$$

Therefore, given any path with T_0-overture identical to (c_t^*), there is another better by ε for any time horizon $T \geqslant T_0$, namely that obtained by changing consumption to c_t for $0 \leqslant t \leqslant T_0$. Consequently (c_t^*, k_t^*) cannot satisfy the definition of agreeability.

(ii) A locally optimal path that is not maximal cannot be agreeable. Let (c_t, k_t) be locally optimal, but not maximal. $(\bar{c}_t, \bar{k}_t)$ is the maximal locally optimal path. Let $T > T_0 > 0$. Denote by (c_t', k_t') the path that maximises $\int_0^T udt$ subject to having the same T_0-overture as $(\bar{c}_t, \bar{k}_t)$. Let (b_t, h_t) be the path that maximises $\int_0^T udt$ without constraint. Then for all $t \leqslant T$, and in particular for $t = T_0$,

$$h_t < \bar{k}_t < k_t. \tag{13.30}$$

We show first that $\int_0^T u(c_t')dt < \int_0^T u(\bar{c}_t')dt$. (The reason is that each integral is a maximum subject to a constraint on the capital stock at T_0, a constraint which is effectively more stringent for the first integral.) Because of (13.30) we can find λ, $0 < \lambda < 1$, such that

$$\lambda h_{T_0} + (1-\lambda)k_{T_0} = \bar{k}_{T_0}. \tag{13.31}$$

The path $[\lambda b_t+(1-\lambda)c_t', \lambda h_t+(1-\lambda)k_t']$ is feasible in $[0, T]$. $(\bar{c}_t')$ maximises $\int_0^T u dt$ subject to the given level of the capital stock at $T_0, \bar{k}_{T_0}$. Therefore

$$\int_0^T u(\bar{c}_t')dt \geqslant \int_0^T u(\lambda b_t+(1-\lambda)c_t')dt$$

$$> \lambda \int_0^T u(b_t)dt+(1-\lambda)\int_0^T u(c_t')dt, \text{ by strict concavity of } u,$$

$$\geqslant \lambda \int_0^T u(\bar{c}_t')dt+(1-\lambda)\int_0^T u(c_t')dt,$$

by the definition of (b_t). Dividing by $(1-\lambda)$, we obtain

$$\int_0^T u(\bar{c}_t)dt > \int_0^T u(c_t')dt \tag{13.32}$$

as promised.

By the concavity of f, the path $(\frac{1}{2}c_t'+\frac{1}{2}\bar{c}_t')$ is feasible. Since u is strictly concave,

$$u(\tfrac{1}{2}c_t'+\tfrac{1}{2}\bar{c}_t') > \tfrac{1}{2}u(c_t')+\tfrac{1}{2}u(\bar{c}_t').$$

Therefore

$$\int_0^{T_0} [u(\tfrac{1}{2}c_t'+\tfrac{1}{2}\bar{c}_t')-\tfrac{1}{2}u(c_t')-\tfrac{1}{2}u(\bar{c}_t')]dt = \varepsilon > 0 \tag{13.33}$$

and

$$\int_0^T u(\tfrac{1}{2}c_t'+\tfrac{1}{2}\bar{c}_t')dt = \int_0^T [u(\tfrac{1}{2}c_t'+\tfrac{1}{2}\bar{c}_t')-\tfrac{1}{2}u(c_t')-$$

$$-\tfrac{1}{2}u(\bar{c}_t')]dt+\tfrac{1}{2}\int_0^T u(c_t')dt+$$

$$+\tfrac{1}{2}\int_0^T u(\bar{c}_t')dt$$

$$> \varepsilon+\tfrac{1}{2}\int_0^T u(c_t')dt+\tfrac{1}{2}\int_0^T u(\bar{c}_t')dt, \quad \text{by (13.31)}$$

$$> \int_0^T u(c_t')dt+\varepsilon \tag{13.34}$$

by (13.32). Notice that ε, given by (13.33), is defined independently of T. Thus (13.32) shows that for all T a path can be found which is better, by at least ε, than any path with the same T_0-overture as (c_t). Therefore (c_t) is not agreeable. This completes the proof.

Corollary. There is at most one agreeable path.

Consider the consumption path (b_t^T) which maximises $\int_0^T u dt$. We know it exists: it is the locally optimal path (in $[0, T]$) for which capital is zero at T. If there is a feasible path (b_t, h_t) such that, for each $t \geqslant 0$,

$$b_t^T \to b_t \quad (T \to \infty) \tag{13.35}$$

we call (b_t, h_t) the asymptotic-optimal path. If it exists, it is clearly unique.

Proposition 3. The asymptotic-optimal path always exists. It is the maximal locally optimal path if and only if a locally optimal path exists; otherwise it has zero consumption at all times.

Proof. Because the paths (b_t^T) are locally optimal, consumption at any time is an increasing function of initial consumption. At the same time, capital at any time is a decreasing function of initial consumption. Therefore initial consumption, b_0^T, must decrease as T increases. It is bounded below by zero, and therefore tends to a limit b_0. At the same time, all the b_t^T must tend to non-negative limits b_t. We have to show that (b_t) is feasible.

If $b_0 > 0$, consider the locally optimal path on which initial consumption is b_0, and denote it by (c_t). Clearly $c_t \leqslant b_t$, since for all T, $c_t < b_t^T$. But if $c_t < b_t$ for some $t > 0$, the locally optimal path on which consumption at t is b_t has initial consumption greater than b_0, so that for all T, $b_0^T \geqslant b_0 + a$ for some $a > 0$ – which is impossible. Therefore (b_t) is the locally optimal path with initial consumption b_0. It must be feasible, since otherwise it would be equal to one of the paths (b_t^T), for $T = T_1$, say. Then $b_t^T < b_t$ for $T > T_1$, which is impossible. Furthermore, it is clear from the definition of (b_t) as a limit of infeasible locally optimal paths that it must be the maximal feasible locally optimal path.

If $b_0 = 0$, then all $b_t = 0$, and there is no locally optimal path.

For suppose first that there is a locally optimal path. It lies below all the paths (b_t^T), and has positive initial consumption. That is inconsistent with $b_0 = 0$.

Suppose that $b_t > 0$ for some t. Then there must be a locally optimal path with consumption b_t at t. This, we have just seen, is impossible.

The proof is complete.

Proposition 4. If consumption is not zero on the asymptotic-optimal path, the path is agreeable.

Proof. Fix T_0 and $\varepsilon > 0$. Choose T_1 so that

$$\int_0^{T_0} [u(b_t^T) - u(b_t)]dt < \varepsilon \tag{13.36}$$

for all $T \geqslant T_1$. This can be done since $b_t > 0$. Let (b_t') be the consumption path that maximises $\int_0^T u dt$ subject to having the same T_0-overture as (b_t). Since h_{T_0}, the capital stock at T_0 on the path (b_t) is greater than the capital stock at T_0 on the path (b_t^T), for any T,

$$\int_0^T u(b_t')dt > \int_0^{T_0} u(b_t)dt + \int_0^T u(b_t^T)dt$$

$$> \int_0^T u(b_t^T)dt - \varepsilon \qquad (13.37)$$

by (13.36). This proves that (b_t) is agreeable.

These propositions together imply the following results:

Theorem 1. If an optimum path exists, it is agreeable.

This follows from the fact, implied by Propositions 3 and 4, that a maximal locally optimal path is agreeable.

Theorem 2. An agreeable path exists if and only if a (perpetually feasible) locally optimal path exists. It is then the maximal locally optimal path.

A maximal locally optimal path exists if and only if a locally optimal path exists. The theorem then follows from Propositions 2, 3 and 4.

IV. THE EXISTENCE OF AGREEABLE PLANS

By using Theorem 2, we can now see for each of the examples discussed in section I whether or not an agreeable path exists, and what path it is. We have already seen that there is no locally optimal path in example (1). Therefore no agreeable path exists. In example (2), agreeability allows a considerable extension over optimality, but does not cover all cases. We saw that no locally optimal path exists if $\rho < (\gamma - 1 + b)m$. But if ρ is greater than this limiting value, an agreeable path exists, even though there is no optimal path unless $\rho \geqslant \gamma m$. Finally, it is apparent that an agreeable path always exists for the case described in example (3).

The following theorem covers many of the cases that would be found most interesting by economists.

Theorem 3. Suppose

$$u_t(c, t) = 0 \quad (c > 0, t \geqslant 0)$$

$$f_t(k, t) \geqslant 0 \quad (k \geqslant 0, t \geqslant 0)$$

and that $u[f(k, t), t]$ *is bounded above for* $c > 0$, $k \geqslant 0$, $t \geqslant 0$. *Then an agreeable path exists.*

Notice that the conditions include cases where there is no technological progress. Boundedness of either the utility function or the production function is sufficient for existence.

Proof. We rely, essentially, upon the Keynes–Ramsey integral of the local optimality conditions, (13.10). Of course it is not valid when f depends upon t, but we have

$$\frac{d}{dt}u+[f-c)uc] = \dot{k}\dot{u}_c+f_k\dot{k}u_c+f_t u_c = f_t u_c \geqslant 0 \qquad (13.38)$$

on any locally optimal path. Therefore

$$u(c_t)+[f(k_t,t)-c_t]u_c(c_t) \geqslant u(c_0)+[f(k_0,0)-c_0]u_c(c_0). \qquad (13.39)$$

As $c_0 \to 0$ (k_0 being held fixed), the right-hand side of this inequality tends to ∞. For, by the concavity of u,

$$\begin{aligned} u(c_0)+(f-c_0)u_c(c_0) &\geqslant u(\tfrac{1}{2}f)-(\tfrac{1}{2}f-c_0)u_c(c_0) \\ &\quad + (f-c_0)u_c(c_0) \\ &= u(\tfrac{1}{2}f)+\tfrac{1}{2}fu_c(c_0) \\ &\to \infty \quad \text{as} \quad c_0 \to 0. \end{aligned}$$

Choose $c_0 > 0$ and $< f(k_0, 0)$, small enough to ensure that the right-hand side is greater than $\sup u(f)$. From (13.39), $f-c$ can never vanish. Since c_t and k_t are continuous, it follows that for all t

$$f(k_t, t)-c_t > 0. \qquad (13.40)$$

Thus $\dot{k}_t > 0$ always on this locally optimal path, which is therefore feasible for all time. This proves the existence of a perpetually feasible locally optimal path, and completes the proof.

Remark. The above proof can be applied also in the case where utility is discounted at a positive rate. We have already seen that an agreeable path (even an optimum path) may exist when u is unbounded and there is discounting. We do not have a general theorem to cover these cases.

V. CONCLUSIONS

Restricting our attention to the familiar one-good model, we have shown that agreeable plans exist in all cases where one can hope for any kind of solution to the 'infinite time horizon' optimum growth problem; namely cases for which there exists a locally optimal path that is always feasible. In other cases, there is no path that cannot be improved by changes confined to a finite period of time. Then one cannot hope for an ideal policy without specifying the time horizon.

We have seen that it is not easy to tell in advance whether a locally optimal path exists or not. If one is prepared to accept a bound on utility or a bound on production, it has been shown that one has an agreeable plan. Bounded production, though a sensible assumption, perhaps is so only in the same sense as is the assumption of a finite time horizon. Agreeability relative to an upper bound (truncation) of the production function does not appear to be a weaker requirement than agreeability relative to a finite time horizon. Yet one might wish, on considering the consumption externalities that appear to arise at high levels of output, to accept an upper bound to possible consumption little higher than that experienced by the middle classes in the industrial economies now. If these considerations are better incorporated in the utility function, the result is the same: an agreeable plan exists.

It has been argued[1] that, since there is a finite probability that utility is unbounded, therefore the utility function used in a planning calculation ought to be unbounded. We do not find this line of argument very persuasive, for the following reason. For definiteness, suppose there is no utility discounting or technological change. If decision-makers now have an unbounded utility function, there is no agreeable plan. If they do, they will still want to recognise that at some future date it may be decided that, properly, utility should be unbounded. If the date at which this happens is sufficiently far away, there is no reason why that should significantly affect the prospective utility loss of following the agreeable plan now (unless these planners reduce consumption to nearly zero for a long time). Therefore it is still reasonable to agree to the agreeable plan, arising from the bounded utility functions. The utility functions used *now* can justifiably be bounded. That it *might* have been different cannot imply that it *must* be wrong.

It will have been noted that an agreeable plan, like an optimum plan, is consistent with the usual competitive decentralisation of the economic system, since the local optimality condition is a shadow price condition, expressing the equality between the rate of interest and the marginal productivity of capital that would have to obtain in competitive equilibrium. No satisfactory means of approximating over time to the optimum path by means of price-guided decentralisation has been proposed, however: one does not know whether this property of the agreeable plan is of great significance.

Finally, we would suggest that agreeable plans are quite amenable to common sense. It is required, we have seen, that the rate at which marginal utility falls be equal to the marginal productivity of capital.

[1] Weizsäcker (1967).

Among paths for which this is true, it is suggested that the economy follow the one on which consumption is a maximum. This seems to be an entirely reasonable policy. Until now, one has had to dismiss this policy as being potentially unreasonable, since there may not in fact be an optimum policy. The concept of agreeability to some extent exorcises that ghost, and allows us to be more content with the path that good economic sense suggests.

REFERENCES

S. Chakravarty, 'The Existence of an Optimum Savings Programme', *Econometrica*, vol. XXX (1962) p. 178.

T. C. Koopmans, 'On the Concept of Optimal Economic Growth', in *The Econometric Approach to Development* (Vatican, 1966).

J. A. Mirrlees, 'Optimum Growth when Technology is Changing', *Review of Economic Studies*, vol. XXXIV (1967) p. 95.

J. Tinbergen, 'Optimum Savings and Utility Maximisation over Time', *Econometrica*, vol. XXX (1959) p. 481.

C. C. von Weizsäcker, 'Existence of Optimal Programmes of Accumulation for an Infinite Time Horizon', *Review of Economic Studies*, vol. XXXII (1965) p. 85.

—— 'Lemmas for a Theory of Approximate Optimal Growth', *Review of Economic Studies*, vol. XXXIV (1967) p. 151.

Discussion of the Paper by Peter J. Hammond and James A. Mirrlees

Professor Mirrlees introduced the paper by Hammond and himself by saying it reflected a certain unease about some of the problems in optimal growth theory. Much effort had been concentrated on existence problems which were difficult but not central to the economics of the problem. He still thought optimal growth theory was interesting – especially with respect to choice of investment projects. He wanted therefore to find a way of steering clear of the existence problems. We should recall that the infinite time horizon is introduced as a simplification, to represent the assumption that the time horizon is 'very distant'. It should not be lightly abandoned.

The framework used in this paper was a one-commodity, continuous-time model since it offered few technical difficulties and was well known to everyone. Mr Hammond was extending the results to many-sector models.

The examples included at the beginning were to remind people of the problems that arose. The third example was perhaps not very important, but it was surprising that bounded production could give rise to non-existence. The most interesting case arose when the intersection of the c, k (in efficiency units) stationaries gave a steady state with the savings rate above golden rule (see Fig. 13.1). The path (P) tending to the saddle-point is not optimal – it is inefficient. It does, however, have the property that any finite-horizon optimal path with 'a fairly long' time horizon starts off 'fairly close' to it (although such a path runs out of capital in finite time). Agreeable plans were defined (p. 289) in order to make this notion precise. The idea was to produce a plan which anyone with a sufficiently long time horizon could accept. If such a plan were unique the argument might be settled. It had been shown for the model of the paper that (i) the agreeable path is unique; (ii) it is locally optimal; (iii) an optimal path is agreeable; (iv) an agreeable path is the highest (in consumption terms) among the permanently feasible Euler paths; (v) if a permanently feasible Euler path exists, then an agreeable path exists. Where an agreeable path does not exist the situation looks hopeless, and this throws some light on the reasons for which an optimal path fails to exist in example (1) (we always want to postpone consumption). In a bounded situation (either utility or production) an agreeable path exists. They did not have as yet any general theorems proving convergence of an agreeable path to a steady state, or for cases involving technical progress.

Professor Stiglitz said he thought this an interesting and important paper. There were two main reasons why an optimum might not exist.

(i) The lollipop problem – we want to maximise $\int_0^T u(c)dt$ by allocating one lollipop over time; the limit of the finite-horizon optimal paths is permanent zero consumption. This was similar to the problem (with no solution) of finding the shortest distance between two points given that we must start at 45° to the line joining them. With such problems the limit of finite-horizon optimal paths as $T \to \infty$ was not feasible – agreeability does not avoid this problem.

(ii) Reasons connected with the non-convergence of the utility integral. Koopman's and Weizsäcker's methods for avoiding this problem were different. Agreeability extended Weizsäcker's notion of overtaking and he wondered if Koopmans's idea could be extended. Agreeability did not avoid the problem of non-existence in example (1). (*Professor Weizsäcker* said that this was similar to the lollipop problem and *Professor Yaari* remarked that this had been called the freewheeling economy by McFadden.) However, the case where the saddle-point corresponds to a savings rate above the golden rule was a very important case and this was covered by agreeability.

He wanted to discuss the nature of the criterion. He had begun to think of two other ways of expressing the idea of agreeability. First, we could specify that the path we are looking for (C_t) be such that the optimal path for a T-horizon plan has initial consumption within ε of C_0 for T sufficiently large. This, however, would include zero consumption as a solution to the lollipop problem which we do not want to do. Secondly, we might have tried to work with only one time, e.g. we want a path with utility integral greater than the integral for any other path less ε, provided T_0 is large enough. This definition did not work well. He had thus become convinced that the formulation of the criterion in the paper was the simplest way of capturing what we are after.

He also wanted to discuss the nature of agreement. We needed agreement about ε, T_0 (planning horizon), T_1 (the lowest estimate of the end of the world). The T_1 implied by ε, T_0 might be too large – if anyone thought the world would last less long than T_1, agreement was not possible. In order to agree, each individual believes that after T_0 he can choose what happens. If an individual thought the government might do something different, he might change his ideas of what was acceptable for the initial period to T_0 – a game-theoretic situation.

Two very strong assumptions in this kind of theory were (a) additive utility, (b) malleable capital. He asked how the concept was extended if these assumptions were relaxed.

Professor Inagaki supposed we were in a situation as in Fig. 13.1 of the paper, where the stationaries intersected at $\bar{x}$ with $\bar{x} > x_G$ (the golden rule capital per efficiency unit of labour), and we began with $x_0 = \bar{x}$. The agreeable path would be $x_t = \bar{x}$ for all t. The agreeable path could be dominated by a path Q of x as shown in Fig. 13.1A. The corresponding consumption path Q is shown in Fig. 13.1B. The reason an agreeable path could get within ε of the Q path was that it caught up between the end of the planning period T_0 and T_1. He would not agree to following the agreeable path.

He suggested it might be possible to reformulate the definition without T_1 since it was possible to catch up with Q in any interval, however small. He thought, however, that other paths would be superior to the one which caught up very quickly.

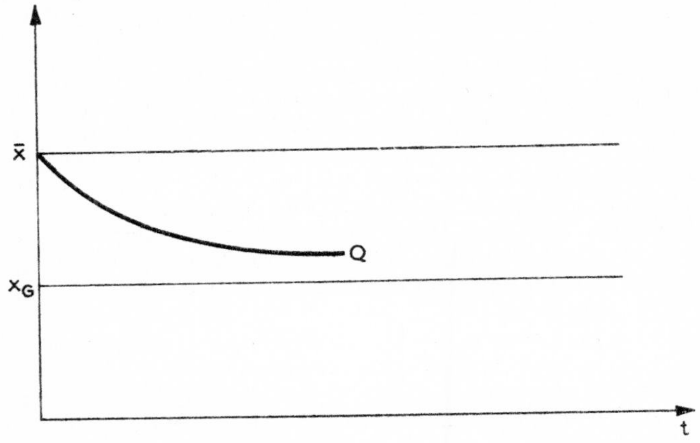

FIG. 13.1A

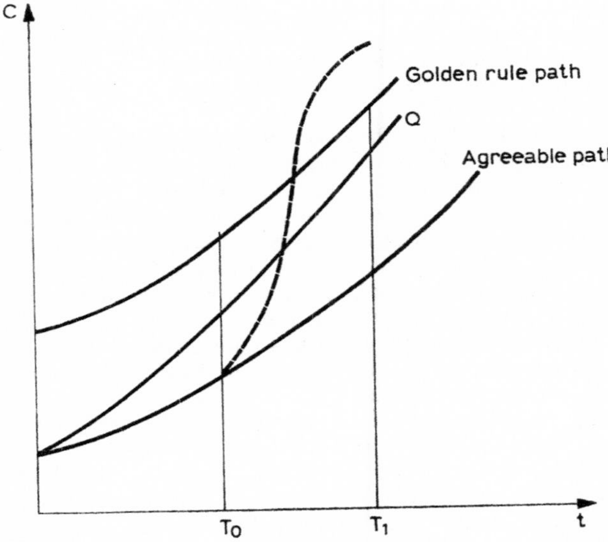

FIG. 13.1B

He said that the criterion should be reformulated using something like

$$1-\left(\int_0^{T_1} u(c')dt\right)\Big/\left(\int_0^{T_1} u(c)dt\right) < \varepsilon,$$

as otherwise we had problems with the definition of the units of ε.

He did not think that agreeability was a way out of non-existence problems as it did not maximise anything.

Professor Weizsäcker said the agreeability notion was a way out of problems that had been worrying us when we should have liked to have been thinking of more important things. In general, for a five-year (T_0) plan we had to decide on terminal capital stocks. Various *ad hoc* propositions had been offered, but such considerations led us to work with infinite horizon plans. The Hammond–Mirrlees proposal was that we adjust capital stocks at T_0 so that they would be acceptable to anyone whose overall horizon is longer than T_1. This showed why T_0 *and* T_1 were needed. We could then give up worrying about existence. The agreeability notion justified his belief that the existence problem was artificial. Inagaki's Q path would not be acceptable as it would have fewer capital stocks.

If we considered a long finite time horizon problem, the optimal solution would stay near the agreeable path in its initial stages. He would agree to the initial stages (to T_0) of an agreeable path, and this is what was being asked.

Professor Inagaki said a finite time horizon path would be very different from an agreeable path since it would finish up with zero capital stocks.

Professor Hahn asked if it was reasonable to agree to a path just because it could catch up with everything else later. We had no existence problems with finite horizons. The agreeability idea was a guide for thinking about finite time horizons.

Professor Mirrlees said that Professor Inagaki's example showed very clearly that we must not actually believe in infinite time horizons if we are to obtain agreement on a plan. If $x_0 = \bar{x}$ and it was proposed staying there indefinitely, I could not agree if my time horizon were infinite. We could, however, obtain agreement to keep x at $\bar{x}$ for the first T_0 years if everyone's horizon was longer than T_1.

Professor Yaari thought agreeability was a reason for feeling better about non-existence rather than a way of avoiding existence problems. That the maximal locally path was agreeable was a nice result since we knew that in certain circumstances it was not optimal. Professor Mirrlees had offered one way of reducing our worries about existence. He wanted to consider alternative methods.

A strong definition (A) of optimality was: (C_t^*) is optimal if

$$\liminf_{T\to\infty} \int_0^T [u(C_t^*)-u(C_t)]dt > 0$$

for all feasible (C_t). We could weaken this to $\geqq$ but this was not much help.

A much weaker condition (B) was to call C^* optimal if no feasible path overtakes it; i.e.

$$\limsup_{T\to\infty} \int_0^T [u(C_t^*)-u(C_t)]dt \geqq 0$$

for all feasible (C_t). Lim sup gave only a partial ordering and this definition gave a greater chance of finding optimal paths. His own work with linear utility functions had shown that we can have existence in the latter sense without existence in the former.

A third condition (C) – Malinvand maximality – was still weaker and this had been used in his paper with Peleg. All three (A, B and C) gave us the competitive pricing solutions we were looking for.

None of these (A, B or C) could fix up the cake problem. He said this problem would not worry us so much if we became used to thinking of finitely additive measures in these problems. In game theory with an infinite number of strategies, we could have a mixed strategy assigning zero probability (p_i) to each strategy but the integral of the p_is could be unity. We would, with this attitude, be happy about spreading butter with zero thickness.

Dr Bliss asked how much of the cake he would receive. *Professor Yaari* replied he would receive the integral of the cake, over him with respect to the measure.

Professor Hahn asked how this dealt with the 'saving above the golden rule' problem. *Professor Weizsäcker* said that the Euler path to the saddle-point was not Malinvand maximal if the savings rate at the saddle-point was above golden rule. Professor Yaari's remarks were not relevant to the problem under discussion and we could return to them tomorrow.

Professor Uzawa said that the differential equation nature of paths was lost with Professor Yaari's way of looking at the cake problem. *Professor Yaari* said this property could be retained if we decomposed the measure into a countably additive and a finitely additive measure.

Professor Inagaki asked if the golden rule had a turnpike property for a finite-horizon plan.

Professor Mirrlees said that the optimal finite horizon plan stayed near the agreeable path. For a long time horizon we would stay near the saddle-point for a long time, even though its saving rate is above golden rule.

Professor Inagaki asked how this fitted in with the sensitivity to final capital stocks shown by Srinivasan in his criticism of Chakravarty. *Professor Weizsäcker* said this was not relevant. Srinivasan had shown that initial consumption levels on the optimum path were very sensitive to terminal capital stocks if the terminal capital stocks were so high that very large savings rates were needed. With smaller capital stocks, initial consumption levels were very insensitive.

Professor Mirrlees said he found Professor Stiglitz's questions very interesting. He agreed it was not very obvious why we needed T_0 and T_1; perhaps a sketch of the situation would help. Consider the usual c, k diagram (Fig. 13.2) and a long finite-horizon plan – the optimal path was A and the agreeable path P. For a long period A would stay close to P and then in the last part of its path turn back to the $k = 0$ axis. Following P until T_0 put us in a position to get very close to the optimal path when we caught up in the last part – from T_0 to T_1. Thus two times were needed.

Stern had raised the question with him that for sensible ε (defined in terms of an equivalent consumption loss) and T_0 it might turn out that T_1 was extremely large so that it would be difficult to obtain agreement, and that numerical information was needed to answer this point. He still thought that people could be expected to modify the loss of utility they would be prepared to accept in the light of the probable difficulty of obtaining agreement. But he agreed that calculations would throw light on the question.

He agreed that expectations about what would actually happen between T_0 and T_1 would affect the possibility of agreement. We might have to agree to postpone that decision. This would be reasonable if we had potential disagreement because of lack of evidence rather than 'wilful' disagreement that later evidence would not upset.

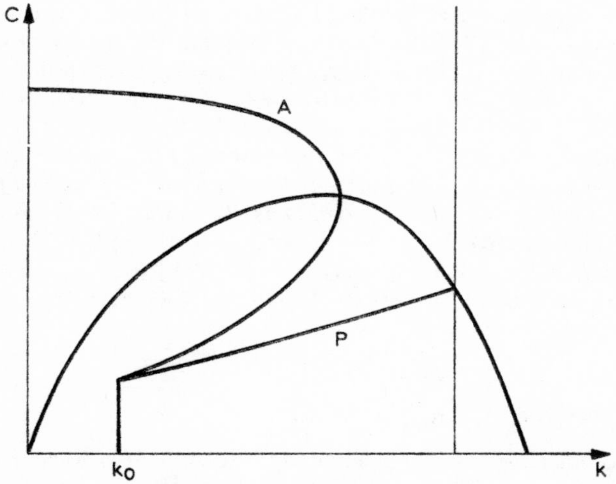

FIG. 13.2

14 Price Properties of Optimal Consumption Programmes*

Bezalel Peleg and Menahem E. Yaari

THE HEBREW UNIVERSITY, JERUSALEM

I. INTRODUCTION

In order to set the stage for the present investigation, it is convenient to start out with a familiar proposition from the theory of concave programming. We shall use the symbol E^n to denote the n-dimensional Euclidean space, and $E_+{}^n$ will be used to denote the non-negative orthant of E^n.

Theorem 1.1: Let Y be a convex subset of $E_+{}^n$. Assume that there exists a point $\mathbf{p}$ *in Y, such that* $\mathbf{p} \gg \mathbf{0}$.[1] *Let u be a real-valued function defined on $E_+{}^n$, and assume that u is increasing [in the sense that $\mathbf{x} \gg \mathbf{x}'$ implies $u(\mathbf{x}) > u(\mathbf{x}')$] and concave. A point $\mathbf{y}^*$ of Y is optimal [that is, it satisfies $u(\mathbf{y}^*) \geqq u(\mathbf{y})$ for all $\mathbf{y} \in Y$] if, and only if, there exists a price vector $\boldsymbol{\pi} > 0$, such that the following two conditions hold:*

(a) $\boldsymbol{\pi}.\mathbf{y}^* \geqq \boldsymbol{\pi}.\mathbf{y}$ for all $\mathbf{y} \in Y$;

(b) $u(\mathbf{y}^*) - u(\mathbf{x}) \geqq \boldsymbol{\pi}.(\mathbf{y}^* - \mathbf{x})$ for all $\mathbf{x} \in E_+{}^n$.[2]

Theorem 1.1 gives a price characterisation to solutions of concave programming problems. It describes optimality in terms of 'competitive' value maximisation [condition (a)] and utility maximisation with cost of consumption measured in utility terms [condition (b)]. The price system $\boldsymbol{\pi}$, which provides this characterisation, might be referred to as a system of *Kuhn–Tucker prices*, to emphasise the family relationship that Theorem 1.1 bears to the Kuhn–Tucker theorem. Note that, in Theorem 1.1, the optimal point, $\mathbf{y}^*$, need not be efficient. However, if the objective function u is increasing in a

* M. E. Yaari's research has been supported by the Maurice Falk Institute for Economic Research in Israel.

[1] The symbol $\mathbf{0}$ will be used for the zero element of whatever space is being considered. If $\mathbf{p} = \langle p(1), \ldots, p(n)\rangle$ belongs to E^n, then $\mathbf{p} \geqq \mathbf{0}$ means $p(j) \geqq 0$ for $j = 1, \ldots, n$; $\mathbf{p} > \mathbf{0}$ means $\mathbf{p} \geqq \mathbf{0}$ and $\mathbf{p} \neq \mathbf{0}$; $\mathbf{p} \gg 0$ means $p(j) > 0$ for $j = 1, \ldots, n$.

[2] A proof of Theorem 1.1 is given, for the sake of completeness, in the Appendix.

stronger sense, namely in the sense that $\mathbf{x} > \mathbf{x}'$ implies $u(\mathbf{x}) > u(\mathbf{x}')$, then $\mathbf{y}^*$ will always be efficient and the price system $\boldsymbol{\pi}$ will satisfy the condition $\boldsymbol{\pi} \gg \mathbf{0}$.

It is our purpose in this essay to try to find Kuhn–Tucker prices for certain optimal growth problems. More specifically, we should like to find out whether there exist propositions analogous to Theorem 1.1, when Y is the set of feasible consumption plans in a general one-sector growth model, and u is a function describing a planner's preferences over all conceivable consumption sequences.

We shall work with a fairly general set of feasible consumption plans. In particular, we refrain from assuming that there exists a state variable (called 'capital') such that knowledge of the value of the state variable at the beginning of each period is all that is required in order to determine production possibilities during the period. It is not that we wish to take sides in the famous Cambridge controversy on 'What Is Capital?' We merely think that possibilities like, say, today's output depending both on today's capital and on yesterday's capital should not be excluded out of hand. On the planner's side, there will be no need to assume that all conceivable consumption sequences can be ranked on a preference ordering. Rather, we shall postulate that the planner ranks just those consumption sequences that have only finitely many positive components. In other words, we shall assume that the utility function is defined only for those non-negative sequences that have but a finite number of components different from zero. We feel that this is perhaps the appropriate way to formalise the notion of planning with an *indefinite* horizon (in contrast to finite or infinite horizons). Of course, the space in which utility is defined is still infinite-dimensional, but it is much smaller than other sequence spaces.

Section II will be devoted to certain preliminaries and to a formal introduction of the model. Sections III and IV will each contain a proposition in the spirit of Theorem 1.1. Some examples at the end of section IV will serve to illustrate the role played by the various assumptions.

Our approach in the present investigation is quite similar in spirit to that of Tjalling C. Koopmans, in his famous article (Koopmans, 1965). By exploring the analogy between the theory of optimal economic growth and the theory of concave programming, Koopmans is able to obtain a good deal of information on the nature of an optimal growth path. One of Koopmans's results (Theorem G in Koopmans, 1965) is, in fact, the analogue for his model of the kinds of results that we are seeking here. Koopmans's study thus provides a prominent illustration of the potential uses that one might expect to have for an investigation like the one being proposed here.

II. FRAMEWORK

We shall be concerned with two linear topological spaces: the space s of all real sequences, and its dual, the space s^* of all real sequences with only finitely many non-zero components. The linear structure is given, both in s and in s^*, by the definitions

$$\mathbf{z} = \mathbf{x}+\mathbf{y} \Leftrightarrow z(t) = x(t)+y(t) \quad \text{for all} \quad t;$$

$$\mathbf{y} = \alpha\mathbf{x} \Leftrightarrow y(t) = \alpha x(t) \quad \text{for all} \quad t.$$

Three linear partial orderings are defined on the space s: $\geqq$, $>$ and $\gg$ (definitions as in note 1, p. 306 above). On s^*, however, only the orderings $\geqq$ and $>$ can be defined. With $\geqq$ as the basic linear partial ordering both in s and in s^*, s^* becomes a partially ordered linear subspace of s. However, we shall not consider s^* to be a topological subspace of the space s. The space s has the topology of coordinate-wise convergence. Thus, a sequence $\langle \mathbf{x}_k \rangle$ of points of s converges to a point $\mathbf{x}$ if, and only if, $x_k(t) \to x(t)$ for each t. In the space s^*, however, we have the topology that is derived from coordinate-wise convergence of uniformly length-bounded sequences. If $\mathbf{z} \in s^*$, then the *length* of $\mathbf{z}$, to be denoted $l(\mathbf{z})$, is defined by

$$\begin{aligned} l(\mathbf{z}) &= 0 \quad \text{if} \quad \mathbf{z} = 0 \\ &= 1+\max\{t \mid z(t) \neq 0\} \quad \text{otherwise.} \end{aligned}$$

A sequence $\langle \mathbf{z}_k \rangle$ of points of s^* converges to a point $\mathbf{z}$ if, and only if, there exists an integer T such that $l(\mathbf{z}_k) < T$ for all k, and $z_k(t) \to z(t)$ for each t. According to this definition, if u is a real function defined on s^*, then u is continuous if and only if it is continuous on every finite-dimensional subspace of s^*.

The symbols s_+ and $s_+{}^*$ will be used to denote the non-negative orthants of s and s^*, respectively. If $\mathbf{x}$ and $\boldsymbol{\pi}$ are two members of s_+, then the scalar product $\boldsymbol{\pi}.\mathbf{x}$ is given by

$$\boldsymbol{\pi}.\mathbf{x} = \sum_{t=0}^{\infty} \pi(t)x(t).$$

$\boldsymbol{\pi}.\mathbf{x}$ is always well defined (for $\boldsymbol{\pi}$ and $\mathbf{x}$ in s_+), but it may equal $+\infty$.

For every member $\mathbf{x}$ of s, and for every non-negative integer t, we now define $\mathbf{x}^t$ to be the member of s^* such that

$$\begin{aligned} x^t(\tau) &= x(\tau) \quad \text{for} \quad 0 \leqq \tau \leqq t \\ &= 0 \quad \text{otherwise.} \end{aligned}$$

We are now ready to describe the simple economy that provides a setting for our investigation. The description consists of two items:

a set of feasible consumption programmes, to be denoted Y, and a utility function, u.

We assume that Y is a non-empty subset of s_+, and that the following conditions are satisfied:

(Y.1) Y is convex.
(Y.2) Y is compact.
(Y.3) For every $\mathbf{x}$ and $\mathbf{y}$ in s_+, if $\mathbf{y} \in Y$ and $\mathbf{y} \geqq \mathbf{x}$, then $\mathbf{x} \in Y$. (Free disposal.)
(Y.4) There exists in Y a point $\mathbf{p}$, such that $\mathbf{p} \gg \mathbf{0}$.

The utility function u is defined on s_+^* (to the real numbers) and it is assumed to satisfy:

(U.1) u is concave.
(U.2) u is continuous.
(U.3) u is increasing, in the sense that $\mathbf{x} > \mathbf{y}$ implies

$$u(\mathbf{x}) > u(\mathbf{y}) \quad \text{for every} \quad x \text{ and } y \text{ in } s_+^*.$$

III. THE CASE OF LOCAL IMPATIENCE

We begin by defining the extension of the utility function u to all of s_+. Given any $\mathbf{x} \in s_+$, let $u(\mathbf{x})$ be given by

$$u(\mathbf{x}) = \lim_{t \to \infty} u(\mathbf{x}^t). \tag{14.1}$$

It follows from assumption U.3 that the limit in (14.1) exists, but it may equal $+\infty$.

Let $\mathbf{x}$ be an arbitrary point of s_+. We shall say that the utility function u exhibits *impatience* at $\mathbf{x}$ if there exists a point $\mathbf{d}$ in s_+^*, such that $u(\mathbf{d}) > u(\mathbf{x})$.

Theorem 3.1: Let $\mathbf{e}$ *belong to* Y, *and assume that* u *exhibits impatience at* $\mathbf{e}$. *Then* $\mathbf{e}$ *is optimal in* Y, *that is,* $u(\mathbf{e}) \geqq u(\mathbf{y})$ *for all* $y \in Y$, *if and only if there exists a price system* $\boldsymbol{\pi} > \mathbf{0}$ *in* s_+, *such that the following two conditions hold:*

(a) $\infty > \boldsymbol{\pi}.\mathbf{e} \geqq \boldsymbol{\pi}.\mathbf{y}$ *for all* $\mathbf{y} \in Y$;

(b) $u(\mathbf{e}) - u(\mathbf{x}) \geqq \boldsymbol{\pi}.(\mathbf{e}-\mathbf{x})$ *for all* $\mathbf{x} \in s_+^*$.

Proof: (i) *Sufficiency*. Let $\mathbf{y}$ belong to Y. By (14.1), $u(\mathbf{y}) = \lim_{t\to\infty} u(\mathbf{y}^t)$. From (a) and (b), we now get

$$\lim_{t\to\infty} u(\mathbf{y}^t) \leqq \lim_{t\to\infty} [u(\mathbf{e}) - \boldsymbol{\pi}.\mathbf{e} + \boldsymbol{\pi}.\mathbf{y}^t] \leqq u(\mathbf{e}).$$

Hence, $\mathbf{e}$ is optimal.

(ii) *Necessity*. Assume that $\mathbf{e}$ is optimal. Since u exhibits impatience at $\mathbf{e}$, there exists a point $\mathbf{d} \in s_+^*$, such that $u(\mathbf{d}) > u(\mathbf{e})$. For integers

T, satisfying $T > l(\mathbf{d})$, and for real numbers ε, satisfying $0 < \varepsilon < u(d) - u(\mathbf{e})$, define

$$Z(T, \varepsilon) = \{\mathbf{z} \in s_+ \,|\, u(\mathbf{z}^t) \geqq u(\mathbf{e}^t) + \varepsilon \quad \text{for} \quad t \geqq T\}.$$

$Z(T, \varepsilon)$ is a closed convex subset of s_+. It is non-empty, since $\mathbf{d} \in Z(T, \varepsilon)$. Furthermore, since $\mathbf{e}$ is optimal, we have $Z(T, \varepsilon) \cap Y = \phi$. Therefore, there exists a non-trivial vector $\boldsymbol{\pi} \in s^*$, such that

$$\boldsymbol{\pi}.\mathbf{z} \geqq \boldsymbol{\pi}.\mathbf{y} \quad \text{for all} \quad \mathbf{z} \in Z(T, \varepsilon) \quad \text{and} \quad \mathbf{y} \in Y.^{1} \qquad (14.2)$$

Now, $Z(T, \varepsilon)$ contains a translate of the non-negative orthant. That is, if $\mathbf{z} \in Z(T, \varepsilon)$ and $\mathbf{x} \geqq \mathbf{z}$, then $\mathbf{x} \in Z(T, \varepsilon)$. From this, it follows that $\boldsymbol{\pi} > \mathbf{0}$. Also, we have $\mathbf{d} \in Z(T, \varepsilon)$ and, by assumption Y.4, there exists a point $\mathbf{p} \gg \mathbf{0}$ in Y. Therefore, from (14.2), we get $\boldsymbol{\pi}.\mathbf{d} \geqq \boldsymbol{\pi}.\mathbf{p} > 0$. Hence, without loss of generality, we may assume that $\boldsymbol{\pi}.\mathbf{d} = 1$. For values of T and ε in the domain of $Z(T, \varepsilon)$, we now define

$$P(T, \varepsilon) = \{\boldsymbol{\pi} \in s_+ \,|\, \boldsymbol{\pi}.\mathbf{d} = 1 \quad \text{and (14.2) holds}\}.$$

For every $\boldsymbol{\pi} \in P(T, \varepsilon)$, we have $\boldsymbol{\pi}.\mathbf{p} \leqq \boldsymbol{\pi}.\mathbf{d} = 1$, where $\mathbf{p} \in Y$ satisfies $\mathbf{p} \gg \mathbf{0}$. Hence, $\pi(t) \leqq 1/p(t)$ for $t = 0, 1, \ldots$, and for all $\boldsymbol{\pi} \in P(T, \varepsilon)$. This means that $P(T, \varepsilon)$ is contained in a compact set. Furthermore, it is easy to verify that the family of sets $\{P(T, \varepsilon)\}$ has the finite intersection property. [For any finite collection $P(T_1, \varepsilon_1), \ldots, P(T_n, \varepsilon_n)$, simply take $T^* = \max(T_1, \ldots, T_n)$ and $\varepsilon^* = \min(\varepsilon_1, \ldots, \varepsilon_n)$, and form the set $P(T^*, \varepsilon^*)$.] Hence, there exists a price vector that belongs to the intersection of the closures of all the sets $P(T, \varepsilon)$. From now on, let the symbol $\boldsymbol{\pi}$ stand for such a price vector. Clearly, $\boldsymbol{\pi} \in s_+$ and $\boldsymbol{\pi}.\mathbf{d} = 1$. Hence, $\boldsymbol{\pi} > \mathbf{0}$.

To conclude the proof, we now proceed through a sequence of four lemmas.

Lemma 3.1: If $\mathbf{x} \in s_+^*$ *and* $u(\mathbf{x}) > u(\mathbf{e})$, *then, for all* $\mathbf{y} \in Y$, *we have that* $\boldsymbol{\pi}.\mathbf{x} \geqq \boldsymbol{\pi}.\mathbf{y}$.

Proof: Let $0 < \varepsilon < \min[u(\mathbf{x}) - u(\mathbf{e}), u(\mathbf{d}) - u(\mathbf{e})]$ and let $T > \max[l(\mathbf{x}), l(\mathbf{d})]$. Then, $\mathbf{x}$ belongs to $Z(T, \varepsilon)$. Since $\boldsymbol{\pi}$ is in the closure of $P(T, \varepsilon)$, there exists a sequence $\langle \boldsymbol{\pi}_k \rangle$, such that $\boldsymbol{\pi}_k \in P(T, \varepsilon)$ for all k, and such that $\lim_{k \to \infty} \boldsymbol{\pi}_k = \boldsymbol{\pi}$. Let t be a non-negative integer. From the fact that $\boldsymbol{\pi}_k$ satisfies (14.2), we get $\boldsymbol{\pi}_k.\mathbf{x} \geqq \boldsymbol{\pi}_k.\mathbf{y} \geqq \boldsymbol{\pi}_k.\mathbf{y}^t$ for all k, where $\mathbf{y}$ is an arbitrary member of Y. By taking the limit on k, we get $\boldsymbol{\pi}.\mathbf{x} \geqq \boldsymbol{\pi}.\mathbf{y}^t$. Hence, $\boldsymbol{\pi}.\mathbf{x} \geqq \lim_{t \to \infty} \boldsymbol{\pi}.\mathbf{y}^t = \boldsymbol{\pi}.\mathbf{y}$. This completes the proof of the lemma.

In particular, Lemma 3.1 tells us that $\boldsymbol{\pi}.\mathbf{d} \geqq \boldsymbol{\pi}.\mathbf{e}$, so that $\boldsymbol{\pi}.\mathbf{e} < \infty$.

Lemma 3.2: $\boldsymbol{\pi}.\mathbf{e} \geqq \boldsymbol{\pi}.\mathbf{y}$ *for all* $\mathbf{y} \in Y$.

[1] See, for example, Kelley and Namioka (1963) p. 119.

Proof: Let $\mathbf{y} \in Y$ and let $\delta > 0$. Choose α so that $0 < \alpha < \min(\delta, 1)$. Let $\beta < (\alpha/(1-\alpha))[u(\mathbf{d})-u(\mathbf{e})]$. There exists an integer T such that, for $t \geqq T$, $u(\mathbf{e}^t) \geqq u(\mathbf{e})-\beta$. Now, for $t \geqq T$, we have

$$\begin{aligned} u[(1-\alpha)\mathbf{e}^t+\alpha\mathbf{d}] &\geqq (1-\alpha)u(\mathbf{e}^t)+\alpha u(\mathbf{d}) \\ &\geqq (1-\alpha)[u(\mathbf{e})-\beta]+\alpha u(\mathbf{d}) \\ &> (1-\alpha)\left[u(\mathbf{e})-\frac{\alpha}{1-\alpha}(u(\mathbf{d})-u(\mathbf{e})\right]+\alpha u(\mathbf{d}) \\ &= u(\mathbf{e}). \end{aligned}$$

Therefore, by Lemma 3.1,

$$(1-\alpha)(\boldsymbol{\pi}.\mathbf{e}^t)+\alpha(\boldsymbol{\pi}.\mathbf{d}) \geqq \boldsymbol{\pi}.\mathbf{y}.$$

But $\boldsymbol{\pi}.\mathbf{e} \geqq \boldsymbol{\pi}.\mathbf{e}^t$, $\boldsymbol{\pi}.\mathbf{d} = 1$ and $\alpha < \delta$. Hence,

$$\boldsymbol{\pi}.\mathbf{e} \geqq \boldsymbol{\pi}.\mathbf{y}-\delta$$

and since δ is arbitrary, we get the desired result.

Lemma 3.3: If $\mathbf{x} \in s_+^*$ *and* $\boldsymbol{\pi}.\mathbf{x} \leqq \boldsymbol{\pi}.\mathbf{e}$, *then* $u(\mathbf{x}) \leqq u(\mathbf{e})$.

Proof: Assume $u(\mathbf{x}) > u(\mathbf{e})$. By Lemma 3.1, $\boldsymbol{\pi}.\mathbf{x} \geqq \boldsymbol{\pi}.\mathbf{e}$. Hence, $\boldsymbol{\pi}.\mathbf{x} = \boldsymbol{\pi}.\mathbf{e}$. By Lemma 3.2, $\boldsymbol{\pi}.\mathbf{e} \geqq \boldsymbol{\pi}.\mathbf{p} > 0$ (see assumption Y.4). Therefore, there exists a t such that $\pi(t)x(t) > 0$. Define a point $\mathbf{z}$ by $z(\tau) = x(\tau)$ for $\tau \neq t$, $z(t) = x(t)-\delta$. For $\delta > 0$ sufficiently small, we have $u(\mathbf{z}) > u(\mathbf{e})$. But $\boldsymbol{\pi}.\mathbf{z} = \boldsymbol{\pi}.\mathbf{x}-\delta\pi(t) < \boldsymbol{\pi}.\mathbf{e}$, contradicting Lemma 3.1.

Lemma 3.4: $u(\mathbf{e})-u(\mathbf{x}) \geqq \boldsymbol{\pi}.(\mathbf{e}-\mathbf{x})$ *for all* $\mathbf{x} \in s_+^*$.

The proof of this lemma is similar to that of Theorem 3.6 in Peleg (1970). (If, in that proof, we replace the set F by s_+^*, we get a proof for Lemma 3.4.)[1]

Lemma 3.2 says that condition (a) holds, and Lemma 3.4 says that condition (b) holds. Thus, the proof of the theorem is now complete.

Corollary: Let C be the cone spanned by Y:

$$C = \{\mathbf{x} \mid \mathbf{x} = \alpha\mathbf{y}, \quad \mathbf{y} \in Y, \alpha \geqq 0\}.$$

Then,

$$u(\mathbf{e})-u(\mathbf{x}) \geqq \pi.(\mathbf{e}-\mathbf{x}) \quad \textit{for all} \quad \mathbf{x} \in C.$$

IV. THE CASE OF AN ADDITIVELY SEPARABLE UTILITY

Let $\mathbf{x}$ and $\mathbf{z}$ be two points of s_+. We shall say that $\mathbf{x}$ is **Malinvaud-superior** to $\mathbf{z}$, and we shall write $\mathbf{x} \underset{M}{>} \mathbf{z}$, if the following two conditions hold:

[1] Note that Lemma 3.1 is actually a statement about cost minimisation over points preferred to *e*, and Lemma 3.3 is a statement about utility maximisation, subject to the 'budget constraint', $\boldsymbol{\pi}.\mathbf{x} \leqq \boldsymbol{\pi}.\mathbf{e}$. These two together form the content of Lemma 3.4.

(i) $\mathbf{x}-\mathbf{z} \in s^*$. That is, **x** and **z** differ only in finitely many components.

(ii) There exists an integer T, which may depend on **x** and **z**, such that $u(\mathbf{x}^t) > u(\mathbf{z}^t)$ for $t \geqq T$.

We shall say that a point **y** of Y is **Malinvaud-maximal** (or **M-maximal**) if no point of Y is Malinvaud-superior to **y**.

We have attached Malinvaud's name to the relation $\underset{M}{>}$ because of an analogy with the definition of Malinvaud prices.

It may be as well at this point to devote a brief comment to a comparison between the ordering $\underset{M}{>}$ and the ordering induced by the so-called overtaking criterion.[1] Let **x** and **z** be points of s_+. Then **x** is said to **overtake z** if

$$\liminf_{t\to\infty} [u(\mathbf{x}^t)-u(\mathbf{z}^t)] \geqq 0.$$

Thus, if $\mathbf{x} \underset{M}{>} \mathbf{z}$, then it is also true that **x** overtakes **z**. (The converse of this assertion, clearly, is false.) From this, it follows that if a point **y** of Y is overtaking-maximal then it is also Malinvaud-maximal. In other words, Malinvaud-maximality is a weaker property than maximality in the ordering induced by the overtaking criterion.

In the present section we shall be concerned with giving a price characterisation to M-maximal consumption programmes. We shall assume, from now on, that the utility function u is additively separable. That is, we assume that there exists a sequence of concave, continuous and strictly increasing real functions, $u_0, u_1, \ldots$, such that u is given by

$$u(\mathbf{x}) = \sum_{t=0}^{\infty} u_t[x(t)] \quad \text{for all} \quad \mathbf{x} \in s_+{}^*.$$

An illustration of why this assumption is necessary will be given in Example 4.1, below.

The first thing to note is:

Remark 4.1: Let **y** *be a point of* Y. *If* **y** *is M-maximal, then* **y** *is efficient.*

Proof: This follows immediately from strict monotonicity.

Before proceeding to the main result of this section, we should like to recall the notion of the **transfer function** of the set Y, to be denoted δ. This notion was defined and discussed extensively in Peleg and Yaari (1971). Let t and s be non-negative integers, and let **y** be a point of Y. Finally, let ε be a real number satisfying $0 \leqq \varepsilon \leqq y(t)$. Then, $\delta(t, s; \mathbf{y}, \varepsilon)$ is defined to be the maximum consumption that can be

[1] See, for example, Gale (1967).

gained in period s by giving up an amount ε of consumption in period t, along the path $\mathbf{y}$. (δ can also be defined, in an analogous fashion, for certain negative values of ε.) The quantity $\delta_+'(t, s; \mathbf{y})$, which appears in the statement of the following theorem, is defined as the right-hand derivative of $\delta(t, s; \mathbf{y}, \varepsilon)$ with respect to ε, evaluated at $\varepsilon = 0$. In what follows, we shall draw freely upon the definitions and results in Peleg and Yaari (1971).

Theorem 4.1: Let $\mathbf{e}$ *be an efficient point of* Y. *Assume that for each integer* t, $t > 0$, *there exists an integer* s, $0 \leqq s < t$, *such that* $\delta_+'(s, t; \mathbf{e}) > 0$. *Then,* $\mathbf{e}$ *is M-maximal in* Y *if, and only if, there exists a vector* $\boldsymbol{\pi} \gg \mathbf{0}$ *in* s_+, *such that the following two conditions hold:*

(a) $\boldsymbol{\pi}$ *is a system of Malinvaud prices for* $\mathbf{e}$.

(b) $u(\mathbf{e}^t) - u(\mathbf{x}^t) \geqq \boldsymbol{\pi}.(\mathbf{e}^t - \mathbf{x}^t)$ *for all* $\mathbf{x} \in s_+^*$ *and* $t = 0, 1, \ldots$.

Proof: Sufficiency is obvious. To prove necessity, we start out by defining, for $t = 0, 1, \ldots$,

$$Y^t(\mathbf{e}) = \left\{ \langle z(0), \ldots, z(t) \rangle \;\middle|\; \begin{array}{l} \text{there exists a } \mathbf{y} \in Y \text{ with} \\ y(j) = z(j) \quad \text{for} \quad 0 \leqq j \leqq t, \\ \text{and} \quad y(j) = e(j) \quad \text{otherwise} \end{array} \right\}.$$

$Y^t(\mathbf{e})$ is clearly a convex subset of E_+^{t+1}. Furthermore, the function that carries a vector $\langle x(0), \ldots, x(t) \rangle$ into $\sum_{j=0}^{t} u_j[x(j)]$, i.e. the restriction of u to E_+^{t+1}, is clearly concave. We now claim that $Y^t(\mathbf{e})$ possesses a vector whose components are all positive. (This will enable us to make use of Theorem 1.1.) By convexity, it is enough to show that, for each j, $0 \leqq j \leqq t$, there exists a point $\hat{\mathbf{y}}_j$ in $Y^t(\mathbf{e})$, with $\hat{y}_j(j) > 0$. By assumption, $\delta_+'(0, 1; \mathbf{e}) > 0$. Hence, $e(0) > 0$, and the point $\langle e(0), \ldots, e(t) \rangle$ clearly belongs to $Y^t(\mathbf{e})$. And if $j > 0$, then there exists a $k < j$, such that $\delta_+'(k, j; \mathbf{e}) > 0$. Hence, for $0 < \varepsilon < e(k)$, the point $\hat{\mathbf{y}}_j$, defined by

$$\begin{aligned} \hat{y}_j(i) &= e(i) \quad \text{for} \quad i \neq j, k, \quad 0 \leqq i \leqq t \\ &= e(k) - \varepsilon \quad \text{for} \quad i = k \\ &= e(j) + \delta(k, j; \mathbf{e}, \varepsilon) \quad \text{for} \quad i = j, \end{aligned}$$

has the property that $\hat{\mathbf{y}}_j \in Y^t(\mathbf{e})$ and $\hat{y}_j(j) > 0$.

Now, $\mathbf{e}$ is M-maximal, and therefore

$$\sum_{=0}^{t} u_j[e(j)] \geqq \sum_{=0}^{t} u_j[\hat{y}(j)] \quad \text{for all} \quad \hat{\mathbf{y}} \in Y^t(\mathbf{e}).$$

Hence, by Theorem 1.1, there exists a strictly positive price vector $\boldsymbol{\alpha} = \langle \alpha(0), \ldots, \alpha(t) \rangle$, such that

$$\boldsymbol{\alpha}.\mathbf{e}^t \geqq \boldsymbol{\alpha}.\hat{\mathbf{y}} \quad \text{for all} \quad \hat{\mathbf{y}} \in Y^t(\mathbf{e}) \tag{14.3}$$

$$u(\mathbf{e}^t) - u(\hat{\mathbf{x}}) \geqq \boldsymbol{\alpha}.(\mathbf{e}^t - \hat{\mathbf{x}}) \quad \text{for all} \quad \hat{\mathbf{x}} \in E_+{}^{t+1}. \tag{14.4}$$

We now define a sequence $\boldsymbol{\beta} \in s_+$, in the following manner:

$$\beta(0) = u_{0-}'[e(0)]$$
$$= \lim_{\varepsilon \to 0-} \{u_0[e(0)+\varepsilon] - u_0[e(0)]\}/\varepsilon.$$

Since $\delta_+'(0, 1; \mathbf{e}) > 0$, we have $e(0) > 0$, so $\beta(0)$ is well defined, and $\beta(0) < \infty$. Proceeding inductively, assume that $\beta(0), \ldots, \beta(t)$ have already been defined. Let

$$r = \min \{s \mid 0 \leqq s \leqq t \quad \text{and} \quad \delta_+'(s, t+1; \mathbf{e}) > 0\}.$$

By assumption, r is well defined. Define $\beta(t+1)$ by

$$\beta(t+1) = \beta(r)/\delta_+'(r, t+1 : \mathbf{e}).$$

The following two lemmas will serve to complete the proof of the theorem.

Lemma 4.1: Let t be a non-negative integer, and let $\boldsymbol{\alpha} = \langle \alpha(0), \ldots, \alpha(t) \rangle$ satisfy (14.3) and (14.4). Then, $\alpha(j) \leqq \beta(j)$ for $j = 0, \ldots, t$.

Proof: Since $\boldsymbol{\alpha}$ satisfies (14.4), and since $e(0) > 0$, it follows that $\alpha(0) \leqq u_{0-}'[e(0)] = \beta(0)$. Now assume that the inequality $\alpha(j) \leqq \beta(j)$ has been shown to hold for $j = 0, \ldots, k$, where $0 \leqq k < t$. Define an integer r by

$$r = \min \{s \mid 0 \leqq s \leqq k \quad \text{and} \quad \delta_+'(s, k+1; \mathbf{e}) > 0\}.$$

Since $\boldsymbol{\alpha}$ satisfies (14.3), we have $\alpha(r) \geqq \alpha(k+1)\delta_+'(r, k+1; \mathbf{e})$. Hence,

$$\alpha(k+1) \leqq \alpha(r)/\delta_+'(r, k+1; \mathbf{e}) \leqq \beta(r)/\delta_+'(r, k+1; \mathbf{e}).$$

But $\beta(r)/\delta_+'(r, k+1; \mathbf{e}) = \beta(k+1)$ by definition. Hence, the proof is complete.

Lemma 4.2: Let k be a non-negative integer, and let $\boldsymbol{\alpha} = \langle \alpha(0), \ldots, \alpha(k) \rangle$ satisfy (14.3) and (14.4), with t replaced by k. Then, for $t = 0, \ldots, k$, the vector $\boldsymbol{\alpha}_t$, defined by $\boldsymbol{\alpha}_t = \langle \alpha(0), \ldots, \alpha(t) \rangle$, also satisfies (14.3) and (14.4). The proof of this assertion is straightforward.

To conclude the proof of the theorem, we now proceed as follows. For each non-negative integer t, we choose a vector $\boldsymbol{\alpha}_t = \langle \alpha_t(0), \ldots, \alpha_t(t) \rangle$ satisfying (14.3) and (14.4). Let $\boldsymbol{\pi}_t \in s_+$ be defined by $\pi_t(k) = \alpha_t(k)$ for $0 \leqq k \leqq t$, and $\pi_t(k) = 0$ for $k > t$. By Lemma 4.1, the sequence $\langle \boldsymbol{\pi}_t \rangle$ is coordinate-wise bounded. Hence, there exists a subsequence $\langle \boldsymbol{\pi}_{t_q} \rangle$ that converges to a point

$\boldsymbol{\pi} \in s_+$. Let t be a non-negative integer. By Lemma 4.2, the vectors $\langle \pi_{t_q}(0), \ldots, \pi_{t_q}(t)\rangle$ satisfy (14.3) and (14.4) for all q such that $t_q \geqq t$. Hence, the vector $\langle \pi(0), \ldots, \pi(t)\rangle$ satisfies (14.3) and (14.4). This means that $\boldsymbol{\pi}$ satisfies the conditions (a) and (b), as asserted. The fact that $\boldsymbol{\pi} \gg \mathbf{0}$ follows from condition (b), in conjunction with strict monotonicity. This completes the proof of the theorem.

We now turn to a pair of examples, designed to illustrate the role of the various assumptions in Theorem 4.1.

Example 4.1: Let Y be given by

$$Y = \left\{\mathbf{y} \in s_+ \,\middle|\, \sum_{t=0}^{\infty} y(t) \leqq 1\right\}$$

and let u be given by

$$u(\mathbf{x}) = 2\{[1+x(0)][1+x(1)]\}^{\frac{1}{2}} + \sum_{t=2}^{\infty} x(t)$$

for all $\mathbf{x} \in s_+^*$. The point $\mathbf{e}$, defined by

$$\begin{aligned} e(t) &= 3/8 \quad \text{for} \quad t = 0, 1 \\ &= 2^{-(t+1)} \quad \text{for} \quad t > 1, \end{aligned}$$

is M-maximal in Y. However, it has no price system $\boldsymbol{\pi} > \mathbf{0}$ which satisfies the conditions (a) and (b) of Theorem 4.1.

Example 4.1 seems to indicate that the assumption on the additive separability of the utility function is essential for the validity of Theorem 4.1.

Example 4.2: Let Y be defined by

$$Y = \{\mathbf{y} \in s_+ \,|\, y(0)+y(t) \leqq 1 \quad \text{for} \quad t = 1, 2, \ldots\}$$

and let u be defined by

$$u(\mathbf{x}) = \sum_{t=0}^{\infty} [x(t)]^{\frac{1}{2}} \quad \text{for all} \quad x \in s_+^*.$$

The point $\mathbf{e}$, such that

$$\begin{aligned} e(t) &= 0 \quad \text{if} \quad t = 0 \\ &= 1 \quad \text{otherwise,} \end{aligned}$$

is M-maximal in Y. However, it has no price system $\boldsymbol{\pi} > \mathbf{0}$ which satisfies the conditions (a) and (b) of Theorem 4.1.

This example shows that our assumption, that for every $t > 0$ there exists an $s < t$ such that $\delta_+'(s, t; \mathbf{e}) > 0$, is probably essential for the validity of Theorem 4.1.

Our next (and final) example is designed to answer the following question. Suppose $\mathbf{e} \in Y$ has a property stronger than M-maximality. In particular, suppose e is maximal in Y on the ordering induced by the overtaking criterion. Will an analogue of Theorem 4.1 then be true, with a price system for **e** having properties *stronger* than those of Malinvaud prices? The example shows the answer to this question to be in the negative.

Example 4.3: Let the point **e** and the set Y be as in Example 8.1 in Peleg and Yaari (1971). That is, let **e** be defined by $e(t) = 2^{-(t+1)}$ for $t = 0, 1, \ldots$, and let Y be the convex hull of the union of the following two sets:

$$A = \left\{ \mathbf{a} \in s_+ \,\middle|\, \sum_{t=0}^{\infty} a(t) \leqq 1 \quad \text{and} \quad a(t) \leqq \frac{t+2}{t+1} e(t) \quad \text{for all} \quad t \right\}$$

and

$$B = \{\mathbf{b} \in s_+ \,|\, b(0) \leqq 2 \quad \text{and} \quad b(t) = 0 \quad \text{for} \quad t > 0\}.$$

Define

$$v_t(\sigma) = 2^{t+1} \min\,[\sigma, e(t)] \quad \text{for} \quad \sigma \geqq 0, \quad t = 0, 1, \ldots.$$

For $\mathbf{x} \in s_+{}^*$, let $v(\mathbf{x}) = \sum_{t=0}^{\infty} v_t[x(t)]$, $w(\mathbf{x}) = \sum_{t=0}^{\infty} x(t)$, and $u(\mathbf{x}) = v(\mathbf{x}) + w(\mathbf{x})$. It can be shown that, with these definitions, the inequality

$$\liminf_{t \to \infty}\, [u(\mathbf{e}^t) - u(\mathbf{y}^t)] \geqq 0$$

holds true for all $\mathbf{y} \in Y$. In other words, **e** is not only maximal in Y with respect to the overtaking order, it is in fact a *maximum* in Y with respect to the overtaking order. However, as shown in Peleg and Yaari (1971), **e** does not have efficiency prices with properties stronger than those of Malinvaud prices.

V. CONCLUDING REMARK

The present investigation can be thought of as a continuation of Peleg's study (1970). In that study, Peleg assumes the utility function to be defined on all of s_+, and to be continuous in the topology of s. He then proves a theorem analogous to Theorem 1.1. However, the continuity of utility in the product topology is generally believed to be a very strong assumption. The present study was motivated, among other things, by a desire to avoid this assumption.

APPENDIX

Proof of Theorem 1.1

Sufficiency is obvious. To prove necessity, let $\mathbf{y}^*$ be optimal and define two sets, $\hat{Y}$ and Z, both contained in E^{n+1}, by

$$\hat{Y} = \{\langle y_0, \mathbf{y}\rangle : y_0 = u(\mathbf{y}^*) \quad \text{and} \quad \mathbf{y} \in Y\};$$
$$Z = \{\langle z_0, \mathbf{z}\rangle : \mathbf{z} \in E_+{}^n \quad \text{and} \quad u(\mathbf{z}) \geqq z_0\}.$$

$\hat{Y}$ and Z are both convex, and $\hat{Y}$ is disjoint from the (non-empty) interior of Z. Therefore, there exists a non-trivial price vector $\langle\pi(0), \pi(1), \ldots, \pi(n)\rangle$, to be written $\langle\pi(0), \boldsymbol{\pi}\rangle$, such that

$$\pi(0)y_0+\boldsymbol{\pi}.\mathbf{y} \leqq \pi(0)z_0+\boldsymbol{\pi}.\mathbf{z} \quad \text{for all} \quad \langle y_0, \mathbf{y}\rangle \in \hat{Y} \quad \text{and} \quad \langle z_0, \mathbf{z}\rangle \in Z. \quad \text{(A.1)}$$

We note the following facts:

(a) Since, for each $\mathbf{x} \in E_+{}^n$, $\langle u(\mathbf{x}), \mathbf{x}\rangle \in Z$, we have

$$\pi(0)u(\mathbf{y}^*)+\boldsymbol{\pi}.\mathbf{y} \leqq \pi(0)u(\mathbf{x})+\boldsymbol{\pi}.\mathbf{x} \quad \text{for all} \quad \mathbf{y} \in Y, \mathbf{x} \in E_+{}^n. \quad \text{(A.2)}$$

(b) For each $\mathbf{x} \in E_+{}^n$ such that $u(\mathbf{x}) \geqq u(\mathbf{y}^*)$, we have $\langle u(\mathbf{y}^*), \mathbf{x}\rangle \in Z$. Hence, from (A.1),

$$u(\mathbf{x}) \geqq u(\mathbf{y}^*) \quad \text{implies} \quad \boldsymbol{\pi}.\mathbf{x} \geqq \boldsymbol{\pi}.\mathbf{y} \quad \text{for all} \quad \mathbf{y} \in Y. \quad \text{(A.3)}$$

(c) From (A.3), together with the monotonicity of u, it follows immediately that the vector $\boldsymbol{\pi} = \langle\pi(1), \ldots, \pi(n)\rangle$ is non-negative.

(d) $\boldsymbol{\pi} \neq \mathbf{0}$. To see this, assume $\boldsymbol{\pi} = \mathbf{0}$. Then, (A.2) reduces to

$$\pi(0)u(\mathbf{y}^*) \leqq \pi(0)u(\mathbf{x}) \quad \text{for all} \quad \mathbf{x} \in E_+{}^n \quad \text{(A.4)}$$

with $\pi(0) \neq 0$. If $\pi(0) < 0$, (A.4) contradicts the monotonicity of u. If $\pi(0) > 0$, then (A.4) implies that $u(\mathbf{y}^*) = u(0)$. But, by the monotonicity of u and by the optimality of $\mathbf{y}^*$, we have $u(\mathbf{y}^*) \geqq u(\mathbf{p}) > u(\mathbf{0})$, where $\mathbf{p} \in Y$ satisfies $\mathbf{p} \gg \mathbf{0}$.

(e) By setting $\mathbf{x} = \mathbf{y}^*$ in (A.2), we now get condition (a).

(f) $\pi(0) < 0$. To see this, set $\mathbf{y} = \mathbf{p} \gg \mathbf{0}$ and $\mathbf{x} = \mathbf{0}$ in (A.2). This leads to $0 < \boldsymbol{\pi}.\mathbf{p} \leqq \pi(0)[u(\mathbf{0})-u(\mathbf{y}^*)]$. But $u(\mathbf{y}^*) > u(\mathbf{0})$. Hence, $\pi(0) < 0$.

(g) In (A.2) set $\mathbf{y} = \mathbf{y}^*$, and normalise prices so that $\pi(0) = -1$. This leads immediately to condition (b).

(h) From condition (b), it follows that if u is assumed to be strongly monotonic (i.e. $\mathbf{x} > \mathbf{x}'$ implies $u(\mathbf{x}) > u(\mathbf{x}')$), then $\boldsymbol{\pi} \gg \mathbf{0}$. To see this, let $\mathbf{x}$ in condition (b) be given by $\mathbf{y}^*+\mathbf{e}_j$, where $\mathbf{e}_j$ is the jth unit vector.

REFERENCES

D. Gale, 'On Optimal Development in a Multi-Sector Economy', *Review of Economic Studies*, vol. XXXIV (1) (1967).

J. L. Kelley and I. Namioka, *Linear Topological Spaces* (Princeton, N.J.: Van Nostrand, 1963).

T. C. Koopmans, 'On the Concept of Optimal Economic Growth', *Semaine d'Étude sur le Rôle de l'analyse économétrique dans la formulation de plans de développement* (Vatican City, 1965).

B. Peleg, 'Efficiency Prices for Optimal Consumption Plans', *Journal of Mathematical Analysis and Applications*, vol. XXIX (1) (1970).

—— and M. E. Yaari, 'Efficiency Prices in an Infinite-Dimensional Space', *Journal of Economic Theory* (1971).

Discussion of the Paper by Bezalel Peleg and Menahem E. Yaari

Professor Yaari said he wanted to give some idea of their motivations and why they found the problem interesting.

The theory of economic growth had recently gone through two stages: (i) descriptive growth – we tried to trace time paths given certain assumptions; (ii) optimal growth – we ask how a planner with a set of preferences should direct an economy under his control. We now had a third stage emerging where we had producers and consumers maximising something and we studied the decentralised growth process that emerged. A fourth stage would be to introduce expectations and uncertainty; we need to introduce a method by which information alters expectations.

They had been interested in the decentralised growth question; this had arisen in Professor Stiglitz's paper. There was no planner – agents determine their own behaviour. Intuition could go only a little way with this problem – a formalism was needed. They had tried to define the meaning of competitive equilibrium and price systems by generalising the static analysis.

They took a Modigliani–Brumberg infinite-lifetime consumer (or equivalently an infinite number of finite-horizon consumers), introduced a technology and examined what came out. It turned out to be very intricate and it was interesting to examine why. It was not any difficulty with fixed-point theorems – they were generalisable to infinite-dimensional spaces; e.g. we have Scarf's theorem on the non-empty core for separable infinite-dimensional spaces. The problem was that the continuity assumptions on preferences required by the two previous papers in this area on infinitely many commodities (Bewley, and Peleg and Yaari) implied impatience. This paper was an attempt to tackle this problem.

In order to avoid the use of fixed-point theorems, they went to a one-consumer economy and the problem was already there. The competitive equilibrium in this one-consumer economy was equivalent to the problem of optimal growth. They wanted to generalise Theorem 1.1 (the Kühn–Tucker theorem). Condition (a) represented decentralised product value maximisation subject to being in the feasible set, and (b) decentralised consumer utility maximisation subject to a budget constraint. This was for a concave utility function. For quasi-concave preferences, we would replace (b) by the statement that the non-negativity of the RHS implies the non-negativity of the LHS. The prices π are competitive equilibrium prices for one consumer.

We now go on to a growth setting. If we replace Y by the space of non-negative real sequence s_+, the theorem is false. We have to add continuity of u with respect to convergence in s_+. This, however, implies impatience in the sense that for all $x \in s_+$ there exists a $z \in s_+^*$ so that $u(z) > u(x)$. This condition is rather strong: it is implied by the Koopmans assumptions, or by discounting. But they had shown (Theorem 3.1) that if continuity was relaxed to local impatience the theorem went through.

They then looked for the weakest continuity assumptions that would yield the theorem. Continuity of u on l_t^∞ (the set of non-negative bounded sequences) with respect to uniform convergence in l_t^∞ does not imply impatience; nor does it give the theorem. They therefore started from here and weakened the topology (strengthened continuity) until the theorem held. They ended up with the Mackey topology, but this implied impatience. So perhaps the theorem *requires* impatience.

They had shown the theorem was true in the additively separable case if one replaced optimality by the fairly weak overtaking criterion which they had called Malinvaud-superiority. Additive separability was a necessary assumption and the theorem may look more reasonable if we think in terms of maximisation of expected utility under uncertainty (so we do have additive separability).

He did not think the natural generalisation of Kühn–Tucker had yet been found. He pointed out that it was natural to tackle the problems associated with the transition from finite time horizons to infinite ones in the one-good case first. Nearly all the theorems for the one-good case had been found to hold in the many-good case.

Professor Weizsäcker said his discussion only involved posing a few questions.

On p. 309 it was assumed that Y is compact: he asked what the implications of this were. *Professor Yaari* replied that if Y is closed then it contains an efficient point if and only if it is compact.

Professor Hahn said compactness involved closedness and boundedness. We frequently had unbounded production functions in optimal growth problems. *Professor Yaari* said this did not lose compactness. The problem was that with topologies that gave compactness of the feasible set, continuity of the utility function was very restrictive.

Professor Weizsäcker said that most economically reasonable spaces gave compact feasible sets. For instance, take any economy which has a golden rule. Then any golden age with savings rate below the golden rule is efficient, so the set of feasible paths is compact. (*Professor Yaari* said c_t should be in consumption per efficiency unit.)

He said that Theorem 4.1 characterised a Malinvaud maximal point. It did not show the existence of such a point.

Professor Yaari agreed it was not an existence theorem. If we could solve (a) and (b) we would have found an optimal point.

Professor Weizsäcker asked whether the definition of utility only on s_+^* covered the kind of infinite-horizon sums and overtaking criteria that we usually used. For instance, could we represent our criterion using an increasing sequence of finite sequences, and could we manipulate the zero level?

Professor Yaari said their definition was always naturally extendable to include the usual infinite sum, but sometimes the infinite sum would diverge and we would be in an overtaking situation. We needed $u(c_t)$ zero for all t greater than some T_0 to be sure that $u = \sum_{t=0}^{\infty} u(c_t)$ converged. u was a well-defined function from s_+^* to the real numbers but not necessarily from s_+ to the real numbers.

Usually the zero level of utility was manipulated to the golden-rule consumption per head. They did not necessarily have a golden rule in their model. He would like to know where to put the zero level.

Professor Mirrlees said that in Theorem 3.1 the assumptions implied that the utility function was finite on the production set. This is restrictive, as we often want to have a utility function such that (with zero consumption) utility can be minus infinity. *Professor Yaari* said that this was not a problem if the optimal consumption plan had only finitely many non-zero components.

Professor Hahn asked if the transfer function was always well defined. *Professor Yaari* said he would give a formal definition:

$$\delta(s, t, y, \varepsilon) = \max \{z(t)-y(t) \,|\, z\, Y s.t.\, z(\tau) \geqq y(\tau)$$
$$\forall\, \tau \neq s, t \quad \text{and} \quad z(s) \geqq y(s)-\varepsilon\}.$$

It represented the most we could get at time t by giving up ε at time s along the path y. s, t were integers as we were in discrete time. In continuous time it was much more difficult to define. *Professor Hahn* asked if it was a bounded steepness property. *Professor Yaari* said the compactness of Y gave bounded steepness.

Professor Rose asked what exactly was meant by the set Y – was it a set of consumption streams or net output streams? *Professor Yaari* said it was all commodity bundles possible with the given primary inputs. It consisted only of final goods which were consumed. *Professor Rose* asked if we should include investment goods. *Professor Mirrlees* said that Gale and Sutherland had shown that there were decentralisation problems if we included intermediate goods.

Professor Weizsäcker asked what exactly were Malinvaud prices. *Professor Yaari* said that if we consider a feasible move from the point we are at so that consumption levels differ at finitely many points, then that move should not be profitable.

Professor Uzawa asked what the relevance of such prices was – what did it mean to announce an infinite sequence of prices? *Professor Yaari* said he was only considering one market. It was not a sequence of markets as in Professor Hahn's paper.

Professor Hahn said that the prices of Professor Yaari's theorem were useful as a reference point, just as steady states had proved useful in growth theory, when we are looking at sequences of markets. *Professor Uzawa* said that steady states had proved useful as paths to which we had convergence. *Professor Hahn* said that reference points for planning paths were also useful.

Professor Uzawa asked why it was considered natural to maximise over an infinite horizon. He did not see the relevance of this framework either in free-market economies or decentralised planning. He could not conceive of prices *announced* for the entire future, or the future in general, and plans then being made for the future by individual units.

Professor Hahn replied that it was interesting to find prices that, if they ruled, would give efficiency.

Professor Yaari said this model could be used to interpret the Samuelson consumption-loan theories. Showing the existence of competitive equilibrium was only a first step to showing the model was consistent.

Professor Hahn said that the theorems obtained from additively separable utility were opaque. Assuming additive separability may involve assuming a lot. Did it, for example, mean anything for continuity? *Professor Yaari* said it did not. An undiscounted sum of utilities was not continuous.

Professor Hahn asked how undiscounted sums could come from an ordering. *Professor Yaari* said the Koopmans result depended on the sensitivity assumption. In their model, introducing additive separability did not imply bringing back continuity.

Professor Shell said most of the existence problems here arose from either no or too little impatience – as in optimal growth theory. They arise when the alleged transversality condition does not hold. Perhaps demanding that some quantity tend to zero was the wrong budget constraint: could we not allow people to run into debt? *Professor Bruno* said the transversality condition only asked for the present value to tend to zero. *Professor Yaari* said that the problem of the conditions on the present value of capital necessary for efficiency was an open question in the general case. In the linear case a zero limit for the present value of capital was necessary and sufficient for efficiency.

Part 6

Developing Economies

15 Models of Dual Economies*

Avinash Dixit
BALLIOL COLLEGE, OXFORD

I. THE PROBLEM OUTLINED

The dual economy has, over the last decade, proved itself to be a useful conceptual framework for analysing several problems of economic development. The basic idea is not new: it goes at least as far back as 1924, when the remarkable Soviet economist, Evgeny Preobrazhensky, used it in the setting of the New Economic Policy and developed the concept of 'primitive socialist accumulation'. He suffered the fate of all prophets (and worse), and the dual economy was resurrected by W. Arthur Lewis and others in the 1950s. With the papers by Jorgenson, and Ranis and Fei, the discipline took off into self-sustained growth.

Growth of the subject over the past decade is too well known to need a simple description, and too rapid to permit a complete one. My aim here is to summarise and organise some major contributions in some areas within the subject, and to relate them to each other. Such a survey must be very selective and subjective. From the models chosen, however, I have once or twice managed to squeeze out more results than their originators did. As a pleasant by-product, some rival models turn out to be far less irreconcilable than thought hitherto.

Dual economy models provide a significantly better description and understanding of the problems of development than any aggregative model, not because two sectors are better than one (several economists including me seem to have grave doubts on that point), but because the sectoral division chosen reflects several vital social and economic distinctions in the type of economy being analysed. First and foremost is the technological fact of product specialisation. The agricultural sector produces food, which, apart from some requirements for seed, can only be used for consumption. Industry produces a different kind of consumption good, which we shall call manufactures, as well as investment goods for use in either

* This is a part of a wider survey of growth and planning in dual economies completed while I was at the University of California, Berkeley. Discussions with Paul Zarembka have led to improvements, not necessarily in directions he would have wished.

sector. There are other related aspects of this asymmetry: the methods of production are quite different in the two sectors. Land may, depending on the resource endowment of the economy, be a scarce resource in agriculture; it is far less important in industry. Capital used in the two sectors is of different forms, and is not easily transferable between them. In these economies, agriculture is mostly 'traditional' and uses 'backward' methods of production; symptoms of this are the high ratios of labour to capital and land, and very low labour productivity. Industry is relatively 'modern' or 'advanced'. There are, of course, exceptions to this, for there exist some modern farms and plantations, while some close substitutes for manufactures are produced using traditional handicraft methods. The economic and social organisation of the two sectors is considerably different. With the exceptions noted, agriculture is largely peasant-owned, uses relatively little wage labour or rented land, and retains some, perhaps even a lot, of output for farm consumption. Industry is largely 'capitalistic' in the sense that wage labour works with capital, whether privately or socially owned, and the output is sold, with some consideration for profit or surplus. Finally, there is the difference in location and community organisation, agriculture being predominantly rural and industry mostly urban.

Each of these distinctions can be used to divide the economy into two sectors. Doubtless the divisions will not be identical, but they will be similar enough to allow us to use the terms 'traditional', 'backward', 'rural' or 'peasant-owned' sector as synonyms for agriculture and the terms 'modern', 'advanced', 'urban' and 'capitalistic' as synonyms for industry. Any exceptions will be pointed out as they arise.

A major drawback of dualistic theories that should be stated at the outset is the total neglect of the service sector, including not only personal services but also transport and communications, trade, banking and finance, professional and government activities. As a very rough approximation, one might suppose these to expand in proportion to industry proper, and be absorbed in it for purpose of analysis. The peasants are then residual: they are all persons not employed in industry. If we wish to emphasise the commercialisation aspects of the division following Lewis (1954), we should classify in the modern sector those services which are available on the market and leave domestic services in the traditional sector. In spite of all such difficulties, the classification is much more meaningful for dual economies than the standard distinction between consumer goods and investment goods used in much of growth theory.

As in all growth theory, dual economy models can be classified into the mechanistic (historical-descriptive) types and the teleological (planning) types. The former assume a complete set of behavioural relations within the economy, and then trace its evolution from a given set of initial conditions. Planning models assume certain freedom of behaviour which is then utilised to achieve some target, typically the maximum of intertemporal social welfare. The descriptive method dominates the dual economy literature, doubtless because it is easier. In a sense, it is a prerequisite for planning, for we need an understanding of the behaviour of the system when left to itself before we can ask the questions of whether and how planning can improve its performance. This is all the more vital in case of a dual economy, where planning for growth may require changes in certain institutions which have come to prevail for decades, and these changes may entail some social cost. By comparing a mechanistic model with the appropriate planning model, we can make explicit the economic benefit to be gained from changes in certain institutions, and thus begin to put on a rational basis the issue of conscious change in social structure.

In this paper I shall confine myself solely to the descriptive dual economy models (I feel that consolidation of existing work in this area is very desirable) even though planning models are probably far more important to development economics. This is partly the fault of the usual approach of descriptive models: their emphasis on conditions for the rate of productivity increase to be positive, the concentration on asymptotic states. Impossibility of development is worse only in degree, not in kind, than very slow development, and yet descriptive theories establish a watershed between the two; planning theories do not. Besides, development is a much more urgent problem, and outcomes in finite time and results about levels of output must form a very important part of the quest of development theories. Planning models have much more to say on this subject; they yield results on initial policies and shadow prices for investment criteria.[1]

The job of a purely historical model is to explain observed phenomena of past development. Descriptive models should go one step beyond this if they are to serve as a basis for planning future development: they should be capable of accounting for phenomena we expect in the light of some incipient changes in the underlying structure. To put the problem in better focus, then, I shall begin with a very brief review of the facts we would like to explain, and the structural changes we expect. The theories discussed here are highly simplified and aggregated, and can at best give a qualitative explanation of the process of development. I shall accordingly state the

[1] The wider survey from which this paper is drawn (Dixit, 1969) has some discussion of planning models; see also Dixit (1971).

facts in a qualitative way. At such a broad level, they are almost universal, the few exceptions being easily accounted for by some special factors. Also, the facts remain basically valid whether in cross-sections or in time series, in the period after the Industrial Revolution. Most important among the sources from which these conclusions are drawn are Kuznets (1959) and Chenery and Taylor (1968). In addition, many theoretical papers and books contain suitable factual material.

The marked shift in labour-force composition is the most important fact: the proportion of labour engaged in agriculture falls from over 70 per cent to under 20 per cent during the course of development. This decrease takes place while population is increasing, and the net effect on the absolute numbers working in agriculture is normally one of slow increase. During phases of rapid industrialisation the agricultural labour force may be virtually constant; a decrease is very rare.

This movement of labour is, of course, accompanied by a shift in the composition of the national product. The share of agriculture declines from around 60 per cent to 15 per cent or even lower. In the meantime, labour productivity in both sectors increases with capital accumulation and technical progress. The increase is, if anything, more dramatic in agriculture. For the illustrative figures given above on shifts in labour and output composition, for example, the ratio of labour productivity in agriculture to that in industry rises from 0·64 to 0·71. Kuznets suggests that there is a slight decline in this ratio during the earlier phases of development, which is more than made up by a marked rise in agricultural productivity subsequently.

With these transformations come important social and economic changes. Increased urbanisation brings about increased commercialisation of economic activities, which is made possible by increased monetisation. This promotes development of capital markets, and allows easier intersectoral movements of savings. There is more transport activity. All these factors lead to an increase in the share of services in national product. As I said earlier, however, we shall not be able to treat these problems in a satisfactory way.

These are merely the broadest facts of development, but further generalisations seem difficult and perhaps even dangerous. I shall consider a model prima facie useful if it accounts for these observations; all the models discussed here meet this test. I shall point out other, more detailed consequences of the different models and consider their relative merits under different circumstances, but I do not feel that the data warrant 'acceptance' or 'rejection' of any of the approaches.

I am sure, however, that we must discard out of hand the thesis of Boeke (1953) and others who maintain that workers in the backward sectors of underdeveloped economies, especially the oriental ones, are so completely tradition-bound, insensitive to the prospects of economic progress and incapable of responding to economic incentives, that methods of economic analysis are totally ineffective when applied to these economies. To the same category belongs the 'unnuanced and unparticularised' picture drawn by Myrdal (1968) of 'silhouettes and shadows . . . a civilisation without qualities' (see Geertz, 1969). For a critique of Boeke I can do no better than refer the reader to Higgins (1956). Several empirical studies of peasant behaviour do show significant ultimate response to changes in their economic environment. This is not to say that there are no serious problems of misallocation and underinvestment in agriculture over the short term, but they are largely explicable in terms of externalities in production and information and lags in the formation of expectations, and as such are eminently suitable problems for economic analysis. Some models which pay a great deal of attention to 'institutional' problems of this nature will appear in this paper. Many models do neglect some fairly vital aspects of institutions in underdeveloped economies, but even these are not without their use. By exhibiting the path of growth that could be followed if constraints were not imposed by the institutions, they go some way towards the rationalisation of discussions of social change – a point mentioned earlier in a different context.

The most widely discussed and controversial question concerning dual economies is undoubtedly that of whether the backward sector of such an economy sustains surplus labour in disguised unemployment. A complete discussion of the debate would fill volumes by itself and yet clarify nothing. Many of the questions raised, and answers where they exist, are much better understood in light of the workings and results of the rival theories. I shall comment on these at the proper times. As a general conclusion from these models and planning models, I have come to believe that the marginal productivity of labour in the backward sector is a far less important parameter compared to some others, especially the elasticity of supply of food to the advanced sector. As an impetus to a shift in emphasis (although quite conceivably productive of precisely the opposite), I shall not discuss the empirical results on the marginal productivity at all. I shall, of course, point out the consequences of alternative assumptions concerning it as they arise.

A brief note on notation will conclude this section. Standard mnemonic symbols for variables will be used wherever possible, but Y will denote output, following usual practice. Subscripts 1 and 2 will denote industry and agriculture, respectively, but when considering one sector in isolation for some length of time, subscripts will be omitted. Letter subscripts on functions will denote partial derivatives with respect to the indicated arguments. If $x(t)$ is a time-series, $G\langle x\rangle$ will denote its proportional rate of growth, $\dot{x}(t)/x(t)$. Given a relationship between various time series, we shall often convert it to a relationship between their rates of growth by logarithmic differentiation. Suppose, for example, we have a relation $z = F(x, y)$. Converting this to rates of growth we get the relation

$$G\langle z\rangle = \frac{Ez}{Ex}\, G\langle x\rangle + \frac{Ez}{Ey}\, G\langle y\rangle \tag{15.1}$$

where Ez/Ex and Ez/Ey are the partial elasticities of z with respect to x and y. Two special cases will be useful and should be mentioned. First, if F is of the Cobb–Douglas form

$$z = Ax^{\alpha}y^{\beta}$$

then $G\langle z\rangle$ is a constant-weight sum of $G\langle x\rangle$ and $G\langle y\rangle$:

$$G\langle z\rangle = \alpha G\langle x\rangle + \beta G\langle y\rangle. \tag{15.1A}$$

Second, if $z = x+y$, then

$$G\langle z\rangle = (x/z)G\langle x\rangle + (y/z)G\langle y\rangle \tag{15.1B}$$

i.e. the weights are the proportions of x and y in z.

II. *AGRICULTURE IN ISOLATION*

The purpose of this section is to consider the vital necessary conditions which the agricultural sector must fulfil before it can perform its dual role of supplier of labour to industry and of food for the industrial labour force. In the process, we shall look at possible effects of the food output per capita on the rate of growth of population. I think that such effects have often been overemphasised in the literature. The birth rate has certainly not been causally related to income. The death rate is related to variables correlated with income, but a causal link is rather tenuous. It seems that the modern medical technology responsible for the lower death rates would have been adopted on purely humanitarian grounds, largely independent of income. An exception should be made for infant mortality: it probably has a component determined by family income. As a result, one would expect a slight rise in the rate of growth of the population followed by a levelling-off as income per capita increases. I would expect the effect to be relatively small, but opinion is divided on the issue, and in any case the importance of the conditions we obtain is independent of the Malthusian effects at a low income.

Let us consider an agrarian economy, with the entire population L (or a constant fraction of it, as usual) engaged in this sector. Agricultural productivity can increase over time as a result of capital accumulation or technical progress or both. Since agriculture does not produce investment goods, we shall have to represent capital accumulation by some exogenous trend in any case, so we shall assume a combined exponential effect and call it technical progress. The effect of capital accumulation on the rate of population growth in an aggregated model is studied by Niehans (1963) and others; our treatment follows Jorgenson (1961). We shall allow for diminishing returns to labour on account of the fixed amount of land, and assume a simple production function

$$Y = Ae^{bt}L^{\beta} \quad 0 < \beta \leqslant 1. \tag{15.2}$$

Let $y = Y/L$, food output per capita. Let us postulate a function $h(y)$ relating $G\langle L\rangle$, the rate of growth of population, to y. This function is assumed to rise with y until it equals ν when y equals $\bar{y}$, and to remain constant thereafter. The shape is depicted in Fig. 15.1; negative $G\langle L\rangle$ for very low y is not an essential aspect of it, and we can generalise Jorgenson's model in a minor way by allowing its rising part to be non-linear.

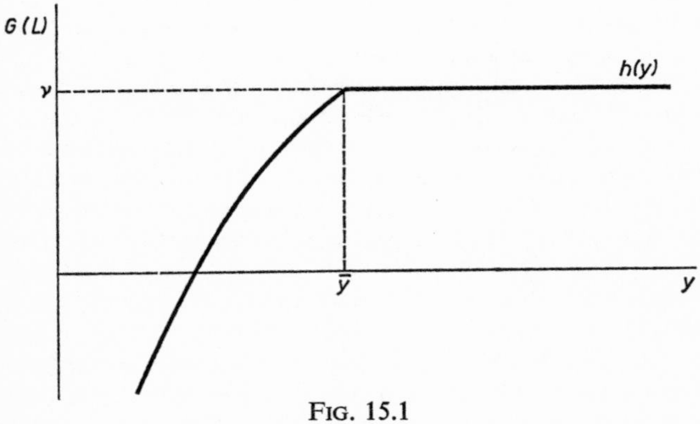

FIG. 15.1

Now let us convert (15.2) to rates of growth. Using (15.1A), we have

$$G\langle Y\rangle = b+\beta G\langle L\rangle$$

and hence

$$\begin{aligned} G\langle y\rangle &= G\langle Y\rangle - G\langle L\rangle \\ &= b-(1-\beta)G\langle L\rangle \\ &= b-(1-\beta)h(y). \end{aligned}$$

Thus y increases when the right-hand side is positive, and decreases when it is negative. Three cases now arise. If $b-(1-\beta)h(0) < 0$, then $G\langle y\rangle$ is always negative and y decreases to zero – clearly a state too dismal to contemplate. If $b-(1-\beta)v > 0$, then y always increases and, after it has passed $\bar{y}$, population grows at the constant rate v and output per capita grows at the constant rate $b-(1-\beta)v$. This is shown in Fig. 15.2A. If $b-(1-\beta)v < 0$, we have a y^* such

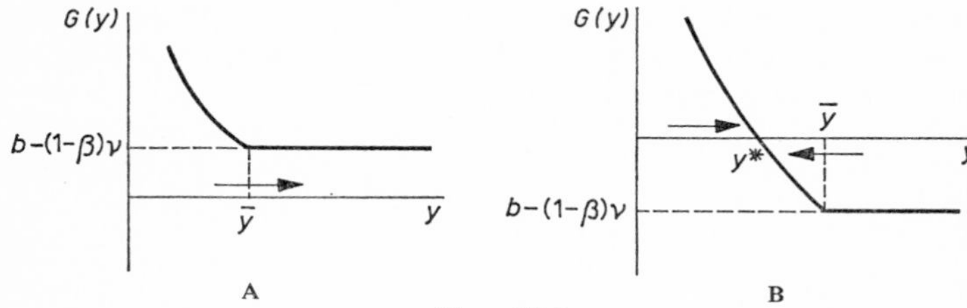

FIG. 15.2

that y decreases when above y^* and increases when below it, thus forming a stable 'trap' for the economy. With technical progress, we do not have a Malthusian trap in the strict sense: population is growing, although at a rate below the maximum. This is shown in Fig. 15.2B. In this case, output per capita is stationary, and clearly agriculture will not be able to release any labour to industry without making matters even worse. Thus the agrarian economy must remain in that state for ever, and if an industrial sector exists initially, it must decay. Jorgenson (1967) gives a rigorous proof for this.

We shall henceforth assume the condition which ensures sustained growth in y, namely

$$b-(1-\beta)v > 0. \tag{15.3}$$

To get a rough idea of what this implies, let us suppose $\beta = 0{\cdot}6$, a value in rough agreement with labour-share data from India and Japan, and $v = 2{\cdot}5$ per cent a year, which is near observed values; then we need $b > 1$ per cent a year for (15.3) to hold. This does not appear unreasonable. Note that if we do not believe in endogeneous effects on population and let it grow at rate v regardless of income per capita, then the same condition (15.3) would ensure growth rather than decay in the standard of living, so that the condition would retain its importance.

Given this condition, the agrarian economy left to itself will eventually surpass the level $\bar{y}$ of food output per capita. Jorgenson assumes that no one wants more food than this, so that beyond this point in time a portion of the population suffices to meet the food requirements of the whole, thus releasing some labour for industrial work. Fei and Ranis (1966, p. 14 n.) point out that this is a restrictive assumption, for the level at which no further improvement in food availability per capita is desired need not coincide with the level at which population growth ceases to be responsive to it, but can be higher. At the level of abstraction at which the point is raised, it is surely trivial, for given the productivity condition (15.3), y will eventually surpass any assigned level, $\bar{y}$ or higher. What is not trivial is the form of the consumption function postulated in either case, namely the sudden drop from one to zero in the income elasticity of demand for food. It is certainly far more reasonable to postulate a smoother demand function for food, with an income elasticity which is always positive but less than one in accordance with Engel's laws. We shall return to this point in section V. The process of release of labour to industry and its consequences will be studied when we look at industrial growth in section IV. For the time being, we merely note that this approach brings out the constraint imposed on growth of industry by the stringent food requirements of the population near a subsistence level.

The theory for agriculture proposed by Fei and Ranis (1961, 1964, 1966) also uses the concept of a subsistence level of income, but differs from the Jorgenson theory in several crucial ways. The marginal product of labour is assumed to be zero beyond a certain level of agricultural employment. Land is owned not by peasants who keep their average product, but by landlords. For reasons of 'a host of environmental factors, such as the land tenure system, the extended family structure, the social consensus with respect to a given community's obligation to individual welfare', they employ all available labour and pay a constant wage, 'usually not far from caloric subsistence and related more or less to the average productivity of agricultural labour' (Fei and Ranis, 1964, pp. 21–2). We shall denote this institutional wage by $\bar{y}$ to bring out the parallel with the Jorgenson model. The story opens with all food exhausted by the wage bill, as is the case at time t in Fig. 15.3. If the marginal product of labour becomes zero at the level L^* of employment, then even without any technical progress and at once, the amount $(L-L^*)$ of labour is potentially available for industrial employment since an agricultural labour force of L^* suffices to meet the institutional wage and food requirement for the whole population. If the economy was vertically integrated to the full extent, the landlords would be able to employ all the excess labour in industry and pay the wage out of agricultural output. When this is not possible on account of the institutional relations, particularly the problems of financial intermediation to secure mobility of savings between the sectors, industrial labour has to be paid its wage out of industrial output. In this case, in an early stage of development when industry is just emerging and does not have very much capital, the potentially available labour will not be employed all at once, since such action will drive down its marginal product below the wage. In the labour-surplus case, then, the size of the capital stock in industry limits the transfer of labour to that sector and thus constrains growth. In the Jorgenson model the binding limitation was the availability of labour. This distinction will be brought out more clearly when we study the development of the industrial sector under the alternative hypotheses in the next two sections. We shall also see that the actual consequences of the distinction are relatively minor.

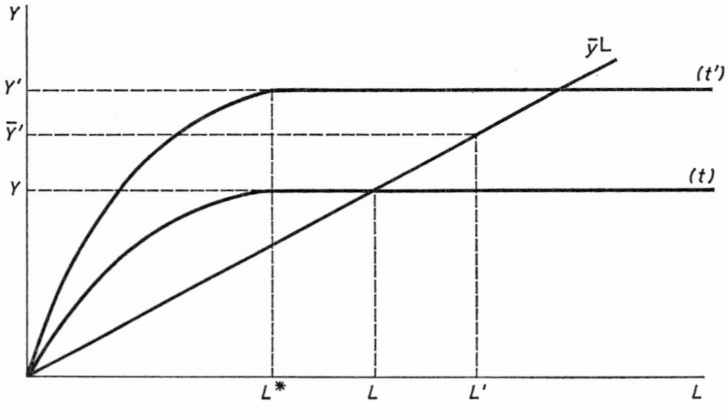

FIG. 15.3

It should be noted that the existence of surplus labour does not override the productivity condition (15.3). From the proportionality in Fig. 15.3, we see at once that if the rate of technical progress exceeds the rate of growth of population (L and L' represent population at instants t and t'), then more labour will become potentially available to industry over time. This is merely a special case of (15.3) when $\beta = 0$. If the condition is violated, all surplus labour will vanish at the instant after t and output will fall short of the institutional wage requirements for the population. Fei and Ranis (1966) discuss the possibility of a Malthusian trap, and also study the possibility that the stagnation is caused by deficiency of induced technical progress.

When surplus labour is transferred to industry, food output exceeds the institutional wage bill of agricultural labour. Fei and Ranis assume that the difference, the agricultural surplus, is appropriated by landlords who place all of it for sale on urban markets. This assumption will be discussed later; its consequence is precisely the same as that of the Jorgenson assumption of zero income elasticity of demand for food beyond the income level $\bar{y}$. Both imply that all food output, in excess of $\bar{y}L_2$ where L_2 is the agricultural labour force, becomes available to feed the industrial workers.

An assumption implicit in Fig. 15.3, as in the work of Jorgenson (1967) and Fei and Ranis (1966), is that technical progress in agriculture is neutral with the result that the point L^* at which the marginal product of labour becomes zero remains unchanged over time. In this case, before surplus labour can be eliminated by industrialisation, there must be an absolute decline in the agricultural labour force. Such decline is rarely observed in practice, and hence Jorgenson claims his model to be better. I believe that the assumption of neutral and exogenous technical change on which the result depends crucially is not justified in this context. If there is surplus labour, a very important role for technical progress to play is surely to secure its elimination. We have given no 'theory' of technical progress, but in actuality it will clearly be undertaken with the object of increasing the marginal product of labour where it is zero. Capital accumulation in agriculture will achieve the same purpose. Thus the level L^* will shift up over time, and it will be possible to end the surplus-labour phase without an absolute decline in agricultural employment. (This point is stated in Dixit, 1970.)

III. INDUSTRY IN ISOLATION

In this section we shall relegate agriculture to a very minor role, namely that of supplier of labour to industry, and study industrial growth assuming simple exogenous wage and price relationships between the sectors. This will give us a theory of industrial growth when agricultural labour is surplus as in the Fei–Ranis model. The techniques of analysis will also prove useful for some more difficult models of later sections.

Fei and Ranis assume, as explained in section II, a constant institutional wage in agriculture. Further, 'As long as surplus labour continues to exist in the agricultural sector, there is no reason to assume that this social consensus changes significantly' (Fei and Ranis, 1964, p. 22). To get a constant industrial product wage, i.e. industrial wage in terms of manufactures, we must also assume constant terms of trade between the sectors. Conditions under which existence of surplus labour guarantees this will be discussed in the next section. If we suppose, following Lewis (1954), that there is a gap between earnings in the two sectors, and that this gap is flexible up to a point, we may for a while be able to cushion the effect of a change in agricultural wages or the terms of trade and keep industrial wage constant. In any case, we have (or assume) a constant industrial wage, and a perfectly elastic supply of labour to industry as long as the agricultural labour surplus persists. It is this aspect that labels this approach to the theory of industrial development as 'classical'. It has become conventional to label the Jorgenson approach 'neo-classical' by contrast. Neo-classical models are often thought to involve as an essential feature the possibility of factor substitution. This is not true here any more than it is when neo-classical models are contrasted with neo-Keynsian ones.

Suppose industry is able to attract labour at a constant wage w. To get the demand curve for industrial labour, we must specify a rule of behaviour in that sector. Following convention – and since I am not going to discuss issues of planning in this paper – I shall suppose this to be maximisation of profits. The demand curve is then simply the marginal product curve, and industrial employment is determined by equating the marginal product to w. Industrial profits Π can be read off as the area between the marginal product curve and the horizontal supply curve. This is shown in Fig. 15.4, which was first introduced by Lewis (1954).

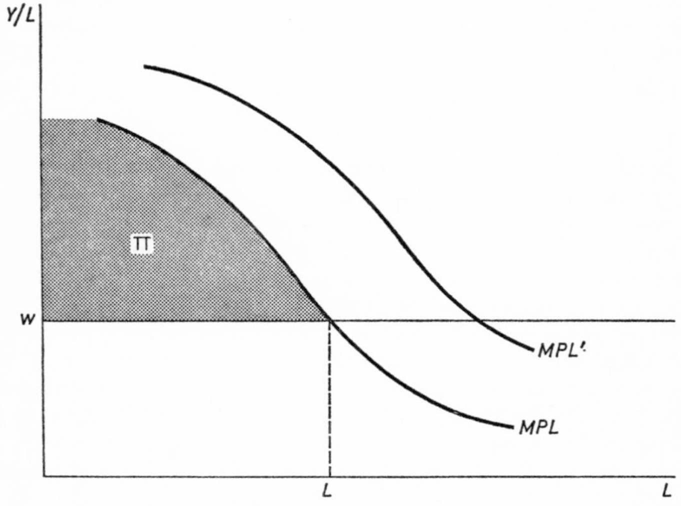

FIG. 15.4

We assume that all wage income is consumed, and that a constant fraction s of profits is saved and invested. The first is probably not far from the truth at the low level of income per capita that prevails in such economies; the second is a simple and convenient assumption. Now, if profits are enough to produce positive net investment, then the capital stock in industry will increase over time, and the marginal product curve in the diagram will shift upward to a position like MPL'. Profits will increase, and there will be further growth. Technical progress will aid this process.

Let us develop a simple model of such a process. We shall assume an industrial production function with constant returns to scale and purely labour-augmenting technical progress at a constant rate; other forms can be dealt with similarly with similar results. At each instant, industrial employment is determined by equating the marginal product of labour to the constant wage w. The saving function is as defined earlier. Thus the basic equations of the model are

$$Y = F(K, e^{bt}L) \tag{15.4}$$

$$w = e^{bt}F_M(K, e^{bt}L) \tag{15.5}$$

where $M = e^{bt}L$ is the labour force in efficiency units, defined merely for notational convenience. Depreciation on capital will be neglected for expositional convenience. Then we have

$$\dot{K} = I = s(Y - wL) = s[F(K, M) - MF_M(K, M)]$$

$$= sKF_K(K, M) \quad \text{by Euler's theorem.}$$

The rate of growth of capital is now seen to be

$$G\langle K\rangle = sF_K(K, e^{bt}L). \tag{15.6}$$

Now let us convert (15.4) and (15.5) to rates of growth. It is well known that the elasticity of F with respect to K is simply π, the share of capital in output, and by Euler's theorem the elasticity with respect to M is $(1-\pi)$. Since F is homogeneous of degree one, F_M is homogeneous of degree zero, so by Euler's theorem its elasticities add up to zero, that with respect to K being

$$EF_M/EK = KF_{MK}/F_M = (KF_K/F_{,}).(FF_{MK}/F_MF_K) = \pi/\sigma$$

where σ is the elasticity of substitution for F. Now we can use (15.1) to get the relations

$$G\langle Y\rangle = \pi G\langle K\rangle + (1-\pi)(b + G\langle L\rangle) \tag{15.4'}$$

$$0 = G\langle w\rangle = b + (\pi/\sigma).(G\langle K\rangle - b - G\langle L\rangle). \tag{155.'}$$

Solving for $G\langle Y\rangle$ and $G\langle L\rangle$ we get

$$G\langle Y\rangle = sF_K + b\sigma(1-\pi)/\pi \tag{15.7}$$

$$G\langle L\rangle = sF_K + b(\sigma/\pi - 1). \tag{15.8}$$

Greater interest centres, however, on other variables such as the labour productivity Y/L and the capital/output ratio K/Y. For these, we find

$$G\langle Y/L\rangle = b(1-\sigma) \tag{15.9}$$

$$G\langle K/Y\rangle = -b\sigma(1-\pi)/\pi \tag{15.10}$$

$$G\langle K/M\rangle = -b\sigma/\pi. \tag{15.11}$$

This yields the following results for the classical model. The capital/output ratio falls over time. So does the ratio of capital to labour in efficiency units. Hence the marginal product of capital rises and, from (15.6), so does the rate of growth of capital stock. Industrial capital, in other words, experiences accelerated growth. Industrial labour productivity behaves ambiguously, growing at a positive rate if $\sigma < 1$. Jorgenson (1967) assumes $\sigma = 1$ and concludes that industrial productivity remains constant in the classical approach, a result he finds (Jorgenson, 1966) in conflict with observation. Marglin (1966), commenting on this, points out that the conclusion depends crucially on Jorgenson's assumption of a Cobb–Douglas production function, and derives (15.9). Even then the rate of productivity growth for the classical model must be rather low; for instance it would equal only 0·9 per cent a year if we take $\sigma = 0{\cdot}7$ and assume labour-augmenting technical progress at 3 per cent a year. Of course everything can be explained by allowing wages to grow over time as a result of increases in agricultural productivity or shifts in the terms of trade: if we assume an exogenous rate of growth $G\langle w\rangle = a$, then we would find

$$G\langle Y/L\rangle = b(1-\sigma) + a\sigma.$$

This is doubtless what happens in practice, but the explanation on the basis of an exogenous wage change is hardly good theory.

In the previous section, agriculture was supposed to have succeeded in contributing to development if it could release labour to industry. When we look at industry in isolation, the natural criterion of success would be its ability to absorb the labour, and for this to happen industrial employment should grow faster than population. This is easily obtained from (15.8). The version given by Fei and

Ranis (1964, p. 121) is much more complex, and allows a different bias in technical progress. They call this a 'critical minimum effort' criterion; the minimum effort is to be understood in the sense of a minimum saving ratio or rate of technical progress, not a minimum necessary level of capital stock. It should be remembered that we really want higher standards of living to be the result of successful development and not a mere transfer of labour. Criteria of success in these terms can be formulated when we come to more complex models in which transfer of labour is related to the income elasticities of demand for food and manufactures.

We can use this model to tackle what Lewis (1954) calls the 'central problem in the theory of economic development', namely 'to understand the process by which a community which was previously saving and investing 4 or 5 per cent of its national income or less, converts itself into an economy where voluntary saving is running at about 12 to 15 per cent of national income or more'. The saving ratio out of national income can be written as a product of two factors: the saving ratio out of industrial income, I/Y, and the share of industry in national income. By manipulations similar to those given above, we can show that

$$G\langle I/Y\rangle = (b-a)(1-\sigma)(1-\pi)/\pi \qquad (15.12)$$

where $G\langle w\rangle = a$. This should be obvious upon reflection: if wages rise slower than the rate of labour-augmenting technical progress and if $\sigma < 1$, then there is not enough substitution of labour for capital and the profit share goes up. This seems to have been what was understood to happen in the earlier phases of industrialisation according to the classical theory.

The other component, the share of industrial income in national income, goes up in the course of development according to all theories. An extreme classical theory with zero marginal product of labour would keep food output constant and the terms of trade constant, and then industrial growth would lead to an increase in industry's share. Of course, a rise in both factors is sufficient but not necessary for a rise in their product. Jorgenson, for instance, uses a Cobb–Douglas production function in industry, thus keeping the profit share there constant and relying entirely on the rise in the relative weight of industry to explain the rise in the economy-wide saving ratio. Moreover, in course of development, agricultural savings would become more important as financial intermediation became better, and this would contribute further to a rise in the saving ratio.

The classical model outlined above describes industrial development only so long as the agricultural labour surplus is supposed to persist. The events that occur when the surplus is exhausted depend on the shifts in the terms of trade between the two sectors, and we shall return to them in the next section. There we shall also compare the results obtained above for the surplus-labour phase of the classical model with the early phase of development in the neo-classical model. Considering the prolonged debate between the proponents of the rival models, we shall discover some remarkable similarities between the two.

IV. SIMPLE TWO-SECTOR MODELS

In this section we shall consider industry and agriculture together, denoting variables pertaining to the former by subscript 1 and those for the latter by subscript 2. Let us continue with the classical model beyond the surplus-labour phase. This is discussed at length by Fei and Ranis (1964, chaps. 5 and 6), and what follows is a summary of the argument. We shall temporarily assume a stationary population

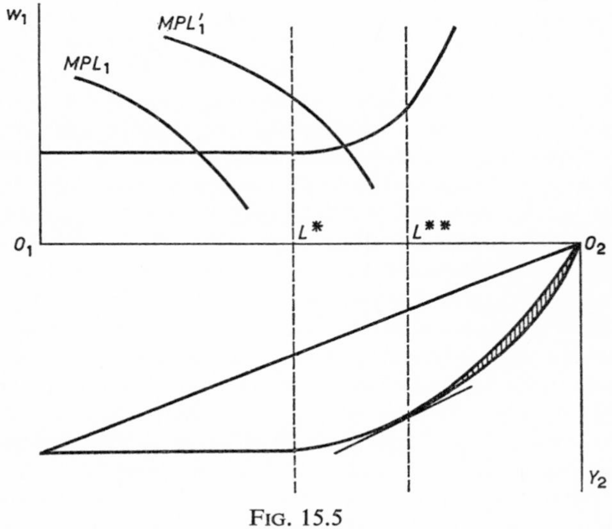

FIG. 15.5

and technology, and show the interaction between the sectors in Fig. 15.5. The horizontal segment O_1O_2 represents the total labour force, with industrial labour measured from O_1 to the right and agricultural labour from O_2 to the left. In the lower half we have the total product curve for food which, as in Fig. 15.3, is flat beyond

L^*. Let L^{**} mark the point where the marginal product of agricultural labour equals the constant institutional wage $\bar{y}$. Then, so long as the labour force exceeds O_2L^{**}, the departure of a labourer will decrease output by an amount less than the wage, and the landlord will be perfectly willing to let him go. Below this, however, the landlord will be willing to bid up the agricultural wage to keep the man on the farm. Thus L^{**} marks the point at which we expect the labour market in agriculture to be commercialised and enter into competition with the industrial labour market.

Suppose the initial situation is one in which the whole population is in agriculture and output equals $\bar{y}L$. As long as the amount withdrawn does not exceed O_1L^*, the wage bill decreases in proportion to the withdrawal while output remains constant. The agricultural surplus is $\bar{y}L_1$, which is proportional to the urban labour force. Fei and Ranis assume that all the surplus is sold by the landlords on the urban market. Then the amount of food available per industrial worker on the urban market remains constant at $\bar{y}$, the agricultural product wage. Thus in effect each worker moves to industry carrying his constant basket of food with him. It is now obvious that a constant industrial product wage and constant terms of trade are a consistent outcome of trade in food; it is easy to show under assumptions of normal indifference curves that this is the only possible equilibrium. This justifies the flat supply curve of labour to industry up to the point L^* as shown in the upper half of the diagram.

When the industrial labour force exceeds O_1L^*, withdrawal of more labour from agriculture leads to some decrease in food output, and the surplus available per urban worker falls. This increases the relative price of food, and the supply curve of labour begins to rise. Thus L^* is the first 'turning-point' of the model: beyond it the classical model discussed in the last section ceases to be valid for the industrial sector. L^{**} is the second turning-point: beyond it the relations between the sectors are fully commercialised, and the value marginal product of labour in the two sectors is equal. Incidentally, since the agricultural wage itself rises beyond L^{**}, there is an even faster loss of food surplus as labour is withdrawn, and this loss is shown by the shaded area in the lower portion of the diagram.

As capital accumulation and technical progress increase the marginal product of labour in industry, the demand curve for labour shifts up, and eventually crosses the first turning-point. Now the industrial wage begins to rise, and this drags down investment and growth. Fei and Ranis assume that the landlords will use a significant amount of their profits from the sale of food to industrial workers for purpose of industrial investment, but even this is not quite enough to carry the economy to the commercialisation point.

At this point, of course, technical progress and investment in agriculture come to the rescue.[1] A shift upward in the total product curve counteracts the decrease in surplus as labour is withdrawn, and this keeps down the price of food. In fact, Fei and Ranis advocate balanced growth with constant industrial wage until the economy is commercialised. The necessary investment and technical progress must be secured by the landlords, and an incentive for them to do this will be provided by the tendency of the price of food to rise.

Successful development of this economy hinges altogether too crucially on the role played by the landlord. He should be eager to save. He should sell his surplus to industry, and should transfer his savings to industrial entrepreneurs. He should be eager to innovate, and thereby improve the technology in agriculture. If such a Schumpeterian entrepreneur, or his equivalent in the form of an omnipotent central government, does not exist, then the dual economy is claimed to be doomed to eternal stagnation (Fei and Ranis, 1964, pp. 166–70). I find it difficult to understand how the landlord, tied down by the 'host of environmental factors', generates enough dynamism for the purpose. Alternatively, if he has all these brilliant qualities, I wonder why he sits passively while agricultural employment remains far above a profitable level. In any case, making development contingent on the existence of such a schizophrenic is a rather harsh sentence for the numerous economies in which a large proportion of output is produced on small family farms and where the government lacks the necessary dictatorial powers. Fortunately, the situation is not quite as bad as that. In spite of all the problems caused by retention of food surpluses on farms, lack of capital markets for chanelling savings, externalities of production and information, lags in expectations and all that, growth is not impossible, and can be aided substantially by policies within the means of ordinary governments. We shall touch on some of these issues again in the next section when we review more complex models.

Let us turn to the neo-classical theory of industrial development, based on the celebrated model of Jorgenson (1961). The theory of the agricultural sector is exactly as outlined in section II. There we let the trend stand for the combined effect of capital accumulation and technical progress in the production function (15.2). When we include industry in the model explicitly, this is hardly appropriate. We must include agricultural capital and assume some rule for

[1] This is not the only reason technical progress is important: it is even more fundamentally necessary if the economy is to pass beyond the first turning-point without an unbearable reduction in food output. This point, discussed in section II, was conveniently forgotten in the discussion here for simplicity of exposition.

investment allocation (not capital allocation: as we said in section I, capital is not likely to be shiftable). Such a complete model has so far proved completely intractable. Jorgenson's solution is to assume that there is no investment in agriculture, so the initial capital if any remains constant over time and can be absorbed in the constant term in the function. Since data on capital accumulation in these countries are very poor, especially in agriculture, it is hard to judge the descriptive accuracy of this, and different authors have expressed different opinions. No matter what the truth concerning the past is, this does make the model rather undesirable from the point of view of the future, since most economists seem to recognise the importance of capital accumulation in agriculture as a source of raising productivity, and agricultural investment is becoming increasingly important in actual plans for development. We shall later consider a model which makes the opposite assumption, and omits labour from the agricultural production function. This has the opposite defect, for it can at best give an inadequate picture of what happens when the assumed surplus-labour phase comes to an end. But each model highlights a different feature of reality, and as yet we have no model which integrates them successfully.

Industrial development in the Jorgenson model can begin when food output per capita reaches $\bar{y}$, population growth becomes exogenous and the income elasticity of demand for food zero. After this point, just enough labour is kept in agriculture to meet the minimum food requirements of the population. Let us choose this instant as $t = 0$. Then we have the following relations, derived from (15.2) with the appropriate subscripts installed:

$$A_2 L_2(0)^{\beta_2} = \bar{y} L_0, \quad L_2(0) = L_0$$

$$A_2 e^{b_2 t} L_2^{\beta_2} = Y_2 = \bar{y} L = \bar{y} L_0 e^{\nu t}.$$

These imply

$$L_2 = L_0 \exp\,[(\nu - b_2)t/\beta_2]. \tag{15.13}$$

Now the productivity condition (15.3) can be written as $\nu > (\nu - b_2)/\beta_2$, which guarantees $L_2 < L$ for all positive t. The difference is L_1, the industrial labour force. If we convert the equation $L = L_1 + L_2$ to rates of growth using (15.1B), we find

$$\nu = l_1 G\langle L_1 \rangle + l_2 G\langle L_2 \rangle \tag{15.14}$$

where l_1 and l_2 are the proportions of labour employed in the two sectors. We start out with $l_1 = 0$ and $l_2 = 1$. From (15.13), $G\langle L_2 \rangle$ is constant and less than ν. It is then easy to see that as t increases from 0 to ∞, l_1 increases from 0 to 1 while $G\langle L_1 \rangle$ decreases from ∞ to ν. The exceedingly rapid growth of industrial labour for small

t is not to be taken seriously: since $L_1 = 0$ and $\dot{L}_1 > 0$ at $t = 0$, the proportional growth is infinite. This gives rise to some consequences near $t = 0$ which are labelled 'statistical artifacts' by Jorgenson. These should not worry us, for in reality we never begin the story with literally zero industrial employment.

For the industrial sector we shall, following Jorgenson, assume a Cobb–Douglas production function, so the elasticity of substitution σ is unity and the share of capital π is constant and equal to α_1, the elasticity of output with respect to capital. The equations (15.4)–(15.6) of section III are still valid, with an important difference in interpretation: instead of taking w to be exogenous and determining L_1, we take L_1 from (15.13) and determine w from (15.5). We can also use (15.4′) and (15.5′), except that $G\langle w\rangle$ need not be zero. Now it is very easy to obtain steady-state paths, and this is the procedure followed by Jorgenson. If $G\langle K_1\rangle$ is constant, since we can write (15.6) as $G\langle K_1\rangle = \alpha_1 Y_1/K_1$, we must have $G\langle Y_1\rangle = G\langle K_1\rangle = \theta$, say. Asymptotically, $G\langle L_1\rangle = v$, so (15.4′) gives $\theta = b+v$ and (15.5′) gives $G\langle w\rangle = G\langle Y_1/L_1\rangle = b$. These are all standard growth-theoretic results: constant capital/output ratio, with wages and productivity rising at the rate of labour-augmenting technical progress.

Jorgenson (1966) now contrasts these with (15.9)–(15.11) to claim superiority for the neo-classical model, for its results are closer to nineteenth-century Japanese data. In my opinion the main difficulty with such a comparison is that the *asymptotic* results of the neo-classical model are being compared with the *short-term* results of the classical model. Besides, since the economy will hopefully cease to be dual in the far-off future, steady-state results are not very interesting in any case.

The behaviour of the neo-classical model in finite time may be studied as follows. Let $r = G\langle K_1\rangle = \alpha_1 Y_1/K_1$. If we convert this to rates of growth, we get

$$\begin{aligned} G\langle r\rangle &= G\langle Y_1\rangle - G\langle K_1\rangle \\ &= (1-\alpha_1)(G\langle L_1\rangle + b_1 - G\langle K_1\rangle \quad \text{from (15.4′)}. \end{aligned}$$

This gives the following differential equation for r:

$$\dot{r} = (1-\alpha_1)r(G\langle L_1\rangle + b_1 - r). \tag{15.15}$$

The solution to this can be shown to be of the form depicted in Fig. 15.6 (Dixit, 1970). For small t, r is small and positive. It rises steadily until, at time t^*, it crosses the declining curve of $G\langle L_1\rangle + b_1$. From (15.15) we see that $\dot{r}$ must be zero at this point. Then r begins to decline, staying above $G\langle L_1\rangle + b_1$, and the two have the same asymptotic value $\theta = b_1 + \nu$.

Up to t^*, r is increasing and below $G\langle L_1\rangle + b_1$. Thus industrial capital is undergoing accelerated growth in this phase. The ratios of capital to output and of capital to labour in efficiency units are both falling, and hence the marginal product of capital is rising. All these results are identical with those of the surplus-labour phase of the classical theory derived earlier. The Japanese data cited by Jorgenson, if they are to be relied upon to reject the classical approach, must now reject the neo-classical approach as well. But the data, especially

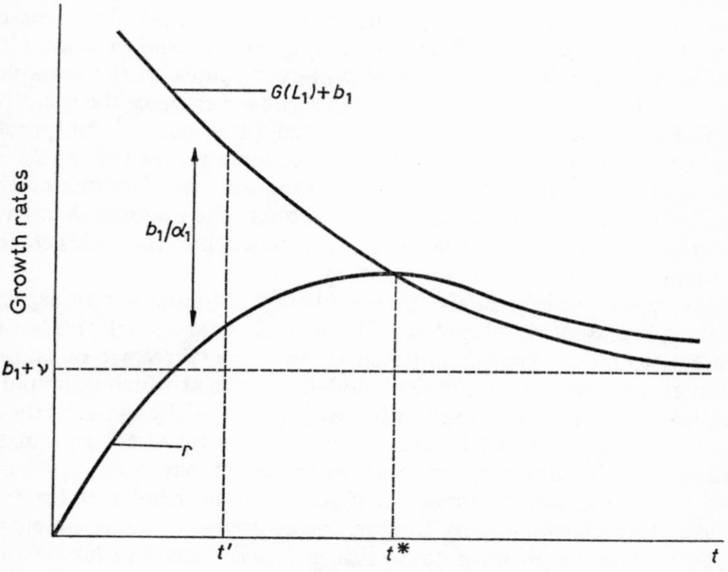

FIG. 15.6

those pertaining to capital stock, are surely too crude to be used as a basis for passing such judgements on these simple and basically qualitative models.

From (15.4′) we get the following expression for the rate of change of labour productivity in the neo-classical model:

$$G\langle Y_1/L_1\rangle = b_1 - \alpha_1(G\langle L_1\rangle + b_1 - r). \qquad (15.16)$$

This is ambiguous; in the early phases of development when $G\langle L_1\rangle + b_1$ is large and r is small, it is certainly negative. It becomes positive and remains so from the instant t' when the gap between these two is reduced to b_1/α_1. We know that t' is less than t^*, and if we carry out simulations with reasonable parameter values on the model (see Dixit, 1970), we find that values of t^* are too large to be neglected while values of t' are quite small and can be ascribed to the 'statistical artifacts' prevailing in the very early phases of the model. On the whole, the neo-classical model does provide a somewhat better explanation of increase in industrial productivity.

Terms of trade play only a passive role in this model: they adjust to equate the income per head in the two sectors. In another version of the theory, we can arrange a preassigned gap between the two; I shall state only the basic version here. If p is the price of food in terms of manufactures, agricultural income per capita in terms of manufactures is pY_2/L_2, which is to be equated to w. Thus $p = wL_2/Y_2$, and we can trace the time-path of p knowing those of the variables on the right. This is not of much interest, however, since the quantity of food demanded is always $\bar{y}$ and the price adjustment purely passive. Since $Y_2 = \bar{y}L$, we can write the equation as $(w - p\bar{y})L_2 = p\bar{y}L_1$, which states that the value in terms of manufactures of the food consumed by industrial workers equals the amount of manufactures consumed by peasants, thus balancing the market for consumer goods.

The two types of models discussed here highlight different aspects of the process of development. The neo-classical model points out the constraint on growth imposed by the rate of release of labour from agriculture. In the classical model, the rate at which potentially available labour can be used in industry is limited by the scarcity of industrial capital. In each case, the more plentiful factor cannot be properly used until the deficiency in the other has been made up, and we should not be surprised if many of the results of the two models turn out to be very similar. In the course of development in both models the effective constraint gradually becomes less severe, and faster growth results. The effect can be obtained by assuming that the marginal propensity to save exceeds the average in an aggregated model. In some generalised sense that is what happens in these models, but both the explanations go deeper than the simple assumption on the propensities to save.

V. THE MARKETABLE SURPLUS PROBLEM

I emphasised earlier that agriculture in a dual economy, in addition to releasing labour for industry, has to produce a food surplus (output over and above its own demand) and deliver it to the urban markets. I also pointed out the weakness of the simple theories in explaining the process by which this supply of marketed surplus of food is obtained. In this section I shall review theories which do a better job in this respect.

Let us begin by allowing a positive income elasticity of demand for food, thus improving on Jorgenson's assumption of a zero elasticity beyond the level $\bar{y}$ of income. The elasticity will be less than one in accordance with Engel's law. Then the greater the inequality of income within the agricultural sector, the greater will be the supply of marketed surplus out of a given level of output. In a model following Jorgenson's, where agriculture is peasant-owned and each peasant gets his average product, the distribution among peasants is completely equal. Such a model will be most conservative as regards marketed surplus. The Fei–Ranis model is at the other extreme, for farm workers are paid an institutional wage and all the surplus is appropriated and sold by landlords. Reality is between these extremes, with peasants accounting for a smaller proportion of marketed surplus than of output. A satisfactory integrated theory will have to find endogenously whether a farm will turn out to be commercially operated or run as a family farm. A framework for such a theory has been provided by Mathur (1964), but not enough has been done to meet our requirements. The Fai–Ranis theory has been explained earlier, and I shall now confine myself to the other extreme of peasant-owned uniform agriculture.

In addition to income effects, marketing will depend on substitution effects as the terms of trade between food and manufactures shift. This poses some most interesting problems which we shall mention later. Let us begin with a simple model of income effects alone. Suppose that, once food output per capita has passed $\bar{y}$ and population is growing exponentially at rate v, the demand for food per capita is a function of income in terms of food, with a constant elasticity ε between 0 and 1. We shall confine ourselves to the case where the income in terms of food is equal for workers in the two sectors, each being equal to the average product in agriculture. The consequences of allowing a gap are discussed by Zarembka (1970). Then the total demand for food in the economy is simply $cL(Y_2/L_2)^\varepsilon$ where c is a constant. This must equal food output on the equilibrium growth path, hence

$$Y_2 = cL(Y_2/L_2)^\varepsilon.$$

The production function for food is, as before,

$$Y_2 = A_2 e^{b_2 t} L_2^{\beta_2}.$$

Converting these to rates of growth, we find

$$(1-\varepsilon)G\langle Y_2\rangle = \nu - \varepsilon G\langle L_2\rangle$$

$$G\langle Y_2\rangle = b_2 + \beta_2 G\langle L_2\rangle.$$

Solving for $G\langle L_2\rangle$ yields

$$G\langle L_2\rangle = (\nu - b_2 + b_2\varepsilon)/(\beta_2 + \varepsilon - \varepsilon\beta_2). \tag{15.17}$$

Note that if we put $\varepsilon = 0$, we get (15.13) as a special case. In the present case, with the population initially all agrarian, the productivity condition which enables release of labour to industry is $G\langle L_2\rangle < \nu$, which is easily seen to reduce to

$$(1-\varepsilon)[b_2 - \nu(1-\beta_2)] > 0. \tag{15.18}$$

Since $0 < \varepsilon < 1$, this is equivalent to (15.3). Thus Engel's law is consistent with industrialisation and imposes no further restriction to ensure the possibility of sustained industrial growth.

This does not mean that the marketed surplus problem is irrelevant. It is easy to see that

$$\partial G\langle L_2\rangle/\partial\varepsilon = [b_2 - \nu(1-\beta_2)]/[\beta_2 + \varepsilon - \varepsilon\beta_2]^2.$$

If the productivity condition is satisfied, this is positive so that higher values of ε entail higher values of $G\langle L_2\rangle$. Correspondingly, given an identical static situation, (15.14) tells us that we will have a smaller $G\langle L_1\rangle$. In other words, when the dual economy has to reckon with the problem of a positive propensity to retain farm output for farm consumption, it must be content with a slower rate of release of labour to industry. Although industrialisation is ultimately possible, the slower rate of command over marketed surplus slows its rate. This is the crux of the marketable surplus problem.

Except for the slower pace of industrialisation, the main features of growth are precisely the ones described in section IV. For $G\langle L_2\rangle$ is constant, and we only have to use the new lower path of $G\langle L_1\rangle$ in (15.15) and proceed with Fig. 15.6 exactly as before.

When we allow substitution effects in demand, the algebra becomes very much more complicated. Zarembka (1970) assumes a constant capital/output ratio to solve for other variables, and this amounts to studying the asymptotic characteristics of growth. The same results prevail, namely that condition (15.3) is necessary and sufficient for viable industrial growth and that the rate of industrialisation is smaller than that for the simple Jorgenson model. We should not be surprised to find that substitution effects matter less in the long run; they do have very important short-run effects which we shall discuss shortly.

Before we do so, we should clarify why we have been speaking of the marketable surplus 'problem'. We saw that the constraint on marketed surplus slows down the rate of industrialisation. It seems a basic fact that this slower rate is often deemed too slow by most developing countries. It is very difficult to pass judgements on the 'propriety' of this view: after all, it boils down to the question of social valuation. If social values require a faster rate of growth, there is every reason for seeking policy tools which will make the constraint less effective. Thus the marketable surplus problem is intimately connected with issues of policy, and a full discussion of it is outside the scope of this paper. I shall therefore mention some policy implications arising from simple descriptive models, without discussing any formal planning models. The model presented here is discussed in much greater depth and in a more complex version by Bose (1968).

For convenience, I shall abstract from technical change in the following exposition. I shall also abstract from population growth. Many of their implications have been studied before and the present model adds little to them. Let industrial output be given by the standard production function, and industrial employment by profit maximisation. Then two of the relations of earlier sections continue to hold:

$$Y_1 = F(K_1, L_1) \tag{15.4'}$$

$$w = F_L(K_1, L_1). \tag{15.5'}$$

As I mentioned earlier, this model will consider the polar case where food output is a function of agricultural capital alone:

$$Y_2 = H(K_2). \tag{15.19}$$

Choice of units can make total population equal to one, and $L_2 = 1 - L_1$. Then income per capita in agriculture is $Y_2/(1-L_1)$, and the condition for equilibrium in the labour market supposing no income gap can be written as

$$w/p = Y_2/(1-L_1). \tag{15.20}$$

With incomes in the two sectors equal, we can write the total demand for food from workers as the sum of individual demands derived from utility maximisation in the general form $f(w, p)$. Let all profit income in industry be saved, so that equilibrium on the food market requires

$$Y_2 = f(w, p) \tag{15.21}$$

and investment equals industrial profits so that, as in (15.6), we have

$$I = K_1 F_K(K_1, L_1). \tag{15.22}$$

At any instant in time, we have as data the stocks K_1 and K_2 of capital in the two sectors. The six equations above define the instantaneous equilibrium and enable us to solve for Y_1, Y_2, L_1, w, p, I. To study the dynamic behaviour we must specify a rule for allocation of investment and solve the differential equations for K_1 and K_2. But we shall be able to understand the effects of some simple allocation rules merely by studying the comparative static properties of the model. This requires us to differentiate the six equations and solve for changes in the endogenous variables – a tedious task which is best concealed. The results depend on the properties of demand functions specified. If ε is the income elasticity and $-\eta$ the price elasticity for $f(w, p)$, the results given below need the following empirically reasonable restrictions:

$$0 < \varepsilon < \eta < 1. \tag{15.23}$$

It is not necessary for ε and η to be constant.

The comparative static exercise shows that an increase in K_1 raises w, p and L_1. It raises Y_1 but by a lower proportion than itself; it may raise or lower total investment but lowers I/K_1. This shows that a policy of forced industrialisation by allocation of all investment to industry will be self-defeating: the growth potential of the economy will become less and less over time. An increase in K_2, on the other hand will lower w and p while raising L_1, Y_1 and I. This will foster growth. Of course, a policy of concentrating investment in agriculture will not be optimal for consumption in the long run on account of Engel's law, but enough agricultural capital in a relative sense will be needed as a base for successful industrialisation. Thus if agriculture is initially capital-poor, we may need a period in which investment is specialised to it, and in the long run there will be some balance to the investment allocation. This will be so in spite of the fact that we have assumed no voluntary saving from the agricultural sector: the importance of food as a capital good – wage fund for industrial workers – is such that it is socially profitable to give away capital to the peasants.

In addition to investment in agriculture, the government can try to alleviate the marketable surplus problem by tax and price policies. These are discussed by Bose (1968), Hornby (1968) and Dixit (1969). Bose shows that direct taxation of agriculture will always be worth while so long as there are no significant disincentive effects on output. Hornby shows that policies of investment and indirect taxation for agriculture are complementary, one being most effective for faster growth when the other is least effective. Dixit obtains the optimum policies for rapid industrialisation. International trade may sometimes provide a way around the problem; this is discussed by Hornby. Discussion of these models in detail will take up far too much space. The whole problem will disappear, of course, if the government has total control over the economy and is able to depress current consumption as low as is compatible with biological subsistence. In this case, we shall be back in the world described by the earlier, simple models.

REFERENCES

I. Adelman and E. Thornbecke (eds.), *Theory and Design of Economic Development* (Baltimore: Johns Hopkins Press, 1960).

J. H. Boeke, *Economics and Economic Policy in Dual Societies* (Haarlem: Tjeenk Willink, 1953).

S. Bose, 'Wage, Price and Investment in the Dual Economy', Brandeis University, MS. (1968).

—— and A. Dixit, *Development Planning: A Theoretical Analysis* (San Francisco: Holden-Day, 1970).

H. B. Chenery and L. Taylor, 'Growth Patterns: Across Countries and Over Time', *Review of Economics and Statistics*, vol. L (4) (1968) pp. 391–416.

A. Dixit, 'Theories of the Dual Economy: A Survey', *Technical Report No.* 30, *Economic Growth Project* (University of California, Berkeley, 1969).

—— 'Growth Patterns in a Dual Economy', *Oxford Economic Papers*, vol. XXII (2) (1970) pp. 229–234.

—— 'Short-run Equilibrium and Shadow Prices in the Dual Economy', *Oxford Economic Papers*, vol. XXIII (3) (1971) pp. 384–400.

J. C. H. Fei and G. Ranis, *Development of the Labor Surplus Economy* (Homewood, Ill.: Irwin, 1964).

—— and —— 'Agrarianism, Dualism and Economic Development', in Adelman and Thornbecke (1966) pp. 3–44.

C. Geertz, 'Myrdal's Mythology', *Encounter* (July 1969) pp. 26–34.

B. Higgins, 'The "Dualistic Theory" of Underdeveloped Areas', *Economic Development and Cultural Change*, vol. IV (2) (1956) pp. 99–115.

J. M. Hornby, 'Investment and Trade Policy in the Dual Economy', *Economic Journal*, vol. LXXVIII (1) (1968) pp. 96–107.

D. W. Jorgenson, 'The Development of a Dual Economy', *Economic Journal*, vol. LXXI (2) (1961) pp. 309–34.

—— 'Testing Alternative Theories of the Development of a Dual Economy', in Adelman and Thornbecke (1966) pp. 45–60.

—— 'Surplus Agricultural Labour and the Development of a Dual Economy', *Oxford Economic Papers*, vol. XIX (3) (1967) pp. 288–312.

S. Kuznets, *Six Lectures on Economic Growth* (Glencoe, Ill.: Free Press, 1959).

W. A. Lewis, 'Economic Development with Unlimited Supplies of Labour', *Manchester School*, vol. XXII (2) (1954) pp. 139–91.

—— 'Unlimited Labour: Further Notes', *Manchester School*, vol. XXVI (1) (1958) pp. 1–32.

S. A. Marglin, 'Comment on Jorgenson', in Adelman and Thornbecke (1966) pp. 60–6.

A. Mathur, 'The Anatomy of Disguised Unemployment', *Oxford Economic Papers*, vol. XVI (2) (1964) pp. 161–93.

G. Myrdal, *Asian Drama* (New York: Twentieth Century Fund, 1968).

J. Niehans, 'Economic Growth with Two Endogenous Factors', *Quarterly Journal of Economics*, vol. LXXVII (3) (1963) pp. 349–71.

E. A. Preobrazhensky, *The New Economics*, trans. B. Pearce (1965) (Oxford: Clarendon Press, 1924).

G. Ranis and J. C. H. Fei, 'A Theory of Economic Development', *American Economic Review*, vol. LI (3) (1961) pp. 533–56.

P. Zarembka, 'Marketable Surplus and Growth in the Low Income Economy', *Journal of Economic Theory* vol. II (2) (1970) pp. 107–21.

Discussion of the Paper by Avinash Dixit

Dr Dixit introduced his paper by saying that it was difficult to summarise as it was a survey. He would indicate the weakest points in the literature.

The sectoral division was never sharp – it could be industrial and agricultural, backward and advanced, or commercial and non-commercial. The choice depends on the context, but some division along these lines was better than other alternatives. A serious omission was a treatment of services, but it was difficult to know how to include these.

The kinds of economies the models were supposed to illuminate were fairly closed, low-income countries with little plantation agriculture and food supply basically foodgrains. Examples were Russia in the 1920s and China and India now.

The problems studied were the conditions for and nature of industrial growth, where we need industrial growth faster than agricultural growth because of the relative magnitudes of income elasticities. The effect of the marketable surplus of foodgrains on growth and problems of investment allocation were also studied.

There had been much discussion on the definition and existence of surplus labour. He suggested that the qualitative aspects of growth paths were very similar with or without surplus labour. Also, the marginal product of labour was much less important in planning problems than other parameters, e.g. the elasticity of supply of food. He suggested that economists should give up worrying about it.

Dr Teubal said the paper gave a combined exposition, an evaluation and some extensions of results in existing models. It presented the classical Lewis, Ranis and Fei model where the marginal product of labour in agriculture was zero beyond a certain point, and the Jorgenson neo-classical model where the marginal product was never zero. Since the preconditions for growth and early behaviour of the two models are very similar, it is difficult to tell which is the right one to use.

He would discuss the necessary and sufficient conditions for industrial growth. He used the notation and referred to the diagrams of the paper. In Jorgenson's model the output of the food sector is $Y = Ae^{bt}.L^{\beta}$ where L is population (assumed for the moment all employed in agriculture). Population growth g was a function of food output per head y (Fig. 15.1): $\dot{y}/y$ is given by Fig. 15.2 as a function of y since $\dot{y}/y = b-(1-\beta)g(y)$. If the productivity condition $b-(1-\beta)v > 0$ holds, we have a possibility (Fig. 15.2A) for indefinite growth in food output per capita, and it is thus claimed that it is a necessary condition for the industrial sector to develop. It is also sufficient, since at $\bar{y}$ Jorgenson assumes the income elasticity of demand for food changes from unity to zero. If it does not hold we have Fig. 15.2B and the low-level equilibrium trap at y^*.

In the paper it is claimed that the productivity condition is also necessary in the Ranis and Fei model, although there might be a temporary process of industrialisation after which the population would have to return to agriculture. Both these discussions were unclear since we cannot have surplus labour without surplus food. A discussion of this point with the author led to the following conclusions.

Suppose we start where $L_0 > L^*$ (the point where the marginal product falls to zero) and keep the (dubious) Ranis–Fei assumption that technical progress does not alter L^*. Then $\dot{y}/y = b - g(y)$ and the productivity condition is $b - v > 0$. Suppose the productivity condition is not satisfied (Fig. 15.2B), $y(0) = y^*$, the labour surplus $L(0) - L^*$ is transferred to industry and the food output per head of the population remaining in agriculture is y'. Then $y' > y^*$. We retain the assumption that the food elasticity goes from 1 to 0 at $\bar{y}$, the point where population growth is maximised, and assume any 'surplus' above $\bar{y}$ is appropriated by landowners for sale to the industrial sector. We have two cases:

(a) $y' < \bar{y}$. Income elasticity of demand for food is still unity and the industrial labour force could not be fed.

(b) $\bar{y} < y'$. In a planning model there might then be a possibility of an industrial labour force, but not in this model. The industrial labour force would have to receive less than y^* whereas the agricultural labour force would receive more than y^*. No one could be persuaded to leave. Thus, while the food output per head is less than $\bar{y}$ industrialisation is not feasible.

He did not think the productivity condition was necessary for industrialisation. Suppose $y^0 < \bar{y}$, where y^0 is the point at which food income elasticity falls from one to zero, and the productivity condition is not satisfied. If $y^0 > y^*$, some labour could be transferred to industry since we can have $L_2(y^* - y^0) = (L_1 + L_2)y^0$ and L_1/L_2 is constant. We could maintain a constant share of the labour force in industry. The productivity condition *is* necessary for the share of the labour force in industry to grow, i.e. for the industrial sector to be dynamic.

Dr Dixit had shown formally that the productivity condition was necessary and sufficient for industrialisation when the food income elasticity falls from unity to a fraction between zero and one. This is intuitively obvious: industrialisation becomes possible as soon as this elasticity falls from unity and a food surplus is possible, and the productivity condition guarantees that this point will be reached. Only the pace of development is affected by the amount of the fall.

He said the closed economy assumption was both crucial and very questionable in these models. The whole character of the analysis is changed if we allow an open economy: the productivity condition is neither necessary nor sufficient for the emergence of an industrial sector. It was not necessary since we could import food by exporting manufactures, and it was not sufficient since we could export food and import manufactures. The significance of the necessary and sufficient arguments turned on the degree of openness of the economy. With foreign exchange bottlenecks the food surplus problem is just part of the foreign exchange problem. Bardhan had done some work on extending these models to accommodate foreign trade.

Professor Spaventa said it was misleading to try to build a descriptive model of a dual economy which ignored such essential factors in the explanation of dualism as international trade and the unproductive service sector.

More generally, he had obtained the impression yesterday that referring any more to reswitching and such arguments was now considered *mauvais goût*. We were told that these were things we had known all along from, e.g., linear programming and the properties of the internal rate of return and that they have no relevance for 'true' modern 'neo-classical' theory, which bears no responsibility for homogeneous capital models and the properties derived from them. If there ever was a black sheep in a respectable family, it is not nice to keep mentioning it all the time.

One could almost believe all this, and decide to spend the rest of one's life trying to learn some notions of fluid dynamics or similar subjects in order to keep up with 'true neo-classical' theory. However, one then realises that the black sheep still has active dealings with the family after all. On opening Dr Dixit's paper he immediately came across a putty–putty homogeneous capital model with well-behaved production functions, factors' shares depending on their marginal productivity and all the rest. The model was used for nothing less than explaining the early phases of industrialisation and the phenomenon of dualism. Dr Dixit's paper is only one of many at this Conference in which homogeneous capital models are nonchalantly used.

He found all this very puzzling. Perhaps we were being so Friedmanesque as to believe that correct results could be derived from false hypotheses. Alternatively, did we have, as happens in most religions, a double standard of morality: one for the initiate, who are allowed to discuss the dogmas, and another for pastoral work with ordinary people?

Professor Mundlak said that agriculture in Israel was more capital-intensive than the rest of the economy, but in the models here there was no capital in agriculture. We might try to build a spectrum of theories applying to situations with varying capital intensities in agriculture; but whether or not a zero agricultural capital model was adequate was an empirical question. If we had capital in agriculture, the relations involving surplus labour and surplus food became endogenous. With low capital–labour ratios the marginal product of capital might be high. In general, more testing of these models was necessary.

He added that if price elasticities were considered to be more important for planning than the marginal product of labour, prices and supply and demand functions should have been brought in explicitly. *Dr Dixit* replied that capital, and especially investment policy, was very important for agriculture and he tried to examine these issues in his own work.

Professor Diamond said he thought the restriction of the subject to descriptive models did not justify the omission of policy tools. *Professor Mirrlees* suggested, as an example, protective tariffs, which are often effectively a tax on agriculture.

Mrs Bharadwaj said that institutional factors cannot be ignored, particularly in the problems of a dual economy. More explicit discussion of how institutional factors affect the process of growth and are, in turn, affected by it, is needed. The 'advanced industrial sector' could not remain competitive when it is a mere island surrounded by a vast 'backward sector' and where growth is initiated amid significant inequalities of income and wealth. The agricultural sector itself needs to be divided into 'surplus' and 'subsistence' sectors, and a consideration of their relative size and interaction would be important to understand the investment and consumption behaviour of the sector, or to assess the extent of 'surplus' labour and means of mobilising it.

Professor Hahn insisted that it was not enough to criticise a theory for its omission of important matters. The onus was on the critic to show how the omissions were important. This was not Friedmanite philosophy (which he did not understand).

Professor Mirrlees said the importance of the omission depended upon the phenomena that the model was addressed to. Here industry was providing the saving for accumulation. Yet with high levels of protection a growing industrial sector may decrease the rate of accumulation.

Dr Boussard said the models presented here were not models of a true dual economy for two reasons. Firstly, 'industry' can produce food, either by selling goods on the international market and buying food in exchange, or by incorporating the modern sector of agriculture in the 'industrial' sector of the model. Thus food production is never a constraint on the growth of the industrial sector. Secondly, there are important transfer costs in changing from a peasant to an industrial worker. Although much higher incomes may be available in the industrial sector, peasants may not have the financial ability to overcome the transfer costs. Thus the main problem of the dual economy is that the industrial sector might grow autonomously, leaving the peasant sector behind. Although these models might give an account of the historical development of now developed countries, they are not of much value in understanding the problems of the development of now underdeveloped countries.

Professor Mundlak said the only way we could decide whether a model was adequate was by seeing whether it explained the important phenomena in which we were interested. If two models gave the same predictions, it did not matter which we chose. We could work with the reduced form rather than the model. *Professor Yaari* asked what constituted an explanation. $k = f(t)$ would 'explain' almost any time path of k if we chose $f(.)$ properly. The philosophers of science had settled these sorts of problem.

Professor Stiglitz thought the appropriate sectoral division of the economy was not obvious. The agricultural–industrial division was not helpful. More appropriate was 'traditional' (including services) and 'advanced', which, e.g. in Israel, Kenya and New Zealand would include agriculture. It was the institutional arrangements and techniques used that determined the split. *Professor Spaventa* agreed the service sector was correctly included in the traditional sector. It constituted a reserve army of labour and might be responsible for inflation.

Professor Hahn requested a formal definition of the sectoral division. *Professor Spaventa* suggested the use of inferior, inefficient techniques characterised the traditional sector.

Professor Lundberg said the split we chose depended on the problem being addressed. In Norway they had successfully explained productivity and price changes in Sweden using two sectors: (a) protected, (b) competitive – e.g. prices given by international trade. In the protected sector (agriculture, services, government) prices were related to production costs, profit margins were stable, and productivity rose by 3 per cent per year. In the competitive sector profits were squeezed and productivity increased at 8½ per cent per year. It also helped explain labour movements. This was yet another way of specifying dualism. *Professor Uzawa* said Ohkawa and Rosovsky had used a traditional/non-traditional split, and in practice it was very easy to decide which activity fell in which sector, although a clear-cut definition was difficult to give.

Professor Hahn demanded some equations. He said the art of economics was to make imprecise things precise. Descriptive accounts did not do that. *Professor Garegnani* thought there were more ways of making things precise than by equations. *Professor Hahn* replied that it was the best way.

In conclusion, *Dr Teubal* agreed that the institutional problems were difficult, but thought the next most important steps to take were to introduce capital into the traditional sector and foreign trade. Dr Dixit himself had some planning models with capital in agriculture. The limits on the survey were too narrow. Investment in agriculture might then accelerate industrial growth. Perhaps we could define the traditional sector as the sector in which everyone was initially.

Dr Dixit quoted Marglin's reply to Jorgenson: their differences were differences in point of view. Jorgenson viewed models as being in perfect competition with oblivion for those that did not fit the data. Marglin thought the models should help us understand processes that occur. Dr Dixit thought that these simple models did a good job. He agreed that institutions were important; but there was no one-way causation between institutions and growth.

He had no definite view on the best sectoral division, but inclined towards the commercial/non-commercial one of Lewis. He agreed that trade, human capital and investment in agriculture were important: these were areas for future research.

He thought that stagnation for the reasons of the failure of productivity conditions in the Jorgenson model was an interesting historical possibility, but he did not believe in it.

Part 7

Summary of the Final Discussion

Summary of the Final Discussion

Professor Weizsäcker introduced the final discussion by saying that he was not going to give a summary of what we did or did not do, but would give some random thoughts that had occurred to him during the Conference.

There was still a big gap between empirical and theoretical research. Even though many participants had done both and had confronted some theories with data, in the past all the problems tackled in papers here arose from theoretical considerations rather than empirical ones.

Another problem was one of *over-precision*. He did not mean that we should decrease our mathematical rigour, but that we should be aware of whether a problem was artificial or intrinsic. This problem arose as follows. We usually have a very simple model, addressed to certain phenomena or problems, which leads us to certain questions. Many of these questions are due to the very simple nature of the set-up and would disappear if we were more general; these are artificial. Two artificial problems in this sense had been intensively discussed at the Conference. The first was the rate of return/rate of profit relation. Both Dr Bliss and Professor Stiglitz had said that we should not expect equality of these two rates where we have any non-utilisation of capacity. In a real economy, however, under-utilisation of capacity arises from an awareness of frictions, etc. If under-utilisation were properly analysed, the problem would probably disappear.

The second was the problem of existence in infinite-horizon optimum growth models. The infinite horizon had only been introduced for convenience and we found ourselves spending a lot of time on problems that arose just from this convenience assumption. Professor Mirrlees had given us a good answer in his paper here and we shoud not waste any more time on this problem. The problem of the optimal rate of investment was very important, but provided $T > 100$ years or so our present optimal rate would not be much affected by T. The outcome of existence discussions was much less important than the analysis of today's decisions. We should be much more rigorous in distinguishing real from artificial problems.

It should be noticed that not only do some problems disappear when we go from a simple to a more complicated setting, but other problems become easier. For example, friction may make stability more likely, or clashes from conflict of interest may be easier to resolve if we leave a static setting and allow a future in our models. We often have agreement now because of different expectations about the future. We should try to make notions like this explicit, but he had not succeeded in formalising them yet.

Problems of income distribution had been neglected at the Conference.

Many of the models had implicitly worked with the neo-classical assumptions on income distribution. The only explicit discussion of the relations between income distribution and growth had been in Professor Helmstädter's paper. Problems in this area need much greater attention.

A frequent question had been whether or not the original Solow model is still worth while. An important, and much more general and hitherto neglected, notion related to this problem is the flexibility of the system. Solow had complete flexibility due to the malleability of capital: we then did not have to look to the future. Heterogeneous models did not have this property. It was important to formalise this concept of flexibility of a system. In this case we could link it to future markets and price expectations. More uncertainty about the future price of capital goods might mean greater flexibility. This might well affect the outcome of stability discussions.

Professor Lundberg said that in Sweden there existed a planning model for wealth rather than income distribution. We could then ask how wealth is distributed over time and whether there was a trade-off between better wealth distribution and growth.

Professor Uzawa said he wanted to make two points. The first was related to Professor Yaari's paper. The set of feasible consumption paths Y in that model reflected not only technological but institutional arrangements. In a static context it might be reasonable to assume these institutional arrangements are fixed, but it is not in a dynamic context: over time, changes in these arrangements become very important. The procedure used in the dynamic analysis was more worrying. It considered how to set institutional arrangements so as to realise an optimal path, based on the set Y. Y was in turn based on the assumption of fixed institutions. This procedure might lead to inconsistency and non-optimality. Although institutional arrangements were very important, they were difficult to formalise precisely and this led us to try to ignore them. There was no guarantee that our results would be compatible with existing institutions.

The second point was that the framework of contemporary welfare economics was based on the notion of Pareto optimality, and this made him uneasy. This criterion did not exclude dictatorship or very uneven income distribution: it was the guiding principle for a feudal society. We are now much more interested in equity, but this idea, partly because it is very difficult to define, lies outside contemporary welfare economics.

Professor Hahn said optimal growth theory was concerned with precisely the problems of equity between generations. The Diamond–Mirrlees paper was concerned with equity inside a generation.

Professor Uzawa said that we had no theory for deriving comparisons between paths. Our criterion was always introduced from outside. This made him uneasy about contemporary welfare economics in general and optimal growth theory in particular. For instance, there had been a very high rate of growth in Japan at the cost of indiscrimate destruction of national and social capital. This was an example of ignoring the inequities between this and future generations. However, as an economist he was unable to say anything about this inside contemporary welfare economics because of the dominance of the concept of Pareto optimality.

Professor Mirrlees agreed that there should be a thorough discussion of criteria and their use. This is very difficult, but up to now it had been too informal and particular. Nevertheless, there was very much more in economics than Debreu. The intention of traditional welfare economics had been very different from, although the analysis was formally similar to, the Arrow–Debreu theorems as popularly received.

Professor Uzawa said that if all Japan voted to hang him he would like to invoke a more basic principle than Pareto optimality to argue against them. Unfortunately, there was no guiding principle in economics to choose between two Pareto optima.

Professor Hahn said that Professor Uzawa had chosen a bad example in Japan's recent growth. It was ideas such as Pareto optimality that made us aware of externalities. It was people who did not understand Pareto optimality who caused a lot of havoc in the world.

There was no science of morals at present and he wondered whether one could be developed. He did not think that biologists were equipped to handle the moral problems of genetic engineering. However, he did not think it would be economists who would carry out this task.

Professor Uzawa said that research was biased by concentrating on easily formulated problems and concepts.

Professor Lundberg said that we should be careful about defining the balance of research from experience here. This was a small minority chosen by a very small minority, and was atypical. There should be more bridges between this kind of group and others.

Professor Uzawa said the primary concern in economics should be to find the crucial determinants of important variables in economics. *Professor Lundberg* asked whether it was the duty of economists to help us decide our needs. *Professor Uzawa* replied that it was.

Dr Dixit said that some of us were well qualified to, and should, look at the problem of the optimal use of fixed national resources.

Professor Rose said that biologists were no more qualified than the rest of us to decide where biological engineering should go. Economists, who were in general no nearer the Archbishop of Canterbury, should not be allowed to tell everyone what was optimal. We lose any right to call economics a science when we do welfare economics.

Professor Weizsäcker said that there was a high correlation between specific knowledge and values. The training of biologists affected their values. They know the facts better than the rest of us, are better able to realise the significance of the issues involved, and are better qualified to judge.

Professor Spaventa said that Professor Uzawa was saying that we should be political economists rather than purely theoretical economists. The kind of theoretical economics presented here was mystifying and led us away from the important problems.

Professor Bruno said that Professor Uzawa's concern about the fast rate of growth in Japan may be justified, but he should show how a slower rate of growth would have helped matters.

Our system of research should proceed as follows. We start from facts and build formal theories. We then formulate policy, go back to the facts and if necessary modify our theories, etc. He was worried about three gaps in this process at present.

The discussion of the first paper had shown how big the gap between data and descriptive theory was. Most of the growth models here had been closed economic systems – largely formulated in countries where international trade was not very important. The opening of the economy makes for more flexibility and changes the important questions, e.g. the choice between consumption and saving becomes less important than that between making goods at home or abroad or that of how much to borrow or lend. Another example of the lack of empirical work was that we did not know the history of the prices of different capital goods, although much of the discussion here had been about these relative prices (*Professor Patinkin* asked what the price of a capital good was).

There was also a gap between theoretical economists concerned with description and theoretical economists concerned with planning. He agreed with Professor Diamond that much of the distinction between policy and description might disappear if theoretical economists were more concerned with empirical work.

The last gap was the one between the theoretical literature on policy and optimal growth and that on planning *per se*. There was little contact between people who work in these fields. Real planners never worry about the existence problems associated with infinite time horizons.

Professor Hahn wondered why economists always put on sackcloth and ashes when they discussed the state of the subject. There had been great progress in the last twenty years: there were many more beautiful theories. He thoroughly disagreed with Professors Weizsäcker and Rose.

The most difficult problem in economic policy is that our material is imprecise. The exciting thing is to make it precise and then put our theories to a logical test. Mathematics was indispensable to this process. All disciplines had complaints from some that people were being too mathematical and from others not enough.

He did not think it was our job to develop a moral calculus, although we should discuss it. We did have to make decisions in complicated situations and it was important to be clear about what our criteria should be.

We should be more critical about the use of steady states: they had been taken as reference points just because they were easy to handle. Heterogeneous capital goods had been overdone. If we did in practice have a tendency to steady state, then it was a proper reference point. However, economic history did not consist of balanced growth and it was not clear that steady state was the appropriate idealisation. In any case, 'Von Neumann growth is hell', to quote Dennis Robertson. Perhaps we should be working with different reference paths and spaces other than commodity spaces.

Dr Boussard said he wanted to raise the problem of uncertainty, not because when you have nothing to say about a model you can always speak of uncertainty, but because it seemed a crucial issue for understanding problems of growth.

Uncertainty is an essential component of the information system described in Professor Weizsäcker's paper. In almost all the other papers, explicitly to take account of uncertainty would have meant strong modifications to even the most sensible-looking assumptions. He hypothesised that the main reason for the gap between the planner's approach and the models treated here was that the planners were obliged to plan in a world of uncertainty.

Professor Garegnani said he wished to raise a general point. As Professor Spaventa has already observed earlier in the week, a contradiction has emerged at the Conference. On the one hand we are told by Professor Stiglitz that the hypothesis of heterogeneous capital alters the conclusions of Solow's model fundamentally. On the other hand more than half the papers at the Conference have used models with only one capital good, without the users showing why their conclusions were not misleading in a world of many capital goods. This contradiction is due to a lack of clarity about certain basic points.

To see this we may again refer to Stiglitz's paper. The physical marginal productivity conditions to which he referred at p. 132 as the true neo-classical theory are in fact only a stepping-stone to demand functions which, when coupled with factor endowments, should yield stable equilibria explaining the rentals of the several capital goods.

When we realise the true role of those propositions in such short-run analysis, we may also see why Wicksell in his long-run theory had more reasons to be worried about reverse capital deepening than Professor Stiglitz allows. In Wicksell, profits appear as a uniform rate over the value of capital and not as rentals. As a result he had to refer to supply and demand for capital considered as a single homogeneous factor – a value substance which could take any physical form. That was necessary because the structure of the capital stock had to adapt itself to the conditions of long-run equilibrium. Wicksell needed then to exclude reverse capital deepening to have a well-shaped demand function for capital and thus ensure the existence and stability of equilibrium in the factor markets.

If instead we attempt to do without the postulate of capital deepening and, with Stiglitz, we treat each kind of capital good as a separate factor, we confine the theory to short-run equilibria and a dynamics made of a sequence of them. We then run into all the difficulties and complications of an analysis where the outcome depends on expectations the assumptions about which can be varied almost indefinitely. As a consequence, the theory becomes barren of definite results.

Thus Wicksell was worried about a proposition that was crucial for the existence of a supply and demand theory which would give definite results about the real world. It was only in the last two or three decades as the weakness of that proposition became increasingly clear that the analysis was shifted on to its new short-run basis. The sterility of this new basis explains the contradiction witnessed at this Conference: when studying real conditions we have to return to the old hypothesis of long-run equilibrium and we accordingly fall back on the notion of homogeneous capital which we admit to be invalid.

Professor Diamond said we had had considerable discussion of the differences between a one-sector growth model and similarly constructed many-capital-good models (see the papers of Professors Hahn and Stiglitz). The discussion had been highly critical of the conclusions of the simple model. On the other hand, many of the papers not dealing directly with this question have used the one-sector model as if the earlier discussion never occurred. It is quite common for a model to be considered satisfactory for some questions and totally unsuitable for others, so we need to examine this further before condemning these practices. It seems that the questions connected with instability with heterogeneous capital are different from those of the failure of monotonicity results (from reswitching) from this point of view.

The stability discussion has shown that the one-sector model behaves very differently from a many-capital-good model which is constructed with similar behavioural assumptions. This raises two questions: the stability of actual economies and the unsatisfactory nature of some behavioural assumptions, especially myopia. Neither of these is really an argument against the use of a one-sector model in optimal growth theory, for example. Nor does it require the one-sector model to be very different in its stability properties from many-capital-good models with different behavioural assumptions.

The monotonicity discussion, however, is a comment on the use of aggregate production functions rather than on the one-sector growth model as a whole. It has made clear the great diversity of behaviour economies can have. This raises two questions on the importance of this diversity. Are there questions, such as the level of savings that optimises growth, whose answers are not sensitive to these additional possibilities? And with what frequency do we find the diversity in behaviour actually occurring? Thus we are asking whether the one-sector model is a special case we rarely expect to find, and so confine to a footnote to warn students away from misleading simplicity, or if the complications of more general models are needed for capital–theoretical considerations and awareness of possible complications, but are not necessarily the standard case we expect to find. This is basically an empirical question. We might get some notion of its importance by considering some measure of the set of many-capital-good models where things look similar to the simpler model.

[*For lack of time, Dr Pasinetti was unable to contribute to the final session. The following is a summary of the written contribution he handed to the chairman at the end of the session.*]

He expressed unease about much of the economic theory discussed at the Conference. Two aspects bothered him most of all. First, it seemed to him there was an uncritical attitude to the specification of the mathematical models. Starting from a sensible problem, the maximisation of the welfare of the community as a whole, subject to technological constraints, we formalise it by making 'simplifications'. We assume that welfare can be expressed by an integral over infinite time of a utility function of aggregate consumption; and that production can be represented by a 'well-behaved' function of 'capital'. Here we are too complacent in accepting the elegant model. On the one hand we introduce complications that in reality do not exist; on the other, many of our 'simplifications' turn out to be critical assumptions. We cannot relax them without affecting the conclusions, and these conclusions are too abstract to be operationally useful.

The second troubling aspect is deeper. Like others, he had doubts about economics being a science dealing with the optimum allocation of scarce resources. By reducing all economic problems to questions of rational behaviour in the face of scarcities, it seemed to him that economists became prisoners of a narrow way of thinking. The more complicated are the problems, the more artificial they have to be made in order to fit into such preconceived schemes. In the case of economic growth, he thought that the artificiality had become so great as to make the analysis almost completely sterile.

Index

Entries in the Index in **bold type** under the names of participants in the conference indicate their papers or discussions of their papers. Entries in *italic* indicate contributions by participants to the discussions.